THE TYPESCRIPT WORKSHOP

A practical guide to confident, effective
TypeScript programming

Ben Grynhaus, Jordan Hudgens, Rayon Hunte, Matt Morgan,
and Wekoslav Stefanovski

THE TYPESCRIPT WORKSHOP

Copyright © 2021 Packt Publishing

Authors: Ben Grynhaus, Jordan Hudgens, Rayon Hunte, Matt Morgan, and Wekoslav Stefanovski

Reviewers: Yusuf Salman and Cihan Yakar

Managing Editor: Mahesh Dhyani

Acquisitions Editors: Royluis Rodrigues and Sneha Shinde

Production Editor: Shantanu Zagade

Editorial Board: Megan Carlisle, Mahesh Dhyani, Heather Gopsill, Manasa Kumar, Alex Mazonowicz, Monesh Mirpuri, Bridget Neale, Abhishek Rane, Brendan Rodrigues, Ankita Thakur, Nitesh Thakur, and Jonathan Wray

First published: July 2021

Production reference: 1280721

ISBN: 978-1-83882-849-3

Published by Packt Publishing Ltd.

Livery Place, 35 Livery Street

Birmingham B3 2PB, UK

Table of Contents

Chapter 3: Functions

Chapter 5: Interfaces and Inheritance

Chapter 6: Advanced Types

Chapter 7: Decorators   257

Chapter 11: Higher-Order Functions and Callbacks   415

PREFACE

ABOUT THE BOOK

By learning TypeScript, developers can start writing cleaner, more readable code that is easier to understand and less likely to contain bugs. What's not to like?

It's certainly an appealing prospect, but learning a new language can be challenging, and it's not always easy to know where to begin. This book is the perfect place to start. It provides the ideal platform for JavaScript programmers to get to grips with writing eloquent, productive TypeScript code.

Unlike many theory-heavy books, *The TypeScript Workshop* balances clear explanations with opportunities for hands-on practice. You'll quickly be up and running building functional websites, without having to wade through pages and pages of history and dull, dry fluff. Guided exercises clearly demonstrate how key concepts are used in the real world, and each chapter is rounded off with an activity that challenges you to apply your new knowledge in the context of a realistic scenario.

Whether you're a hobbyist eager to get cracking on your next project or a professional developer looking to unlock your next promotion, pick up a copy and make a start! Whatever your motivation, by the end of this book, you'll have the confidence and understanding to make it happen with TypeScript.

ABOUT THE AUTHORS

Ben Grynhaus is a full-stack developer with a passion for the frontend. With over 7 years of experience, most of them in web development working with various tech stacks, he specializes in TypeScript, React, and Angular. Ben has worked on several products at Microsoft and is now part of an innovative start-up in the marketing domain. He has published numerous open source npm modules that help in Angular app development, especially when integrating with React.

Jordan Hudgens is a full-stack developer and the founder of DevCamp and the Bottega Code School. As a developer over the past 15 years, he specializes in Ruby on Rails, React, Vue.js, and TypeScript with a focus on API development. He has built applications for a wide variety of organizations, including Eventbrite and Quip. He has published and maintains multiple open source **Node Package Manager** (**npm**) modules that help individuals automate the development process for JavaScript and TypeScript applications. Additionally, he has published over 30 courses, taught 42,000 students globally, and written several programming books.

Rayon Hunte has been working with Angular and TypeScript for more than 3 years. He has built complex web applications, such as a vehicle management system and a land management web application for the local government. TypeScript has enabled Rayon to leverage his knowledge of JavaScript and web frameworks to build complex, scalable web applications. Having been a development team lead, Rayon has firsthand knowledge of how large projects can become too complicated and impossible to modify and scale as time passes and more features are added. He realizes that adding strong typing to your projects is essential in modern web development and for him, TypeScript has been a real game-changer.

Matt Morgan has been a software engineer, architect, and technology leader for more than 20 years. He's worked with many technologies over the years, such as RDBMS, Java, and Node.js, and seen many generations of web frameworks rise and fall. He is an occasional OSS contributor and a frequent blogger. Matt is most interested in finding ways to improve workflows and developer experience. A great toolchain is a force multiplier.

Wekoslav Stefanovski has about two decades of professional developer experience using a variety of development technologies. He has been using JavaScript since the previous millennium and has a long and fruitful love/hate relationship with it. On the other hand, with TypeScript it was love at first compilation, and it's only gotten better since then. His passions include building better programs and building better programmers.

WHO THIS BOOK IS FOR

The TypeScript Workshop is designed for software developers who want to broaden their skill set by learning TypeScript. To get the most out of this book, you should have a basic knowledge of JavaScript or experience of using another similar programming language.

ABOUT THE CHAPTERS

Chapter 1, *TypeScript Fundamentals*, equips you with TypeScript fundamentals. You'll first learn how to set up your compiler options. Then, you'll perform various exercises on TypeScript types and objects.

Chapter 2, *Declaration Files*, gets you started with declaration files in TypeScript. You'll learn how to create declaration files from scratch and implement common development patterns for creating declaration files.

Chapter 3, Functions, dives deep into TypeScript functions. The chapter begins by introducing basic functions in TypeScript and then progresses to teach you advanced topics, such as type inference, currying, and the use of import, export, and the **require** syntax.

Chapter 4, Classes and Objects, teaches you how to define classes and instantiate them to create objects. You'll learn how to create classes that take in multiple objects as arguments to build dynamic behavior and confidently use TypeScript to generate HTML code.

Chapter 5, Interfaces and Inheritance, shows how you can use the power of interfaces and inheritance in TypeScript to write better, more maintainable code with well-structured functions, classes, and objects, and also be able to reuse your existing code efficiently.

Chapter 6, Advanced Types, teaches you how to use type literal and type alias. The chapter also discusses the fundamentals of how you can implement complex types such as intersection and union types.

Chapter 7, Decorators, first establishes the motivation for decorators and then teaches you how you can use them to add complex logic to your code without getting your application logic cluttered up.

Chapter 8, Dependency Injection in TypeScript, introduces **dependency injection (DI)** in TypeScript. The chapter begins with some fundamentals of design patterns in TypeScript and teaches you how to use the DI design pattern in a simple application.

Chapter 9, Generics and Conditional Types, describes the fundamentals of generics and conditional types in TypeScript. The chapter then describes how you can use generics to make your code more type-safe and avoid errors at runtime.

Chapter 10, Event Loop and Asynchronous Behavior, first establishes the motivation for events loops and asynchronous behavior, and then through several exercises teaches you how you use the asynchronous approach in TypeScript.

Chapter 11, Higher-Order Functions and Callbacks, begins with the fundamentals of higher-order functions and callbacks in TypeScript and then teaches you how you can implement them in TypeScript through several exercises and examples.

Chapter 12, Guide to Promises in TypeScript, first establishes the motivation for using Promises and then teaches you how you can implement them in TypeScript.

Chapter 13, Async/Await in TypeScript, covers common uses of **async/await** and discusses the landscape of asynchronous programming in TypeScript.

Chapter 14, TypeScript and React, covers the React library and how to build enhanced user interfaces with TypeScript. You will bootstrap React applications using the **Create React App** command-line interface.

CONVENTIONS

Code words in the text, database table names, folder names, filenames, file extensions, pathnames, dummy URLs, user input, and Twitter handles are shown as follows: "This code invokes **myFunction** with an argument of **'world'** and assigns the result of the function call to a new constant message (**const message**)."

A block of code is set as follows:

```
const message = myFunction('world');
console.log(message);
// Hello world!
```

BEFORE YOU BEGIN

Please make sure you have followed the instructions given below regarding the installation of the required compilers and code editors before you begin executing the code provided in the book.

HARDWARE REQUIREMENTS

For an optimal experience, we recommend the following hardware configuration:

- Processor: Intel Core i5 or equivalent
- Memory: 4 GB RAM
- Storage: 35 GB available space

SOFTWARE REQUIREMENTS

You'll also need the following software installed in advance:

- OS: Windows 7 SP1 64-bit, Windows 8.1 64-bit, or Windows 10 64-bit, Ubuntu Linux, or the latest version of macOS
- Browser: The latest version of either Google Chrome or Mozilla Firefox

INSTALLATION AND SETUP

VS Code

This book uses VS Code as the IDE to save and run TypeScript and JavaScript files. You can download VS Code from the following website: https://code.visualstudio.com/download. Scroll to the bottom of the page and click on the download button relevant to your system. Follow the instructions displayed on your screen.

Node.js

You need to install the latest version of Node.js, which includes **npm**. You can download and install Node.js from https://nodejs.org/en/download/. Click and download the installer relevant to your system.

TypeScript

This book uses TypeScript version 4.1.3. Once you have VS Code and Node.js installed in your system, you can install TypeScript by opening a terminal and running the following command:

```
npm install -g typescript@4.1.3
```

The preceding command will install version 4.1.3 globally. There are several other libraries and dependencies that you might have to install as part of executing the code given in the exercises and activities in this book. However, instructions for doing so have been provided in the relevant chapter/section.

INSTALLING THE CODE BUNDLE

Download the code files from GitHub at https://github.com/PacktWorkshops/The-TypeScript-Workshop. The files here contain the code for the exercises and activities for each chapter. This can be a useful reference as you go through the book. You can either download the code files in the `.zip` format or clone the entire repository to your desktop using GitHub Desktop.

GET IN TOUCH

Feedback from our readers is always welcome.

General feedback: If you have any questions about this book, please mention the book title in the subject of your message and email us at `customercare@packtpub.com`.

Errata: Although we have taken every care to ensure the accuracy of our content, mistakes do happen. If you have found a mistake in this book, we would be grateful if you could report this to us. Please visit www.packtpub.com/support/errata and complete the form.

Piracy: If you come across any illegal copies of our works in any form on the internet, we would be grateful if you could provide us with the location address or website name. Please contact us at `copyright@packt.com` with a link to the material.

If you are interested in becoming an author: If there is a topic that you have expertise in, and you are interested in either writing or contributing to a book, please visit authors.packtpub.com.

PLEASE LEAVE A REVIEW

Let us know what you think by leaving a detailed, impartial review on Amazon. We appreciate all feedback – it helps us continue to make great products and help aspiring developers build their skills. Please spare a few minutes to give your thoughts – it makes a big difference to us. You can leave a review on Amazon via the following link: https://packt.link/r/1838828494.

1

TYPESCRIPT FUNDAMENTALS

OVERVIEW

In this chapter, we'll briefly illustrate the problems that exist in JavaScript development environments, and we'll see exactly how TypeScript helps us write better and more maintainable code. This chapter will first help you set up the TypeScript compiler and then teach you the fundamentals. Additionally, we'll begin our journey into types, as they are the core feature of TypeScript – it's right in the name. Finally, you will be able to test your newly gained TypeScript skills by creating your own library.

INTRODUCTION

The world of online applications has grown tremendously in the past few decades. With it, web-based applications have grown not only in size but also in complexity. JavaScript, a language that was originally thought of and used as a go-between between the core application logic and the user interface, is being seen in a different light. It is the de facto language with which web apps are being developed. However, it just was not designed for the building of large applications with lots of moving parts. Along came TypeScript.

TypeScript is a superset of JavaScript that provides lots of enterprise-level features that JavaScript lacks, such as modules, types, interfaces, generics, managed asynchrony, and so on. They make our code easier to write, debug, and manage. In this chapter, you will first learn how the TypeScript compiler works, how transpilation occurs, and how you can set up the compiler options to suit your needs. Then, you will dive straight into TypeScript types, functions, and objects. You will also learn how you can make your own types in TypeScript. Finally, you can test your skills by attempting to create your own library to work with strings. This chapter serves as a launchpad with which you can jump-start your TypeScript journey.

THE EVOLUTION OF TYPESCRIPT

TypeScript was designed by Microsoft as a special-purpose language with a single goal – to enable people to write better JavaScript. But why was that an issue at all? To understand the problem, we have to go back to the roots of the scripting languages for the web.

In the beginning, JavaScript was designed to enable only a basic level of interactivity on the web.

> **NOTE**
>
> JavaScript was initially developed in 1995 by Brendan Eich for use in Netscape Navigator.

It was specifically not designed to be the main language that runs within a web page, but to be a kind of glue between the browser and the plugins, such as Java applets that run on the site. The heavy lifting was supposed to be done by the plugin code, with JavaScript providing a simple layer of interoperability. JavaScript did not even have any methods that would enable it to access the server. Another design goal for JavaScript was that it had to be easy to use for non-professional developers. That meant that the language had to be extremely forgiving of errors, and quite lax with its syntax.

For a few years, that was the task that JavaScript (or, more properly, ECMAScript, as it was standardized) was actually doing. But more and more web pages came into existence, and more and more of them needed dynamic content. Suddenly, people needed to use a lot of JavaScript. Web pages started getting more and more complex, and they were now being referred to as web *applications*. JavaScript got the ability (via AJAX) to access servers and even other sites, and a whole ecosystem of libraries appeared that helped us write better web applications.

However, the language itself was still lacking lots of features that are present in most languages – primarily features that are targeted toward professional developers.

> **NOTE**
>
> Some of the most talked-about features included a lack of module/namespace support, type-checked expressions, better scoping mechanisms, and better support for asynchronous functionality.

Since it was designed for small-scale usage, it was very troublesome to build, and especially to maintain, large applications built with JavaScript. On the other hand, once it was standardized, JavaScript became the *only* way to actually run code inside the browser. So, one solution that was popular in the 2000s was to make an emulation layer – a kind of a tool that enabled developers to use their favorite language to develop an application that will take the original source code as input and output equivalent JavaScript code. Such tools became known as *transpilers* – a portmanteau of the words "translator" and "compiler." While traditional compilers take source code as input and output machine code that can execute directly on the target machine, transpilers basically translated the source code from one language to another, specifically to JavaScript. The resulting code is then executed on the browser.

> **NOTE**
>
> The code actually gets compiled inside the browser, but that's another story.

There were two significant groups of transpilers present – ones that transpiled from an existing language (C#, Java, Ruby, and so on) and ones that transpiled from a language specifically designed to make web development easier (CoffeeScript, Dart, Elm, and so on).

> **NOTE**
>
> You can see a comprehensive list at https://packt.link/YRoA0.

The major problem with most transpilers was that they were not native to the web and JavaScript. The JavaScript that was generated was confusing and non-idiomatic – it looked like it was written by a machine and not a human. That would have been fine, except that generated mess was the code that was actually executing. So, using a transpiler meant that we had to forgo the debugging experience, as we could not understand what was actually being run. Additionally, the file size of the generated code was usually large, and more often than not, it included a huge base library that needed to load before we would be able to run our transpiled code.

Basically, by 2012 there were two options in sight – write a large web application using plain JavaScript, with all the drawbacks that it had, or write large web applications using a transpiler, writing better and more maintainable code, but being removed from the platform where our code actually runs.

Then, TypeScript was introduced.

> **NOTE**
>
> A video of the introductory lecture is available at https://channel9.msdn.com/Events/Build/2012/3-012.

DESIGN GOALS OF TYPESCRIPT

The core idea behind it was one that, in hindsight, seems quite obvious. Instead of replacing JavaScript with another language, why not just add the things that are missing? And why not add them in such a way that they can be very reasonably removed at the transpiling step, so that the generated code will not only look and be idiomatic but also be quite small and performant? What if we can add things such as static typing, but in an optional way, so that it can be used as much or as little as we want? What if all of that existed while we're developing and we can have nice tooling and use a nice environment, yet we're still able to debug and understand the generated code?

The design goals of TypeScript, as initially stated, were as follows:

- Extend JavaScript to facilitate writing large applications.

- Create a strict superset of JavaScript (that is, any valid JavaScript is valid TypeScript).

- Enhance the development tooling support.

- Generate JavaScript that runs on any JavaScript execution environment.

- Easy transfer between TypeScript and JavaScript code.

- Generate clean, idiomatic JavaScript.

- Align with future JavaScript standards.

Sounds like a pie-in-the-sky promise, and the initial response was a bit lukewarm. But, as time progressed, and as people actually tried it and started using it in real applications, the benefits became obvious.

> **NOTE**
>
> The author's lecture on TypeScript, which was the first one to be broadcast worldwide by a non-Microsoft employee, can be found at https://www.slideshare.net/sweko/typescript-javascript-done-right.

Two areas where TypeScript became a power player were JavaScript libraries and server-side JavaScript, where the added strictness of type checking and formal modules enabled higher-quality code. Currently, all of the most popular web development frameworks are either natively written in TypeScript (such as Angular, Vue, and Deno) or have tight integrations with TypeScript (such as React and Node).

GETTING STARTED WITH TYPESCRIPT

Consider the following TypeScript program – a simple function that adds two numbers:

Example 01.ts

```
1 function add (x, y) {
2     return x + y;
3 }
```

Link to the example on GitHub: https://packt.link/P9k6d

No, that's not a joke – that's real-life TypeScript. We just did not use any TypeScript-specific features. We can save this file as **add.ts** and can compile it to JavaScript using the following command:

```
tsc add.ts
```

This will generate our output file, **add.js**. If we open it and look inside, we can see that the generated JavaScript is as follows:

Example 01.js

```
1 function add(x, y) {
2     return x + y;
3 }
```

Link to the example on GitHub: https://packt.link/mTfWp

Yes, aside from some spacing, the code is identical, and we have our first successful transpilation.

THE TYPESCRIPT COMPILER

We will add to the example, of course, but let's take a moment to analyze what happened. First of all, we gave our file the **.ts** file extension. All TypeScript files have this extension, and they contain the TypeScript source code of our application. But, even if our code is valid JavaScript (as in this case), we cannot just load the **.ts** files inside a browser and run them. We need to compile/transpile them using the tool called the "TypeScript compiler," or **tsc** for short. What this tool does is takes TypeScript files as arguments and generates JavaScript files as outputs. In our case, our input was **add.ts** and our output was **add.js**. The **tsc** compiler is an extremely powerful tool, and it has a lot of options that we're able to set. We can get a full list of the options using this command:

```
tsc --all
```

The most common and important ones are as follows:

- **-outFile**: With this option, we can specify the name of the output file we want to be generated. If it's not specified, it defaults to the same name as the input file, but with the **.js** extension.

- **-outDir**: With this option, we can specify the location of the output file(s). By default, the generated files will be in the same location as the source files.

- **-types**: With this option, we can specify additional types that will be allowed in our source code.

- **-lib**: With this option, we specify which library files need to be loaded. As there are different execution environments for JavaScript, with different default libraries (for example, browser JavaScript has a **window** object, and Node.js has a **process** object), we can specify which one we want to target. We can also use this option to allow or disallow specific JavaScript functionality. For example, the **array.include** method was added in the **es2016** JavaScript version. If we want to assume that the method will be available, then we need to add the **es2016.array.include** library.

- **-target**: With this option, we specify which version of the ECMAScript (that is, JavaScript) language we're targeting. That is, if we need to support older browsers, we can use the **ES3** or **ES5** values, which will compile our code to JavaScript code that will execute in any environment that supports, correspondingly, versions 3 and 5 of the JavaScript language. If, on the other hand, we know that we'll run in an ultra-modern environment, as the latest Node.js runtime, we can use the **ES2020** target, or even **ESNEXT**, which is always the next available version of the ECMAScript language.

- There are several more options; however, we have only discussed a few here.

SETTING UP A TYPESCRIPT PROJECT

Since the TypeScript compiler has lots of options, and we'll need to use quite a few of them, specifying all of them each and every time we transpile a file will get tedious very fast. In order to avoid that, we can save our default options in a special file that will be accessed by the **tsc** command. The best way to generate this special file called **tsconfig.json** is to use **tsc** itself with the **--init** option. So, navigate to the folder where you want to store your TypeScript project and execute the following command:

```
tsc --init
```

This will generate a **tsconfig.json** file with the most commonly used option. The rest of the options are commented out, so if we want to use some other set of options, we can simply uncomment what we need. If we ignore the comments (which include a link to the documentation about the options), we get the following content:

```
{
  "compilerOptions": {
    "target": "es5",
    "module": "commonjs",
    "strict": true,
    "esModuleInterop": true,
    "skipLibCheck": true,
    "forceConsistentCasingInFileNames": true
  }
}
```

You can see that each and every option in the **tsconfig.json** file has a corresponding command-line switch, for example, **module**, **target**, and so on. If a command-line switch is specified, it takes precedence. However, if a command-line switch is not defined, then **tsc** looks for the nearest **tsconfig.json** file up the directory hierarchy and takes the value specified there.

EXERCISE 1.01: USING TSCONFIG.JSON AND GETTING STARTED WITH TYPESCRIPT

In this exercise, we'll see how to command TypeScript using the **tsconfig.json** file. We'll see how to create TypeScript files and transpile them to JavaScript, based on the options we specify:

> **NOTE**
>
> Please make sure you have installed **Visual Studio** (**VS**) Code and followed the installation steps as mentioned in the *Preface*. The code files for this exercise can be found here: https://packt.link/30NuU.

1. Create a new folder and execute the following command in a new terminal within it:

```
tsc --init
```

2. Verify that a new **tsconfig.json** file is created within the folder and that its target value is **es5**.

3. Create a new file called **squares.ts** inside it.

4. In **squares.ts**, create a function called **squares**:

```
function squares(array: number[]) {
```

5. Create a new array from the input argument, using the JavaScript **map** function with an arrow function argument:

```
const result = array.map(x => x * x);
```

6. Return the new array from the function:

```
    return result;
}
```

7. Save the file and run the following command in the folder:

```
tsc squares.ts
```

8. Verify that there is a new file in the folder called **squares.js** with the following content:

```
function squares(array) {
    var result = array.map(function (x) { return x * x; });
    return result;
}
```

Here, we can see that the transpilation step did several things:

- It removed the type annotation from the **array: number[]** parameter, transpiling it to **array**.

- It changed the **const result** variable declaration to a **var result** declaration.

- It changed the arrow function, **x=>x*x**, to a regular function, **function (x) { return x * x; }**.

While the first is TypeScript-specific code, the second and third are examples of TypeScript's backward compatibility – both the arrow functions and the **const** declarations are JavaScript features that were introduced in the ES6 version of the language.

9. Run the following command in the folder:

```
tsc --target es6 squares.ts
```

This will override the setting from the **tsconfig.json** file and it will transpile the TypeScript code to **ES6**-compatible JavaScript.

10. Verify that the contents of the **squares.js** file are now as follows:

```
function squares(array) {
    const result = array.map(x => x * x);
    return result;
}
```

You can note that, in contrast to the results in *step 8*, now the **const** keyword and the arrow functions are intact, because the target we specified supports them natively. This is an extremely important feature of TypeScript. With this feature, even if we don't use the rich type system that TypeScript provides, we can still write code in the most modern version of JavaScript available, and TypeScript will seamlessly transpile our code to a version that can actually be consumed by our customers.

TYPES AND THEIR USES

We've mentioned that TypeScript's type system is its distinguishing feature, so let's take a better look at it. JavaScript is what's called a loosely typed language. That means that it does not enforce any rules on the defined variables and their values. Consider, for example, that we define a variable called **count** and set it to the value of **3**:

```
let count = 3;
```

There is nothing that prevents us from setting that variable to a value that is a string, a date, an array, or basically any object. All of the following assignments are valid:

```
count = "string";
count = new Date();
count = false;
count = [1, 2, 3];
count = { key: "value" };
```

In almost all scenarios, this is not a behavior we actually want. Moreover, since JavaScript does not know when we are writing the code whether a variable contains a string or a number, it cannot stop us from trying to, for example, convert it to lowercase. We cannot know whether that operation will succeed or fail until the moment we actually try it, when running the code.

Let's take the following example:

```
let variable;
if (Math.random()>0.5) {
    variable = 3;
} else {
    variable = "String";
}
console.log(variable.toLowerCase());
```

This code will either output **"String"** or throw a **variable.toLowerCase is not a function** error. The only way to determine whether this code will break is to actually run it. In a nutshell, in a loosely typed language, while values themselves have types, variables, on the other hand, don't. They just take the type of the value they are currently holding. So, any checks whether a method is possible on a variable, such as **variable.toLowerCase()**, can only be done when we have the actual value, that is, when we run the code. Once more, this is quite fine for small-sized applications, but it can become tedious for large-scale applications. In contrast, strongly typed languages enforce the type rules for both the values and the variables they live in. This means that the language itself can detect the error as you are typing the code, as it has more information about what is going on in your code.

So, in a large software product, (in most cases) we don't want variables that have values of different types. So, we want to be able to somehow say "this variable has to be a number, and if someone tries to put something that is not a number inside it, issue an error."

This is where TypeScript, as a strongly typed language, comes in. We have two ways that we can use to bind a variable to a type. The simpler one is to simply annotate the variable with the type we want it to be, like this:

```
let variable: number;
```

The : **number** part of the code is called a *type* annotation, and we're doing just that – saying "this variable has to be a number, and if someone tries to put something that is not a number inside it, issue an error."

Now, if we try to assign a number to that variable, everything is fine. But the minute we try to assign a string to the variable, we'll get an error message:

```
let variable: number;

Type 'string' is not assignable to type 'number'. ts(2322)

let variable: number                         .

View Problem (Alt+F8)    No quick fixes available
variable = "string"
```

Figure 1.1: Error message from assigning an incorrect type

This type of annotation is explicit and specific to TypeScript. Another way is simply to assign a value to a variable and let TypeScript work its magic. The magic is called *type inference*, and that means that TypeScript will try to guess the type of the variable based on the value provided.

Let's define a variable and initialize it with a value, like this:

```
let variable = 3;
```

Now, if we try to assign a string to that variable, TypeScript will issue an error:

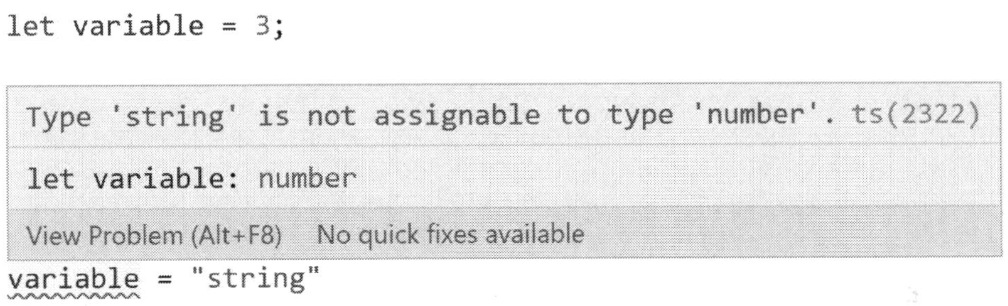

```
let variable = 3;
```

```
Type 'string' is not assignable to type 'number'. ts(2322)

let variable: number

View Problem (Alt+F8)    No quick fixes available

variable = "string"
```

Figure 1.2: Error message from assigning an incorrect type

From the error message, we can see the type that TypeScript correctly inferred for the variable – **number**. Actually, in most cases, we won't even need to add type annotations, as TypeScript's powerful type inference engine will correctly infer the type of the variable.

TYPESCRIPT AND FUNCTIONS

Another huge benefit of TypeScript is automatic function invocation checking. Let's say that we have the function we used for our first TypeScript file:

```
function add (x, y) {
    return x + y;
}
```

Even without any type annotations, TypeScript still has some information about this function – namely, that it takes two, and exactly two, parameters.

In contrast, JavaScript does not enforce that the number of actual arguments has to conform to the number of parameters defined, so all of the following invocations are valid calls in JavaScript:

```
add(1, 2); // two arguments
add(1, 2, 3); // three arguments
add(1); // one argument
add(); // no arguments
```

In JavaScript, we can call a function with more arguments than parameters, fewer arguments, or even without any arguments at all. If we have more arguments than needed, the extra arguments are simply ignored (and stored in the magical **arguments** variable), and if we have fewer arguments than needed, the extra parameters are given the value **undefined**. So, in essence, the preceding calls will be correspondingly transformed into the following:

```
add(1, 2); // no changes, as the number of arguments match the number of
parameters.
add(1, 2); // the third argument is ignored
add(1, undefined); // the second parameter is given a value of undefined
add(undefined, undefined); // both parameters are given a value of undefined
```

In the third and fourth cases, the return value of the function will be the special numeric value **NaN**.

TypeScript has a radically different approach to this issue. A function can only be called using valid arguments – both in number and in type. So, if we write the same code, but this time in a TypeScript file, we'll get appropriate error messages. For a case where we have extra arguments, we'll get an error message on the extra arguments:

```
function add (x, y) {
    return x + y;
}

                    Expected 2 arguments, but got 3. ts(2554)
add(1, 2); View Problem (Alt+F8)    No quick fixes available
add(1, 2, 3); // three arguments
add(1); // one argument
add(); // no arguments
```

Figure 1.3: Error message from using an incorrect number of arguments – too many in this case

For cases with too few arguments, we get the error message on the method itself:

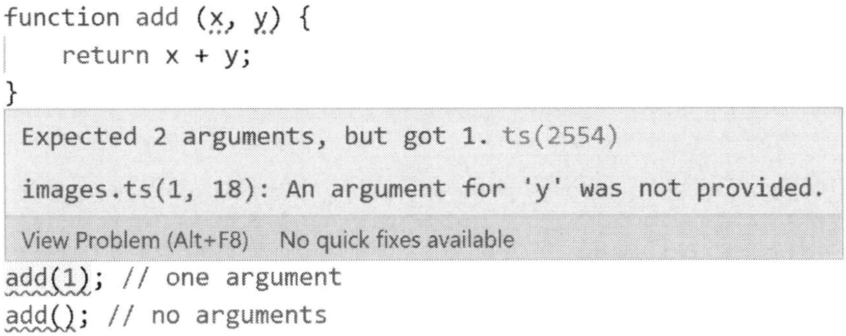

```
function add (x, y) {
    return x + y;
}
```
```
Expected 2 arguments, but got 1. ts(2554)

images.ts(1, 18): An argument for 'y' was not provided.

View Problem (Alt+F8)    No quick fixes available
```
```
add(1); // one argument
add(); // no arguments
```

**Figure 1.4: Error message from using an incorrect number
of arguments – too few in this case**

In this case, we're notified that a required parameter is missing, as well as what the name and the type of that parameter should be. Note that it's a common JavaScript technique to have methods that accept a variable number of parameters, accept optional parameters, or provide some defaults if a parameter is not specified. All those cases (and many more) are correctly handled by TypeScript.

> **NOTE**
>
> Details on how to write such methods using TypeScript are inlcuded in *Chapter 3, Functions*.

Of course, parameter checking works not only on the number but also on the type of the parameters as well. We would want the **add** function to work only with numbers – it does not make sense to add a Boolean and an object, for example. In TypeScript, we can annotate our function like this:

```
function add (x: number, y: number) {
    return x + y;
}
```

This will cause the compiler not only to check that the number of arguments matches the number of parameters but also to verify that the types used for the arguments are actually valid. Since JavaScript can't check for that, adding a Boolean and an object is actually a valid call to the JavaScript equivalent of our **add** method. Furthermore, since JavaScript tries to be as forgiving as possible, we won't even get a runtime error – the call will be successful, as JavaScript will coerce both the object and Boolean to a common string representation, and then try (and succeed) to add those two values together.

Let's interpret the following call to our function as both JavaScript and TypeScript:

```
const first = { property: 'value'};
const second = false;


const result = add(first, second);
```

This is valid, albeit nonsensical, JavaScript code. If run, it will yield the result **[object Object] false**, which would not be useful in any context.

The same code, interpreted as TypeScript, will yield the following compile type error:

```
function add (x: number, y: number) {
    return x + y;
}
```

Argument of type '{ property: string; }' is not assignable to parameter of type 'number'. ts(2345)

```
const first: {
    property: string;
}
```

```
const first = { pro
const second = fals
```

View Problem (Alt+F8)   No quick fixes available

```
const result = add(first, second);
```

Figure 1.5: Error message on VS Code

We can also annotate the return type of the function, adding a type annotation after the parameter list:

```
function add (x: number, y: number): number {
    return x + y;
}
```

That is usually not necessary, as TypeScript can actually infer the return type from the return statements given. In our case, since **x** and **y** are numbers, **x+y** will be a number as well, which means that our function will return a number. However, if we do annotate the return type, TypeScript will enforce that contract as well:

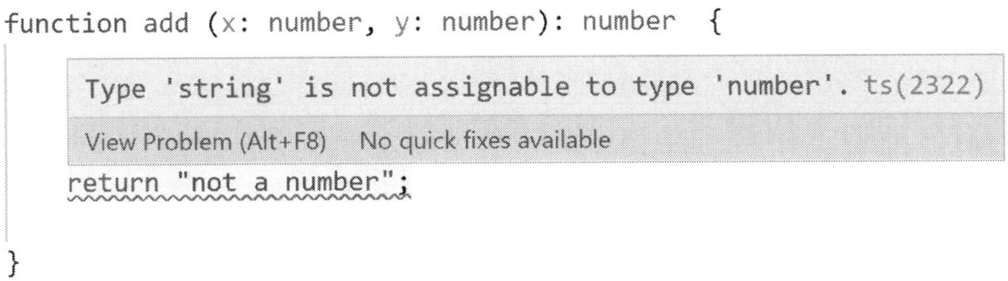

```typescript
function add (x: number, y: number): number  {
```
> Type 'string' is not assignable to type 'number'. ts(2322)
> View Problem (Alt+F8)   No quick fixes available
```typescript
    return "not a number";

}
```

Figure 1.6: TypeScript enforcing the correct type

In either case, whether we explicitly annotate the return type or it's inferred, the type of the function will be applied to any values that are produced by calling the function. So, if we assign the return value to some variable, that variable will have the type of **number** as well:

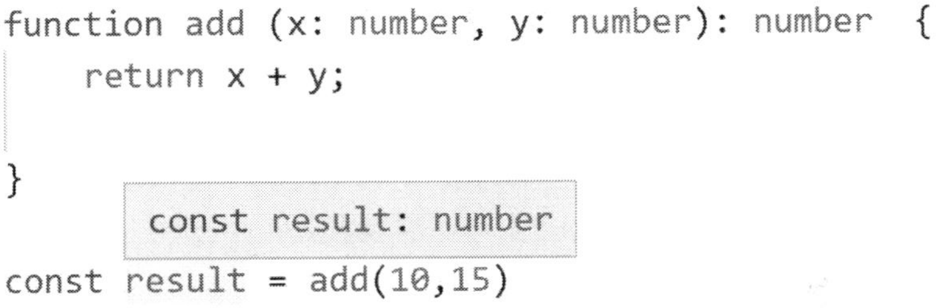

```typescript
function add (x: number, y: number): number  {
    return x + y;

}
```
> const result: number
```typescript
const result = add(10,15)
```

Figure 1.7: VS Code showing the type of the variable

Also, if we try to assign the return value to a variable that is already known to be something else other than a number, we'll get an appropriate error:

```
function add (x: number, y: number): number  {
    return x + y;

}
```

```
Type 'number' is not assignable to type 'string'. ts(2322)

const result: string

View Problem (Alt+F8)    No quick fixes available
```

```
const result: string  = add(10,15)
```

Figure 1.8: Error message on VS Code

Let's make another great point about TypeScript and its type system. As can be seen, the screenshots in this chapter don't show actual compiler error messages – they are taken from inside a code editor (VS Code, an editor that is itself written in TypeScript).

We did not even have to actually compile the code. Instead, we got the error messages while we typed the code – an experience that is familiar to developers in other strongly typed languages, such as C# or Java.

This happens because of the design of the TypeScript compiler, specifically its Language Service API. This enables the editor to easily use the compiler to check the code as it's written so that we can get a nice and intuitive GUI. Additionally, since all the editors will use the same compiler, the development experience will be similar across different editors. This is a dramatic change from the situation that we started with – fully writing, loading, and actually executing the JavaScript code in order to know whether it even makes sense.

> **NOTE**
>
> In recent years, some editors have started using the TypeScript Language Service API on JavaScript code as well, so TypeScript improves even the plain JavaScript development experience.

In a nutshell, using TypeScript changes one of the most prevalent pain points for JavaScript development – inconsistent and sometimes even impossible tooling support – into a much easier and more convenient experience. In our case, we need only to open a parenthesis when calling the **add** function, and we'll see the following:

```
add(x: number, y: number): number
add()
```

Figure 1.9: List of parameters that the function can take

We are shown a list of parameters that shows that the function – which can be defined in another file, by another developer – takes two numbers and also returns a number.

EXERCISE 1.02: WORKING WITH FUNCTIONS IN TYPESCRIPT

In this exercise, we'll define a simple function and see how we can and can't invoke it. The function we will be developing will be a string utility function that shortens a string to a snippet. We'll basically cut off the text after a given length, but take care that we don't chop a word in half. If the string is larger than the maximum length, we'll add an ellipsis (...) to the end:

> **NOTE**
>
> The code files for this exercise can be found here: https://packt.link/BHj53.

1. Create a new file called **snippet.ts**.

2. In **snippet.ts**, define a simple function called **snippet**:

```
function snippet (text: string, length: number) : string {
```

3. Check whether the text is smaller than the specified length, and if it is, return it unchanged:

```
if (text.length < length) {
    return text;
}
```

4. If the text is larger than the maximum length, we'll need to add an ellipsis. The maximum number of characters that we'll be able to show is the specified length minus the length of our ellipsis (as it takes up space too). We'll use the **slice** string method to extract that many characters from the text:

```
const ellipsis = "...";
let result = text.slice(0, length - ellipsis.length);
```

5. We'll find the last word boundary before the cutoff, using **lastIndexOf**, and then combine the text up to that point with the ellipsis:

```
const lastSpace = result.lastIndexOf(" ");
result = `${result.slice(0, lastSpace)}${ellipsis}`;
```

6. Return the result from the function:

```
    return result;
}
```

7. After the function, create a few calls to the function with different parameter types:

```
// correct call and usage
const resultOne = snippet("TypeScript is a programming language that
is a strict syntactical superset of JavaScript and adds optional
static typing to the language.", 40);
console.log(resultOne);
// missing second parameter
const resultTwo = snippet("Lorem ipsum dolor sit amet");
console.log(resultTwo);
// The first parameter is of incorrect type
const resultThree = snippet(false, 40);
console.log(resultThree);
// The second parameter is of incorrect type
const resultFour = snippet("Lorem ipsum dolor sit amet", false);
console.log(resultFour);
// The result is assigned to a variable of incorrect type
var resultFive: number = snippet("Lorem ipsum dolor sit amet", 20);
console.log(resultFive);
```

8. Save the file and run the following command in the folder:

```
tsc snippet.ts
```

9. Verify that the file did not compile correctly. You will get specifics from the compiler about the errors found, and the compilation will end with the following message:

```
Found 3 errors.
```

10. Comment out or delete all invocations except the first one:

```
// correct call and usage
var resultOne = snippet("TypeScript is a programming language that is
a strict syntactical superset of JavaScript and adds optional static
typing to the language.", 40);

console.log(resultOne);
```

11. Save the file and compile it again:

```
tsc snippet.ts
```

12. Verify that the compilation ended successfully and that there is a **snippet.js** file generated in the same folder. Execute it in the **node** environment with the following command:

```
node snippet.js
```

You will see an output that looks as follows:

```
TypeScript is a programming language...
```

In this exercise, we developed a simple string utility function, using TypeScript. We saw the two main strengths of TypeScript. For one, we can see that the code is idiomatic JavaScript – we could leverage our existing JavaScript knowledge to write the function. *Steps 3* through *6*, the actual body of the function, are exactly the same in JavaScript and TypeScript.

Next, we saw that TypeScript takes care that we invoke the function correctly. In *step 7*, we tried five different invocations of the function. The last four invocations are incorrect ones – they would have been errors either in JavaScript or TypeScript. The important difference is that with TypeScript, we immediately got feedback that the usage is invalid. With JavaScript, the errors would have only been visible when we, or a client, actually executed the code.

TYPESCRIPT AND OBJECTS

One great thing about JavaScript is its object literal syntax. While in some languages, to create an object we have to do a lot of groundwork, such as creating classes and defining constructors, in JavaScript, and by extension in TypeScript, we can just create the object as a literal. So, if we want to create a **person** object, with **firstName** and **lastName** properties, we only need to write the following:

```
const person = {
    firstName: "Ada",
    lastName: "Lovelace"
}
```

JavaScript makes it easy to create and use the object, just like any other value. We can access its properties, pass it as an argument into **methods**, receive it as a **return** value from functions, and so on. And because of JavaScript's dynamic nature, it's very easy to add properties to our object. If we wanted to add an **age** property to our object, we could just write the following:

```
person.age = 36;
```

However, because of the loose typing, JavaScript has no knowledge of our object. It does not know what the possible properties of our object are, and what methods can and cannot use it as an argument or a return value. So, say we make a typo, for example, writing out something like this:

```
console.log("Hi, " + person.fristName);
```

JavaScript will happily execute this code and write out **Hi undefined**. That is not what we intended, and will only be visible and detectible when the code is actually run in the browser. Using TypeScript, we have a few options to remedy that. So, let's rewrite our **person** object using TypeScript:

```
const person = {
    firstName: "Ada",
    lastName: "Lovelace"
}

console.log(`Hi, ${person.fristName}`);
```

This code will immediately be marked as invalid by the compiler, even when we haven't added any type information:

```
const person = {
    firstName: "Ada",
    lastName: "Lovelace"
}
```

```
Property 'fristName' does not exist on type '{
firstName: string; lastName: string; }'. Did you mean
'firstName'? ts(2551)

images.ts(2, 5): 'firstName' is declared here.

any

View Problem (Alt+F8)    Quick Fix... (Ctrl+.)
```

```
console.log(`Hi, ${person.fristName}`);
```

Figure 1.10: TypeScript compiler inferring the type of the object

From the error message, we can see what the TypeScript compiler inferred for the type of our object – it thinks that its type consists of two properties, **firstName** of type **string** and **lastName** of type **string**. And according to that definition, there is no place for another property called **fristName**, so we are issued an error.

> **NOTE**
>
> Notice the suggestion **Did you mean 'firstName'?** along with the link to the definition of the **person** class. Since typos are common, the type inference algorithm tries to detect and offer suggestions on common typos.

So, once more, we have detected a bug in our code just by using TypeScript, with no additional code written. TypeScript does this by analyzing the definition of the object and extracts the data from there. It will allow us to write code such as the following:

```
person.lastName = "Byron";
```

But it will not allow us to write code where we set **lastName** to a number:

```
const person = {
    firstName: "Ada",
    Type 'number' is not assignable to type 'string'. ts(2322)

    (property) lastName: string

    View Problem (Alt+F8)    No quick fixes available
person.lastName = 7
```

Figure 1.11: Error message by assigning an incorrect type to lastName

Sometimes, we know more about the shape of our objects than TypeScript does. For example, TypeScript inferred that our type has only the **firstName** and **lastName** properties. So, if we set the age in TypeScript, with **person.age = 36;**, we will get an error. In this case, we can explicitly define the type of our object, using a TypeScript interface. The syntax that we can use looks as follows:

```
interface Person {
    firstName: string;
    lastName: string;
    age? : number;
}
```

With this piece of code, we're defining an abstract – a structure that some object will need to satisfy in order to be allowed to be treated as a **Person** object. Notice the question mark (**?**) next to the **age** variable name. That denotes that that property is in fact optional. An object does not have to have an **age** property in order to be a **Person** object. However, if it does have an **age** property, that property has to be a number. The two other properties (**firstName** and **lastName**) are mandatory.

Using this definition, we can define and use our object using the following:

```
const person: Person = {
    firstName: "Ada",
    lastName: "Lovelace"
}


person.age = 36;
```

We can use interfaces as type annotations for function arguments and return types as well. For example, we can define a function called **showFullName** that will take a person object and display the full name to the console:

```
function showFullName (person: Person) {
    console.log(`${person.firstName} ${person.lastName}`)
}
```

If we invoke this function with **showFullName(person)**, we'll see that it will display **Ada Lovelace** on the console. We can also define a function that will take two strings, and return a new object that fits the **Person** interface:

```
function makePerson (name: string, surname: string): Person {
    const result = {
        firstName: name,
        lastName: surname
    }
    return result;
}

const babbage = makePerson("Charles", "Babbage");
showFullName(babbage);
```

One important thing that we need to point out is that, unlike in other languages, the interfaces in TypeScript are structural and not nominal. What that means is that if we have a certain object that fulfills the "rules" of the interface, that object can be considered to be a value of that interface. In our **makePerson** function, we did not specify that the **result** variable is of the **Person** type – we just used an object literal with **firstName** and **lastName** properties, which were strings. Since that is enough to be considered a person, the code compiles and runs just fine. This is a huge boon to the type inference system, as we can have lots of type checks without having to explicitly define them. In fact, it's quite common to omit the return type of functions.

EXERCISE 1.03: WORKING WITH OBJECTS

In this exercise, we'll define a simple object that encapsulates a book with a few properties. We'll try to access and modify the object's data and verify that TypeScript constrains us according to inferred or explicit rules. We will also create a function that takes a book object and prints out the book's details:

> **NOTE**
>
> The code files for this exercise can be found here: https://packt.link/N8y1f.

1. Create a new file called **book.ts**.

2. In **book.ts**, define a simple interface called **Book**. We will have properties for the author and the title of the book, optional properties for the number of pages of the book, and a Boolean that denotes whether we have read the book:

```
interface Book {
    author: string;
    title: string;
    pages?: number;
    isRead?: boolean;
}
```

3. Add a function called **showBook** that will display the book's author and title to the console. It should also display whether the book has been read or not, that is, whether the **isRead** property is present:

```
function showBook(book: Book) {
    console.log(`${book.author} wrote ${book.title}`);
    if (book.isRead !== undefined) {
        console.log(`  I have ${book.isRead ? "read" : "not read"}
this book`);
    }
}
```

4. Add a function called **setPages** that will take a book and a number of pages as parameters, and set the **pages** property of the book to the provided value:

```
function setPages (book: Book, pages: number) {
    book.pages = pages;
}
```

5. Add a function called **readBook** that will take a book and mark it as having been read:

```
function readBook(book: Book) {
    book.isRead = true;
}
```

6. Create several objects that fulfill the interface. You can, but don't have to, annotate them with the interface we have created:

```
const warAndPeace = {
    author: "Leo Tolstoy",
    title: "War and Peace",
    isRead: false
}
const mobyDick: Book = {
    author: "Herman Melville",
    title: "Moby Dick"
}
```

7. Add code that will call methods on the books:

```
setPages(warAndPeace, 1225);
showBook(warAndPeace);

showBook(mobyDick);
readBook(mobyDick);
showBook(mobyDick);
```

8. Save the file and run the following command in the folder:

```
tsc book.ts
```

9. Verify that the compilation ended successfully and that there is a **book.js** file generated in the same folder. Execute it in the **node** environment with the following command:

```
node book.js
```

You will see an output that looks as follows:

```
Leo Tolstoy wrote War and Peace
  I have not read this book
Herman Melville wrote Moby Dick
```

```
Herman Melville wrote Moby Dick
   I have read this book
```

In this exercise, we created and used an interface, a purely TypeScript construct. We used it to describe the shape of the objects we will use. Without actually creating any specific objects of that shape, we were able to use the full power of TypeScript's tooling and type inference to create a couple of functions that operate on the objects of the given shape.

After that, we were able to actually create some objects that had the required shape (with and without making the declaration explicit). We were able to use both kinds of objects as parameters to our functions, and the results were in line with the interface we declared.

This demonstrated how a simple addition of an interface made our code much safer to write and execute.

BASIC TYPES

Even though JavaScript is a loosely typed language, that does not mean that values do not have types. There are several primitive types that are available to the JavaScript developer. We can get the type of the value using the **typeof** operator, available both in JavaScript and TypeScript. Let's inspect some values and see what the results will be:

```
const value = 1234;
console.log(typeof value);
```

The execution of the preceding code will write the string **"number"** to the console. Now, consider another snippet:

```
const value = "textual value";
console.log(typeof value);
```

The preceding expression will write the string **"string"** to the console. Consider the following snippet:

```
const value = false;
console.log(typeof value);
```

This will write out **"boolean"** to the console.

All of the preceding types are what are called "primitives." They are baked directly into the execution environment, whether that is a browser or a server-side application. We can always use them as needed. There is an additional primitive type that has only a single value, and that's the undefined type, whose only value is undefined. If we try to call **typeof** undefined, we will receive the string **"undefined"**. Other than the primitives, JavaScript and by extension TypeScript have two so-called "structural" types. Those are, respectively, objects, that is, custom-created pieces of code that contain data, and functions, that is, custom-created pieces of code that contain logic. This distinction between data and logic is not a clear-cut border, but it can be a useful approximation. For example, we can define an object with some properties using the object literal syntax:

```
const days = {
    "Monday": 1,
    "Tuesday": 2,
    "Wednesday": 3,
    "Thursday": 4,
    "Friday": 5,
    "Saturday": 6,
    "Sunday": 7,
}
```

Calling the **typeof** operator on the **days** object will return the string **"object"**. We can also use the **typeof** operator if we have an **add** function as we defined before:

```
function add (x, y) {
    return x + y;
}

console.log(typeof add);
```

This will display the string **"function"**.

> **NOTE**
>
> Recent versions of JavaScript added **bigint** and **symbol** as primitive types, but they won't be encountered outside of specific scenarios.

EXERCISE 1.04: EXAMINING TYPEOF

In this exercise, we'll see how to use the **typeof** operator to determine the type of a value, and we will investigate the responses:

> **NOTE**
>
> The code files for this exercise can be found here: https://packt.link/uhJqN.

1. Create a new file called **type-test.ts**.

2. In **type-test.ts**, define several variables with differing values:

```typescript
const daysInWeek = 7;
const name = "Ada Lovelace";
const isRaining = false;
const today = new Date();
const months = ["January", "February", "March"];
const notDefined = undefined;
const nothing = null;
const add = (x:number, y: number) => x + y;
const calculator = {
    add
}
```

3. Add all the variables into a containing array, using the array literal syntax:

```typescript
const everything = [daysInWeek, name, isRaining, today, months,
notDefined, nothing, add, calculator];
```

4. Loop all the variables using a **for..of** loop, and for each value, call the **typeof** operator. Show the result on the console, along with the value itself:

```typescript
for (const something of everything) {
    const type = typeof something;
    console.log(something, type);
}
```

5. Save the file and run the following command in the folder:

```
tsc type-test.ts
```

6. After the compilation is done, you will have a **type-test.js** file. Execute it in the **node** environment with the following command:

```
node type-test.js
```

You will see that the output is as follows:

```
7 number
Ada Lovelace string
false boolean
2021-04-05T09:14:56.259Z object
[ 'January', 'February', 'March' ] object
undefined undefined
null object
[Function: add] function
{ add: [Function: add] } object
```

Note specifically the output from the **months** and **nothing**. **typeof** variables will return the string **"object"** both for arrays and the **null** value. Also note that the **calculator** variable is an object whose only property is actually a function; that is, we have an object whose piece of data is actually a piece of logic. This is possible because functions are first-class values in JavaScript and TypeScript, which means that we can manipulate them just like we would regular values.

STRINGS

Words and text are part of any application, just as they are part of everyday life. In JavaScript, they are represented by the **string** type. Unlike in other languages, such as C++ or Java, strings in JavaScripts are not treated as an array-like object that consists of smaller parts (characters). Instead, strings are a first-order citizen of JavaScript. In addition, JavaScript strings natively support Unicode, so we won't get any problems with characters with, for example, Cyrillic or Arabic script. Just like in JavaScript, to define a string in TypeScript, we can use single quotes (') or double quotes ("). Of course, if we start the string with a single quote, we have to end it with a single quote, and vice versa. We can also use a special type of string definition, called *template strings*. These strings are delimited with the backtick character (`) and support two very important things for web development – newlines and embedded expressions. They are supported in all environments that support ES2015, but TypeScript is able to compile to any JavaScript target environment.

Using embedded expressions and newlines inside a string enables us to generate nice HTML, because instead of string concatenation, we're able to use embedded expressions to have a much clearer view of the generated output. For example, if we had a **person** object with **firstName** and **lastName** properties, and we wanted to display a simple greeting inside a **<div>** tag, we would have to write code as follows:

```
const html = "<div class=\"greeting\">\nHello, " + firstName + " " +
lastName + "\n</div>";
```

From this code (which can get much more complex), it's difficult to see what will actually be written and where. Using template strings transforms this into the following:

```
const html = `<div class="greeting">
    Hello, ${firstName} ${lastName}
</div>";
```

In order to output the **firstName** and **lastName** values, we have to surround them with brackets (**{ }**), preceded by a dollar sign (**$**). We are not limited to variable names, but can have whole expressions, including the conditional operator (**? :**).

NUMBERS

Numbers are an important aspect of the world. We use them to quantify everything around us. And, it's worth noting, that there are two quite different kinds of numbers that you encounter in your daily life – integers and real numbers. One distinguishing difference between the two kinds of numbers is that integers are numbers without any fractional part. These often result from counting things; for example, the number of people in town. On the other hand, real numbers can have a fractional component to them. For example, the weight or height of a person is often a real number.

In most programming languages, these two types of numbers are represented with (at least) two different primitive types; for example, in C#, we have a type called **int** for integers and a type called **float** for real numbers.

In JavaScript, and consequently in TypeScript, they are indeed the same primitive type. That primitive type is simply called **number**. Under the hood, it's a 64-bit floating-point number, fully implementing the IEEE 754 standard. This standard is specified for real numbers, and this leads to some weirdness that is specific to JavaScript. For example, in most environments, dividing by zero results in an error. In JavaScript and TypeScript, division by zero results in some special numbers such as **Infinity** or **NaN**. Additionally, there is no concept of integer division in JavaScript, as division is always done using real numbers.

However, even if everything is stored as floating-point real numbers, JavaScript guarantees that all operations that can be done using only integer arithmetic will be done exactly. One famous example of this behavior is adding **0.1** to **0.2**. In all compliant JavaScript engines, we get the result **0.30000000000000004** because of the finite precision of the underlying type. What we are guaranteed is that we can never get a decimal result if we are adding integers. The engine makes sure that **1+1=2** with no decimal remainder. All integer operations are completely safe, but only if the results are within a specified range. JavaScript has a special constant defined (**Number.MAX_SAFE_INTEGER**) with a value of **9007199254740991** (with digit grouping, this is represented as **9.007.199.254.740.991**) over which we might get precision and rounding errors.

BOOLEANS

Booleans are one of the simplest, and also one of the most used and useful, primitive types. This datatype has exactly two values, **true** and **false**. The useful thing is that if a variable of this type does not have a certain value, well, then it automatically has the other, as that is the only other possible option. In theory, this is sound, but in JavaScript, there are a lot of possibilities for things to go wrong. Since it has no type information, it cannot guarantee that a certain variable actually holds a Boolean value, which means that we always have to be careful of our Boolean checks.

TypeScript completely defines away this problem. Say we define a variable as a Boolean, using either a type annotation or type inference, as follows:

```
let isRead = false;
```

We can be absolutely sure that the variable will always have exactly one of the two possible values.

ARRAYS

One of the reasons computers are popular, aside from accessing social networking sites and playing video games, is that they are able to run the same processing algorithm on a whole collection of values, as many times as needed, without getting bored or making any errors. In order to be able to do that, we need to somehow organize the data into a collection of similar values that we can access one at a time. In JavaScript, the primary mechanism for such processing is the array. JavaScript has an extremely simple interface for creating arrays using the array literal syntax. We just list the elements, surrounded by brackets (**[ ]**), and we have an array:

```
const numbers = [1, 2, 3, 4, 5];
```

We can access that array using an index:

```
console.log(numbers[3]) // writes out 4, as arrays in JavaScript are
//...0-based
numbers[1] = 200; // the second element becomes 200
```

That makes it easy to use a **for** loop to go through the elements and process them all with a single piece of code:

```
for (let index = 0; index < numbers.length; index += 1) {
    const element = numbers[index];
    console.log(`The element at index ${index} has a value of
${element}`);
}
```

We can also use a **for..of** loop to iterate through the values, and the following snippet will calculate the sum of all the numbers in the array:

```
let sum = 0;
for (const element of numbers) {
    sum += element;
}
```

As with anything in JavaScript, it has no mechanism to enforce that all the items in an array satisfy the "similarity" requirement we mentioned previously. So, there's nothing stopping us from adding a string, a Boolean, an object, or even a function to the array of numbers we have defined. All of these are valid JavaScript commands that will execute successfully:

```
numbers[1] = false;
numbers[2] = new Date();
numbers[3] = "three";
numbers[4] = function () {
    console.log("I'm really not a number");
};
```

In almost all cases, it is not to our benefit to have an array with vastly different types as elements. The main benefit of arrays is that we can group similar items together and work with all of them with the same code. If we have different types, we lose that advantage, so we might as well not use an array at all.

With TypeScript, we can restrict the type so that an array will only allow a single type of value for its elements. Arrays have something that is referred to as a *composite* or *generic* type. That means that when we are specifying the type of the array, we're specifying it indirectly, via another type.

In this case, we define the type of the array through the type of the array's elements, for example, we can have an array whose elements will be numbers or an array whose elements will be strings. In TypeScript, we denote that by writing the type of the element and then appending brackets to the type name. So, if we needed our **numbers** array to only accept values whose type is **number**, we will denote that as follows:

```
let numbers: number[];
```

Even better, if we are initializing our array, we can omit the type annotation and let TypeScript infer the value:

```
const numbers = [1, 2, 3, 4, 5];

    Type 'string' is not assignable to type 'number'. ts(2322)

    const numbers: number[]

    View Problem (Alt+F8)    No quick fixes available
numbers[3] = "six";


numbers.push("six")
```

Figure 1.12: TypeScript inferring the type of the elements in the array

As shown previously, TypeScript will not let us use the **push** method with a value whose type does not match the type of the elements, nor will it allow elements to be set to invalid values.

Another, equivalent way to denote the type of the array is to use generic type syntax. In that case, we can use the **Array** type, with the type of the actual elements in angle brackets:

```
let numbers: Array<number>;
```

Generic classes and methods will be covered in detail in *Chapter 9, Generics and Conditional Types*.

The benefit here is that we can be certain that if an array claims to have elements of a certain type, it will indeed have that kind of element, and we can process them without worrying that a bug introduced an incompatible element.

TUPLES

Another common usage of arrays in JavaScript is to group data – just like objects, but without the hassle (and benefit) of property names. We could, for example, instead of creating a **person** object create a **person** array where, by convention, we'll use the first element to hold the first name, the second element to hold the last name, and the third element to hold the age. We could define such an array using the following:

```
const person = ["Ada", "Lovelace", 36];

console.log(`First Name is: ${person[0]}`);
console.log(`Last Name is: ${person[1]}`);
console.log(`Age is: ${person[2]}`);
```

In this case, even as we are using the same structure – an array – we're not using it to group an unknown number of unrelated data of the same type, we're using it to group a known number of related data that can be of separate types. This kind of array is called a *tuple*. Once more, JavaScript has no mechanism to enforce the structure of a tuple, so in our code we can do lots of things that are syntactically valid, but nonsensical semantically. We could add a fourth element in the array, we can set the first element to be a number, the third to be a function, and so on.

With TypeScript, we can formally define the number and types of the data elements that we need inside a tuple, using syntax such as the following:

```
const person: [string, string, number] = ["Ada", "Lovelace", 36];
```

The **[string, string, number]** declaration tells TypeScript that we intend to use a tuple of three elements, that the first two elements will be a string, and the third will be a number. TypeScript now has enough information to enforce the structure. So, if we write code that will call the **toLowerCase** method on the first element of the tuple and multiply the third element by 10, that will work, as the first operation is valid on a string and the second is valid on a number:

```
console.log(person[0].toLowerCase());
console.log(person[2] * 10);
```

But if we try the operations the other way around, we'll get errors on both calls:

```
const person: [string, string, number] = ["Ada", "Lovelace", 36];

console.log(person[0].
console.log(person[2]
```

> Property 'toLowerCase' does not exist on type
> 'number'. ts(2339)
>
> any
>
> View Problem (Alt+F8)   No quick fixes available

```
console.log(person[2].toLowerCase());
console.log(person[0] * 10);
```

Figure 1.13: TypeScript error when performing incorrect operations

Additionally, if we try to access an element that is outside of the defined range, we'll get an error as well:

```
const person: [string, string, number] = ["Ada", "Lovelace", 36];
```

> Tuple type '[string, string, number]' of length '3' has no
> element at index '3'. ts(2493)
>
> View Problem (Alt+F8)   No quick fixes available

```
console.log(person[3]);
```

Figure 1.14: TypeScript when accessing elements outside the defined range

SCHWARTZIAN TRANSFORM

Arrays have a helpful sort function, which we can use to sort the objects contained in the array. However, during the sorting process, multiple comparisons will be done on the same objects. For example, if we sort an array of 100 numbers, the method that compares two numbers will be called more than 500 times, on average. Let's say that we have a **Person** interface, defined with the following:

```
interface Person {
    firstName: string;
    lastName: string;
}
```

If we want to get the full name of the person, we might use a function such as this:

```
function getFullName (person: Person) {
    return `${person.firstName} ${person.lastName}`;
}
```

If we have an array of **Person** objects, called **persons**, and want to sort it according to full name, we might use the following code:

```
persons.sort((first, second) => {
    const firstFullName = getFullName(first);
    const secondFullName = getFullName(second);
    return firstFullName.localeCompare(secondFullName);
})
```

This will sort the **persons** array, albeit in an inefficient manner. If we have 100 **Person** objects, this means that we have 100 different targets for the **getFullName** functions. But if we have more than 500 calls to the comparison function, that would mean that we have more than 1,000 calls to the **getFullName** function, so at least 900 calls are redundant.

> **NOTE**
>
> The relation gets worse: for 10,000 persons, we will have around a quarter of a million redundant calls.

Our method is fast and trivial, but if some expensive calculations were needed, simple sorting could slow down our application.

Fortunately, there's a simple technique called a Schwartzian transform that can help us with that. The technique has three parts:

- We will transform each element in the array into a tuple of two elements. The first element of the tuple will be the original value, and the second will be the result of the ordering function (colloquially, the Schwartz).

- We will sort the array on the second element of the tuple.

- We will transform each tuple, discarding the ordering element and taking the original value.

We will employ this technique in the following exercise.

EXERCISE 1.05: USING ARRAYS AND TUPLES TO CREATE AN EFFICIENT SORT OF OBJECTS

In this exercise, we are going to employ the Schwartzian transform to sort and print a predefined array of programmers. Each programmer object will be an instance of the **Person** interface, defined in the previous section.

We'll want to sort the programmers based on their full name, which can be calculated using the **getFullName** function, also from the previous section.

In order to implement a Schwartzian transform, we'll take the following steps:

We'll use the **map** method of the array in order to transform our programmers into a tuple of the **[Person, string]** type, where the first element is the actual programmer and the second element is the full name string.

We'll use the **sort** method of the array to sort the tuples, using the second element of each tuple.

We'll use the **map** method once more to transform the tuples back to an array of programmers by just taking the first element and discarding the second element.

Let's start:

> **NOTE**
>
> The code files for this exercise can be found here: https://packt.link/EgZnX.

1. Create a new file called **person-sort.ts**.

2. Inside the file, create the interface for the **Person** objects:

```
interface Person {
    firstName: string;
    lastName: string;
}
```

3. Create the function that will get the full name of a given person:

```
let count = 0;

function getFullName (person: Person) {
    count += 1;
    return `${person.firstName} ${person.lastName}`;
}
```

We will use the **count** variable to detect the total number of calls of the function.

4. Define an array of persons and add a few objects with **firstName** and **lastName** properties:

```
const programmers: Person[] = [
    { firstName: 'Donald', lastName: 'Knuth'},
    { firstName: 'Barbara', lastName: 'Liskow'},
    { firstName: 'Lars', lastName: 'Bak'},
    { firstName: 'Guido', lastName: 'Van Rossum'},
    { firstName: 'Anders', lastName: 'Hejslberg'},
    { firstName: 'Edsger', lastName: 'Dijkstra'},
    { firstName: 'Brandon', lastName: 'Eich'},
    // feel free to add as many as you want
];
```

5. Define a naïve and straight forward sorting function:

```
// a naive and straightforward sorting function
function naiveSortPersons (persons: Person[]): Person[] {
    return persons.slice().sort((first, second) => {
        const firstFullName = getFullName(first);
        const secondFullName = getFullName(second);
        return firstFullName.localeCompare(secondFullName);
    })
}
```

6. Use a Schwartzian transform and define a function that will take an array of persons and return (a sorted) array of persons:

```
function schwartzSortPersons (persons: Person[]): Person[] {
```

7. Use the array's **map** function to transform each element into a tuple:

```
    const tuples: [Person, string][] = persons.map(person => [person, getFullName(person)]);
```

8. Sort the **tuples** array of tuples, using the standard **sort** method:

```
    tuples.sort((first, second) => first[1].localeCompare(second[1]));
```

We should note that the **sort** function takes two objects, in our case, two tuples, and we sort the tuples according to their second element – the result of the **getFullName** call.

9. Transform the sorted array of tuples into the format we want – just an array of **person** objects – by taking the first element of each tuple, discarding the Schwartz:

```
const result = tuples.map(tuple => tuple[0]);
```

10. The last three steps are the three parts of the Schwartzian transform.

11. Return the new array from the function:

```
    return result;

}
```

12. Add a line that will call the **naiveSortPersons** function on our defined array:

```
count = 0;
const sortedNaive = naiveSortPersons(programmers);
```

13. Output both the sorted array, and the count variable.

```
console.log(sortedNaive);
console.log(`When called using the naive approach, the function was called ${count} times`);
```

14. Add a line that will call the **schwartzSortPersons** function on our defined array:

```
count = 0;
const sortedSchwartz = schwartzSortPersons(programmers);
```

15. Output both the **sorted** array and the **count** variable. The **count** variable should be identical to the number of items in the array, which is 7 in our example. Without the optimization, the method would have been called 28 times:

```
console.log(sortedSchwartz);
console.log(`When called using the Schwartzian transform approach, the function was called ${count} times`);
```

16. Save and compile the file:

```
tsc person-sort.ts
```

17. Verify that the compilation ended successfully and that there is a **person-sort.js** file generated in the same folder. Execute it in the **node** environment with the following command:

```
node person-sort.js
```

You will see an output that looks as follows:

```
[
    { firstName: 'Anders', lastName: 'Hejslberg' },
    { firstName: 'Barbara', lastName: 'Liskow' },
    { firstName: 'Brandon', lastName: 'Eich' },
    { firstName: 'Donald', lastName: 'Knuth' },
    { firstName: 'Edsger', lastName: 'Dijkstra' },
    { firstName: 'Guido', lastName: 'Van Rossum' },
    { firstName: 'Lars', lastName: 'Bak' }
]
When called using the naive approach, the function was called 28
times
[
    { firstName: 'Anders', lastName: 'Hejslberg' },
    { firstName: 'Barbara', lastName: 'Liskow' },
    { firstName: 'Brandon', lastName: 'Eich' },
    { firstName: 'Donald', lastName: 'Knuth' },
    { firstName: 'Edsger', lastName: 'Dijkstra' },
    { firstName: 'Guido', lastName: 'Van Rossum' },
    { firstName: 'Lars', lastName: 'Bak' }
]
When called using the Schwartzian transform approach, the function
was called 7 times
```

We can easily check that the values that are outputted are sorted according to their full names. We can also notice a 7 at the end of output – that's the total number of calls of the **getFullName** function. Since we have 7 items in the programmers array, we can conclude that the function was called just once for each object.

We could have instead sorted the programmers array directly, using code such as the following:

```
programmers.sort((first, second) => {
    const firstFullName = getFullName(first);
    const secondFullName = getFullName(second);
    return firstFullName.localeCompare(secondFullName);
});

console.log(count);
```

In this case, for this array, the count of execution of the **getFullName** function would have been 28, which is four times as high as our optimized version.

ENUMS

Often we have some types that have a predefined set of values, and no other value is valid. For example, there are four and only four cardinal directions (East, West, North, and South). There are four and only four different suits in a deck of cards. So, how do we define a variable that should have such a value?

In TypeScript, we can use an **enum** type to do that. The simplest way to define an enum would be as follows:

```
enum Suit {
    Hearts,
    Diamonds,
    Clubs,
    Spades
}
```

We can then define and use a variable of such type, and TypeScript will help us use it:

```
let trumpSuit = Suit.Hears;
```

TypeScript will infer that the type of the **trumpSuit** variable is **Suit** and will only allow us to access those four values. Any attempt to assign something else to the variable will result in an error:

```
let trumpSuit = Suit.Hearts;
```

```
Type '"invalid-value"' is not assignable to type
'Suit'. ts(2322)

let trumpSuit: Suit

View Problem (Alt+F8)    No quick fixes available
trumpSuit = "invalid-value"
```

Figure 1.15: TypeScript inferring the type of trumpSuit

So far, all the types we've encountered were JavaScript types that were augmented with TypeScript. Unlike that, enums are specific to TypeScript. Under the hood, the **Suit** class actually compiles into an object with values like this:

```
{
    '0': 'Hearts',
    '1': 'Diamonds',
    '2': 'Clubs',
    '3': 'Spades',
    Hearts: 0,
    Diamonds: 1,
    Clubs: 2,
    Spades: 3
}
```

TypeScript will automatically assign numbers starting with zero to the options provided and add a reverse mapping as well, so if we have the option, we can get the value, but if we have the value, we can map to the option as well. We can also explicitly set the provided numbers as well:

```
enum Suit {
    Hearts = 10,
    Diamonds = 20,
    Clubs = 30,
    Spades = 40
}
```

We can also use strings instead of numbers, with syntax like this:

```
enum Suit {
    Hearts = "hearts",
    Diamonds = "diamonds",
    Clubs = "clubs",
    Spades = "spades"
}
```

These enums are called string-based enums, and they compile to an object like this:

```
{
  Hearts: 'hearts',
  Diamonds: 'diamonds',
  Clubs: 'clubs',
  Spades: 'spades'
}
```

ANY AND UNKNOWN

So far, we have explained how TypeScript inference works, and how powerful it is. But sometimes we actually want to have JavaScript's "anything goes" behavior. For example, what if we genuinely need a variable that will sometimes hold a string and sometimes hold a number? The following code will issue an error because we're trying to assign a string to a variable that TypeScript inferred to be a number:

```
let variable = 3;
if (Math.random()>0.5) {
    variable = "not-a-number";
}
```

This is how the code will appear on VS Code with the error message:

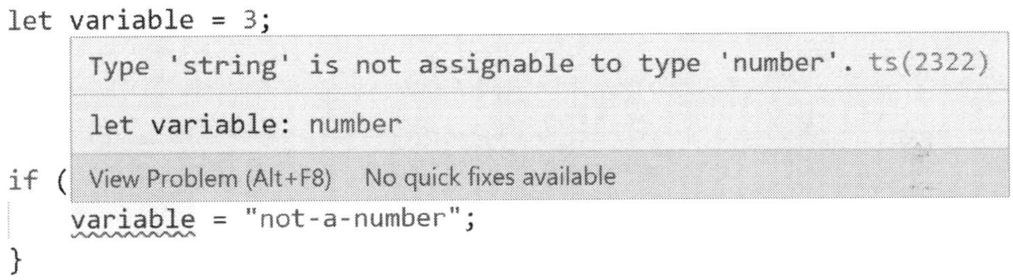

```
let variable = 3;
     Type 'string' is not assignable to type 'number'. ts(2322)

     let variable: number

if ( View Problem (Alt+F8)    No quick fixes available
    variable = "not-a-number";
}
```

Figure 1.16: TypeScript inferring the type of variable

What we need to do is somehow suspend the type inference for that specific variable. To be able to do that, TypeScript provides us with the **any** type:

```
let variable: any = 3;
if (Math.random()>0.5) {
    variable = "not-a-number";
}
```

This type annotation reverts the **variable** variable to the default JavaScript behavior, so none of the calls involving that variable will be checked by the compiler. Additionally, most calls that include a variable of the **any** type will infer a result of the same type. This means that the **any** type is highly contagious, and even if we define it in a single place in our application, it can propagate to lots of places.

Since using **any** effectively negates most of TypeScript's benefits, it's best used as seldom as possible, and only when absolutely necessary. It's a powerful tool to use the opt-in/opt-out design of TypeScript so that we can gradually upgrade existing JavaScript code into TypeScript.

One scenario that is sometimes used is a combination of the dynamic nature of **any** and the static nature of TypeScript – we can have an array where the elements can be anything:

```
const everything: any[] = [ 1, false, "string"];
```

Starting from version 3.0, TypeScript also offers another type with dynamic semantics – the **unknown** type. While still dynamic, it's much more constricted in what can be done with it. For example, the following code will compile using **any**:

```
const variable: any = getSomeResult(); // a hypothetical function //with
some return value we know nothing about

const str: string = variable;   // this works, as any might be a //string,
and "anything goes";
variable.toLowerCase();         // we are allowed to call a method, //and
we'll determine at runtime whether that's possible
```

On the other hand, the same code with an **unknown** type annotation results in the following:

```
const variable: unknown = 7; // a hypothetical function //with some
```

Type 'unknown' is not assignable to type 'string'. ts(2322)

const str: string

View Problem (Alt+F8)   No quick fixes available

```
const str: string = variable;   // this works, as any might be a //s
variable.toLowerCase();         // we are allowed to call a method,
```

Figure 1.17: TypeScript compiler error message

The **unknown** type basically flips the assertion and the burden of proof. With **any**, the flow is that, since we don't know that it's not a string, we can treat it as a string. With **unknown**, we don't know whether it's a string, so we can't treat it as a string. In order to do anything useful with an **unknown**, we need to explicitly test its value and determine our actions based on that:

```
const variable: unknown = getSomeResult(); // a hypothetical function
with some return value we know nothing about


if (typeof variable === "string") {
    const str: string = variable; // valid, because we tested if the
value inside `variable` actually has a type of string
    variable.toLowerCase();
}
```

NULL AND UNDEFINED

One of the specifics of JavaScript is that it has two separate values that signify that there isn't a value: **null** and **undefined**. The difference between the two is that **null** has to be specified explicitly – so if something is **null**, that is because someone set it to **null**. Meanwhile, if something has the value **undefined** usually it means that the value is not set at all. For example, let's look at a **person** object defined with the following:

```
const person = {
    firstName: "Ada",
    lastName: null
}
```

The value of the **lastName** property has been set to **null** explicitly. On the other hand, the **age** property is not set at all. So, if we print them out, we'll see that the **lastName** property has a value of **null**, while the **age** property has a value of **undefined**:

```
console.log(person.lastName);
console.log(person.age);
```

We should note that if we have some optional properties in an object, their default value will be **undefined**. Similarly, if we have optional parameters in a function, the default value of the argument will be **undefined** as well.

NEVER

There is another "not a value" type that's specific to TypeScript, and that is the special **never** type. This type represents a value that never occurs. For example, if we have a function where the end of the function is not reachable and has no return statements, its return type will be **never**. An example of such a function will be as follows:

```
function notReturning(): never {
    throw new Error("point of no return");
}

const value = notReturning();
```

The type of the **value** variable will be inferred as **never**. Another situation where **never** is useful is if we have a logical condition that cannot be **true**. As a simple example, let's look at this code:

```
const x = true;

if (x) {
    console.log(`x is true: ${x.toString()}`);
}
```

The conditional statement will always be **true**, so we will always see the text in the console. But if we add an **else** branch to this code, the value of **x** inside the branch cannot be **true** because we're in the **else** branch, but cannot be anything else because it was defined as **true**. So, the actual type is inferred to be **never**. Since **never** does not have any properties or methods, this branch will throw a compile error:

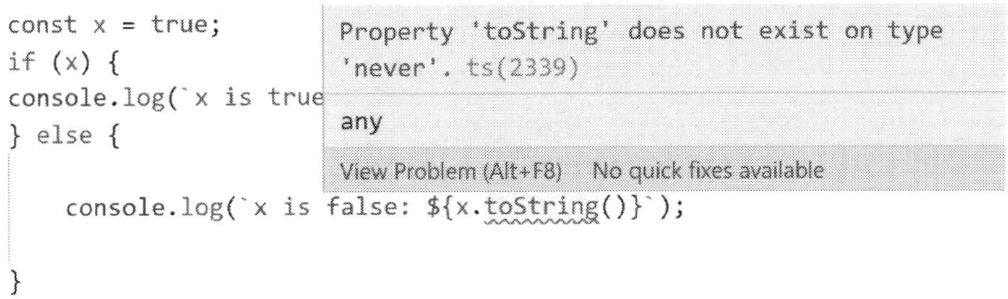

```
const x = true;
if (x) {
console.log(`x is true
} else {

    console.log(`x is false: ${x.toString()}`);


}
```

Property 'toString' does not exist on type 'never'. ts(2339)

any

View Problem (Alt+F8)   No quick fixes available

Figure 1.18: Compiler error from using the never type

FUNCTION TYPES

The last built-in type in JavaScript that we'll take a look at is not really a piece of data – it's a piece of code. Since functions are first-order objects in JavaScript, they remain so in TypeScript as well. And just like the others, functions get types as well. The type of a function is a bit more complicated than the other types. In order to identify it, we need all the parameters and their types, as well as the return values and their types. Let's take a look at an **add** function defined with the following:

```
const add = function (x: number, y: number) {
    return x + y;
}
```

To fully describe the type of the function, we need to know that it is a function that takes a number as the first parameter and a number as the second parameter and returns a number. In TypeScript, we'll write this as **(x: number, y: number) => number**.

MAKING YOUR OWN TYPES

Of course, aside from using the types that are already available in JavaScript, we can define our own types. We have several options for that. We can use the JavaScript **class** specification to declare our own classes, with properties and methods.
A simple class can be defined with the following:

```
class Person {
    constructor(public firstName: string, public lastName: string, public age?: number) {
    }

    getFullName() {
        return `${this.firstName} ${this.lastName}`;
    }
}
```

We can create objects of this class and use methods on them:

```
const person = new Person("Ada", "Lovelace");
console.log(person.getFullName());
```

Another way to formalize our complex structures is to use an interface:

```
interface Person
{
    firstName: string;
    lastName: string;
    age?: string;
}
```

Unlike classes, which compile to JavaScript classes or constructor functions (depending on the compilation target), interfaces are a TypeScript-only construct. When compiling, they are checked statically, and then removed from the compiled code.

Both classes and interfaces are useful if implementing a class hierarchy, as both constructs are suitable for extension and inheritance.

Yet another way is to use type aliases, with the **type** keyword. We can basically put a name that we will use as a type alias to just about anything available in TypeScript. For example, if we want to have another name for the primitive **number** type, for example, **integer**, we can always do the following:

```
type integer = number;
```

If we want to give a name to a tuple, **[string, string, number?]**, that we use to store a person, we can alias that with the following:

```
type Person = [string, string, number?];
```

We can also use objects and functions in the definition of a type alias:

```
type Person = {
    firstName: string;
    lastName: string;
    age?: number;
}

type FilterFunction = (person: Person) => boolean;
```

We will go into more details and intricacies of the **class**, **interface**, and **type** keywords in *Chapter 4, Classes and Objects*, *Chapter 5, Interfaces and Inheritance*, and *Chapter 6, Advance Types*, respectively.

EXERCISE 1.06: MAKING A CALCULATOR FUNCTION

In this exercise, we'll define a calculator function that will take the operands and the operation as parameters. We will design it so it is easy to extend it with additional operations and use that behavior to extend it:

> **NOTE**
>
> The code files for this exercise can be found here: https://packt.link/dKoCZ.

1. Create a new file called **calculator.ts**.

2. In **calculator.ts**, define an enum with all the operators that we want to support inside our code:

```
enum Operator {
    Add = "add",
    Subtract = "subtract",
    Multiply = "multiply",
    Divide = "divide",
}
```

3. Define an empty (for now) **calculator** function that will be our main interface. The function should take three parameters: the two numbers that we want to operate on, as well as an operator:

```
const calculator = function (first: number, second: number, op:
Operator) {

}
```

4. Create a type alias for a function that does a calculation on two numbers. Such a function will take two numbers as parameters and return a single number:

```
type Operation = (x: number, y: number) => number;
```

5. Create an empty array that can hold multiple tuples of the **[Operator, Operation]** type. This will be our dictionary, where we store all our methods:

```
const operations: [Operator, Operation][] = [];
```

6. Create an **add** method that satisfies the **Operation** type (you don't need to explicitly reference it):

```
const add = function (first: number, second: number) {
    return first + second;
};
```

7. Create a tuple of the **Operator.Add** value and the **add** function and add it to the **operations** array:

```
operations.push([Operator.Add, add]);
```

8. Repeat *steps 6* and *7* for the subtraction, multiplication, and division functions:

```
const subtract = function (first: number, second: number) {
    return first - second;
};
operations.push([Operator.Subtract, subtract]);


const multiply = function (first: number, second: number) {
    return first * second;
};
operations.push([Operator.Multiply, multiply]);


const divide = function (first: number, second: number) {
    return first / second;
};
operations.push([Operator.Divide, divide]);
```

9. Implement the **calculator** function, using the **operations** array to find the correct tuple by the **Operator** provided, and then using the corresponding **Operation** value to do the calculation:

```
const calculator = function (first: number, second: number, op:
Operator) {
    const tuple = operations.find(tpl => tpl[0] === op);
    const operation = tuple[1];
    const result = operation(first, second);
    return result;
}
```

Note that, as long as a function has the required type, that is, it takes two numbers and outputs a number, we can use it as an operation.

10. Let's take the calculator for a test run. Write some code that will call the **calculator** function with different arguments:

```
console.log(calculator(4, 6, Operator.Add));
console.log(calculator(13, 3, Operator.Subtract));
console.log(calculator(2, 5, Operator.Multiply));
console.log(calculator(70, 7, Operator.Divide));
```

11. Save the file and run the following command in the folder:

```
tsc calculator.ts
```

12. Verify that the compilation ended successfully and that there is a **calculator. js** file generated in the same folder. Execute it in the **node** environment with the following command:

```
node calculator.js
```

You will see the output looks as follows:

```
10
10
10
10
```

13. Now, let's try to extend our calculator by adding a modulo operation. First, we need to add that option to the **Operator** enum:

```
enum Operator {
    Add = "add",
    Subtract = "subtract",
    Multiply = "multiply",
    Divide = "divide",
    Modulo = "modulo"
}
```

14. Add a function called **modulo** of the **Operation** type, and add a corresponding tuple to the **operations** array:

```
const modulo = function (first: number, second: number) {
    return first % second;
};
operations.push([Operator.Modulo, modulo]);
```

15. At the end of the file, add a call to the **calculator** function that uses the **Modulo** operator:

```
console.log(calculator(14, 3, Operator.Modulo));
```

16. Save and compile the file and run the resulting JavaScript with the following command:

```
node calculator.js
```

You will see an output that looks as follows:

```
10
10
10
10
2
```

Note that when we extended our calculator with the modulo function, we did not change the **calculator** function at all. In this exercise, we saw how we can use the tuples, arrays, and function types to effectively design an extensible system.

ACTIVITY 1.01: CREATING A LIBRARY FOR WORKING WITH STRINGS

Your task is to create a series of simple functions that will help you do some common operations on strings. Some of the operations are already supported in the standard JavaScript library, but you will use them as a convenient learning exercise, both of JavaScript internals and TypeScript as a language. Our library will have the following functions:

1. **toTitleCase**: This will process a string and will capitalize the first letter of each word but will make all the other letters lowercase.

   Test cases for this function are as follows:

   ```
   "war AND peace" => "War And Peace"
   "Catcher in the Rye" => "Catcher In The Rye"
   "tO kILL A mOCKINGBIRD" => "To Kill A MockingBird"
   ```

2. **countWords**: This will count the number of separate words within a string. Words are delimited by spaces, dashes (-), or underscores (_).

   Test cases for this function are as follows:

   ```
   "War and Peace" => 3
   "catcher-in-the-rye" => 4
   "for_whom the-bell-tolls" => 5
   ```

3. **toWords**: This will return all the words that are within a string. Words are delimited by spaces, dashes (–), or underscores (_).

Test cases for this function are as follows:

```
"War and Peace" => [War, and, peace]
"catcher-in-the-rye" => [catcher, in, the, rye]
"for_whom the-bell-tolls"=> [for, whom, the, bell, tolls]
```

4. **repeat**: This will take a string and a number and return that same string repeated that number of times.

Test cases for this function are as follows:

```
"War", 3 => "WarWarWar"
"rye", 1 => "rye"
"bell", 0 => ""
```

5. **isAlpha**: This will return **true** if the string only has alpha characters (that is, letters). Test cases for this function are as follows:

```
"War and Peace" => false
"Atonement" => true
"1Q84" => false
```

6. **isBlank**: This will return **true** if the string is blank, that is, consists only of whitespace characters.

Test cases for this function are as follows:

```
"War and Peace" => false
"         " => true
"" => true
```

When writing the functions, make sure to think of the types of the parameters and the types of the return values.

> **NOTE**
>
> The code files for this activity can be found here: https://packt.link/TOZuy.

Here are some steps to help you create the preceding functions (note that there are multiple ways to implement each of the functions, so treat these steps as suggestions):

1. Creating the **toTitleCase** function: In order to change each word, we'll need first to get all the words. You can use the **split** function to make a single string into an array of words. Next, we'll need to **slice** off the first letter from the rest of the word. We can use the **toLowerCase** and **toUpperCase** methods to make something lower- and uppercase, respectively. After we get all the words properly cased, we can use the **join** array method to make an array of strings into a single large string.

2. Creating the **countWords** function: In order to get the words, we can split the original string on any occurrence of any of the three delimiters (**" "**, **"_"**, and **"-"**). Fortunately, the **split** function can take a regular expression as a parameter, which we can use to our benefit. Once we have the words in an array, we just need to count the elements.

3. Creating the **towards** function: This method can use the same approach as the preceding one. Instead of counting the words, we'll just need to return them. Take note of the return type of this method.

4. Creating the **repeat** function: Create an array with the required length (using the **Array** constructor), and set each element to the input value (using the array's **fill** method). After that, you can use the **join** method of the array to join the values into a single long string.

5. Creating the **isAlpha** function: We can design a regular expression that will test this, but we can also split the string into single characters, using the string **split** method. Once we have the character array, we can use the map function to transform all the characters to lowercase. We can then use the filter method to return only those characters that are not between "a" and "z". If we don't have such characters, then the input only has letters, so we should return true. Otherwise, we should return false.

6. Creating the **isBlank** function: One way to create such a function is to repeatedly test whether the first character is empty, and if it is, to remove it (a **while** loop works best for this). That loop will break either on the first non-blank characters or when it runs out of the first elements, that is, when the input is empty. In the first case, the string is not blank, so we should return **false**; otherwise, we should return **true**.

> **NOTE**
>
> The solution to this activity can be found on page 590.

SUMMARY

In this chapter, we looked at the world before TypeScript and described the problems and issues that TypeScript was actually designed to solve. We had a brief overview of how TypeScript operates under the hood, got ourselves introduced to the **tsc** compiler, and learned how we can control it using the **tsconfig.json** file.

We familiarized ourselves with the differences between TypeScript and JavaScript and saw how TypeScript infers the types from the values that we provide. We learned how different primitive types are treated in TypeScript, and finally, we learned how to create our own types to structure the building blocks of a large-scale, enterprise-level web application. Equipped with the fundamentals, you are now in a position to delve further into TypeScript, with the next chapter teaching you about declaration files.

2

DECLARATION FILES

OVERVIEW

This chapter gets you started with declaration files in TypeScript. You will learn how to work with declaration files, including how to build your own declaration files from scratch, and then work with types in external libraries. By the end of this chapter, you will be able to create declaration files from scratch, implement common development patterns for creating declaration files, and produce type checking when working with third-party NPM code libraries.

INTRODUCTION

In this chapter, you will learn about TypeScript declaration files. Declaration files give you the ability to give TypeScript more information about how a function or class is structured.

Why is it important to understand how declaration files work? Technically, declaration files speak directly to the core motivations for why TypeScript is becoming so popular. One of the common rationales for using TypeScript is because it guides developers through the application process. Let's walk through a real-world example as a case study.

In pure JavaScript, if we start working with a code library that we've never used before that formats dates, such as **Moment JS**, we would have to start by looking through the documentation in order to know what type of data we can pass to the Moment JS functions. When working with a new library, it is tedious work to figure out requirements, such as how many function arguments are required for each function and what data type each argument needs to be.

With the declaration files, however, TypeScript informs the text editor of the requirements for every function that a library has. So, instead of having to rely solely on documentation and Google searches, the text editor itself informs the developer how to work with each function. For example, the text editor, with the help of TypeScript, would inform us that the Moment JS format function takes in zero to one arguments, and the optional argument needs to be a string. And declaration files make all of this possible.

DECLARATION FILES

Anytime we're asked to write additional boilerplate code, our first question is: why is it important to do this? With that in mind, before we walk through creating and managing declaration files, let's first analyze the role of declaration files in the development process.

The entire reason why we use TypeScript in the first place is to give our applications a specified structure based on types. Declaration files extend this functionality by allowing us to define the shape of our programs.

In this section, we will walk through two ways to work with declaration files. The first approach will be to create our own declaration files from scratch. This is a great place to start since it provides insight into how the declaration process works. In the second part, we will see how we can integrate types into third-party NPM libraries.

> **NOTE**
>
> Declaration files are not a new concept in the programming world. The same principle has been used for decades in older programming languages such as Java, C, and C++.

Before we get into this chapter's example project, let's look at the core elements that comprise a declaration file in TypeScript. Consider the following code, which assigns a string value to a variable:

```
firstName = "Kristine";
```

The preceding code in TypeScript will generate a compiler warning that says **Cannot find name 'firstName'**, which can be seen in the following screenshot:

```
TS hello.ts
1    firstName ="Kristine";
2
     Cannot find name 'firstName'. ts(2304)

     any        .

     View Problem (Alt+F8)   Quick Fix... (Ctrl+.)
```

Figure 2.1: Compiler error when TypeScript cannot find a variable declaration

This error is shown because whenever we attempt to assign a value to a variable, TypeScript looks for where a variable name is defined. We can fix this by utilizing the **declare** keyword. The following code will correct the error that we encountered in the previous case:

```
declare let firstName: string;
firstName = "Kristine";
```

As you can see in the following screenshot, the compiler warning disappeared with the use of the **declare** keyword:

```
TS hello.ts > ...
1    declare let firstName: string;
2    firstName = "Kristine";
3
```

Figure 2.2: Example of a variable being defined in TypeScript

Now, that may not seem like a big deal, because we could accomplish the same goal by simply defining a **let** variable, such as the following:

```
let firstName: string;
firstName = "Kristine"
```

The preceding code would not generate an error when viewed in the Visual Studio Code editor.

So, what is the point of using **declare**? As we build out complex modules, the declare process allows us to describe the complete shape of our modules in a way that cannot be done by simply defining a variable. Now that you know the role of declaration files along with the basic syntax, let's walk through the full workflow of creating a declaration file from scratch in the following exercise.

EXERCISE 2.01: CREATING A DECLARATION FILE FROM SCRATCH

In this exercise, we'll create a declaration file from scratch. We'll declare file conventions, import, and then use declared files. Consider that you are developing a web app that requires users to register themselves with credentials such as email, user roles, and passwords. The data types of these credentials will be stated in the declaration file that we'll be creating. A user won't be allowed to log in if they fail to enter the correct credentials.

> **NOTE**
>
> The code files for this exercise can be found here: https://packt.link/bBzat.

Perform the following steps to implement this exercise:

1. Open the Visual Studio Code editor.

2. Create a new directory and then create a file named **user.ts**.

3. Start the TypeScript compiler and have it watch for changes to the file with the following terminal compile command:

```
tsc user.ts --watch
```

The following screenshot shows how the command appears inside the terminal:

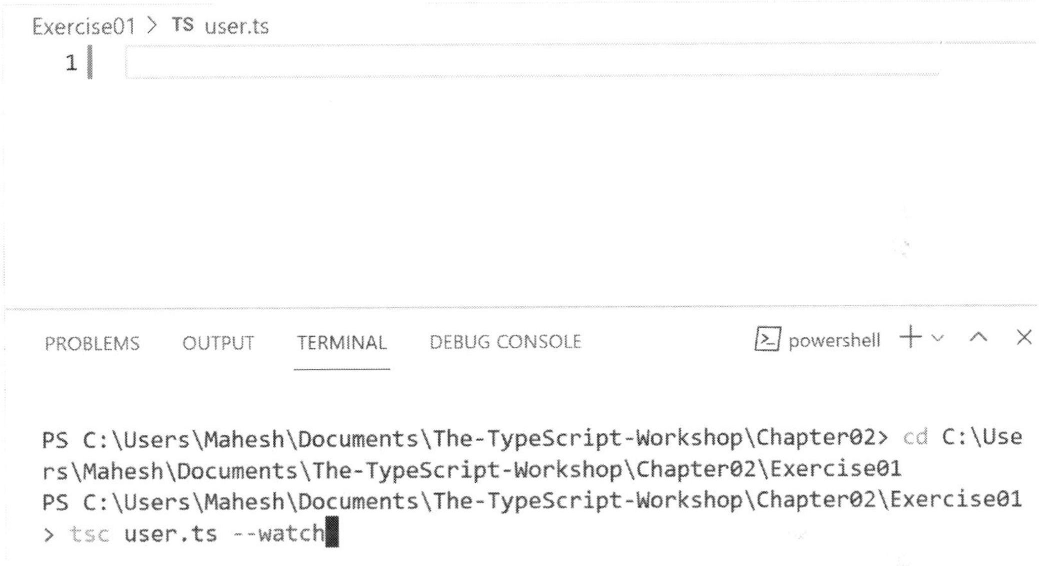

```
Exercise01 > TS user.ts
  1 |

PROBLEMS    OUTPUT    TERMINAL    DEBUG CONSOLE              powershell + ∨ ∧ ✕


PS C:\Users\Mahesh\Documents\The-TypeScript-Workshop\Chapter02> cd C:\Use
rs\Mahesh\Documents\The-TypeScript-Workshop\Chapter02\Exercise01
PS C:\Users\Mahesh\Documents\The-TypeScript-Workshop\Chapter02\Exercise01
> tsc user.ts --watch
```

Figure 2.3: Running the TypeScript compiler with the watch flag

It's fine to leave this file empty for now. We'll start building out our implementation shortly. Now let's create our declaration file.

4. Create a directory called **types/** at the root of our program and then create a file inside it called **AuthTypes.d.ts**.

    Our project's directory should now look like this:

Figure 2.4: AuthTypes file structure

> **NOTE**
>
> Traditionally, declaration files are kept in their own directory called **types/** and are then imported by the modules that they are defining. It's also the standard convention to use the file extension of **.d.ts** instead of **.ts** for your declaration files.

5. Within the new declaration file, define the shape of our **AuthTypes** module. Use the **declare** keyword at the top of the file. This tells TypeScript that we are about to describe how the **AuthTypes** module should be structured:

```
declare module "AuthTypes" {
    export interface User {
        email: string;
        roles: Array<string>;
    }
}
```

In the preceding code, another bit of syntax that might be different than what you're used to writing is that we wrap the module name in quotation marks. When we implement the program, you'll see that if we remove the quotation marks, we won't be able to import the module. Inside the module, we can place any number of exports that we want the module to have. One of the most important concepts to keep in mind is that declaration files do not have any implementation code; they simply describe the types and structure for the elements used in the module. The following screenshot gives a visual representation of the code:

```
Exercise01 > types > TS AuthTypes.d.ts > {} "AuthTypes"
1    declare module "AuthTypes" {
2        export interface User {
3            email: string;
4            roles: Array<string>;
5            source?: string;
6        }
7    }
```

Figure 2.5: AuthTypes interface

The compiler messages suggest that the import should happen successfully as there have not been any errors up to this point.

In this step, we're exporting a user interface that defines two data points: email and roles. As far as the data types are concerned, the **email** attribute needs to be a string, and **roles** needs to be an array filled with strings. Such type definitions will ensure that anyone using this module will be informed immediately if they attempt to use the incorrect data structure.

Now that we have defined the **AuthTypes** module, we need to import it into our TypeScript file so that we can use it. We're going to use the reference import process to bring the file into our program.

6. Go to the **user.ts** file and add the following two lines of code:

```
/// <reference path = "./types/AuthTypes.d.ts" />
import auth = require("AuthTypes");
```

The code in the editor will look something like this:

```
TS hello.ts  U      TS user.ts  M  ✕      TS AuthTypes.d.ts

Exercise01 > TS user.ts
  1   /// <reference path = "./types/AuthTypes.d.ts" />
  2   import auth = require("AuthTypes");
  3
```

```
PROBLEMS   OUTPUT   TERMINAL   DEBUG CONSOLE                    [>] PowerShell

[12:12:58 pm] File change detected. Starting incremental compilation...

[12:12:58 pm] Found 0 errors. Watching for file changes.
```

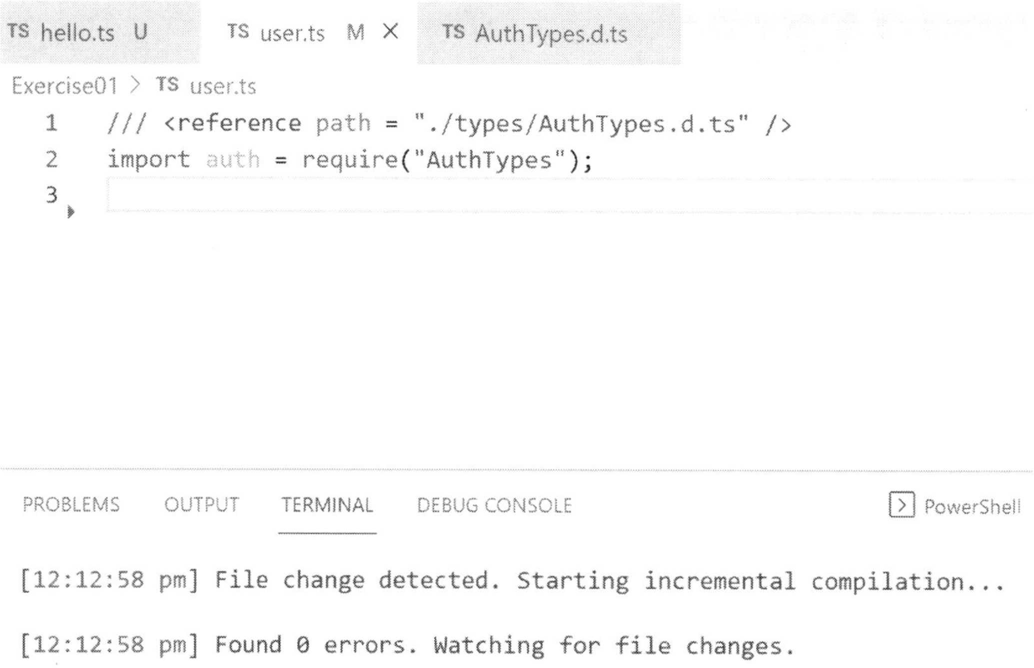

Figure 2.6: Importing a declaration file

The first line in the preceding code will make **AuthTypes.d.ts** available to our program, and the second line imports the module itself. Obviously, you can use any variable name for the import statement that you prefer. In this code, we're importing the **AuthTypes** module and storing it in the **auth** keyword.

With our module imported, we can now start building the implementation for our program. We'll start out by defining a variable and assigning it to our user interface type that we defined in the declaration files.

7. Add the following code to the **user.ts** file:

```
let jon: auth.User;
```

The updated code of **user.ts** file will look something like this:

```
/// <reference path = "./types/AuthTypes.d.ts" />
import auth = require("AuthTypes");
let jon: auth.User;
```

What we've done here is quite impressive. We've essentially created our own type/interface in a separate file, imported it, and told the TypeScript compiler that our new variable is going to be of the **User** type.

8. Add the actual values of **email** and **roles** for the **jon** variable with the help of the following code:

```
jon = {
    email: "jon@snow.com",
    roles: ["admin"]
};
```

With the required shape in place, the program compiles properly, and you can perform any tasks that you need to do.

9. Create another **User** and see how we can work with optional attributes. Add the following code to add details of the user **alice**:

```
let alice: auth.User;

alice = {
    email: "alice@snow.com",
    roles: ["super_admin"]
};
```

Now, let's imagine that we sometimes keep track of how a user found our application. Not all users will have this attribute though, so we'll need to make it optional without breaking the other user accounts. You can mark an attribute as optional by adding a question mark before the colon.

10. Add a **source** attribute to the declaration file:

```
declare module "AuthTypes" {
    export interface User {
        email: string;
        roles: Array<string>;
        source?: string;
    }
}
```

11. Update our **alice** user with a **source** value of **facebook**:

```
/// <reference path = "./types/AuthTypes.d.ts" />
import auth = require("AuthTypes");
let jon: auth.User;
jon = {
    email: "jon@snow.com",
    roles: ["admin"]
};
let alice: auth.User;

alice = {
    email: "alice@snow.com",
    roles: ["super_admin"],
    source: "facebook"
}
```

Notice that the **jon** variable still works perfectly fine, even without the **source** value. This helps us to build flexible interfaces for our programs that define both optional and required data points.

12. Open the terminal and run the following command to generate a JavaScript file:

```
tsc user.ts
```

Let's now look at the generated **user.js** file, which can be seen in the following screenshot:

```
Exercise01 > JS user.js > ...
1    "use strict";
2    exports.__esModule = true;
3    var jon;
4    jon = {
5        email: "jon@snow.com",
6        roles: ["admin"]
7    };
8    var alice;
9    alice = {
10       email: "alice@snow.com",
11       roles: ["super_admin"],
12       source: "facebook"
13   };
14
```

Figure 2.7: Declaration file rules not added to the generated JavaScript code

Well, that's interesting. There is literally not a single mention of the declaration file in the generated JavaScript code. This brings up a very important piece of knowledge to know when it comes to declaration files and TypeScript in general: declaration files are used solely for the benefit of the developer and are only utilized by the IDE.

Declaration files are completely bypassed when it comes to what is rendered in the program. And with this in mind, hopefully the goal of declaration files is becoming clearer. The better your declaration files are, the easier it will be for the IDE to understand your program and for yourself and other developers to work with your code.

EXCEPTIONS

Let's see what happens when we don't follow the rules of our interface. Remember in the previous exercise that our interface required two data elements (**email** and **roles**) and that they need to be of the **string** and **Array<string>** types. So, watch what happens when we don't implement the proper data type with the following code:

```
jon = {
    email: 123
}
```

This will generate the following compiler error, as shown in the following screenshot:

```
TS hello.ts  U      Type 'number' is not assignable to type 'string'. ts(2322)
Exercise01 >        AuthTypes.d.ts(3, 9): The expected type comes from property
    1    ///        'email' which is declared here on type 'User'
    2    impo
    3    let         (property) auth.User.email: string
    4    jon         View Problem (Alt+F8)    No quick fixes available
    5       email: 123,
    6
    7    };
    8
    9    |
```

Figure 2.8: TypeScript showing the required data types for an object

That is incredibly helpful. Imagine that you are working with a library that you've never used before. If you were using vanilla JavaScript, this implementation would silently fail and would force you to dig through the library's source code to see what structure it required.

This compiler error makes sense, and in a real-life application, such as a **React** or an **Angular** app, the application wouldn't even load until the issue was fixed. If we update the data structure to match the declaration file for **AuthTypes** with the following code:

```
jon = {
    email: "jon@snow.com"
}
```

We can see that the compiler will move the error message up to the **jon** variable name. If you hover over it, or look at the terminal output, you'll see the error shown in the following screenshot:

```
1    /// <reference path = "./types/AuthTypes.d.ts" />
2    import auth = require("AuthTypes");
3    let jon: auth.User;
4    jon = {
5
6        Property 'roles' is missing in type '{ email: string; }' but
         required in type 'User'. ts(2741)
7
8        AuthTypes.d.ts(4, 9): 'roles' is declared here.
9
         let jon: auth.User

         View Problem (Alt+F8)    No quick fixes available
```

Figure 2.9: TypeScript showing the required attributes for an object

This is an incredibly useful functionality. If you're new to development, this may not seem like a very big deal. However, this type of information is the exact reason why TypeScript continues to grow in popularity. Error messages such as this instantly provide the information that we need in order to fix the bug and work with the program. In the preceding screenshot, the message is telling us that the program won't compile as we are missing a required value, namely, **roles**.

Now that we have built out our own declaration file from scratch, it's time to move on and see how declaration files are utilized by other libraries.

THIRD-PARTY CODE LIBRARIES

Depending on the types of applications that you build, you may never need to build your own declaration files. However, if you're using TypeScript and working with third-party modules, you will need to understand how declaration files work because you will then be able to work seamlessly with external libraries.

DEFINITELYTYPED

Let's jump back in time for a moment. When TypeScript was originally developed, there was quite a bit of excitement around the idea of integrating types into JavaScript applications. However, developers began to get frustrated, because even though they were building their programs with types, every time that they imported an external library, such as lodash, they were forced to write code with no type signatures and little to no IDE guidance.

Essentially, this meant that each time we were to call a function from an external library, we didn't have a high level of assurance that we were working with it properly.

Thankfully, the open source community had the answer, and the DefinitelyTyped library was created. DefinitelyTyped is a very large repository that contains literally thousands of declaration files for JavaScript code libraries. This means that libraries such as **react**, **lodash**, and pretty much every other popular library has a full set of declaration files that we can use in our TypeScript programs.

> **NOTE**
>
> For more information on DefinitelyTyped, visit https://definitelytyped.org.

ANALYZING AN EXTERNAL DECLARATION FILE

Before we learn how to import and use types with external libraries, let's peek into what they look like:

Figure 2.10: Example of how DefinitelyTyped uses declaration files

In the preceding screenshot, if you look at the **lodash** declaration file for the array data structure, you'll see that a single declaration file is over 2,000 lines long. That can be a little intimidating to look at, so let's try to simplify it.

> **NOTE**
>
> **lodash** is a utility library that provides functionality for working with objects, strings, arrays, and suchlike. The **lodash** library's declaration file for the array data structure, as shown in the preceding screenshot, can be found here: https://github.com/DefinitelyTyped/DefinitelyTyped/blob/master/types/lodash/common/array.d.ts.

You'll be pleased to know that the elements in the preceding declaration file are exactly what we built out in *Exercise 1.01: Creating a Declaration File from Scratch*. It starts by declaring a **module** instance, and from that point, it lists out interfaces for each of the elements that utilize the array data structure. In fact, if you dissect the code, you'll see that **lodash** provides three interfaces for each of the functions in the library. You don't have to know what these do; however, it is helpful to realize that you can provide as many interfaces as needed when you're building your own code libraries.

Let's now look at the interface for the **last** function:

```
836        interface LoDashStatic {
837            /**
838             * Gets the last element of array.
839             *
840             * @param array The array to query.
841             * @return Returns the last element of array.
842             */
843            last<T>(array: List<T> | null | undefined): T | undefined;
844        }
```

Figure 2.11: How lodash implements interfaces

This is a good function to look at, because we'll use it when we get to the example for this section. You can see that the majority of the interface is actually a comment. If you've never seen this syntax before, it is using JSDoc syntax. This is very helpful, because IDEs such as Visual Studio Code will pull the comment, parameters, and return type directly into the IntelliSense interface. This means that when we start typing the **last** function when working with **lodash**, the IDE will automatically pull in the comment data so we can easily read how to use the function.

After that, the declaration is pretty basic. It simply describes the shape of the last function, specifically, that it takes a list of values as the argument and then returns either **T** or **undefined**. Don't worry about all the references to **T**; you'll learn about what this represents in *Chapter 8, Generics*. For now, just know that it means that it is returning a value.

Following the same pattern from when we created the declaration file from scratch, in the next section, let's create a new TypeScript project and walk through a practical example of why types are needed.

EXERCISE 2.02: CREATING TYPES WITH EXTERNAL LIBRARIES

In this exercise, we'll install types and integrate our types with external libraries. We will also be exploring a scenario wherein we'll check how the function behaves when the wrong type of parameter is passed to it. You'll need to start with an empty directory for this exercise.

> **NOTE**
>
> The code files for this exercise can be found here: https://packt.link/k7Wbt.

Perform the following steps to implement this exercise:

1. Open the Visual Studio Code editor.

2. Create an empty directory on your computer and run the following command to create a new NPM project:

```
npm init -y
```

The preceding code will generate a **package.json** file.

3. To install the Lodash library, open the terminal and type the following command:

```
npm i lodash
```

The preceding command installs the Lodash library. The **package.json** file should now look something like this, with **lodash** installed in the dependencies list:

```
> {} package.json > ...
{
  "name": "Example",
  "version": "1.0.0",
  "description": "",
  "main": "index.js",
  ▷ Debug
  "scripts": {
    "test": "echo \"Error: no test specified\" && exit 1"
  },
  "keywords": [],
  "author": "",
  "license": "ISC",
  "dependencies": {
    "loadash": "^1.0.0"
  }
}
```

Figure 2.12: The generated package.json file

4. Create a file in that directory named **lodash_examples.ts**, start the TypeScript compiler, and have it watch for changes. Inside of the new .**ts** file, add the following code:

```
import _ = require("lodash");
const nums = [1, 2, 3];
console.log(_.last(nums));
```

5. Run the preceding program in the terminal by writing the following commands:

```
tsc lodash_examples.ts
node lodash_examples.js
```

The console generates an output of **3**, as you can see in the following screenshot:

```
PS C:\Users\Mahesh\Documents\TypeScript_code\Chapter02_demo> tsc lodash_examples.ts

PS C:\Users\Mahesh\Documents\TypeScript_code\Chapter02_demo> node lodash_examples.js

3
```

Figure 2.13: Running the generated lodash_example.js program

6. Create another variable named **number** and assign it the value **10**. We'll then pass this number as an argument to the Lodash library's **_.last()** function. Write the following code to do this:

```
import _ = require("lodash");
//const nums = [1, 2, 3];
//console.log(_.last(nums));
const number = 10;
console.log(_.last(number));
```

Since we've looked at the declaration file, we know that the last function expects an array or some type of list. However, for now, let's pretend that we don't have that information, and this is the first time that we're working with the Lodash library.

> **NOTE**
>
> The Lodash library's **last** function also works with strings because it views the string of characters like a collection of characters. For example, **_.last("hey")** will return **"y"** since it's the last character in the string.

7. Run the preceding program in the terminal by writing the following commands:

```
tsc lodash_examples.ts
node lodash_examples.js
```

The following output is generated when the preceding commands are executed:

```
PS C:\Users\Mahesh\Documents\TypeScript_code\Chapter02_demo> node lodash_examples.js

undefined
PS C:\Users\Mahesh\Documents\TypeScript_code\Chapter02_demo> []
```

Figure 2.14: What happens when the wrong argument is passed to the last function

In such a small program, this may seem like a trivial issue. However, in a large system, getting an undefined value while expecting an actual value can be time-consuming, as we have to spend more time on debugging.

In order to fix this issue, let's leverage the DefinitelyTyped repository and bring in the **lodash** types. If you hover over the **import** statement at the top of the file, you'll even see the following warning and recommendation, as shown in the following screenshot:

```
import _ = require("lodash");
//const nums = [1,   Could not find a declaration file for module 'lodash'.
//console.log(_.las   'c:/Users/Mahesh/Documents/TypeScript_code/chapter02_example/node_modules/lc
const number = 10;   implicitly has an 'any' type.
console.log(_.last(    Try `npm i --save-dev @types/lodash` if it exists or add a new
                     declaration (.d.ts) file containing `declare module 'lodash';` ts(7016)
                     Quick Fix... (Ctrl+.)
```

Figure 2.15: TypeScript recommending to install Lodash types from DefinitelyTyped

That's quite helpful. The warning itself is showing us how we can install the types for the library.

8. Follow the recommendation and run the following command in the terminal to install **lodash** types:

```
npm install @types/lodash
```

> **NOTE**
>
> Any time that you see an **install** command that starts with @**types/**, that means that NPM is going to pull from the DefinitelyTyped repository.

If you run that command, the warning in the **import** statement should go away automatically. But even more importantly, you should now see that the IDE is now complaining about the line of code where we're trying to pass a number to the **last** function. If you hover over the word **number**, you should see the error shown in the following screenshot:

```
import _ = require("lodash");
//const nums = [1, 2, 3];
//console.log(_.last(nums));
const number = 10;    Argument of type 'number' is not assignable to parameter of
                      type 'List<any>'. ts(2345)

                      const number: 10

                      View Problem (Alt+F8)    No quick fixes available
console.log(_.last(number));
```

Figure 2.16: IntelliSense revealing the correct type to use with the last function

From the preceding screenshot, it is clear that the **last** function won't take any argument of the **number** type. It accepts either an array or a list as an argument. So, let's imagine that we're building a real-world application, and we try to use the **last** function. If we were using vanilla JavaScript, we wouldn't realize our error until we, or even a user, encountered the error while running the program. However, by leveraging TypeScript and DefinitelyTyped, the program won't even compile if we attempt to use a function in the incorrect manner.

DEVELOPMENT WORKFLOW WITH DEFINITELYTYPED

Now that you've seen how to install and work with types, we will walk through a full development workflow so that you can observe the benefits of working with types. Without the integration of types into external libraries, we are forced to either have prior knowledge of the library or dig through the documentation to discover the proper usage.

However, with types, we're going to see how much more streamlined the process is when it comes to working with libraries such as **lodash**. Let's solve an exercise in the next section to get a proper understanding of this.

EXERCISE 2.03: CREATING A BASEBALL LINEUP CARD APPLICATION

In this exercise, we'll create a baseball lineup application, wherein we have an array of player names that we'll be retrieving from an API, and then we have a constant variable in the application called **lineupOrder**. Our lineup card application needs to pair the names from the API with **lineupOrder**:

> **NOTE**
>
> The code files for this exercise can be found here: https://packt.link/01spl.

1. Open the Visual Studio Code editor.

2. Create a file named **lodash_newexamples.ts** and add the following code, wherein we have an array variable, **playerNames**, and a list, **lineupOrder**:

```
import _ = require("lodash");

const playerNames = [
    "Springer",
    "Bregman",
    "Altuve",
    "Correa",
    "Brantley",
    "White",
    "Gonzalez",
    "Kemp",
    "Reddick"
];

const lineupOrder = [1, 2, 3, 4, 5, 6, 7, 8, 9];
```

This is a perfect situation for using the **zip** function from the Lodash library. Let's imagine that we've heard about the **zip** function, but aren't quite aware of how to use it yet. Start by writing the following code in the same file:

```
_.zip()
```

3. Once you've typed the preceding code, place the cursor in between the parentheses. You'll get some guidance on how to use the function straight from DefinitelyTyped, as shown in the following screenshot:

```
(method) _.LoDashStatic.zip<T1, T2>(arrays1: _.List<T1>,
arrays2: _.List<T2>): [T1, T2][] (+4 overloads)
```

Creates an array of grouped elements, the first of which contains the first elements of the given arrays, the second of which contains the second elements of the given arrays, and so on.

@param `arrays` — The arrays to process.

@return — Returns the new array of grouped elements.

```
_.zip|
```

Figure 2.17: IntelliSense guidance on how to use the zip function in lodash

> **NOTE**
>
> From the preceding screenshot, we can see that the **zip** function takes two arguments. Both arguments need to be **ArrayLike**, which means they need to function as a type of collection. Also, the function groups the elements together and returns the grouped collection. Thus, without having to dig through the **lodash** documentation, we were able to leverage the type definition as we were building the program. It gives us the guidance we need while working with the function.

Let's now test it out. We know that the **zip** function takes in two arrays. So, let's provide it with the **playerNames** and **lineupOrder** arrays.

4. Add the following code to provide the **zip** function with two arrays, **playerNames** and **lineupOrder**:

```
console.log(_.zip(lineupOrder, playerNames));
```

If you run the preceding code, you'll see that the **zip** function does exactly what it said it would do. It groups the elements and returns the exact data structure that we needed. The rendered lineup card would look something like that shown in the following screenshot:

```
PS C:\Users\Mahesh\Documents\TypeScript_code\Chapter02_demo>
js

[
  [ 1, 'Springer' ],
  [ 2, 'Bregman' ],
  [ 3, 'Altuve' ],
  [ 4, 'Correa' ],
  [ 5, 'Brantley' ],
  [ 6, 'White' ],
  [ 7, 'Gonzalez' ],
  [ 8, 'Kemp' ],
  [ 9, 'Reddick' ]
]
```

Figure 2.18: Running the zip function properly from lodash

In completing this process, you can see how DefinitelyTyped allows you to extend types directly into third-party libraries so that you can get type guidance in your programs.

ACTIVITY 2.01: BUILDING A HEAT MAP DECLARATION FILE

In this activity, you will build a TypeScript application named **heat map log system** for tracking baseball pitch data and ensuring data integrity. You will utilize a TypeScript declaration file to build the type system for the program. From that point, you will import the Lodash library and will add type checking to the program by implementing type definitions from DefinitelyTyped.

The steps are as follows:

1. Visit the following GitHub repository and download the activity project containing the specs and configuration elements: https://packt.link/vnj1R.

2. Create a file called **heat_map_data.ts**.

3. Run the TypeScript compiler on the file and watch for changes.

4. Create a declaration file and define a module called **HeatMapTypes** and export the interface named **Pitcher**.

5. Define three attributes for the **Pitcher** module: **batterHotZones**, **pitcherHotZones**, and **coordinateMap**.

6. The data structures should be the same for all three attributes, **Array<Array<number>>**, but **coordinateMap** should be optional.

7. Then, import the declaration files into the **heat_map_data.ts** file. Then, create and export a **let** variable called **data** and assign it to the **Pitcher** type.

8. Add values that adhere to the declaration rules, ensuring that one of the nested arrays is identical in the **batterHotZones** and **pitcherHotZones** attributes.

9. Create a new function called **findMatch** that takes in both the **batterHotZones** and **pitcherHotZones** arrays and utilize the **lodash** function, **intersectionWith**, to return the identical nested array. You will need to import the Lodash library, which was installed when you initially ran **npm install**. Finally, store the value of **findMatch** in the **coordinateMap** attribute that was defined in the declaration file.

The expected output of this activity will be a nested array that looks similar to this:

```
[[10.2, -5], [3, 2]]
```

> **NOTE**
>
> The solution to this activity can be found on page 598.

SUMMARY

In this chapter, we've walked through how to utilize declaration files in TypeScript. We've analyzed how declaration files can assist the IDE in guiding how programs should be structured. We've seen examples of structuring the declaration files. Importing declaration files into TypeScript files assists in the development life cycle. We learned to assign objects to custom types that were defined in the declaration files. It injects typed guidance into the IDE's IntelliSense process. We also learned about DefinitelyTyped and how it can be leveraged to layer on types for third-party libraries and work with them like typed programs.

With all this knowledge of declaration files, in the next chapter, we'll be taking a deep dive into working with functions in TypeScript. We'll be defining a function using types, building a suite of functions in a module, building a class of functions to perform a specific task, and exploring unit testing.

3

FUNCTIONS

OVERVIEW

Functions are a basic building block of any application. This chapter teaches you how to unleash the power of TypeScript using versatile functions that have capabilities you may not find in other programming languages. We will talk about the **this** key and look at function expressions, member functions, and arrow functions. This chapter also discusses function arguments, including rest and default parameters. We will also look at the **import** and **export** keywords.

This chapter also teaches you how to write tests that pass different combinations of arguments and compare the expected output with the actual output. We will close the chapter by designing a prototype application and completing it with unit tests.

INTRODUCTION

So far, we've learned some of the basics of TypeScript, how to set up a project, and the use of definition files. Now we will delve into the topic of functions, which are going to be the most important tools in your arsenal. Even object-oriented programming paradigms depend heavily on functions as a basic building block of business logic.

Functions, sometimes called routines or methods, are part of every high-level programming language. The ability to reuse segments of code is critical, but functions provide an even more important role than that in that they can be given different arguments, or variables, to act against and produce different results. Writing good functions is the difference between a good program and a great one. You first need to start by learning the syntax before thinking about crafting a good function by considering what arguments it should take and what it should produce.

In this chapter, we will cover three different ways to create functions. We will describe the pitfalls and the proper use of the **this** keyword. We will look at powerful programming techniques, including currying, functional programming, and the use of closures. We will explore the TypeScript module system and how to share code between modules by means of the **import** and **export** keywords. We'll see how functions can be organized into classes and how to refactor JavaScript code into TypeScript. Then we will learn how to use the popular Jest testing framework.

Putting these skills to use, we will design, build, and test a prototype flight booking system.

FUNCTIONS IN TYPESCRIPT

A simple definition of function is a set of statements that can be invoked; however, the use and conventions of functions cannot be summarized so easily. Functions in TypeScript have greater utility than in some other languages. In addition to being invoked as normal, functions can also be given as arguments to other functions and can be returned from functions. Functions are actually a special kind of object that can be invoked. This means that in addition to parameters, functions can actually have properties and methods of their own, though this is rarely done.

Only the smallest of programs will ever avoid making heavy use of functions. Most programs will be made up of many `.ts` files. Those files will typically export functions, classes, or objects. Other parts of the program will interact with the exported code, typically by calling functions. Functions create patterns for reusing your application logic and allow you to write **DRY (don't repeat yourself)** code.

Before diving into functions, let's perform an exercise to get a glimpse of how functions in general are useful. Don't worry if you do not understand some of the function-related syntax in the exercise. You will be studying all of this later in the chapter. The purpose of the following exercise is only to help you understand the importance of functions.

EXERCISE 3.01: GETTING STARTED WITH FUNCTIONS IN TYPESCRIPT

To give an example of the usefulness of functions, you will create a program that calculates an average. This exercise will first create a program that does not make use of any functions. Then, the same task of calculating the average will be performed using functions.

Let's get started:

> **NOTE**
>
> The code file for this exercise can be found at https://packt.link/ZHrsh.

1. Open VS Code and create a new file called **Exericse01.ts**. Write the following code that makes no use of functions other than the **console.log** statement:

```
const values = [8, 42, 99, 161];
let total = 0;
for(let i = 0; i < values.length; i++) {
    total += values[i];
}
const average = total/values.length;
console.log(average);
```

2. Run the file by executing **npx ts-node Exercise 01.ts** on the terminal. You will get the following output:

```
77.5.
```

3. Now, rewrite the same code using built-in functions and a function of our own, **calcAverage**:

```
const calcAverage = (values: number[]): number =>
    (values.reduce((prev, curr) =>
    prev + curr, 0) / values.length);
```

```
const values = [8, 42, 99, 161];
const average = calcAverage(values);
console.log(average);
```

4. Run the file and observe the output:

```
77.5.
```

The output is the same, but this code is more concise and more expressive. We have written our own function, but we also make use of the built-in **array. reduce** function. Understanding how functions work will both enable us to write our own useful functions and make use of powerful built-in functions.

Let's continue to build upon this exercise. Instead of just getting the average, consider a program to calculate a standard deviation. This can be written as procedural code without functions:

Example01_std_dev.ts

```
1  const values = [8, 42, 99, 161];
2  let total = 0;
3  for (let i = 0; i < values.length; i++) {
4      total += values[i];
5  }
6  const average = total / values.length;
7  const squareDiffs = [];
8  for (let i = 0; i < values.length; i++) {
9      const diff = values[i] - average;
10     squareDiffs.push(diff * diff)
11 }
12 total = 0;
13 for (let i = 0; i < squareDiffs.length; i++) {
14     total += squareDiffs[i];
15 }
16 const standardDeviation = Math.sqrt(total / squareDiffs.length);
17 console.log(standardDeviation);
```

Link to the preceding example: https://packt.link/YdTYD

You will get the following output once you run the file:

```
58.148516748065035
```

While we have the correct output, this code is very inefficient as the details of implementation (summing an array in a loop, then dividing by its length) are repeated. Additionally, since functions aren't used, the code would be difficult to debug as individual parts of the program can't be run in isolation. If we have an incorrect result, the entire program must be run repeatedly with minor corrections until we are sure of the correct output. This will not scale to programs that contain thousands or millions of lines of code, as many major web applications do. Now consider the following program:

Example02_std_dev.ts

```
1   const calcAverage = (values: number[]): number =>
2   (values.reduce((prev, curr) => prev + curr, 0) / values.length);
3   const calcStandardDeviation = (values: number[]): number => {
4     const average = calcAverage(values);
5     const squareDiffs = values.map((value: number): number => {
6       const diff = value - average;
7       return diff * diff;
8     });
9     return Math.sqrt(calcAverage(squareDiffs));
10  }
11  const values = [8, 42, 99, 161];
12  console.log(calcStandardDeviation(values));
```

Link to the preceding example: https://packt.link/smsxT

The output is as follows:

```
58.148516748065035
```

Again, the output is correct and we've reused **calcAverage** twice in this program, proving the value of writing that function. Even if all the functions and syntax don't make sense yet, most programmers will agree that more concise and expressive code is preferable to large blocks of code that offer no patterns of reuse.

THE FUNCTION KEYWORD

The simplest way to create a function is with a function statement using the **function** keyword. The keyword precedes the function name, after which a parameter list is given, and the function body is enclosed with braces. The parameter list for a function is always wrapped in parentheses, even if there are no parameters. The parentheses are always required in TypeScript, unlike some other languages, such as Ruby:

```
function myFunction() {
   console.log('Hello world!');
}
```

A function that completes successfully will always return either one or zero values. If nothing is returned, the **void** identifier can be used to show nothing was returned. A function cannot return more than one value, but many developers get around this limitation by returning an array or object that itself contains multiple values that can be recast into individual variables. Functions can return any of the built-in types in TypeScript or types that we write. Functions can also return complex or inline types (described in later chapters). If the type a function might return can't easily be inferred by the body of the function and a **return** statement, it is a good idea to add a return type to the function. That looks like this. The return type of **void** indicates that this function doesn't return anything:

```
function myFunction(): void {
   console.log('Hello world!');
}
```

FUNCTION PARAMETERS

A parameter is a placeholder for a value that is passed into the function. Any number of parameters can be specified for a function. As we are writing TypeScript, parameters should have their types annotated. Let's change our function so that it requires a parameter and returns something:

Example03.ts

```
1 function myFunction(name: string): string {
2    return `Hello ${name}!`;
3 }
```

In contrast to the previous example, this function expects a single parameter identified by **name**, the type of which has been defined as **string** – **(name: string)**. The function body has changed and now uses a string template to return our greeting message as a template string. We could invoke the function like this:

```
4 const message = myFunction('world');
5 console.log(message);
```

Link to the preceding example: https://packt.link/ITlEU

You will get the following output once you run the file:

```
Hello world!
```

This code invokes **myFunction** with an argument of **'world'** and assigns the result of the function call to a new constant, **message**. The **console** object is a built-in object that exposes a **log** function (sometimes called a method as an object member) that will print the given string to the console. Since **myFunction** concatenates the given parameter to a template string, **Hello world!** is printed to the console.

Of course, it isn't necessary to store the function result in a constant before logging it out. We could simply write the following:

```
console.log(myFunction('world'));
```

This code will invoke the function and log its result to the console, as shown in the following output:

```
Hello world!
```

Many of the examples in this chapter will take this form because this is a very simple way to validate the output of a function. More sophisticated applications use unit tests and more robust logging solutions to validate functions, and so the reader is cautioned against filling applications with **console.log** statements.

ARGUMENT VERSUS PARAMETER

Many developers use the terms argument and parameter interchangeably; however, the term argument refers to a value passed to a function, while parameter refers to the placeholder in the function. In the case of **myFunction('world');**, the **'world'** string is an argument and not a parameter. The **name** placeholder with an assigned type in the function declaration is a parameter.

OPTIONAL PARAMETERS

One important difference from JavaScript is that TypeScript function parameters are only optional if we postfix them with **?**. The function in the previous example, **myFunction**, expects an argument. Consider the case where we don't specify any arguments:

```
const message = myFunction();
```

This code will give us a compilation error: **Expected 1 arguments, but got 0**. That means the code won't even compile, much less run. Likewise, consider the following snippet, where we provide an argument of the wrong type:

```
const message = myFunction(5);
```

Now, the error message reads: **Argument of type '5' is not assignable to parameter of type 'string'**.

It's interesting that this error message has given the narrowest possible type for the value we tried to pass. Instead of saying **argument of type 'number'**, the compiler sees the type as simply the number **5**. This gives us a hint that types can be far narrower than the primitive **number** type.

TypeScript automatically prevents us from making mistakes such as this by enforcing types. But what if we actually do want to make the parameter optional? One option is, as previously mentioned, to postfix the parameter with **?**, as shown in the following code snippet:

Example04.ts

```
1 function myFunction(name?: string): string {
2   return `Hello ${name}!`;
3 }
```

Now we can successfully invoke it:

```
4 const message = myFunction();
5 console.log(message);
```

Link to the preceding example: https://packt.link/cnW4c

Running this command will display the following output:

```
Hello undefined!
```

In TypeScript, any variable that has yet to be assigned will have the value of **undefined**. When the function is executed, the **undefined** value gets converted to the **undefined** string at runtime, and so **Hello undefined!** is printed to the console.

DEFAULT PARAMETERS

In the preceding example, the **name** parameter has been made optional and since it never got a value, we printed out **Hello undefined!**. A better way to do this would be to give **name** a default value, as shown here:

Example05.ts

```
1 function myFunction(name: string = 'world'): string {
2    return `Hello ${name}!`;
3 }
```

Link to the preceding example: https://packt.link/zS5Ej

Now, the function will give us the default value if we don't provide one:

```
4 const message = myFunction();
5 console.log(message);
```

The output is as follows:

```
Hello world!
```

And it will give us the value we passed if we do provide one using the following code:

```
const message = myFunction('reader');
console.log(message);
```

This will then display the following output:

```
Hello reader!
```

This was pretty straightforward. Now, let's try working with multiple arguments.

MULTIPLE ARGUMENTS

Functions can have any number or type of arguments. The argument list is separated by commas. Although your compiler settings can allow you to omit argument types, it is a best practice to enable the **noImplicitAny** option. This will raise a compiler error if you accidentally omit a type. Additionally, the use of the broad **any** type is discouraged whenever possible, as was covered in *Chapter 1, TypeScript Fundamentals and Overview of Types*. *Chapter 6, Advanced Types*, will give us a deeper dive into advanced types, in particular, intersection and union types, that will help us to ensure that all of our variables have good, descriptive types.

REST PARAMETERS

The spread operator (...) may be used as the final parameter to a function. This will take all arguments passed into the function and place them in an array. Let's look at an example of how this works:

Example06.ts

```
1 function readBook(title: string, ...chapters: number[]): void {
2   console.log(`Starting to read ${title}...`);
3   chapters.forEach(chapter => {
4     console.log(`Reading chapter ${chapter}.`);
5   });
6   console.log('Done reading.');
7 }
```

Link to the preceding example: https://packt.link/Fw2iC

Now, the function can be called with a variable argument list:

```
readBook('The TypeScript Workshop', 1, 2, 3);
```

The first argument is required. The rest will be optional. We could just decline to specify any chapters to read. However, if we do give additional arguments, they must be of the **number** type because that's what we've used as the type (**number[]**) for our rest parameter.

You will obtain the following output once you run the preceding code:

```
Starting to read The TypeScript Book...
Reading chapter 1.
Reading chapter 2.
Reading chapter 3.
Done reading.
```

Note that this syntax specifically requires single arguments of the **number** type. It would be possible to implement the function without a rest parameter and instead expect an array as a single argument:

Example07.ts

```
1 function readBook(title: string, chapters: number[]): void {
2   console.log(`Starting to read ${title}...`);
3   chapters.forEach(chapter => {
4     console.log(`Reading chapter ${chapter}.`);
5   });
6   console.log('Done reading.');
7 }
```

Link to the preceding example: https://packt.link/AvlnF

The function will now require precisely two arguments:

```
readBook('The TypeScript Book', [1, 2, 3]);
```

The output is as follows:

```
Starting to read The TypeScript Book...
Reading chapter 1.
Reading chapter 2.
Reading chapter 3.
Done reading.
```

Which is better? That's something you'll need to decide for yourself. In this case, the chapters we want to read are already in array form, and then it probably makes the most sense to pass that array to the function.

Notice that the **readBook** function includes an arrow function inside it. We'll cover arrow functions in an upcoming section.

DESTRUCTURING RETURN TYPES

At times, it may be useful for a function to return more than one value. Programmers who have embraced functional programming paradigms often want a function that will return a tuple, or an array of two elements that have different types. Going back to our previous example, if we wanted to calculate both the average and standard deviation for a number array, it might be convenient to have a single function that handles both operations, rather than having to make multiple function calls with the same number array.

A function in TypeScript will only return one value. However, we can simulate returning multiple arguments using destructuring. Destructuring is the practice of assigning parts of an object or array to different variables. This allows us to assign parts of a returning value to variables, giving the impression we are returning multiple values. Let's look at an example:

Example08.ts

```
1 function paritySort(...numbers: number[]): { evens: number[], odds: 2 number[] }
  {
3   return {
4     evens: numbers.filter(n => n % 2 === 0),
5     odds: numbers.filter(n => n % 2 === 1)
6   };
7 }
```

Link to the preceding example: https://packt.link/SHkuW

This code uses the **filter** method of the built-in array object to iterate through each value in an array and test it. If the test returns a **true** Boolean, the value is pushed into a new array, which is returned. Using the modulus operator to test the remainder will filter our number array into two separate arrays. The function then returns those arrays as properties of an object. We can take advantage of this destructuring. Consider the following code:

```
const { evens, odds } = paritySort(1, 2, 3, 4);
console.log(evens);
console.log(odds);
```

Here, we give the function the arguments **1, 2, 3, 4**, and it returns the following output:

```
[2, 4]
[1, 3]
```

THE FUNCTION CONSTRUCTOR

Note that the TypeScript language contains an uppercase **Function** keyword. This is not the same as the lowercase **function** keyword and should not be used as it is not considered to be secure due to its ability to parse and execute arbitrary code strings. The **Function** keyword only exists in TypeScript because TypeScript is a superset of JavaScript.

EXERCISE 3.02: COMPARING NUMBER ARRAYS

TypeScript comparison operators such as **===** or **>** only work on primitive types. If we want to compare more complex types, such as arrays, we need to either use a library or implement our own comparison. Let's write a function that can compare a pair of unsorted number arrays and tell us whether the values are equal.

> **NOTE**
>
> The code file for this exercise can be found at https://packt.link/A0IxN.

1. Create a new file in VS Code and name it **array-equal.ts**.

2. Start with this code, which declares three different arrays and outputs, irrespective of whether or not they are equal:

```typescript
const arrayone = [7, 6, 8, 9, 2, 25];
const arraytwo = [6, 8, 9, 2, 25];
const arraythree = [6, 8, 9, 2, 25, 7];
function arrayCompare(a1: number[], a2: number[]): boolean {
  return true;
}
console.log(
  `Are ${arrayone} and ${arraytwo} equal?`,
  arrayCompare(arrayone, arraytwo)
);
console.log(
  `Are ${arrayone} and ${arraythree} equal?`,
  arrayCompare(arrayone, arraythree)
);
console.log(
  `Are ${arraytwo} and ${arraythree} equal?`,
  arrayCompare(arraytwo, arraythree)
);
```

The output will be true for all three comparisons because the function has not been implemented and just returns **true**.

Our function, **arrayCompare**, takes two arrays as arguments and returns a Boolean value to represent whether or not they are equal. Our business rule is that arrays can be unsorted and will be considered equal if all their values match when sorted.

3. Update **arrayCompare** with the following code:

```
function arrayCompare(a1: number[], a2: number[]): boolean {
  if(a1.length !== a2.length) {
    return false;
  }
  return true;
}
```

In the preceding code, we are testing to see whether the two arrays passed in are equal. The first check we should make is to test whether the arrays have equal length. If they aren't equal in length, then the values can't possibly be equal, so we'll return **false** from the function. If we hit a return statement during execution, the rest of the function won't be executed.

At this point, the function will only tell us whether the arrays are equal in length. To complete the challenge, we'll need to compare each value in the arrays. This task will be considerably easier if we sort the values before trying to compare them. Fortunately, the array object prototype includes a **sort()** method, which will handle this for us. Using built-in functions can save a lot of development hours.

4. Implement the **sort()** method to sort array values:

```
function arrayCompare(a1: number[], a2: number[]): boolean {
  if(a1.length !== a2.length) {
    return false;
  }
  a1.sort();
  a2.sort();
  return true;
}
```

The **sort()** method sorts the array elements in place, so it isn't necessary to assign the result to a new variable.

Finally, we need to loop over one of the arrays to compare each element at the same index. We use a **for** loop to iterate through the first array and compare the value at each index to the value at the same index in the second array. Since our arrays use primitive values, the **!==** comparison operator will work.

5. Use the following **for** loop to loop over the arrays:

```
function arrayCompare(a1: number[], a2: number[]): boolean {
  if(a1.length !== a2.length) {
    return false;
  }
  a1.sort();
  a2.sort();
  for (let i = 0; i < a1.length; i++) {
    if (a1[i] !== a2[i]) {
      return false;
    }
  }
  return true;
}
```

Again, we'll return **false** and exit the function if any of the comparisons fail.

6. Execute the program using **ts-node**:

```
npx ts-node array-equal.ts
```

The program will produce the following output:

```
Are 7,6,8,9,2,25 and 6,8,9,2,25,8 equal? false
Are 2,25,6,7,8,9 and 6,8,9,2,25,7 equal? true
Are 2,25,6,8,8,9 and 2,25,6,7,8,9 equal? False
```

7. Experiment with different array combinations and validate the program is working correctly.

A good function takes an argument list and returns a single value. You now have experience writing a function as well as utilizing built-in functions to solve problems.

FUNCTION EXPRESSIONS

Function expressions differ from function declarations in that they can be assigned to variables, used inline, or invoked immediately – an immediately invoked function expression or IIFE. Function expressions can be named or anonymous. Let's look at a few examples:

Example09.ts

```
1 const myFunction = function(name: string): string {
2   return `Hello ${name}!`;
3 };
4 console.log(myFunction('function expression'));
```

Link to the preceding example: https://packt.link/2JeGQ

You will get the following output:

```
Hello function expression!
```

This looks quite a lot like a previous example we looked at, and it works almost exactly the same. Here is the function declaration for comparison:

```
function myFunction(name: string = 'world'): string {
  return `Hello ${name}!`;
}
```

The one slight difference is that function declarations are *hoisted*, meaning they are loaded into memory (along with any declared variables) and, as such, can be used before they are declared in code. It is generally considered bad practice to rely on hoisting and, as such, it is now allowed by many linters. Programs that make heavy use of hoisting can have bugs that are difficult to track down and may even exhibit different behaviors in different systems. One of the reasons why function expressions have become popular is because they don't allow hoisting and therefore avoid these issues.

Function expressions can be used to create anonymous functions, that is, functions that do not have names. This is impossible with function declarations. Anonymous functions are often used as callbacks to native functions. For example, consider the following code snippet with the **Array.filter** function:

Example10.ts

```
1 const numbers = [1, 3, 2];
2 const filtered = numbers.filter(function(val) {return val < 3});
3 console.log(filtered);
```

Link to the preceding example: https://packt.link/aJyhj

The output is as follows:

```
[1, 2]
```

Remember that in TypeScript (as well as JavaScript), functions are can be given as arguments to, or returned from, other functions. This means that we can give the anonymous function, **function(val) { return val < 3 }**, as an argument to the **Array.filter** function. This function is not named and cannot be referred to or invoked by other code. That's fine for most purposes. If we wanted to, we could give it a name:

```
const filtered = numbers.filter(function myFilterFunc(val) {return val <
3});
```

There's little point in doing this in most cases, but it might be useful if the function needed to be self-referential, for example, a recursive function.

> **NOTE**
>
> For more information about callbacks, refer to *Chapter 11, Higher-Order Functions and Callbacks in TypeScript*.

Immediately invoked function expressions look like this:

Example11.ts

```
1 (function () {
2    console.log('Immediately invoked!');
3 })();
```

Link to the preceding example: https://packt.link/iQoSX

The function outputs the following:

```
"Immediately invoked!"
```

The function is declared inline and then the additional **()** parentheses at the end invoke the function. The primary use case for an IIFE in TypeScript involves another concept known as closure, which will be discussed later in this chapter. For now, just learn to recognize this syntax where a function is declared and invoked right away.

ARROW FUNCTIONS

Arrow functions present a more compact syntax and also offer an alternative to the confusing and inconsistent rules surrounding the **this** keyword. Let's look at the syntax first.

An arrow function removes the **function** keyword and puts a "fat arrow" or **=>** between the parameter list and the function body. Arrow functions are never named. Let's rewrite the function that logs **Hello**:

```
const myFunction = (name: string): string => {
    return `Hello ${name}!`;
};
```

This function can be made even more compact. If the function simply returns a value, the braces and the **return** keyword can both be omitted. Our function now looks like this.

```
const myFunction = (name: string): string => `Hello ${name}!`;
```

Arrow functions are very frequently used in callback functions. The callback to the preceding filter function can be rewritten using an arrow function. Again, callbacks will be discussed in more detail in *Chapter 11, Higher-Order Functions and Callbacks in TypeScript*. Here is another example of an arrow function:

Example12.ts

```
1 const numbers = [1, 3, 2];
2 const filtered = numbers.filter((val) => val < 3);
2 console.log(filtered);
```

Link to the preceding example: https://packt.link/lUTCm

The output is as follows:

```
[1, 2]
```

This concise syntax may look confusing at first, so let's break it down. The **filter** function is a built-in method of the array object in TypeScript. It will return a new array containing all the items in the array that match the criteria in the callback function. So, we are saying for each **val**, add it to the new array if **val** is less than **3**.

Arrow functions are more than just a different syntax. While function declarations and function expressions create a new execution scope, arrow functions do not. This has implications when it comes to using the **this** (see below) and **new** (see *Chapter 4, Classes and Objects*) keywords.

TYPE INFERENCE

Let's consider the following code:

```
const myFunction = (name: string): string => `Hello ${name}!`;
const numbers = [1, 3, 2];
const filtered = numbers.filter((val) => val < 3);
console.log(filtered);
```

The output is as follows:

```
[1, 2]
```

Notice that in the preceding code, we aren't specifying a type for the **numbers** constant. But wait, isn't this a book on TypeScript? Yes, and now we come to one of the best features of TypeScript: type inference. TypeScript has the ability to assign types to variables when we omit them. When we declare **const numbers = [1, 2, 3];**, TypeScript will intuitively understand that we are declaring an array of numbers. If we wanted to, we could write **const numbers: number[] = [1, 2, 3];**, but TypeScript will see these declarations as equal.

The preceding code is 100% valid ES6 JavaScript. This is great because any JavaScript developer will be able to read and understand it, even if they have no experience with TypeScript. However, unlike JavaScript, TypeScript will prevent you from making an error by putting the wrong type of value into the **numbers** array.

Because TypeScript has inferred the type of our **numbers** array, we would not be able to add a value other than a number to it; for example, **numbers.push('hello');** will result in a compiler error. If we wanted to declare an array that would allow other types, we'd need to declare that explicitly – **const numbers: (number | string)[] = [1, 3, 2];**. Now, we can later assign a string to this array. Alternatively, an array declared as **const numbers = [1, 2, 3, 'abc'];** would already be of this type.

Going back to our **filter** function, this function is also not specifying any type for the parameter or the return type. Why is this allowed? It's our friend, type inference, again. Because we're iterating over an array of numbers, each item in that array must be a number. Therefore, **val** will always be a number and the type need not be specified. Likewise, the expression **val < 3** is a Boolean expression, so the return type will always be a Boolean. Remember that optional means you can always opt to provide a required type and you definitely should if that improves the clarity or readability of your code.

When an arrow function has a single parameter and the type can be inferred, we can make our code slightly more concise by omitting the parentheses around the parameter list. Finally, our **filter** function may look like this:

Example13.ts

```
1 const numbers = [1, 3, 2];
2 const filtered = numbers.filter(val => val < 3);
3 console.log(filtered);
```

Link to the preceding example: https://packt.link/hvbsc

The output is as follows:

```
[1, 2]
```

The syntax you choose is really a matter of taste, but many experienced programmers gravitate to the more concise syntax, so it's important to at least be able to read and understand it.

EXERCISE 3.03: WRITING ARROW FUNCTIONS

Now, let's write some arrow functions and get used to that syntax, as well as start to build our utility library. A good candidate for a utility library is a function that might be called. In this exercise, we'll write a function that takes a subject, verb, and list of objects and returns a grammatically correct sentence.

> **NOTE**
>
> The code file for this exercise can be found at https://packt.link/ylQnz.

1. Create a new file in VS Code and save it as **arrow-cat.ts**.

2. Start with a pattern for the function we need to implement, along with some calls to it:

```
export const sentence = (
  subject: string,
  verb: string,
  ...objects: string[]
): string => {
  return 'Meow, implement me!';
};
console.log(sentence('the cat', 'ate', 'apples', 'cheese',
'pancakes'));
console.log(sentence('the cat', 'slept', 'all day'));
console.log(sentence('the cat', 'sneezed'));
```

Our **sentence** function obviously isn't doing what we need it to do. We can modify the implementation to use a template string to output the subject, verb, and objects.

3. Use the following code to implement a template string to output the subject, verb, and objects:

```
export const sentence = (
  subject: string,
  verb: string,
  ...objects: string[]
): string => {
  return `${subject} ${verb} ${objects}.`;
};
```

Now, when we execute our program, we get the following output:

```
the cat ate apples,cheese,pancakes.
the cat slept all day.
the cat sneezed .
```

This is readable, but we have a number of issues with capitalization and word spacing. We can add some additional functions to help with these problems. Thinking through what should logically happen for these cases, if there are multiple objects, we'd like commas between them and to use "and" before the final object. If there's a single object, there shouldn't be commas or "and," and if there's no object, there shouldn't be an empty space, as there is here.

4. Implement a new function to add this logic to our program:

```
export const arrayToObjectSegment = (words: string[]): string => {
  if (words.length < 1) {
    return '';
  }
  if (words.length === 1) {
    return ` ${words[0]}`;
  }
  ...
};
```

Here, we implement the easier cases. If there are no objects, we want to return an empty string. If there is just one, we return that object with a leading space. Now, let's tackle the case of multiple objects.

We will need to add the objects to a comma-separated list, and if we have reached the last object, join it with "and".

5. To do this, we'll initialize an empty string and loop over the array of objects:

```
export const arrayToObjectSegment = (words: string[]): string => {
  if (words.length < 1) {
    return '';
  }
  if (words.length === 1) {
    return ` ${words[0]}`;
  }
  let segment = '';
  for (let i = 0; i < words.length; i++) {
    if (i === words.length - 1) {
      segment += ` and ${words[i]}`;
    } else {
      segment += ` ${words[i]},`;
    }
  }
  return segment;
};
```

By breaking the problem down into small components, we've come up with a function that solves all our use cases. Our **return** statement from **sentence** can now be **return** `` `${subject} ${verb}${arrayToObjectSegment(objects)}.` ``;.

Notice how the function that returns a string can fit right into our string template. Running this, we get the following output:

```
the cat ate apples, cheese, and pancakes.
the cat slept all day.
the cat sneezed.
```

That's almost correct, but the first letter of the sentence should be capitalized.

6. Use another function to handle capitalization and wrap the whole string template with it:

```
export const capitalize = (sentence: string): string => {
  return `${sentence.charAt(0).toUpperCase()}${sentence
    .slice(1)
    .toLowerCase()}`;
};
```

7. This function uses several built-in functions: **charAt**, **toUpperCase**, **slice**, and **toLowerCase**, all inside a string template. These functions grab the first character from our sentence, make it uppercase, and then concatenate it with the rest of the sentence, all cast to lowercase.

Now, when we execute the program, we get the desired result:

```
The cat ate apples, cheese, and pancakes.
The cat slept all day.
The cat sneezed.
```

To complete this exercise, we wrote three different functions, each serving a single purpose. We could have jammed all the functionality into a single function, but that would make the resulting code less reusable and more complicated to read and test. Building software from simple, single-purpose functions remains one of the best ways to write clean, maintainable code.

UNDERSTANDING THIS

Many developers have been frustrated by the **this** keyword. **this** nominally points to the runtime of the current function. For example, if a member function of an object is invoked, **this** will usually refer to that object. The use of **this** across other contexts may seem inconsistent, and its use can result in a number of unusual bugs. Part of the problem lies in the fact that the keyword is relatively straightforward to use in languages such as C++ or Java and programmers with experience in those languages may expect the TypeScript **this** to behave similarly.

Let's look at a very simple use case for **this**:

```
const person = {
    name: 'Ahmed',
    sayHello: function () {
        return `Hello, ${this.name}!`
    }
}
console.log(person.sayHello());
```

Here we declare an object that has a property, **name**, and a method, **sayHello**. In order for **sayHello** to read the **name** property, we use **this** to refer to the object itself. There's nothing wrong with this code and many programmers will find it quite intuitive.

The problem will come in when we need to declare another function inline, likely as a callback function for something like the **filter** function we looked at earlier.

Let's imagine we want to encapsulate the **arrayFilter** function in an object that can have a property to specify the maximum number allowed. This object will have some resemblance to the previous one, and we might expect to be able to employ **this** to get that maximum value. Let's see what happens when we try:

```
const arrayFilter = {
    max: 3,
    filter: function (...numbers: number[]) {
        return numbers.filter(function (val) {
            return val <= this.max;
        });
    }
}
console.log(arrayFilter.filter(1, 2, 3, 4));
```

TypeScript doesn't like my code. I'll have a red squiggly line under **this**, depending on my editor, and I won't be able to execute my program. Even if the program executes, you will not obtain the intended output.

The problem here is that my use of the **function** keyword creates a new scope and **this** no longer has the value I want it to. In fact, it has no value. It is **undefined**.

The reason for this is that unlike object-oriented languages, such as C++ and Java, the value of **this** will be determined at runtime and it will be set to the calling scope. In this case, our callback function is not part of any set context or object, and so **this** is **undefined**. The fact that it's **undefined** is really immaterial here. The important part is that it's not what we want.

There have been a number of workarounds to this problem over the years. One of them is that we cache the **this** reference to another variable and make that variable available in our callback function. Another is that we use the **bind** member function of the **Function** prototype to set the **this** reference. You may come across code that looks like this.

A better solution is to simply use arrow functions instead of function expressions. Not only is the syntax more concise and more modern, but arrow functions do not create a new **this** context. You get the **this** reference that you want, that of a top-level object. Let's rewrite the code using an arrow function:

Example14.ts

```
1 const arrayFilter = {
2     max: 3,
3     filter: function(...numbers: number[]) {
4         return numbers.filter(val => {
5             return val <= this.max;
6         });
7     }
8 }
9 console.log(arrayFilter.filter(1, 2, 3, 4));
```

Link to the preceding example: https://packt.link/90JSJ

The function produces the following output:

```
[1, 2, 3]
```

TypeScript no longer complains about **this** and the code works correctly.

But wait, why are we using a function expression for the **filter** function and an arrow function for the callback? It's because we actually need the scope-creating capability of **function** in order for **this** to have a value. If we rewrote the **filter** function as an arrow function, **this** would never be set and we wouldn't be able to access the **max** property.

This is confusing, to be sure, and it's the reason **this** is dreaded in TypeScript and JavaScript more than in other languages. The important thing to remember is that when you are programming with **this**, you want any object or class methods to be function expressions and any callbacks to be arrow functions. That way, you'll always have the correct instance of **this**.

Chapter 4 , *Classes and Objects*, will contain a deeper dive into classes and explore other patterns. Let's now use **this** in an object in the following exercise.

EXERCISE 3.04: USING THIS IN AN OBJECT

For this exercise, we will imagine that we have to implement some accounting software. In this software, each account object will track the total amount due, along with the amount that has been paid, and will have a couple of utility methods to get the current state of the account and the balance that needs to be paid.

Let's start by creating the object with its methods unimplemented. This example will demonstrate a simplified workflow where we print out the account, attempt to pay more than is due (receiving an error), then pay the amount due, and finally the full amount due:

> **NOTE**
>
> The code file for this exercise can be found at https://packt.link/P6YIf.

1. Write the following code, which is the basis for starting our program:

```
export const account = {
  due: 1000,
  paid: 0,
  status: 'OPEN',
  payAccount: function (amount: number): string {
    return 'unimplemented!';
  },
  printStatus: function (): string {
    return 'unimplemented!';
  },
};
```

```
console.log(account.printStatus());
console.log(account.payAccount(1500));
console.log(account.payAccount(500));
console.log(account.payAccount(500));
```

We need to implement both methods. The **printStatus** method will just output the total that was due, the amount paid so far, and whether the account is open or closed (or fully paid).

2. Use a string template to output the status, but in order to access the properties on the **account** object, use the **this** keyword:

```
printStatus: function (): string {
  return `$${this.paid} has been paid and $${
    this.due - this.paid
  } is outstanding. This account is ${this.status}.`;
},
```

We implement the **printStatus** function expression as a string template that uses **this** to access properties on the same object. As a reminder, we must use a function expression here and cannot use an arrow function, even if we might prefer that syntax, because arrow functions do not create a new execution context.

In case there's any confusion, there's no double dollar sign operator here. The first is a literal indicating the currency, and the second is part of the template string.

Now let's handle the payment. Our requirements are that if the amount paid exceeds the amount due, we should throw an error and not apply any payment. Otherwise, we track the additional payment. If the balance reaches $0, then we close the account. We should also print the current status following each transaction.

3. Write the code to handle the payment:

```
payAccount: function (amount: number): string {
  if (amount > this.due - this.paid) {
    return `$${amount} is more than the outstanding balance of $${
      this.due - this.paid
    }.`;
  }
```

```
      this.paid += amount;
      if (this.paid === this.due) {
        this.status = 'CLOSED';
      }
      return this.printStatus();
    },
```

4. Execute the program and check the output:

```
$0 has been paid and $1000 is outstanding. This account is OPEN.
$1500 is more than the outstanding balance of $1000.
$500 has been paid and $500 is outstanding. This account is OPEN.
$1000 has been paid and $0 is outstanding. This account is CLOSED
```

In this exercise, we used function expressions as object methods to access properties on the object. Methods can not only read properties on an object, they can also update them. It's a common pattern in object-oriented programming to have objects that both contain data and have the methods available to access and mutate them. Sometimes, those methods will be set to private and only accessed via accessors such as **get** and **set**. More on this subject will be covered in *Chapter 4, Classes and Objects*.

As we've seen in this exercise, when implementing object-oriented patterns, function expressions are still important to know and understand.

CLOSURES AND SCOPE

In addition to everything else we've discussed so far, functions do something special in TypeScript. When a function is declared (be it a function statement, expression, or arrow function), it encloses any variables in a higher scope. This is called a closure. Any function can be a closure. A closure is simply a function that has enclosed variables.

The concept of scope simply means that each function creates a new scope. As we've seen, functions can be declared inside other functions. The **inner** function can read any variables declared in the outer function, but the outer function cannot see variables declared in the inner function. This is scope. The following code establishes an outer scope and an inner scope by declaring a second function inline inside an outer function. The inner function is able to access the variables in the outer scope, but the **world** variable declared in the inner scope is not visible outside that function:

Example15.ts

```
1  const outer = (): void => {
2      const hello = 'Hello';
3      const inner = (): void => {
4          const world = 'world!';
5          console.log(`${hello} ${world}`);
6      }
7      inner();
8
9      console.log(`${hello} ${world}`);
10 }
11 outer();
```

Link to the preceding example: https://packt.link/USZ74

The function produces the following output:

```
Hello world!
ReferenceError: world is not defined
```

When this function is invoked, the inner log statement is reached and logs **"Hello world!"**, and then the outer log statement is reached and we get **ReferenceError**. We can fix **ReferenceError** by adding **let world;** to the outer function:

Example16.ts

```
1   const outer = (): void => {
2       const hello = 'Hello';
3       let world;
4       const inner = (): void => {
5           const world = 'world!';
6           console.log(`${hello} ${world}`);
7       }
8       inner();
8
9       console.log(`${hello} ${world}`);
10  }
11  outer();
```

Link to the preceding example: https://packt.link/yC0Zq

The function produces the following output:

```
Hello world!
Hello undefined!
```

This is because the **inner** function declared a new **world** variable that the **outer** function cannot access. We can drop **const** from the **inner** declaration:

Example17.ts

```
1  const outer = (): void => {
2      const hello = 'Hello';
3      let world;
4      const inner = (): void => {
5          world = 'world!';
6          console.log(`${hello} ${world}`);
7      }
8      inner();
9
10     console.log(`${hello} ${world}`);
11 }
12
13 outer();
```

Link to the preceding example: https://packt.link/fCsaY

The function produces the following output:

```
Hello world!
Hello world!
```

The function finally works because the **inner** function operates against a variable that was declared in the scope of the **outer** function. It is still visible after the inner scope is exited, so it can be printed out.

Let's look at a more useful example. The Fibonacci sequence is a number set in which the next number is the sum of the two previous numbers: **[0, 1, 1, 2, 3, 5, 8, 13, 21, …]**. The Fibonacci sequence is often used to help explain recursive functions. In this case, we will instead use it to demonstrate closures by writing a function that will return the next value in the sequence each time it is called.

The logic of our program will be that we will track the current number being returned by our function, the next one that should be, and the amount to increment the number. Each time it is called, all three numbers will be updated to prepare for the next call. One way to do that is to define these values as global scoped variables and write a simple function to update and track them. That might look like this:

Example_Fibbonacci_1.ts

```
1 let next = 0;
2 let inc = 1;
3 let current = 0;
4
5 for (let i = 0; i < 10; i++) {
6     [current, next, inc] = [next, inc, next + inc];
7     console.log(current);
8 }
```

Link to the preceding example: https://packt.link/17Hda

The function produces the following output:

```
0
1
1
2
3
5
8
13
21
34
```

This program works and returns the desired result, but since it isn't a function, the program will just execute once and stop. If you wanted to get the next Fibonacci number as part of some other process, you wouldn't be able to. If you just wrap it in a function, that won't work either:

`Example_Fibbonacci_2.ts`

```
1   const getNext = (): number => {
2       let next = 0;
3       let inc = 1;
4       let current = 0;
5
6       [current, next, inc] = [next, inc, next + inc];
7       return current;
8   };
9
10  for (let i = 0; i < 10; i++) {
11      console.log(getNext());
12  }
```

`Link to the preceding example:` https://packt.link/rfDuz

The function produces the following output:

```
0
0
//...
```

This function will just return **0** every time it's called because all the variables get re-declared when it's invoked. We can fix that by moving the variables outside the function. That way, they are declared once and modified by the function being invoked.

Our function now sets up the next value to be returned, the amount to increment, and the most recent returned value. On each function call in the loop, it will replace the current value with the next value, the next value with the increment amount, and the increment amount to the sum of the next value plus the previous increment amount. Then it logs out the current value:

Example_Fibbonacci_3.ts

```
1   let next = 0;
2   let inc = 1;
3   let current = 0;
4
5   const getNext = (): number => {
6       [current, next, inc] = [next, inc, next + inc];
7       return current;
8   };
9
10  for (let i = 0; i < 10; i++) {
11      console.log(getNext());
12  }
```

Link to the preceding example: https://packt.link/mAEds

The function produces the following output:

```
0
1
1
2
3
5
8
13
21
34
```

This works! The reason it works is that the **getNext** function is able to access the variables in the higher scope. The function is a closure. This will seem standard and expected, but what might be unexpected is that this will work even if the function is exported and called by some other part of the program. This can be illustrated better by creating another function:

`Example_Fibbonacci_4.ts`

```
1   const fibonacci = () => {
2       let next = 0;
3       let inc = 1;
4       let current = 0;
5       return () => {
6           [current, next, inc] = [next, inc, next + inc];
7           return current;
8       };
9   };
10  const getNext = fibonacci();
11  for (let i = 0; i < 10; i++) {
12      console.log(getNext());
13  }
```

`Link to the preceding example:` https://packt.link/CdKte

The output hasn't changed:

```
0
1
1
2
3
//...
```

Calling the **fibonacci** function will return a new function that has access to the variables declared in **fibonacci**. If we wanted to run another Fibonacci sequence, we could call **fibonacci()** again to get a fresh scope with initialized variables:

Example_Fibbonacci_5.ts

```
1   const fibonacci = () => {
2       let next = 0;
3       let inc = 1;
4       let current = 0;
5       return () => {
6           [current, next, inc] = [next, inc, next + inc];
7           return current;
8       };
9   };
10  const getNext = fibonacci();
11  const getMoreFib = fibonacci();
12  for (let i = 0; i < 10; i++) {
13      console.log(getNext());
14  }
15  for (let i = 0; i < 10; i++) {
16      console.log(getMoreFib());
17  }
```

Link to the preceding example: https://packt.link/0nGph

We'll see the same output again, but twice this time:

```
0
1
1
2
//...
21
34
0
1
1
2
//...
```

> **NOTE**
>
> For ease of presentation, only a section of the actual output is displayed.

In both cases, the closures have closed over the variables in a higher scope and are still available on function calls. This is a powerful technique, as has been shown, but could potentially lead to memory leaks if not used correctly. Variables declared in a closure like this cannot be garbage-collected while a reference to them still exists.

EXERCISE 3.05: CREATING THE ORDER FACTORY WITH CLOSURES

Closures can be tricky to work with, but a common pattern that really brings out the usefulness is sometimes called a factory pattern. This is, simply, a function that returns another function that is all set up and ready for use. In this pattern, a closure is used to make sure that variables can persist between function calls. We'll explore this pattern in this exercise.

Let's start with some code that almost does what we want it to do. We are working on an order system for some sort of garment. Each order that comes in will specify a quantity of the garment in identical color and size. We just have to produce a record of each garment with a unique ID for tracking:

> **NOTE**
>
> The code file for this exercise can be found at https://packt.link/fsqdd.

1. Create a new file in VS Code and save it as **order.ts**. Begin with the following code with some sample calls:

```
interface Order {
  id: number;
  color: string;
  size: string;
}
export const createOrder = (
  color: string,
  size: string,
  quantity: number
): Order[] => {
  let id = 0;
  const orders = [];
  for (let i = 0; i < quantity; i++) {
    orders.push({ id: id++, color, size });
  }
  return orders;
```

```
};
const orderOne = createOrder('red', 'M', 4);
console.log(orderOne);
const orderTwo = createOrder('blue', 'S', 7);
console.log(orderTwo);
```

The code looks OK. Let's run it and see how it works. You will obtain the following output:

```
[
  { id: 0, color: 'red', size: 'M' },
  { id: 1, color: 'red', size: 'M' },
  { id: 2, color: 'red', size: 'M' },
  { id: 3, color: 'red', size: 'M' }
]
[
  { id: 0, color: 'blue', size: 'S' },
  { id: 1, color: 'blue', size: 'S' },
  { id: 2, color: 'blue', size: 'S' },
  { id: 3, color: 'blue', size: 'S' },
  { id: 4, color: 'blue', size: 'S' },
  { id: 5, color: 'blue', size: 'S' },
  { id: 6, color: 'blue', size: 'S' }
]
```

That's not right. We can't start the ID numbers over at zero again each time. How can we fix this problem?

There are a couple of ways to fix this. The easiest way to do it would be to declare the ID number outside of **orderFactory**. However, doing that might lead to bugs as system complexity grows. Variables that are in a topmost or even global scope are accessible to every part of the system and may get modified by some edge case.

2. Use a closure to solve this problem instead. Create an **orderFactory** function that returns an instance of **createOrder**, which will put the ID number in the scope just over **createOrder**. That way, the ID will be tracked between multiple calls of **createOrder**:

```
export const orderFactory = (): ((
  color: string,
  size: string,
  qty: number
```

```
) => Order[]) => {
  let id = 0;
  return (color: string, size: string, qty: number): Order[] => {
    const orders = [];
    for (let i = 0; i < qty; i++) {
      orders.push({ id: id++, color, size });
    }
    return orders;
  };
};
```

This factory function returns another function, which is defined inline as an arrow function. Before that function is returned, the **id** variable is declared in the scope just above it. Each invocation of the returned function will see the same instance of **id** and thus it will retain its value between calls.

3. In order to make use of the factory, call the function once:

```
const createOrder = orderFactory();
```

Calling **orderFactory** once will initialize the ID variable and make it available in the returned function that is now assigned to **createOrder**. That variable is now enclosed. No other code will be able to access it or, more importantly, modify it.

4. Run the program and observe that we now get the correct output:

```
[
    { id: 0, color: 'red', size: 'M' },
    { id: 1, color: 'red', size: 'M' },
    { id: 2, color: 'red', size: 'M' },
    { id: 3, color: 'red', size: 'M' }
]
[
    { id: 4, color: 'blue', size: 'S' },
    { id: 5, color: 'blue', size: 'S' },
    { id: 6, color: 'blue', size: 'S' },
```

```
    { id: 7, color: 'blue', size: 'S' },
    { id: 8, color: 'blue', size: 'S' },
    { id: 9, color: 'blue', size: 'S' },
    { id: 10, color: 'blue', size: 'S' }
]
```

Closures can be very difficult to understand without practice. Beginner TypeScript programmers shouldn't worry about mastering them immediately, but it's very important to recognize factory patterns and the behavior of enclosed variables.

CURRYING

Currying (named after Haskell Brooks Curry, the mathematician after whom the Haskell, Brooks, and Curry programming languages are also named) is the act of taking a function (or a formula in mathematics) and breaking it down into individual functions, each with a single parameter.

> **NOTE**
>
> For more information on currying, refer to the following URL: https://javascript.info/currying-partials.

Since functions in TypeScript can return functions, arrow syntax gives us a special concise syntax that makes currying a popular practice. Let's start with a simple function:

`Example_Currying_1.ts`

```
1 const addTwoNumbers = (a: number, b: number): number => a + b;
2 console.log(addTwoNumbers(3, 4));
```

`Link to the preceding example:` https://packt.link/InDVT

The output is as follows:

```
7
```

Here, we've used arrow syntax to describe a function body without braces or the **return** keyword. The function returns the result of the single expression in the body. This function expects two parameters and can be rewritten as curried functions with a single parameter each:

Example_Currying_2.ts

```
1 const addTwoNumbers = (a: number): ((b: number) => number) => (b:
2 number): number => a + b;
3 console.log(addTwoNumbers(3)(4));
```

Link to the preceding example: https://packt.link/975cf

The output is as follows:

```
7
```

This is actually two function declarations. The first function returns another function, which actually does the calculation. Because of closures, the **a** parameter is available within the second function, as well as its own parameter, **b**. The two sets of parentheses mean that the first one returns a new function that is then invoked immediately by the second one. The preceding code could be rewritten in a longer form:

Example_Currying_3.ts

```
1 const addTwoNumbers = (a: number): ((b: number) => number) => {
2     return (b: number): number => {
3         return a + b;
4     }
5 }
6
7 const addFunction = addTwoNumbers(3);
8
9 console.log(addFunction(4));
```

Link to the preceding example: https://packt.link/TgC17

The output is as follows:

```
7
```

It looks a bit silly when written that way, but these do exactly the same thing.

So what use is currying?

Higher-order functions are a variety of curried functions. Higher-order functions both take a function as an argument and return a new function. These functions are often wrapping or modifying some existing functionality. How can we wrap our REST client in a higher-order function to ensure that all responses, whether successful or in error, are handled in a uniform way? This will be the focus of the next exercise.

EXERCISE 3.06: REFACTORING INTO CURRIED FUNCTIONS

Currying makes use of closures and is closely related to the last exercise, so let's return to it and establish the solution from the last exercise as the starting point for this one. Our **orderFactory** function is doing its job and tracking IDs properly, but the initialization of each type of garment is too slow. The first time an order for red medium comes in, we expect some time will be taken in spinning up this particular recipe, but subsequent red mediums suffer the same latency. Our system isn't efficient enough to handle the demand for popular items. We need some way to cut into the setup time each time a similar order comes in:

> **NOTE**
>
> The code file for this exercise can be found at https://packt.link/jSKic.

1. Review the code from *Exercise 3.05, Creating the Order Factory with Closures* (**order-solution.ts**):

```
interface Order {
  id: number;
  color: string;
  size: string;
}
export const orderFactory = (): ((
  color: string,
  size: string,
  qty: number
) => Order[]) => {
  let id = 0;
  return (color: string, size: string, qty: number): Order[] => {
    const orders = [];
    for (let i = 0; i < qty; i++) {
      orders.push({ id: id++, color, size });
    }
```

```
      return orders;
    };
  };
const createOrder = orderFactory();
const orderOne = createOrder('red', 'M', 4);
console.log(orderOne);
const orderTwo = createOrder('blue', 'S', 7);
console.log(orderTwo);
```

How can we use currying to increase efficiency? You need to refactor the code into curried functions.

2. Refactor **orderFactory** to return a curried function by breaking up the returned function into three separate functions, each of which returns the next function:

```
export const orderFactory = () => {
  let id = 0;
  return (color: string) => (size: string) => (qty: number) => {
    const orders = [];
    for (let i = 0; i < qty; i++) {
      orders.push({ id: id++, color, size });
    }
    return orders;
  };
};
```

In this case, our refactor is as simple as putting an arrow in between each parameter. Note that this code omits return types from the functions. There are two reasons for this. One is that the type can be reasonably inferred from the code and is quite clear. The other is that adding all of the return types will significantly clutter the code.

If we add all the return types together, the code will look like this:

```
export const orderFactory = (): ((
  color: string
) => (size: string) => (qty: number) => Order[]) => {
  let id = 0;
  return (color: string): ((size: string) => (qty: number) =>
Order[]) => (
    size: string
```

```
  ) => (qty: number): Order[] => {
    const orders = [];
    for (let i = 0; i < qty; i++) {
      orders.push({ id: id++, color, size });
    }
    return orders;
  };
};
```

TypeScript gives us the flexibility of choosing between explicitly declaring types and allowing type inference, when clear, to supply the correct types.

Now that **orderFactory** returns a curried function, we can take advantage of it.

3. Instead of passing every argument to **createOrder**, call **createOrder** with just the first argument to establish our line of red garments:

```
const redLine = createOrder('red');
```

4. Then, further break out the individual items available:

```
const redSmall = redLine('S');
const redMedium = redLine('M');
```

5. When necessary or appropriate, create an item on one line:

```
const blueSmall = createOrder('blue')('S')
```

6. Try creating many different combinations of orders and printing out the results:

```
const orderOne = redMedium(4);
console.log(orderOne);


const orderTwo = blueSmall(7);
console.log(orderTwo);


const orderThree = redSmall(11);
console.log(orderThree);
```

7. When you run the program, you'll see the following output:

```
[
    { id: 0, color: 'red', size: 'M' },
    { id: 1, color: 'red', size: 'M' },
    { id: 2, color: 'red', size: 'M' },
    { id: 3, color: 'red', size: 'M' }
]
//...
```

> **NOTE**
>
> For ease of presentation, only a section of the actual output is shown here.

Currying is a powerful technique for caching variables and partial function results. At this point, we've explored closures, higher-order functions, and currying, all of which show the power and versatility of functions in TypeScript.

FUNCTIONAL PROGRAMMING

Functional programming is a deep topic and the subject of many books by itself. This book can only touch on the topic. One of the foundational concepts in functional programming is to use simple functions that have an input and an output and do not modify variables that are outside their scope:

Example_Functional_1.ts

```
1 let importantNumber = 3;
2
3 const addFive = (): void => {
4     importantNumber += 5;
5 };
6
7 addFive();
8
9 console.log(importantNumber);
```

Link to the preceding example: https://packt.link/CTn1X

The function produces the following output:

```
8
```

The output of this program is correct. We have indeed added **5** to the initial value of **3**, but the **addFive** method accesses a variable in a higher scope and mutates it. It is greatly preferred in functional programming paradigms to instead return the new value and allow the outer scope to control the variables that have been declared in it. We can change **addFive** so that it no longer operates on variables outside its scope and instead only operates against its argument and returns the correct value:

Example_Functional_2.ts

```
1 let importantNumber = 3;
2
3 const addFive = (num: number): number => {
4     return num + 5;
5 };
6
7 importantNumber = addFive(importantNumber);
8
9 console.log(importantNumber);
```

Link to the preceding example: https://packt.link/6fWcF.

The function produces the following output:

```
8
```

The function is now much more portable. It would be easier to test or reuse since it's not reliant on something in a higher scope. A functional programming paradigm encourages the use of smaller functions. Sometimes, programmers can write functions that do too many different things and are hard to read and maintain. This is often a source of bugs or a negative impact on team velocity. By keeping functions small and simple, we can chain logic together in ways that support maintenance and reusability.

A popular concept in functional programming is immutability. That is the concept whereby once a variable is declared, its value should not change. To understand why this would be a desirable trait, consider a program that has a requirement to print out a customer ID after the customer's name:

Example_Functional_3.ts

```
1 const customer = {id: 1234, name: 'Amalgamated Materials'}
2
3 const formatForPrint = ()=> {
4   customer.name = `${customer.name} id: ${customer.id}`;
5 };
6
7 formatForPrint();
8
9 console.log(customer.name);
```

Link to the preceding example: https://packt.link/TX81Z

This program does as expected. When the customer's name is printed out, it has the ID behind it; however, we've actually changed the name in the customer object:

```
Amalgamated Materials id: 1234
```

What happens If **formatForPrint** is called repeatedly? With a minor refactor, our code is much safer and more consistent:

```
const customer = {id: 1234, name: 'Amalgamated Materials'}

const formatForPrint = ()=> {
  return `${customer.name} id: ${customer.id}`;
};

console.log(formatForPrint());
```

The output is as follows:

```
Amalgamated Materials id: 1234
```

It would be even better to pass in the customer object rather than having **formatForPrint** access it in a higher scope.

TypeScript supports both functional programming and object-oriented paradigms. Many applications borrow from both.

ORGANIZING FUNCTIONS INTO OBJECTS AND CLASSES

Sometimes, it makes sense to organize functions into member functions of objects and classes. These concepts will be addressed in greater detail in *Chapter 4*, *Classes and Objects*, but for now we can examine how we take a function declaration and add it to an object or class.

Let's take a simple function:

Example_OrganizingFuncs_1.ts

```
1 function addTwoNumbers(a: number, b: number) { return a + b; }
```

If we wanted to have an object that contains a number of math functions, we could simply add the following function to it:

```
2 const mathUtils = {
3     addTwoNumbers
4 };
5
6 console.log(mathUtils.addTwoNumbers(3, 4));
```

Link to the preceding example: https://packt.link/qX1QO

The output is as follows:

```
7
```

Note that the syntax used in the **mathUtils** object is shorthand, meaning the left and right side of the assignment are the same. This could also be written like this:

Example_OrganizingFuncs_2.ts

```
5 const mathUtils = {
6     addTwoNumbers: addTwoNumbers
7 };
```

We also have the option of defining the method inline with a function expression:

```
5 const mathUtils = {
6     addTwoNumbers: function(a: number, b: number) { return a + b; }
7 };
```

Link to the preceding example: https://packt.link/Ew4vi

The output in either case will be as follows:

```
7
```

Remember that function expressions are usually the best thing to use in objects because they will have the correct **this** reference. In the case of our **mathUtils** object, we aren't using the **this** keyword, so an arrow function *could* be used, but bear in mind that if, later on, another developer refactors this object, they might not think to change from an arrow function to a function expression and you might wind up with buggy code.

Adding functions to classes can be done in exactly the same way and, in fact, the syntax is very similar. Let's say we want to use a class instead of a plain object and we want to define **addTwoNumbers** inline. The **MathUtils** class might look something like this:

```
class MathUtils {
    addTwoNumbers(a: number, b: number) { return a + b; }
};
```

Now that we're using a class, in order to call the function, we need to instantiate an object:

```
const mathUtils = new MathUtils();
console.log(mathUtils.addTwoNumbers(3, 4));
```

The output is as follows:

```
7
```

For more information on classes, see *Chapter 4, Classes and Objects*.

EXERCISE 3.07: REFACTORING JAVASCRIPT INTO TYPESCRIPT

Updating older JavaScript code to TypeScript isn't difficult. If the original code was well written, we can retain much of the structure, but enhance it with interfaces and types. In this exercise, we will use an example legacy JavaScript code that prints the area of various shapes given the dimensions:

> **NOTE**
>
> The code file for this exercise can be found at https://packt.link/gRVxx.

1. Start with the following legacy code and make some decisions about what we'd like to improve by converting it to TypeScript:

```
var PI = 3.14;
function getCircleArea(radius) {
  return radius * radius * PI;
}
//...
```

> **NOTE**
>
> Only a section of the actual code is presented here. You can find the complete code at https://packt.link/pahq2.

A few of the changes are easy. We'll substitute **var** with **const**. The functions that determine area are pretty good, but **getArea** mutates the shape objects. It would be better to just return the area. All of our shapes are pretty well defined, but they would be improved with interfaces.

2. Let's create some interfaces. Create a new file in VS Code and save it as **refactor-shapes-solution.ts**.

3. First, create a **Shape** interface that includes an enumerated type and an area property. We can extend our **Circle**, **Square**, **Rectangle**, and **RightTriangle** interfaces from that one:

```
const PI = 3.14;
interface Shape {
  area?: number;
  type: 'circle' | 'rectangle' | 'rightTriangle' | 'square';
}
interface Circle extends Shape {
  radius: number;
  type: 'circle';
}
interface Rectangle extends Shape {
  length: number;
  type: 'rectangle';
  width: number;
}
interface RightTriangle extends Shape {
```

```
    base: number;
    height: number;
    type: 'rightTriangle';
  }
  interface Square extends Shape {
    type: 'square';
    width: number;
  }
```

4. Now, let's improve and simplify **getArea**. Instead of accessing properties on each shape, **getArea** can simply pass the shape to the correct function to determine the area and then return the calculated value:

```
const getArea = (shape: Shape) => {
  switch (shape.type) {
    case 'circle':
      return getCircleArea(shape as Circle);
    case 'rectangle':
      return getRectangleArea(shape as Rectangle);
    case 'rightTriangle':
      return getRightTriangleArea(shape as RightTriangle);
    case 'square':
      return getSquareArea(shape as Square);
  }
};
```

This change requires that we make minor changes to all the functions that calculate area.

5. Instead of each individual property being passed in, now pass in the shape and then grab the props inside the functions:

```
const getCircleArea = (circle: Circle): number => {
  const { radius } = circle;
  return radius * radius * PI;
};
const getRectangleArea = (rectangle: Rectangle): number => {
  const { length, width } = rectangle;
  return length * width;
};
const getSquareArea = (square: Square): number => {
  const { width } = square;
  return getRectangleArea({ length: width, type: 'rectangle', width
```

```
  });
};
const getRightTriangleArea = (rightTriangle: RightTriangle): number
=> {
  const { base, height } = rightTriangle;
  return (base * height) / 2;
};
```

This pattern is very common among modern web app development and works very well in TypeScript development.

6. Add some type hints to our object declarations:

```
const circle: Circle = { radius: 4, type: 'circle' };
console.log({ ...circle, area: getArea(circle) });


const rectangle: Rectangle = { type: 'rectangle', length: 7, width: 4
};
console.log({ ...rectangle, area: getArea(rectangle) });


const square: Square = { type: 'square', width: 5 };
console.log({ ...square, area: getArea(square) });


const rightTriangle: RightTriangle = {
  type: 'rightTriangle',
  base: 9,
  height: 4,
};
console.log({ ...rightTriangle, area: getArea(rightTriangle) });
```

7. Running the program yields the correct output:

```
{ radius: 4, type: 'circle', area: 50.24 }
{ type: 'rectangle', length: 7, width: 4, area: 28 }
{ type: 'square', width: 5, area: 25 }
{ type: 'rightTriangle', base: 9, height: 4, area: 18 }
```

This exercise provided us with practical experience in refactoring legacy JavaScript code into TypeScript. These skills can help us to identify what constituted code quality problems in the original JavaScript code and improve them as we move the code to TypeScript.

IMPORT, EXPORT, AND REQUIRE

Very small programs, such as the kind often found in books on programming, can work just fine with all the code in a single file. Most of the time, applications will be made up of multiple files, often referred to as modules. Some modules may be dependencies installed from Node Package Manager (**npm**) and some may be modules you or your team have written. When you look at other projects, you may see the keywords **import**, **export**, **module**, and **require** used to link different modules together. **import** and **require** both serve the same purpose. They allow you to use another module in the module (file) you are currently working in. **export** and **module** are the opposite. They allow you to make part or all of your module available for other modules to use.

We'll go over the different syntax options here. The reason for multiple ways to do things has, as usual, to do with the way the languages and runtimes have evolved. Node.js is by far the most popular runtime for server-side JavaScript, and this is where most of our compiled server-side TypeScript will run. Node.js was released in 2009 and, at that time, there was no standard module system for JavaScript. Many JavaScript web applications at that time would simply attach functions and objects to the global window object. This could work fine for web applications, since the window object is refreshed upon loading the page and exists in the web browser, so it's only used by a single user.

Although there is a global object in Node.js, this is not a practical way to link modules together. Doing so would risk one module overwriting another, memory leaks, exposing customer data, and all manner of other catastrophes. The great thing about the module system is that you can share only the bits of your module that you intend to.

Because there was a need for a more robust solution, Node.js adopted the CommonJS spec and the **module** and **require** keywords. **module** is used to share all or part of your module and **require** is used to consume another module. These keywords were standard in Node.js for many years until ECMAScript 6 introduced the **import** and **export** syntax. The latter has been supported in TypeScript for many years and is preferred, although the **require** syntax is still valid and can be used.

This book will use **import** and **export** syntax, as this is standard. The examples that follow will use this syntax, but will also feature the **require** syntax as a comment so readers can compare.

Any file with the **import** or **export** keyword is considered to be a module. Modules may export any variables or functions they declare, either as part of the declaration or by explicitly doing so:

```
// utils.ts
export const PI = 3.14;
export const addTwoNumbers = (a: number, b: number): number => a + b;
```

That is equivalent to explicit exports. Here is the complete code for **utils.ts**:

Example_Import_Exports/utils.ts

```
1 // utils.ts
2 const PI = 3.14;
3
4 const addTwoNumbers = (a: number, b: number): number => a + b;
5
6 export { PI, addTwoNumbers };
7 // module syntax:
8 // module.exports = { PI, addTwoNumbers };
```

Link to the preceding example: https://packt.link/3FEbm

We can now import our exports into another module (another **.ts** file – **app.ts**):

Example_Import_Exports/app.ts

```
1 // app.ts
2 import { PI, addTwoNumbers } from './utils';
3 // require syntax:
4 // const { PI, addTwoNumbers } = require('./utils');
5 console.log(PI);
6 console.log(addTwoNumbers(3, 4));
```

Link to the preceding example: https://packt.link/ozz9N

Once you run **app.ts**, you will obtain the following output:

```
3.14
7
```

> **NOTE**
>
> The code files for the preceding example can be found here:
> https://packt.link/zsCDe

Modules that are part of our application are imported via the relative path from the root of the project. Modules that are imported from our installed dependencies are imported by name. Note that the file extension is not part of the required path, just the filename.

Modules can also have default exports that use the **default** keyword. Default exports are imported without brackets. Consider the following examples:

Example_Import_Export_2/utils.ts

```
1 // utils.ts
2 const PI = 3.14;
3 const addTwo = (a: number, b: number): number => {
4   return a + b;
5 };
6 const fetcher = () => {
7   console.log('it is fetched!');
8 };
9 export default { addTwo, fetcher, PI };
```

Link to the preceding example: https://packt.link/h3R4r

The code for **app.ts** is as follows:

```
1 // app.ts
2 import utils from './utils';
3 console.log(utils.addTwo(3, 4));
```

Link to the preceding example: https://packt.link/oamFn

Once you run the **app.ts** file, you will get the following output:

```
7
```

EXERCISE 3.08: IMPORT AND EXPORT

Looking back at the last exercise, we have a single file that has a bunch of utility functions, and then we have procedural code that establishes some objects, calls the functions, and logs out the output. Let's refactor the result from Exercise 3.07, Refactoring JavaScript into TypeScript to use the **import** and **export** keywords and move those functions to a separate module:

> **NOTE**
>
> The code file for this exercise can be found at https://packt.link/2K4ds.
> The first step of this exercise requires you to copy-paste some lines of
> code to your exercise file. Hence, we suggest you either download the
> code files from this repository or migrate it your desktop before you begin
> this exercise.

1. Cut and paste the first 61 lines of **shapes.ts** into **shapes-lib.ts**. Your IDE should start warning you that it can no longer find the relevant functions.

2. Look over the code in **shapes-lib.ts**. Which functions and interfaces need to be exported? Square, circle, and the rest are utilized directly in **shapes.ts**, but the shapes interface isn't, so only those four need to be exported. Likewise, the PI constant is only used in **shapes-lib.ts**, so no need to export that one:

```
const PI = 3.14;
interface Shape {
  area?: number;
  type: 'circle' | 'rectangle' | 'rightTriangle' | 'square';
}
```

```
export interface Circle extends Shape {
  radius: number;
  type: 'circle';
}
export interface Rectangle extends Shape {
  length: number;
  type: 'rectangle';
  width: number;
}
export interface RightTriangle extends Shape {
  base: number;
  height: number;
  type: 'rightTriangle';
}

export interface Square extends Shape {
  type: 'square';
  width: number;
}
```

3. The only function that needs to be exported is **getArea**, as that's the only one referenced in **shapes.ts**:

```
export const getArea = (shape: Shape) => {
  switch (shape.type) {
    case 'circle':
      return getCircleArea(shape as Circle);
    case 'rectangle':
      return getRectangleArea(shape as Rectangle);
    case 'rightTriangle':
      return getRightTriangleArea(shape as RightTriangle);
    case 'square':
      return getSquareArea(shape as Square);
  }
};
```

4. Now, let's import the exported interfaces and function into **shapes.ts**. Your IDE may assist you in this task. For example, in VS Code, if you hover over a module that can be imported, it should ask you whether you'd like to add the import:

```
import {
  Circle,
  getArea,
  Rectangle,
  RightTriangle,
  Square,
} from './shapes-lib-solution';
```

5. With all the imports and exports set, run the program again. You should get the correct result:

```
{ radius: 4, type: 'circle', area: 50.24 }
{ type: 'rectangle', length: 7, width: 4, area: 28 }
{ type: 'square', width: 5, area: 25 }
{ type: 'rightTriangle', base: 9, height: 4, area: 18 }
```

One of the more challenging things about learning a new programming language is how to structure modules. A good rule of thumb is to always be prepared to break them into smaller chunks if they grow too large. This exercise helps us to understand how we can separate our application logic from utilities or reusable functions, a practice that will lead to clean, maintainable code.

ACTIVITY 3.01: BUILDING A FLIGHT BOOKING SYSTEM WITH FUNCTIONS

As a developer at a start-up for online bookings, you need to implement a system that manages airline bookings. The architecture for this system has already been decided upon. There will be a system for managing flights and seat availability on them and a system for managing bookings. Users will interact directly with the booking system and it, in turn, will search and update flight information.

For the sake of keeping this activity to a manageable size, we'll abstract a number of things, such as customer information, payments, the dates of flights, and even the city of origin. In understanding the problem we need to solve, it can be very helpful to create a diagram describing the flows we need to implement. The following diagram shows the expected workflow for our user:

> **NOTE**
>
> The code files for this activity can be found here: https://packt.link/o5n0t.

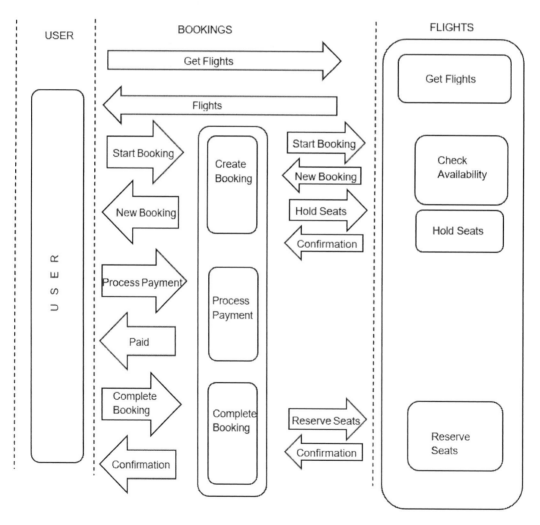

Figure 3.1: Flows that need to be implemented in the flight booking system

Here's how the program flows:

1. Get a list of flights to choose from.

2. Start a booking with one of those flights.

3. Pay for the flight.

4. Complete the booking with seats reserved on the flight.

As the diagram shows, the user will interact with two different systems, a Bookings system and a Flights system. In most scenarios, the user interacts with the Bookings system, but they go directly to the Flights system to search for flights.

In this activity, these systems can be represented by a **bookings.ts** file and a **flights.ts** file, which are two TypeScript modules. To complete the activity, implement these two modules in TypeScript. Here are some steps to help you:

1. Since both the user and the Bookings system depend on the Flights system, start with flights – **flights.ts**. As the activity is simplified, we can simply return a list of destinations when the user wants to access flights. To allow access to the **bookings.ts** module, we'll want to use the **export** keyword on a function.

2. Although the user has already fetched the flights, we need to check availability before initiating a booking. This is because our system will have many users and availability can change minute by minute. Expose a function for checking availability and another to hold seats while the transaction is completed.

3. The process payment step really hints at a third system for payments, but we won't include that system in this activity, so just mark the booking as paid when the user gets to the payment step. The Flights system doesn't need to be aware of payment status as that is managed by Bookings.

4. When we complete the booking, held seats convert to reserved seats. Our booking is finalized and the seats are no longer available on the flight.

5. A typical output for such an activity would look like this:

```
Booked to Lagos {
  bookingNumber: 1,
  flight: {
    destination: 'Lagos',
    flightNumber: 1,
    seatsHeld: 0,
    seatsRemaining: 29,
    time: '5:30'
```

```
    },
    paid: true,
    seatsHeld: 0,
    seatsReserved: 1
  //...
```

> **NOTE**
>
> For ease of presentation, only a part of the actual output is shown here.
> The solution to this activity can be found on page 602.

There are many other scenarios here that could be explored. Try holding all remaining seats, failing to start a new booking for that flight, and then complete the original booking. That should work with the logic we've implemented here! This exercise uses several functions to create a cohesive program. It uses closures, currying, functional programming concepts, and the **import** and **export** keywords to share functions between modules.

UNIT TESTING WITH TS-JEST

Large systems require constant testing to ensure they are correct. This is where unit testing comes in. Some of the biggest software projects in the world have hundreds of millions of lines of code and thousands of features and views. It's simply not possible to manually test every feature. This is where unit tests come in. Unit tests test the smallest unit of code, often a single statement or function, and give us quick feedback if we've done something to change the behavior of an application. Short feedback cycles are a developer's best friend and unit tests are one of the most powerful tools to achieve them.

There are many testing frameworks that can help us to unit test our code. Jest is a popular testing framework from Facebook. You may also come across other frameworks, such as Jasmine, Mocha, or Ava. Jest is a "batteries included" framework that will seem familiar to users of those other frameworks as it has tried to incorporate the best features of all of them.

Jest, Mocha, Ava, and the rest are JavaScript libraries, not TypeScript libraries, and so some special preparation is required to use them. **ts-jest** is a library that helps us to write TypeScript tests written in TypeScript and to use the Jest test runner and all the good parts of Jest.

To get started, we'll install **jest**, **ts-jest**, and **typings** for **jest** (@**types/ jest**):

```
npm install -D jest ts-jest @types/jest
```

Once the library is installed, we can use **npx** to initialize **ts-jest** with a default configuration that will let us write our first test:

```
npx ts-jest config:init
```

Running this command will create a config file called **jest.config.js**. As you become more comfortable writing tests with Jest, you may wish to modify this file, but for now, the default will work just fine.

Some developers put unit tests in a tests directory, and some put the tests directly alongside the source code. Our default Jest config will find both kinds of tests. The convention for unit tests is the name of the module under test, followed by a dot, then the word **spec** or **test**, and then the file extension, which will be **ts** in our case. If we create files with that naming convention anywhere under our project root, Jest will be able to find and execute the tests.

Let's add a simple test. Create a file named **example.spec.ts**. Then add this code to the file. This code is just a placeholder for the test and doesn't actually do anything other than verify that Jest is working correctly:

```
describe("test suite for `sentence`", () => {
  test("dummy test", () => {
    expect(true).toBeTruthy();
  });
});
```

We can run Jest by typing **npx jest** at the console or we can add an **npm** script. Try typing **npm test** at the console. If you haven't changed the default test, you should see something like the following:

```
npm test
> ex1@1.0.0 test /Users/mattmorgan/typescript/function-chapter/exercises
> echo "Error: no test specified" && exit 1
Error: no test specified
npm ERR! Test failed.  See above for more details.
```

Let's now update the **package.json** file so that it runs Jest instead of just failing. Find the **package.json** file and you'll see this configuration inside it:

```
"scripts": {
  "test": "echo \"Error: no test specified\" && exit 1"
},
```

We can replace the entire test with simply **jest**:

```
"scripts": {
  "test": "jest"
},
```

Now, try **npm test** again:

```
npm test

> ex1@1.0.0 test /Users/mattmorgan/typescript/function-chapter/exercises
> jest

 PASS  ./example.spec.ts
  test suite for `sentence`
    ✓ dummy test (1ms)

Test Suites: 1 passed, 1 total
Tests:       1 passed, 1 total
Snapshots:   0 total
Time:        1.449s
Ran all test suites
```

Of course, this test doesn't do anything useful. Now, let's import the functions we want to test and write some tests that are actually useful. First, let's clean up the **arrow-cat-solution.ts** file (from Exercise 3.03, Writing Arrow Functions) a little. We can remove all the console statements because we're going to validate our code by writing tests, not by just logging the console. Then, let's add the **export** keyword to each of the functions so that our test can import them. **arrow-cat-solution.ts** now looks like this:

```
export const arrayToAnd = (words: string[]) => {
  return words.reduce((prev, curr, index) => {
    if (words.length === 1) {
      return ` ${curr}`;
    }
```

```
    if (words.length - 1 === index) {
      return `${prev} and ${curr}`;

    }
    return `${prev} ${curr},`;
  }, "");
};

export const capitalize = (sentence: string) => {
  return `${sentence.charAt(0).toUpperCase()}${sentence
    .slice(1)
    .toLowerCase()}`;
};

export const sentence = (
  subject: string,
  verb: string,
  ...objects: string[]
): string => {
  return capitalize(`${subject} ${verb}${arrayToAnd(objects)}.`);
};
```

Let's try writing a test for the **capitalize** function. We simply need to call the function and test the outcome against the expected outcome. First, import the function in a new file (**arrow-cat-solution.spec.ts**):

```
import { capitalize } from './arrow-cat-solution';
```

Then, write an expectation. We expect our function to turn all-caps "HELLO" into "Hello". Let's now write that test and execute it:

```
describe("test suite for `sentence`", () => {
  test("capitalize", () => {
    expect(capitalize("HELLO")).toBe("Hello");
  });
});
```

Did it work?

```
npm test


> ex1@1.0.0 test /Users/mattmorgan/typescript/function-chapter/exercises
> jest
 PASS   ./example.spec.ts
```

```
  test suite for `sentence`
    ✓ capitalize (1ms)


Test Suites: 1 passed, 1 total
Tests:       1 passed, 1 total
Snapshots:   0 total
Time:        0.502s, estimated 2s
Ran all test suites.
```

The **describe** keyword is used to group tests and its only purpose is to affect the output of your test report. The **test** keyword should wrap the actual test. Instead of **test**, you can write **it**. Tests that use **it** are often written as an assertion with **should**:

```
it("should capitalize the string", () => {
    expect(capitalize("HELLO")).toBe("Hello");
});
```

Now, write tests for the other functions.

ACTIVITY 3.02: WRITING UNIT TESTS

In the last activity, we built a booking system for airlines and applied TypeScript functions to the scenarios involved in securing a flight reservation. We executed these scenarios from a single **index.ts** file, representing user interactions. This approach works well enough while we're learning, but it's a bit messy and doesn't actually assert that any of the scenarios are correct. To put that another way, it's almost a unit test, but it's not as good as a unit test.

We've learned about how to install Jest, so let's use it to unit test *Activity 3.01, Building a Flight Booking System with Functions*. For each function we wrote, we'll write a test that invokes the function and tests the output:

> **NOTE**
>
> The code files for this activity can be found at https://packt.link/XMOZO.

1. The code stubs provided for this activity include **bookings.test.ts** and **flights.test.ts** with a number of unimplemented tests. Implement those tests to complete this activity.

   You can execute the tests by running **npm test**. You can also run just the solutions with **npm run test:solution**.

2. To test a function, you will need to **import** it into your test file.

3. Invoke the function with sample input, and then use Jest's **expect** assertions to test the output, for example, **expect(value).toBe(5);**.

4. Error scenarios can be tested with **try/catch** blocks, catching the error thrown by the function, and then testing the error condition. When using **catch** in a unit test, it's a best practice to use **expect.assertions** to indicate how many assertions you want to test. Otherwise, your test might complete without the **catch** block being invoked.

5. Try to reach 100% line coverage in the coverage report (already configured with **--coverage**).

> **NOTE**
>
> The solution to this activity can be found on page 606.

In this activity, we took a program we'd written and applied best practices with some good unit tests. It will now be much easier to add additional functionality and scenarios knowing that the existing code is tested. Instead of writing out an index file to call various functions, we now have things logically grouped, ordered, and tested. We have a mechanism to track line coverage and understand how much of our code is under test.

ERROR HANDLING

When we write functions, we need to bear in mind that not everything always works perfectly. What will we do if the function receives unexpected input? How will our program react if some other function that we need to call doesn't work perfectly? It's always a good idea to validate function input. Yes, we're using TypeScript, and we can be reasonably sure that if we expect a string, we won't get an object instead, but sometimes, external input doesn't conform to our types. Sometimes, our own logic may be erroneous. Consider this function:

```
const divide = (numerator: number, denominator: number) => {
    return numerator / denominator;
}
```

It looks fine, but what if I pass in the number **0** as the denominator? We cannot divide by zero, and so the result will be the constant, **NaN. NaN**, when used in any mathematical equation, will always return **NaN**. This could introduce a serious bug into our system, and this needs to be avoided.

To solve this problem, we need to figure out what should happen if we get invalid input. Log it? Throw an error? Just return zero? Exit the program? Once that is decided, we can add some validation to our function:

```
const divide = (numerator: number, denominator: number) => {
    if(denominator === 0) {
        throw 'Cannot divide by zero!'
    }
    return numerator / denominator;
}
```

Now at least we won't fail silently as we are displaying a warning on the screen, **Cannot divide by zero!**. It's always better to raise an exception than for a function to fail without anybody noticing.

SUMMARY

By now, you know how to create the most important building blocks of any TypeScript program – functions. We have explored the difference between function expressions and arrow functions and when to use which. We looked at immediately invoked function expressions, closures, currying, and other powerful TypeScript techniques.

We talked about functional programming paradigms and looked at how to include functions in objects and classes. We've looked at how to convert legacy JavaScript code into modern TypeScript and how we can improve our software by doing so.

We have had an overview of the TypeScript module system and the critically important **import** and **export** keywords. We wrote a lot of our own TypeScript code and learned how to test it with **ts-jest**.

Finally, we rounded out this chapter with a discussion of error handling. We'll look at more advanced error-handling techniques in *Chapters 12, Guide to Promises in TypeScript*, and *Chapter 13, Async Await in TypeScript*, when it comes to asynchronous programming.

We covered quite a few topics in this chapter, and most readers won't retain all of them immediately. That's OK! You have written a number of functions in this chapter and you'll write many more in chapters to come. Writing good functions is a skill that comes with practice and you'll be able to refer back to this chapter to check your learning as you progress in your mastery of TypeScript.

In the next chapter, we will further explore the object-oriented programming paradigm by studying the **class** keyword and how we can construct type-safe objects.

4

CLASSES AND OBJECTS

OVERVIEW

In this chapter, you will learn how to define classes and instantiate them to create objects. You will also learn how to define the data types that can be passed to a class using interfaces. By the end of this chapter, you will be able to build a basic class that includes data attributes, a constructor, methods, and an interface. You will be able to create classes that take in multiple objects as arguments to build dynamic behavior and confidently use TypeScript to generate HTML code.

INTRODUCTION

Object-Oriented Programming (**OOP**) has been around since the 1960s and many popular programming languages utilize it, including **Java**, **Ruby**, and **Python**. Prior to OOP, developers typically followed the procedural programming style. Languages that utilize procedural programming processes run from the top of the code file to the bottom. Eventually, developers started wanting to wrap entire processes and data so that they could be called from different parts of a program at different times. And that's how OOP was born.

From a high-level perspective, OOP allows programs to wrap data and behavior together to create complete systems. So, instead of programs running code from top to bottom, as with procedural programs, OOP programs allow you to create code blueprints and establish rules for how a program will run, and then you can call those blueprints from other parts of an application.

Don't worry if that doesn't make sense quite yet – we're going to walk through exactly how to work with OOP in TypeScript in this chapter. And we're going to start by learning about the fundamental building blocks of OOP – **classes** and **objects**.

In the previous chapters, we've covered a wide assortment of topics, including various ways to declare variables, how to work with advanced types, aliases, union types, and assertions, and how to check for types. You've already added quite a bit of knowledge to your TypeScript skill set.

In this chapter, we're going to build a scoreboard application in TypeScript and will be learning about classes and objects along the way. Do not worry if you have no previous knowledge or familiarity with OOP, or how it applies to TypeScript. If you have some experience with classes and objects, then you can skip ahead to some of the more advanced material later in the chapter – though you may still benefit from a refresher on these key concepts.

WHAT ARE CLASSES AND OBJECTS?

Before we build out our class, let's take a step back and understand how classes work. You can think of a class as a blueprint. It establishes a structure for what we want to build and has some behavior inside it. Now, the class by itself does nothing. It is simply a blueprint. In order to work with it, we have to perform a process called **instantiation**.

Instantiation is the process of taking a class and creating an actual object of the class that we can use. Let's walk through an example to understand instantiation further. Imagine that you're building a house and, like a good builder, you have a blueprint of what you want to build. That blueprint is like our class. The blueprint for a home is simply a set of rules, attributes, and behavior for a home. A blueprint for a house defines elements such as square footage, the number of rooms, the number of bathrooms, and where the plumbing goes. Technically, a blueprint is simply a set of rules that are printed out or stored on a computer; it's not the house itself, or the program itself, in this case. In order to create the house, someone needs to take the blueprint and then actually build the house, and it's the same in programming.

A class by itself does nothing besides establishing the rules for the program. In order to work with the class, we need to create an instance or object of that class. So, returning to the building analogy, you can think of instantiation as taking the blueprint for the house and building it.

Let's look at the following code snippet to understand how classes and objects appear in TypeScript:

```typescript
class Person {
    name:string;

    constructor(name) {
        this.name = name;
    }

    read() {
        console.log(this.name+ "likes to read.");
    }
}
const obj = new Person("Mike");
obj.read();
```

Let's walk through each of the elements in the preceding code so that you can have a mental model of the key terminology associated with classes and objects in TypeScript, and then we'll go through an in-depth exercise where you will see how to work with each element:

- **class Person {}** creates or defines a class.
- **name: string;** creates the class attributes.

- **constructor()** allows you to perform setup work for when an object is created.

- **read()** is a method that allows you to implement custom behavior in a class.

- **const obj = new Person("Mike");** creates an object from a class and stores it in a variable so that it can be used.

- **obj.read();** calls a method on an object. In this example, it would console log out the value **Mike likes to read**.

In the next section, we will solve an exercise wherein we'll be building our first TypeScript class.

EXERCISE 4.01: BUILDING YOUR FIRST CLASS

In this exercise, we'll build a class named **Team** and add a behavior or method named **generateLineup** inside it. We'll also create an object of this class and access its method. Perform the following steps to implement this exercise:

> **NOTE**
>
> The code files for this exercise can be found here: https://packt.link/UJXSY.

1. Open the Visual Studio Code editor.

2. Create a new directory and then a new file called **scoreboard.ts**. You will be running the TypeScript compiler on it to have it generate a JavaScript file as well. Add the following command in the TypeScript compiler to generate a JavaScript file:

```
tsc scoreboard.ts
```

Once this command is executed, a **scoreboard.js** file is generated, as you can see in the following screenshot:

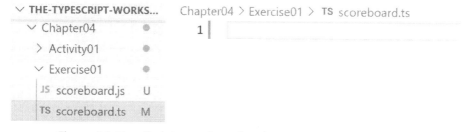

Figure 4.1: TypeScript scoreboard and generated JavaScript files

3. Now, create a class called **Team**, and then utilize the instantiation process to create an object of that class. Write the following code inside the **scoreboard.ts** file to create a class:

```
class Team {

}
```

Right now, this is simply an empty class that doesn't do anything. Let's fix that by adding some behavior to the class. We can add behavior by defining functions. For our **Team** class, we're going to generate a lineup, so we define a function called **generateLineup**, and it doesn't take in any arguments.

> **NOTE**
>
> From a syntax perspective, notice that we're using the **class** keyword. The term **class** is a reserved word in TypeScript and JavaScript, and it tells the compiler that we're about to define a class. In this case, we're calling the **Team** class.

4. Write the following code to define a **generateLineup()** function inside the class:

```
class Team {
    generateLineup() {
        return "Lineup will go here...";
    }
}
```

As you can see, functions in classes, which are also referred to as methods, look similar in syntax to standard functions in JavaScript. Now, our **generateLineup** method simply returns a string. Later in the chapter, we'll see how we can implement dynamic behavior in this method.

Once we've created a class and defined its behavior, we can create an object. In order to create an object of the **Team** class, we call the **new** keyword in front of the **Team** class name and assign that to a variable. In this case, we'll store the instantiated object in a variable called **astros**.

5. Add the following code to create an object of the **Team** class:

```
const astros = new Team();
```

Notice that in the preceding code, we're also adding parentheses after the **Team** class name, mimicking how we call functions in TypeScript.

With all of this in place, we can now use the **astros** variable to call the **generateLineup** method on it.

6. Add the following code to call the **generateLineup** method:

```
console.log(astros.generateLineup());
```

7. In the terminal, type the following commands to generate the JavaScript code and run it:

```
tsc scoreboard.ts
node scoreboard.js
```

Once we run the preceding commands, the following output is displayed in the terminal: **Lineup will go here**...

Hence, we've created our first class, and then from there, we've taken that class, that blueprint, and then used instantiation to create an object. From that point, we're able to call the method inside the class. Now that we've created a class and used its object to access its methods, in the next section, we'll explore the concept of the **constructor**.

EXTENDING CLASS BEHAVIOR WITH A CONSTRUCTOR

In the previous section, we established the syntax for classes in TypeScript. Before we get started with the next phase of the previous program, let's take a step back and discuss an element that we're going to use, called the constructor. The concept of constructors can be confusing if you've never used them before.

Returning to our blueprint/house analogy, if a class is like a home's blueprint and an object is the home that is created, the constructor is the process of going to the hardware shop and purchasing the materials needed to build the home. A constructor is run automatically anytime that you create an object. Typically, constructors are used to do the following:

- Set data for attributes, which we're about to explore.

- Run any setup processes. Examples of this include calling outside APIs to get data and communicating with a database.

NOTE

More on constructors will be covered in *Chapter 8, Dependency Injection in TypeScript*.

THE THIS KEYWORD

The concept of **this** is one of the most confusing aspects of OOP. The **this** keyword refers to the instance of the class that is currently being executed. It has access to the data and behavior of the created object. Let's say we have the following code within a class:

```
constructor(name) {
    this.name = name;
}
```

In the preceding code, if **this.name** is referring to the instance of the class and the attribute of **name**, what does the **name** parameter in the constructor represent? In order to use data in our class, we need to have a mechanism for passing data into the object, and that's what the constructor parameters are doing. So, why do we need to assign **this.name** to **name**? It does seem redundant; however, it is helpful for understanding how variable scope works in TypeScript classes. We need to assign the values passed into the object to **this.attributeName** so that the other methods in the class can have access to the values. If we simply passed the value into the constructor and didn't perform the **this.name** assignment, the other methods in the class wouldn't have access to the **name** value. Now, let's extend the behavior of the program in the next exercise, where we will explore the attributes of the class.

EXERCISE 4.02: DEFINING AND ACCESSING THE ATTRIBUTES OF A CLASS

In this exercise, we'll add attributes to the **Team** class, which we created in the previous exercise. We'll be using constructors to define and access the attributes of the objects. Perform the following steps to implement this exercise.

> **NOTE**
>
> In this exercise, we'll continue the work we performed earlier in the chapter with our **Team** class, so make sure to reference it as a starting point. The code files for this exercise can be found here: https://packt.link/Diuyl.

We begin by listing the names of the attributes at the top of the **Team** class and then we set the value with a **constructor** function by passing in a **name** parameter. From there, we set the value of **this.name** to the value that gets passed into the **constructor** function:

1. Write the following code to create a **constructor** function:

```
class Team {
    name: string;

    constructor(name) {
        this.name = name;
    }
    generateLineup() {
        return "Lineup will go here …";
    }
}
```

When we create the **astros** object, the **this** keyword represents the object that was created.

2. Create another object to see how the **this** keyword works with multiple objects. Add the following code to the **scoreboard.ts** file to create objects of the **Team** class:

```
const astros = new Team();
console.log(astros.generatLineup());

const bluJays = new Team();
console.log(blueJays.generateLineup());
```

In the preceding code, we've created another **Team** class object called **blueJays**. From there, we called the **generateLineup** method on the object. When we say **this.name**, what we're referring to is the instance of the class. This means that when we say **this.name** for the first object, we're referring to the **astros** object. And then, for the new object we've created, **this.name** is referencing the **blueJays** object.

Our **generateLineup** method has access to the value of **name** because we assigned it in the constructor.

3. Pass values to the constructors of both the objects by writing the following code:

```
const astros = new Team("Astros");
console.log(astros.generateLineup());


const blueJays = new Team("Blue Jays");
console.log(blueJays.generateLineup());
```

> **NOTE**
>
> If you ever get asked the difference between parameters and arguments in TypeScript, parameters are what you place inside the function's declarations in your class. Arguments are what you pass to an object or a function.

In order to pass arguments to a class, you can pass them in the same way that you do with functions, as you can see above. Additionally, when we perform an assignment such as **this.name = name**, this means that when an object is created, it can call the data value as well.

4. Write the following code to call the relevant data values:

```
const astros = new Team("Astros");
//console.log(astros.generateLineup());
console.log(astros.name);

const blueJays = new Team("Blue Jays");
//console.log(blueJays.generateLineup());
console.log(blueJays.name);
```

5. In the terminal, type the following commands to generate the JavaScript code and run it:

```
tsc scoreboard.ts
node scoreboard.js
```

Once we run the preceding commands, the following output is displayed in the terminal:

```
Astros
Blue Jays
```

As you can see in the code in the previous step, when we call **astros.name**, this outputs the name value that was passed into the instantiated object. When we pass the name value **Blue Jays** into the new object, the new value is printed in the terminal.

We are now able to understand the basic workings of classes and objects. We've also learned how to pass data into an object via a constructor. Now it's time to extend that knowledge and see how we can integrate types directly into our classes.

Even though the current implementation works, we're not taking advantage of the key benefits that TypeScript offers. In fact, the current implementation is very close to how you would build a class in vanilla JavaScript. By using types in classes, we can define exactly how to work with the code, which will help to make our code more manageable and scalable.

A real-world example of this would be a React application that utilizes TypeScript versus vanilla JavaScript. One of the most common errors that developers run into is passing the wrong type of data to a class or method, resulting in an error for the user. Imagine accidentally passing a string to a class that requires an array. When the user tries to access the page that is associated with that class, they won't see any data, as the wrong data was passed to the method.

When you utilize TypeScript and types in a React class, the text editor won't allow the program to even compile as it will explain to you exactly what type of data is required by each class and process. In the next section, we'll solve an exercise wherein we'll integrate different types into our class.

EXERCISE 4.03: INTEGRATING TYPES INTO CLASSES

In this exercise, we'll add another attribute named **players** inside our **Team** class. This parameter takes arrays of strings. Perform the following steps to implement this exercise:

> **NOTE**
>
> We'll continue the work we performed in the previous exercise with our **Team** class, so make sure to reference it as a starting point. The code files for this exercise can be found here: https://packt.link/tbav7.

1. Open the **scoreboard.ts** file.

2. Inside the **Team** class, declare another attribute named **players**, which takes arrays of strings. Write the following code to declare the **string** array:

    ```
    players: string[];
    ```

3. Update the **constructor** function by adding the **name** and **players** parameters. Set the values of the **name** and **players** parameters to **this.name** and **this.players**, respectively. Write the following code to update our **constructor** function:

    ```
    constructor(name, players){
        this.name = name;
        this.players = players;
    }
    ```

4. Update the **generateLineup()** method so that it joins the player names that will get passed into the object. This method will return a plain string. Here is the updated code of the **generateLineup()** method:

    ```
    generateLineup(){
        return this.players.join(", ");
    }
    ```

5. Create two arrays of players, namely, **astrosPlayers** and **blueJaysPlayers**. Assign four player names to each array and pass those arrays as second arguments to the **Team** class objects. Write the following code to accomplish this:

```
const astrosPlayers = ["Altuve", "Bregman", "Correa", "Springer"];
const astros = new Team("Astros", astrosPlayers);
console.log(astros.generateLineup());
console.log(astros.name);


const blueJaysPlayers = ["Vlad", "Smoak", "Tellez", "Sogard"];
const blueJays = new Team("Blue Jays", blueJaysPlayers);
console.log(blueJays.generateLineup());
console.log(blueJays.name);
```

6. Now, in the terminal, type the following commands to generate the JavaScript code and run it:

```
tsc scoreboard.ts
node scoreboard.js
```

Once we run the preceding commands, the following output is displayed in the terminal:

```
Altuve, Bregman, Correa, Springer
Astros
Vlad, Smoak, Tellez, Sogard
Blue Jays
```

We've now integrated types into our **Team** class. If you're able to view the names that you passed to the class in the console, this means that you're working with the class and their types properly. In the next section, we'll learn why **interfaces** are needed and how they are useful.

TYPESCRIPT INTERFACES

We'll go through a deep dive into TypeScript interfaces in the next chapter. But for now, just know that an interface allows you to describe the data passed to a class when you're creating an object. In the previous exercise code, if we hover over the **Team** class on Visual Studio Code, we get the following message:

```
const astrosPlayers  constructor Team(name: any, players: any): Team
const astros = new Team("Astros", astrosPlayers);
console.log(astros.generateLineup());
console.log(astros.name);

const blueJaysPlayers = ["Vlad", "Smoak", "Tellez", "Sogard"];
const blueJays = new Team("Blue Jays", blueJaysPlayers);
console.log(blueJays.generateLineup());
console.log(blueJays.name);
```

Figure 4.2: Vague IntelliSense guidance

As you can see in the preceding screenshot, the Visual Studio Code editor's IntelliSense is saying that the **players** parameter uses the **any** data type. It's not giving us any usage hints here, and this starts to speak to the reason why we need interfaces, because right now, the **players** array could be anything. It could be a string, it could be an object, and so on. This is essentially breaking one of the main benefits of using TypeScript in the first place. Ideally, our programs should be declarative to the point that we know exactly what type of data should be passed to our functions and classes. We're going to leverage interfaces in order to do that. The way you define an interface is by starting with the **interface** keyword followed by the name of the interface. The common convention in the TypeScript community is to start with a capital **I**, followed by whatever class you're building the interface for.

Once we have created the interface and update the constructor, we'll establish a way of defining our arguments and our types. This will break any of the previously created objects with the old argument syntax since the previous arguments no longer match up with our new interface. In the next section, we'll complete an exercise wherein we'll build an interface.

EXERCISE 4.04: BUILDING AN INTERFACE

In this exercise, we'll build an interface and set the types of data that need to be passed to our functions and classes. Perform the following steps to implement this exercise:

> **NOTE**
>
> We'll continue the work we performed in the previous exercise with our **Team** class, so make sure to reference it as a starting point. The code files for this exercise can be found here: https://packt.link/FWUA6.

1. Open the **scoreboard.ts** file.

2. Create an interface named **ITeam** and list out the attributes and data types with the same key/value syntax that you would use with an object. Write the following code to create an interface:

```
interface ITeam{
    name: string;
    players: string[];
}
```

3. Inside our **Team** class, alter the parameter list in the **constructor** function so that the data is passed in as a single object that is of the **ITeam** type. Write the following code to accomplish this:

```
constructor(args: ITeam){
    this.name = args.name;
    this.players = args.players;
}
```

Notice in the preceding code that, instead of listing out each of the parameters separately, we're declaring the exact structure that is needed for a **Team** object to be created. From that point, we're calling the **name** and **players** values from the **args** parameter since our parameter list has now been refactored to use a single argument.

4. Create an object of the **Team** class by writing the following code:

```
const astros = new Team();
```

Now notice what happens when we hover over the parentheses. It says that it expected one argument but got zero. Look at the following screenshot to view the message:

```
generateLineup(){
    return this players join(" ");
}
```

Expected 1 arguments, but got 0. ts(2554)

Untitled-1(11, 17): An argument for 'args' was not provided.

constructor Team(args: ITeam): Team

View Problem (Alt+F8)   No quick fixes available

```
const astros = new Team();
```

Figure 4.3: IntelliSense listing out the arguments needed by the class

5. Let's update how we create the objects. Start typing in the **name** attribute. Write the following code to create the object:

```
const astros = new Team({
    name
})
```

After adding in the **name** argument, we'll see the following error:

Argument of type '{ name: any; }' is not assignable to parameter of type 'ITeam'.
  Property 'players' is missing in type '{ name: any; }' but required in type 'ITeam'. ts(2345)

Untitled-1(3, 5): 'players' is declared here.

(property) ITeam.name: string

View Problem (Alt+F8)   No quick fixes available

```
        name   = }
);
```

Figure 4.4: IntelliSense describing the data types needed to create the object

If you hover over the **name** attribute, you can see that TypeScript is helping us understand the other arguments we need to pass in, because the **players** property is missing. So, this is already giving us so much more information on how our class needs to work.

6. Now, pass the values for both the attributes, **name** and **players**, and update the values for both the objects, **astros** and **blueJays**. Write the following code to accomplish this:

```
const astrosPlayers = ["Altuve", "Bregman", "Correa", "Springer"];
const astros = new Team({
    name: "Astros",
    players: astrosPlayers
});
console.log(astros.generateLineup());
console.log(astros.name);


const blueJaysPlayers = ["Vlad", "Smoak", "Tellez", "Sogard"];
const blueJays = new Team({
    name: "Blue Jays",
    players: blueJaysPlayers
});
console.log(blueJays.generateLineup());
console.log(blueJays.name);
```

7. Now, in the terminal, type the following commands to generate the JavaScript code and run it:

```
tsc scoreboard.ts
node scoreboard.js
```

Once we run the preceding commands, the following output is displayed in the terminal:

```
Altuve, Bregman, Correa, Springer
Astros
Vlad, Smoak, Tellez, Sogard
Blue Jays
```

We've now built an interface and set the types of data that need to be passed to our functions and classes. Although we got the same output as we got in the previous exercise, we are now aware of what type of data needs to be passed to our functions and classes.

Another great benefit of using interfaces and object-based arguments with classes is that the arguments do not have to be in a specific order. You can pass in the keys in any order that you want, and the class can still parse them properly. If you use standard parameter names, you'll always need to know the order to pass arguments to the class and function.

GENERATING HTML CODE IN METHODS

Now that we have learned how to build an interface and have the ability to pass data, along with having some help from IntelliSense in knowing the types of data that we're passing in, we can actually generate some HTML. It's fun to see the code we write generate its own code. Part of the reason why we chose to include this example is that this is very close to the same type of process that you will be using when building React JS or Angular applications. At their very core, the goal of a standard React app is to leverage JavaScript/TypeScript code to render HTML code that can be rendered to the user.

In the next section, we'll complete an exercise wherein we generate HTML code and view it in the browser.

EXERCISE 4.05: GENERATING AND VIEWING HTML CODE

In this exercise, we will generate some HTML by cleaning up some of the code. We'll get rid of the **name** attribute and the interface. Perform the following steps to implement this exercise:

> **NOTE**
>
> We'll continue the work we performed in the previous exercise with our **Team** class, so make sure to reference it as a starting point. The code files for this exercise can be found here: https://packt.link/Bz5LV.

1. Open the **scoreboard.ts** file.

2. Inside the **Team** class, declare the **players** array and create a **constructor** function. Write the following code to implement this:

```
players: string[];
constructor(players){
    this.players = players;
}
```

3. Update the **generateLineup()** function by writing the following code:

```
generateLineup(): string{
    const playersWithOrderNumber =
        this.players.map((player, idx) => {
            return `<div>${idx + 1} - ${player}</div>`;
        });
    return playersWithOrderNumber.join("");
}
```

The **map** function is a helpful iterator tool that loops over the player array. You can pass it as a function that performs some type of operation. In the preceding code, the line `<div>${idx + 1} - ${player}</div>` states that in every iteration, each player's data is wrapped inside the HTML code. Also, each element that is returned is stored in a new array, **playersWithOrderNumber**.

> **NOTE**
>
> Notice the return type that we've declared for the **generateLineup** method. This means that we're telling the TypeScript compiler that the method will always return a string value. The reason why this is so important is that if any other part of the application calls this method and tries to perform a task that does not work with the string data type, they'll get a clear error and recommendation on how to fix it.

4. Now, in the terminal, type the following commands to generate the JavaScript code and run it:

```
tsc scoreboard.ts
node scoreboard.js
```

Once we have run the preceding commands, the following output is displayed in the terminal:

```
<div>1 - Altuve</div><div>2 - Bregman</div><div>3 - Correa</div><div>4 - Springer</div>
<div>1 - Vlad</div><div>2 - Smoak</div><div>3 - Tellez</div><div>4 - Sogard</div>
```

Figure 4.5: Output showing the lineup of players for both teams

In the preceding output, you'll see that we're getting HTML returned that prints out the lineup of players for both teams.

But let's not stop here. Let's see what this looks like in the browser.

5. Save the generated code in an HTML file named **index.html** and view it in the browser. The following output will be displayed in the browser:

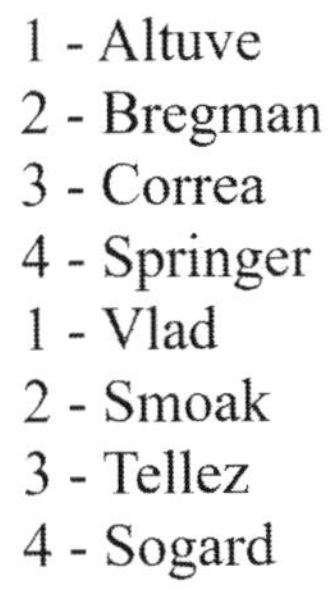

> 1 - Altuve
> 2 - Bregman
> 3 - Correa
> 4 - Springer
> 1 - Vlad
> 2 - Smoak
> 3 - Tellez
> 4 - Sogard

Figure 4.6: Viewing the generated HTML code in the browser

> **NOTE**
>
> You may get a different image depending on your default browser; however, the text displayed will be the same as listed in the preceding screenshot.

You can see that we have a full lineup of players for both teams. However, we have not yet formatted the text on the page, and so it is difficult to ascertain the teams to which the players belong unless you have access to the code. We will be enhancing this page with more information and formatting as we progress in this chapter.

Note that we can pass the objects themselves to another class that will put them together for us and generate a full scoreboard. In the next section, we'll learn how to work with multiple classes and objects.

WORKING WITH MULTIPLE CLASSES AND OBJECTS

In this section, we're going to learn how to create a class that combines other classes to give us more advanced behavior. The reason why this is an important concept to understand is that you will need to implement this type of behavior in many different types of applications. For example, if you are building a contact form in a React application, you might need to have classes for an API, form elements, form validations, and other form features all working together. In the next section, we will look at an exercise where we'll combine classes.

EXERCISE 4.06: COMBINING CLASSES

In this exercise, we will be creating a **scoreboard** class that will allow us to pass in objects and work with their data and behavior. This will allow us to take instantiated objects that were created from other classes such as our **Team** class. Then, we're going to add in some other behavior that will generate a full scoreboard that shows off both the lineups along with the data. Perform the following steps to implement this exercise:

> **NOTE**
>
> We'll continue the work we performed in the previous exercise with our **Team** class, so make sure to reference it as a starting point. The code files for this exercise can be found here: https://packt.link/UY5NP.

1. Open the **scoreboard.ts** file.

2. Create a **Scoreboard** class and list three attributes, namely, **homeTeam**, **awayTeam**, and **date**. Here, **homeTeam** and **awayTeam** will be of the **Team** type, and **date** will be of the **string** type. Write the following code to accomplish this:

```
class Scoreboard{
    homeTeam: Team;
    awayTeam: Team;
    date: string;
}
```

In the preceding code, notice how we were able to call the **Team** class. This is because when we create a class, we're able to treat that class like a type in TypeScript. So, TypeScript now knows that our **homeTeam** and **awayTeam** data attributes must be a **Team** object. The **date** attribute will represent the date of the scoreboard. If we tried to pass in **string**, **array**, or anything else for a **Team** object, the program would not compile.

3. Now that we know the type of data that our scoreboard needs to have, let's create an interface for it. Write the following code to create an interface:

```
interface IScoreboard{
    homeTeam: Team;
    awayTeam: Team;
```

```
    date: string;
}
```

This is similar to what we implemented with the **ITeam** interface, but with a nice twist. Because our **homeTeam** and **awayTeam** attributes are not associated with a basic data type such as **string** or **number**, we're letting the interface know that these values are required to be objects of the **Team** class.

4. Now, in the terminal, type the following commands to generate the JavaScript code and run it:

```
tsc scoreboard.ts
```

When the preceding command is executed, the **scoreboard.js** file is created.

5. Open the **scoreboard.js** file and you'll see the following code at the beginning:

```
var Scoreboard = /** @class */ (function () {
    function Scoreboard() {
    }
        return Scoreboard;
}());
```

Figure 4.7: Generated JavaScript that shows interfaces are only used by the text editor

In the preceding screenshot, what we're essentially doing here is almost like a mini declaration file for this class. We're defining the shape of the class. If you remember, those interfaces and those declaration files do not get compiled down into JavaScript. You can confirm this by looking at the generated JavaScript code in the preceding screenshot.

Now that we've defined the interface, we have essentially defined the shape of our **Scoreboard** class.

6. Now we implement a **constructor** function, allowing the **Scoreboard** class to know what parameters to expect when creating a new object. Write the following code to accomplish this:

```
constructor(args: IScoreboard){
    this.homeTeam = args.homeTeam;
    this.awayTeam = args.awayTeam;
    this.date = args.date;
}
```

With this in place, any functions inside our **Scoreboard** class can work with these values.

7. Now let's create a function called **scoreboardHtml()** inside the **Scoreboard** class. Write the following code to accomplish this:

```
scoreboardHtml(): string{
    return `
    <h1>${this.date}</h1>
    <h2>${this.homeTeam.name}</h2>
    <div>${this.homeTeam.generateLineup()}</div>
    <h2>${this.awayTeam.name}</h2>
    <div>${this.awayTeam.generateLineup()}</div>
    `;
}
```

In the preceding code, we have an **<h1>** heading tag for **date** and an **<h2>** heading tag wrapping the team names. This is great, as even though the **Scoreboard** class has no knowledge of the **Team** class, the IDE can let us know that we have access to the name value. Lastly, we're able to call the **Team** functions. So, inside the **<div>** tags wrapper, we're calling the **generateLineup()** function of **Team**, which we know from earlier returns a list of HTML elements. Also, notice that this function will always return a string and that we're using backticks so that we can use string literals, which can be dynamic.

> **NOTE**
>
> In TypeScript and JavaScript, string literals can be written on multiple lines, which is not allowed with quotation marks.

8. Update the **Team** class with the **name** attribute and **constructor** function. Write the following code to accomplish this:

```
name: string;
players: string[];

constructor(name, players){
    this.name = name;
    this.players = players;
}
```

9. To view the final scoreboard, first create two team objects followed by the **Scoreboard** class object, and then pass in dates and both of our team objects to it. Write the following code to accomplish this:

```
const astrosPlayers = ["Altuve", "Bregman", "Correa", "Springer"];
const astros = new Team("Astros", astrosPlayers);
//console.log(astros.generateLineup());

const blueJaysPlayers = ["Vlad", "Smoak", "Tellez", "Sogard"];
const blueJays = new Team("Blue Jays", blueJaysPlayers);
//console.log(blueJays.generateLineup());

const todaysGame = new Scoreboard({
    date: "5/24/19",
    homeTeam: astros,
    awayTeam: blueJays
});


console.log(todaysGame.scoreboardHtml());
```

10. Now, in the terminal, type the following commands to generate the JavaScript code and run it:

```
tsc scoreboard.ts
node scoreboard.js
```

Once we run the preceding commands, the following output is displayed in the terminal:

```
<h1>5/24/19</h1>
<h2>Astros</h2>
<div><div>1 - Altuve</div><div>2 - Bregman</div><div>3 - Correa</div><div>4 - Springer</div></div>
<h2>Blue Jays</h2>
<div><div>1 - Vlad</div><div>2 - Smoak</div><div>3 - Tellez</div><div>4 - Sogard</div></div>
```

Figure 4.8: Generated HTML code

11. Add this code to an HTML file and view it in the browser. You will see that we have a full scoreboard like the one shown in the following screenshot:

5/24/19

Astros

1 - Altuve
2 - Bregman
3 - Correa
4 - Springer

Blue Jays

1 - Vlad
2 - Smoak
3 - Tellez
4 - Sogard

Figure 4.9: Generated code in the browser

Finally, we combined two classes, namely, **Scoreboard** and **Team**. In the **Scoreboard** class, we created attributes of the **Team** type and added a few behaviors that will help to generate a full scoreboard consisting of the lineups of both teams.

So far, we've introduced classes and objects in TypeScript, and with this knowledge, we're ready to move on to the code activity in the next section, where we will create a user model.

ACTIVITY 4.01: CREATING A USER MODEL USING CLASSES, OBJECTS, AND INTERFACES

In this activity, you will build a user authentication system that mimics how a TypeScript application would pass login data to a backend API to register and sign users into our baseball scorecard application. This will entail building multiple TypeScript classes and combining classes and objects together to mimic an authentication feature. Perform the following steps to implement this activity:

1. Visit the GitHub repository and download the activity project containing the specs and configuration elements: https://packt.link/vJxBm.

2. Open the Visual Studio Code editor.

3. Create a file called **auth.ts**.

4. Run the TypeScript compiler on the file and watch for changes.

5. Create a **Login** class that takes in an object containing the string attributes of **email** and **password**.

6. Build an interface called **ILogin** that defines the **email** and **password** attributes.

7. Pass it as a parameter to the **constructor** function.

8. Create an **Auth** class that takes in an object containing the attributes of **user** and **source**.

9. Build an interface called **IAuth** that defines the **user** and **source** attributes and pass it as the **constructor** function parameter. Have the **user** attribute be of the **Login** type and the **source** attribute of the **string** type.

10. Add a **validUser()** method to the **Auth** class that returns **true** if **email** is equal to **admin@example.com** and if **password** is equal to **secret123**.

11. Ensure that you can access the **source** attribute from the instantiated **Auth** object and that it's a string.

12. Test the user model by first checking a valid user and then an invalid user.

    The expected output should look something like this:

```
Validating user...User is authenticated: true
Validating user...User is authenticated: false
```

NOTE

The solution to this activity can be found on page 611.

SUMMARY

Learning OOP development patterns for the first time can be a challenging task. In this chapter, you learned about OOP development, how to define classes in TypeScript, how to instantiate classes and create objects, how to combine data and methods in a class to encapsulate a full set of behavior, how to utilize interfaces in order to define the data that can be passed to a TypeScript class, and finally, how to pass the objects to classes of various types.

You also now have a basic understanding of how an authentication system works and how to utilize TypeScript to generate HTML code.

Now that you have a basic understanding of how classes and objects work in TypeScript, in the next chapter, you'll learn how to work with the concept of class inheritance and take a deeper dive into interfaces.

5

INTERFACES AND INHERITANCE

OVERVIEW

This chapter introduces you to interfaces and inheritance. You will learn how to use an interface to shape your classes, objects, and functions. You will also gain an appreciation of how interfaces will help you to write better code. By the end of this chapter, you will be able to write better, more maintainable code with well-structured functions, classes, and objects, and also be able to reuse your existing code efficiently.

INTRODUCTION

The previous chapter discussed classes and objects. You learned that classes define objects and their functionality. Classes are the blueprint followed while constructing these objects. Now, we will go up one level of abstraction. We are now going to construct interfaces. Interfaces are descriptors and allow you to define the structure of your object. Interfaces allow you to define contracts, which are rules that govern how your data is shaped.

Interfaces are important because they enable your objects to be strongly typed, which gives you the ability to write cleaner code. Defining the shape of your objects may not be much of an issue with smaller applications, but when working with large applications, interfaces will prove their worth as they will make it possible for your application to scale without your code becoming confusing and hard to support.

Inheritance allows new objects to take the properties of existing objects, enabling you to extend your code functionality without having to redefine common properties. Inheritance will give you a better understanding of how you should structure your code to be more efficient and logical in your approach. This chapter will first address interfaces and equip you with the skills you need to use them and will then progress onto the topic of inheritance.

INTERFACES

Here we have an example of a simple interface that defines the shape of a user object:

```
interface UserInterFace {
    email: string,
    token: string,
    resetPassword: ()=> boolean
}
```

In the preceding code, we have defined an interface that we can implement on any object that should follow rules defined in our interface. The advantage this gives us over other web languages such as vanilla JavaScript is that all objects that implement this interface have to follow the structure defined by the interface. This means that our objects are now strongly typed and have language support such as syntax highlighting, autocompletion, and the throwing of exceptions when implemented incorrectly. If you are a developer working on a large application, this is very important as you have defined the rules and can now be sure that all the objects that implement **UserInterFace** will have the same properties as those defined in the interface.

Here is an example of an object that implements the **UserInterface** interface:

```
const User: UserInterFace = {
    email: 'home@home.com',
    token: '12345678',
    resetPassword(): boolean{
        return true
    }
}
```

As you can see in the preceding example, we are now able to implement an object that adheres to the guidelines defined in the **UserInterFace** interface. When working with large teams or on complex web applications, it is important to have transparent, well-understood rules for your code.

Interfaces allow for the creation of a common point of reference for your objects, a place where rules are defined on how objects should be constructed. In the following section, we will cover in-depth interfaces in TypeScript.

Interfaces are used when you want to set up rules for how your objects, classes, and functions should be implemented. They are a contract that governs structure but not functionality. Here we have a diagram that shows an interface and its relationship to two classes – **User** and **Admin**:

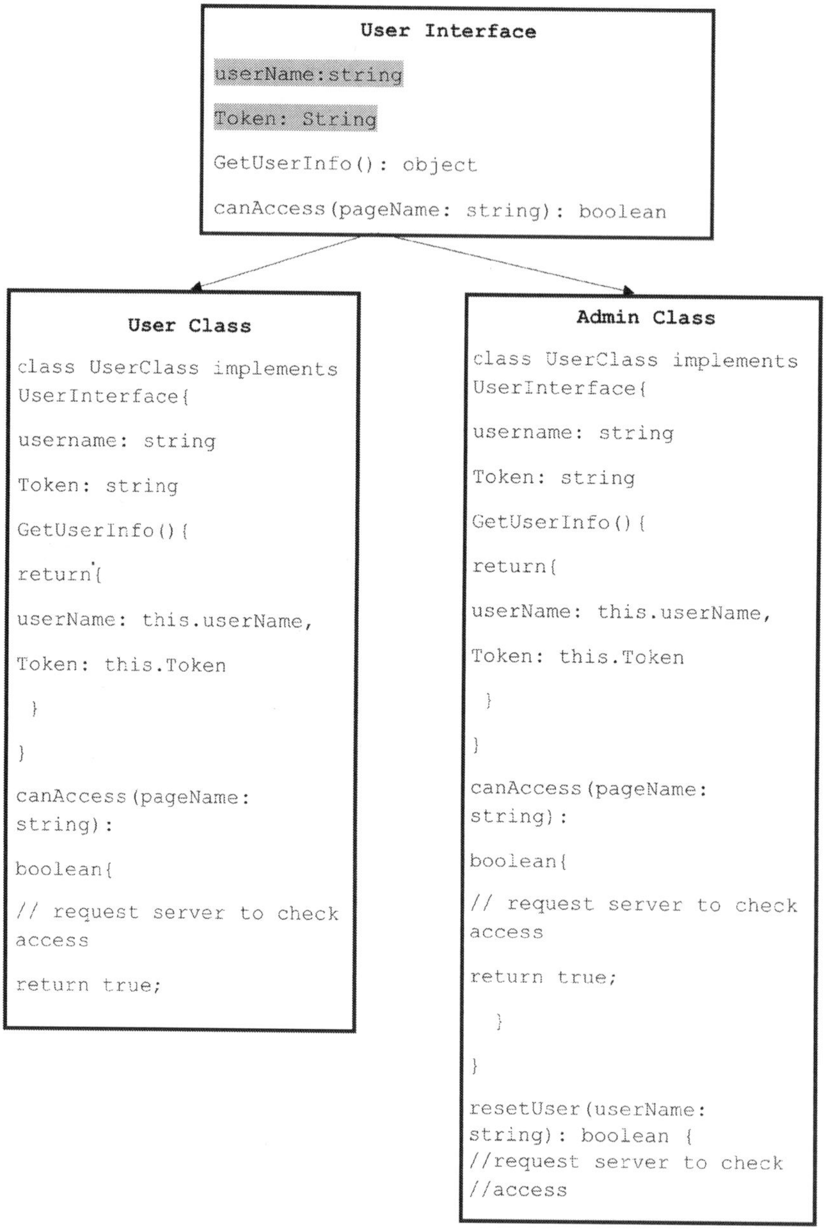

```
                    User Interface

    userName:string

    Token: String

    GetUserInfo(): object

    canAccess(pageName: string): boolean
```

```
         User Class

class UserClass implements
UserInterface{

username: string

Token: string

GetUserInfo(){

return{

userName: this.userName,

Token: this.Token

  }

}

canAccess(pageName:
string):

boolean{

// request server to check
access

return true;
```

```
         Admin Class

class UserClass implements
UserInterface{

username: string

Token: string

GetUserInfo(){

return{

userName: this.userName,

Token: this.Token

  }

}

canAccess(pageName:
string):

boolean{

// request server to check
access

return true;

  }

}

resetUser(userName:
string): boolean {
//request server to check
//access
```

Figure 5.1: Relation between interface and classes

In the diagram, we have a user interface that describes how a class belonging to this interface should be implemented. As you can see, we have a few properties (highlighted code in User Interface) and methods provided in two classes. The interface provides only basic information for the property's name, type, method structures, and return types, if not void. Note that the interface provides no rules related to how the methods work, only how they are structured. The actual functionality of the methods is defined in the class itself. As stated earlier, interfaces in TypeScript give you the rules and you implement them as you see fit. This is evident from the preceding diagram. The **AdminUser** class has a method not defined in **UserInterface**; however, this is not an issue because the class is in compliance with all the elements of the interface. There is no rule that says that you cannot add to your class, only that you need to meet the requirements of the interface that your class implements.

CASE STUDY – WRITING YOUR FIRST INTERFACE

Imagine you are working with an application development team building an application for warehouse floor workers. You have the task of building the product creation classes and functions. You have developed a plan for your classes based on the functional requirements of your application. You start by creating a product interface called **ProductTemplate**. **ProductTemplate** defines the structure of our product object and base requirements. Note that we could also use a type object in the same way, and it may be preferable since this is a simple object, not a class, which could not be represented by a type. However, for the sake of this example and also to enlighten you to the fact that interfaces can also be used as types when defining a simple object, we have constructed the **ProductTemplate** interface:

Example_Interface_1.ts

```
1 //first interface
2 interface ProductTemplate {
3     height: number
4     width: number
5     color: string
6 }
```

Link to the preceding example: https://packt.link/wYJis.

When defining an interface, we start with the interface keyword, followed by the name of our interface, **ProductTemplate**, as shown in the preceding snippet. We have three properties that our product requires – height, width, and color. Now that we have described what our product data should look like, let's use it:

```
7 //make product function
8 const productMaker = (product: ProductTemplate) => {
9     return product
10 }
```

We have built a function, **productMaker**, that takes a product object as an argument. To ensure that only objects with the properties required by our **productMaker** function get passed to the function, we use our **ProductTemplate** interface, as shown in the preceding snippet. Now, all we need to do is define our product object; we will use our interface there as well:

```
11 // implement interface
12 const myProduct: ProductTemplate = {
13     height: 10,
14     width: 12,
15     color: 'red',
16 }
```

We have declared a product object, **myProduct**, with our **ProductTemplate** interface and added the properties required by our interface. Using the interface in this way ensures that we are fully compliant when creating the product object. Now, if we add a property not defined or remove a property that is defined in our **ProductTemplate** interface, the IDE and or TypeScript compiler will throw a helpful error message. IDE highlighting will depend on your IDE and the level of support for TypeScript. VS Code should highlight the following error messages for the preceding two scenarios.

The following error message appears when you add a property length that is not defined in the interface:

```
(property) length: number
Type '{ height: number; width: number; color: string; length: number; }'
is not assignable to type 'ProductTemplate'.
   Object literal may only specify known properties, and 'length' does not
exist in type 'ProductTemplate'.ts(2322)
```

The following error message appears when you don't use the color property, which is defined in the interface:

```
const myProduct: ProductTemplate

Property 'color' is missing in type '{ height: number; width: number; }'
but required in type 'ProductTemplate'.ts(2741)
Example_Interface.ts(5, 5): 'color' is declared here.
```

Now that we have our product object, let's pass it to our productMaker function:

```
// call the function using console log to show the output
console.log(productMaker(myProduct));
```

Once you run the file using **npx ts-node Example_Interface.ts**, you will obtain the following output:

```
{ height: 10, width: 12, color: 'red' }
```

This is the ideal scenario. But what would happen if you pass an object that does not comply with the **ProductTemplate** interface? Consider the following code representing this scenario:

```
const myBadProduct = {
    height: '20',
    color: 1
}
console.log (productMaker(myBadProduct))
```

You will receive the following error message when you run the file using **tsc [filename].ts**:

```
error TS2345: Argument of type '{ height: string; color: number; }' is
not assignable to parameter of type 'ProductTemplate'.
  Property 'width' is missing in type '{ height: string; color: number;
}' but required in type 'ProductTemplate'.
```

VS Code prevents you from making such errors. If you hover over the red-underlined code in the VS Code window, you will see a warning similar to the preceding error message.

Let's go back to our interface example (**Example_Interface.ts**). Now, we have an interface for our product. Let's do the same for our **productMaker** function. We want to make sure that whenever a function takes our product as an argument, it is constructed in the right way. Hence, we construct the following interface – **productInterfaceFunction**:

Example_Interface_2.ts

```
 1 // first interface
 2 interface ProductTemplate {
 3     height: number
 4     width: number
 5     color: string
 6 }
 7 //function interface
 8 interface productInterfaceFunction {
 9     (product: ProductTemplate): ProductTemplate
10 }
```

Link to the preceding example: https://packt.link/Dzogj.

We added the function interface, **productInterfaceFunction**, just after **ProductTemplate**. As you can see, the syntax is simple and just defines what arguments the function can take and what it should return. We can now use the function interface in our function declaration, as shown here:

```
//make product function
const productMaker: productInterfaceFunction = (product: ProductTemplate) => {
    return product }
```

You should again get the same output as before:

```
{ height: 10, width: 12, color: 'red' }
```

We have now used interfaces in two ways: to shape an object and a function. The only issue here is that it's not very efficient to work this way. As good developers, we want to be as efficient as possible and comply with object-oriented standards of coding. To this end, we will now refactor our code to define a class that will encapsulate our product properties and methods:

Example_Interface_3.ts

```
 9  //product class interface
10 interface ProductClassInterface {
11     product: ProductTemplate
12     makeProduct(product: ProductTemplate) :ProductTemplate
13 }
```

Link to the preceding example: https://packt.link/kF4Ee.

In the preceding snippet, we have built an interface for our class where we have defined a **product** property and the makeProduct method.

We are also making good use of the interfaces we created previously for our product object and **makeProduct**. Next, we will use the new interface, **ProductClassInterface**, to instantiate a new class:

```
16 //class that implements product class interface
17 class ProductClass implements ProductClassInterface  {
18    product: ProductTemplate
19    constructor(product: ProductTemplate){
20        this.product = product
21    }
22    makeProduct():ProductTemplate {
23        return this.product;
24    }
25 }
26
27 //new product object
28 const product: ProductTemplate = {height:100, width:200, color: 'pink'}
```

In the preceding snippet, we are using the **implements** keyword to apply the interface rules to our **ProductClass**. The syntax structure is as follows: **class ProductClass** followed by the **implements** keyword, and then the interface you would like to apply to the class: **class ProductClass implements ProductClassInterface**. As you can see, this code is a bit less verbose and easy to manage. Using an interface to define our product class allows us to be more descriptive as we can not only define our class but the methods and properties associated with it.

ype aliases can also be used in a similar manner, but types are more of a validator than a descriptor, hence it is recommended to use types more to verify objects returned from a function or arguments received by a function.

Interfaces and types can be used together, and they should be. However, how they are used, where they are used, and how they are applied in code is down to you, as they are similar in many respects and even more so in recent updates of the TypeScript language. Let's now make a product object and use our class instance, **newProduct**:

```
27 //new product object
28 const product: ProductTemplate = {height:100, width:200, color: 'pink'}
29
30 //call make Product function
31 // instantiate product class with new product object
32 const newProduct = new ProductClass(product)
33 // console our new product instance
34 console.log(newProduct.product)
```

In the preceding snippet, we build a product object and then pass it to our class's **makeProduct** function. We then console out the results, which is the same as before, except now our functional code is wrapped in a class.

You will obtain the following output:

```
{ height: 100, width: 200, color: 'pink' }
```

Now that we have a basic understanding of how to implement an interface with TypeScript, let's build a more realistic product creation process in the following exercise.

EXERCISE 5.01: IMPLEMENTING INTERFACES

In this exercise, we will implement an interface on an object, function, and class. Some of the code is verbose and you may not implement it this way in a real-world application. However, this exercise will expose you to the different ways in which you can implement interfaces in your code. We will construct a class that manages product objects and use interfaces to enforce rules related to how our class should be implemented. We will also use interfaces to shape our product object and class methods. In a typical web application, this code would probably be part of a product management interface – an inventory management application, for example. Alternativley, it could also be part of the product creation process, where you have a form that takes user data and processes it:

> **NOTE**
>
> The code file for this exercise can be found here: https://packt.link/SR8eg. For this chapter, in order to run any TypeScript file, you need to go into the file directory and execute **npx ts-node filename.ts**.

1. Create an interface called **ProductObjectTemplate**:

```
interface ProductObjectTemplate {
    height: number
    width: number
    color: string
}
```

When creating an interface or a type object for that matter, you should take into consideration what are the common elements your interface or type will need. This could be based on the application requirements or dependent only on the functionality the application is required to have. **ProductObjectTemplate** is a simple object and, in most cases, should be a type, but in order to show that interfaces can also be used in this way, we have opted to make it an interface. As you can see, we have just defined some basic properties that we may have for a product – **height**, **width**, and **color**.

2. Using the interface defined in the preceding step, define a function called **ProductClass**Template:

```
interface ProductFunctionTemplate {
    (product: ProductObjectTemplate)
}
```

In the preceding step, we used an interface to define a function and, by doing this, we are providing the rules on what arguments your function can take. This will ensure that any implementation of this function will only take **ProductObjectTemplate** as an argument.

3. Build an interface for a class called **ProductClassTemplate**. Reuse **ProductFunctionTemplate** and **ProductObjectTemplate** in your new class:

```
interface ProductClassTemplate {
    makeProduct: ProductFunctionTemplate
    allProducts():ProductObjectTemplate[]
}
```

In the preceding step, we are reusing the function and product interfaces defined in *Steps 1 and 2* to build our class interface. We can simplify the code in this step because we are reusing interfaces that we created in the first two steps. *Step 3* is a good example of how you can build complexity while also making your code less verbose.

4. Create a **Product** class and implement our class interface:

```
class Product implements ProductClassTemplate {
    products: ProductObjectTemplate []
    constructor() {
        this.products = []
    }
    makeProduct(product: ProductObjectTemplate) {
```

```
        this.products.push(product)
    }


    allProducts():ProductObjectTemplate[] {
        return this.products
    }}
```

In this preceding step, we created our class implementing the **ProductClassTemplate** interface. This will ensure that our class adheres to the rules defined in our interface. We are also reusing the **ProductTemplate** interface to verify that our class method takes the right arguments and returns the correct data. In the previous steps, we did a bit of prep work setting up interfaces, and now we can reuse them in our code base, making the overall code easier to write, well supported, and understandable.

5. Instantiate our class as follows:

```
const productInstance: ProductClassTemplate = new Product()const
productInstance: ProductClassTemplate = new Product()
productInstance.makeProduct({})
```

Here again, we are making use of an interface, **ProductClassTemplate** to ensure the class we implement matches our ruleset.

If we try to call **makeProduct** with an empty object, we get a helpful error message we can use to resolve our issue. Feel free to perform a test to make sure that your interfaces are working as they should. Here, we have the correct implementation of our class instance method, **makeProduct**.

6. Call the **makeProduct** method and provide a valid product object as defined in our product interface:

```
productInstance.makeProduct(
    {
    color: "red",
    height: 10,
    width: 14
    }
)
```

7. Call the **allProducts** method and console out the results:

```
console.log(productInstance.allProducts())
```

The **allProducts** method returns an array of products. This would be the equivalent of an API call that returns a list of products to your frontend.

8. Now, console out the results of the **allProducts** method:

```
console.log(productInstance.allProducts())
```

9. Run the file by executing **npx ts-node Exercise01.ts**.

You will obtain the following output:

```
[ { color: 'red', height: 10, width: 14 } ]
```

Once you have followed the steps correctly, your output should be an array or product object as shown in the preceding screenshot. Interfaces provide you with the means to define contracts that govern how your code should be implemented, which is the point of a strongly typed language such as TypeScript and its main advantage over JavaScript. By using interfaces as shown in the exercise, we now have code that is less prone to errors and easier to support when working with large applications or on a large team. Interfaces can be invaluable to the development process if they are implemented correctly.

EXERCISE 5.02: IMPLEMENTING INTERFACES – CREATING A PROTOTYPE BLOGGING APPLICATION

Imagine that you are a developer working on a social networking site. You are tasked with setting up a blogging system that will allow users to post to the site. The project is intended to scale up globally, so it will be quite large. Hence, your code needs to be well defined with all the necessary contexts. The main theme here is context. You are coding in a manner that will lead to bug-free code that is well supported and understood.

First, we start with the main object – the blog post. In order to build a blogging system, we need to define what a blog post is. Because this is a simple object, we create a type alias, **BlogPost**. As mentioned previously, we can use an interface to define this object, but types are more suited to simple, non-complex objects. A type is more of a descriptor of a unit of something, for example, a number or a string, while an interface is more like directions on how to interact with something, not what it is:

> **NOTE**
>
> The code file for this exercise can be found here: https://packt.link/6uFmG.

1. Define a blog type as shown in the following snippet:

```
type BlogPost = {
    post: string,
    timeStamp: number,
    user: string
}
```

2. Create an interface called **AddToPost**:

```
interface AddToPost {
    (post: BlogPost): BlogPost []
}
```

This interface will serve as the main interface for the method we will use to add to our blog list. As we elaborated in the previous exercise, the **AddToPost** interface defines how we will interact with our main method and also what it will return when called.

3. Create an interface to define a class, **BlogPostClass**:

```
interface IBlogPost {
    allPost: BlogPost [],
    addToPost: AddToPost
}
```

Here, we define our class interface. We know we need a place to hold our blogs, so we define an **allPost** global object that is of the **BlogPost** type array. We also define a method, **addToPost**, that implements the **AddPost** interface.

4. Create a class called **blogPostClass** that implements the **blogPostClass** interface:

```
class blogPostClass implements IBlogPost{
    allPost: BlogPost [] = []
    addToPost(post: BlogPost): BlogPost[] {
        this.allPost = [
            ...this.allPost,
            post
        ]
        return this.allPost
    }
}
```

In the preceding class, we reuse our type to enforce and validate. The logic of the **addToPost** method is up to you, the developer. In this step, the code implements the method once it adheres to the interface by taking an argument of the **BlogPost** type and returns a **BlogPost** array.

5. Create an instance of **blogPostClass**:

```
const blog = new blogPostClass();
```

6. Build three objects of the **BlogPost** type:

```
let post1: BlogPost = {post: 'Goodbye, 2020', timeStamp: 12345678,
user: 'Rayon'}
let post2: BlogPost = {post: 'Welcome, 2021', timeStamp: 12345678,
user: 'Mark'}
let post3: BlogPost = {post: 'What happened to 1999?', timeStamp:
12345678, user: 'Will'}
```

This step simulates a user posting to your blog site. In a real-world application, this will be a web form that creates the object when submitted.

7. Call the **addToPost** method three times and pass the post objects you created in *Step 6*:

```
blog.addToPost(post1)
blog.addToPost(post2)
blog.addToPost(post3)
```

In an actual web application, the call to **addToPost** would entail making an API call to send the updated data to the backend of your application, but for the purpose of this exercise, we are just updating an array. If, for example, you are using some kind of state management for your frontend, the preceding code could look very similar to the state management handling the backend updates.

8. Console out the **allPost** global from the class instance created in *Step 5*:

```
console.log(blog.allPost)
```

9. Run the file by executing **npx ts-node Exercise02.ts**.

You should see the following output:

```
[
  { post: 'Goodbye, 2020', timeStamp: 12345678, user: 'Rayon' },
  { post: 'Welcome, 2021', timeStamp: 12345678, user: 'Mark' },
  { post: 'What happened to 1999?', timeStamp: 12345678, user: 'Will'
  }
]
```

EXERCISE 5.03: CREATING INTERFACES FOR A FUNCTION FOR UPDATING A USER DATABASE

As part of a web app developer team, you have been tasked with building an interface for a function that will update a user database. In a real-world application, this function might be part of a user registration form that updates a user database via an API call. The requirements are simple: the function should take an argument of the **User** type, which consists of **email** and **userId** properties.

For the sake of this exercise, assume that you are just working out the logic of the function and that the code is just temporary for testing purposes before you implement it in your working application. As such, we will have an array that will represent the database, which will be preloaded with some user objects:

> **NOTE**
>
> The code file for this exercise can be found here: https://packt.link/XLlz9.

1. Create a user type with **email** and **userId** properties, as shown here:

```
type User = {
    email: string,
    userId: number
}
```

Creating a user type allows you to simplify your function interface. Now, you can reuse your **User** type when defining your interface in the next step.

2. Build a function interface called **SuperAddMe**, as shown here:

```
interface SuperAddMe {
    (user: User): User[]
};
```

In doing this, we have defined how we will interact with our function. This is a small thing, but now, all functions of this type will have set rules. We will know what it needs and what it will return.

3. Initialize an array of the **User** type and populate it with a few users:

```
let allUsers: User[] = [
    { email: 'home@home.com', userId: 1 },
    { email: 'out@side.com', userId: 2 }
];
```

This array will simulate a database of users that we will add to.

4. Define a function of the **SuperAddMe** interface type:

```
let adduser: SuperAddMe

adduser = function (user: User): User[] {
    return [
        ...allUsers,
        user
    ]
}
```

When implementing a function in this way, you must first declare it as being of the interface type, which in this case is the **SuperAddMe** interface. Next, use the function variable and assign a function to it that adheres to the specification of our interface. This implementation is very similar to a type assignment, but because of the complexity of the function, an interface is used. Also, note that this code could be simplified by doing the declaration and assignment on one line, but in order to show the process and make it more readable, the assignment is implemented in parts.

5. Display the results of a call to a new function, **adduser**, and pass a user object of the **User** type. Console out the results to show that the code is working:

```
console.log(
    adduser(
        { email: 'slow@mo', userId: allUsers.length }
    )
)
```

6. Run the code using the **npx ts-node** command. You should see the following output:

```
[
  { email: 'home@home.com', userId: 1 },
  { email: 'out@side.com', userId: 2 },
  { email: 'slow@mo', userId: 2 }
]
```

ACTIVITY 5.01: BUILDING A USER MANAGEMENT COMPONENT USING INTERFACES

Imagine that you are working on a web application and are tasked with building a user management component. You need to build a class to encapsulate the user management aspects of the application and, because you are a good developer, you will be using interfaces to ensure that your code is easy to reuse and support. For this activity, you can assume that your user interface will have at least three properties: email, token, and loginAt. These properties relate to a user's email ID, the web token, and the time on the system when the user logged in.

> **NOTE**
>
> The code file for this activity can be found here: https://packt.link/xsOhv.

Here are some steps that will help you to complete this activity:

1. Create a user object interface with the following properties: **email : string**, **loginAt : number**, and **token: string**. The **loginAt** and **token** properties should be optional properties.

2. Build a class interface with a global property, **user**, and use the interface created in the preceding step to apply user object rules.

    You need to define a **getUser** method that returns the **user** object and then use the interface to ensure that the return object is a user object. Finally, define a **login** method that takes a **user** object and **password(type string)** as arguments. Use the **user** object interface as the **user** argument type.

3. Declare a class called **UserClass** that implements the class interface from the preceding step. Your login method should assign the local function's **user** argument to the global user property and return the global user. The **getUser** method should return the global user.

4.   Create an instance of your class declared in *Step 2*.

5.   Create a **user** object instance.

6.   Console out our methods to ensure that they are working as expected.

The expected output is as follows:

```
{ email: 'home@home.com', loginAt: 1614068072515, token: '123456' }
{ email: 'home@home.com', loginAt: 1614068072515, token: '123456' }
```

> **NOTE**
>
> The solution to this activity can be found on page 615.

TypeScript was born out of the need to build less confusing, clearly defined code. Interfaces allow you to build out your code in the most structured way possible. Everything has rules and there is no confusion, unlike with vanilla JavaScript.

To summarize the importance of interfaces, you can say that now you can produce code that is better structured and easier for third parties to use.

Let's say, for example, that you built a **user** class as you did in the preceding activity, and now you need to move on to a different part of your project. The interfaces you have built will be a great help to the developer taking over the user section of the application, or maybe some other developer wants to build a user class with a similar structure to your user class. By using the interfaces you have defined, they can build a structure that follows all the rules you have put in place. This is also helpful as regards debugging, as now they know how things are expected to function and can find where the issues are by using the interfaces as a guideline.

The next section of this chapter is dedicated to inheritance in TypeScript.

TYPESCRIPT INHERITANCE

We will now dive into inheritance, which is one of the core principles of object-oriented programming. It allows us to stay DRY (don't repeat yourself). Inheritance also allows us to be polymorphic, by abstracting functionality. Inheritance gives you the ability to extend your classes from the original class to a child class, which allows you to retain the functionality from the parent or original class and add or override what you don't need.

Child classes can override methods of their parents and have their own methods and objects. Inheritance only allows you to build on the parent class; how you implement your child class is up to you. However, the rule is that there must be some code you need to reuse from your parent class in your child class or you should create a new class as there would be no need to extend a class you don't plan to use any code from.

Let's say you have a user class created to manage users in your application. You are working on a web application and, in the planning stages, you come to the realization that you need more than one user type, as different users will have different levels of access and be able to perform different actions depending on their roles. This is the perfect case for the use of inheritance. Any time you have common properties and functionality, you can extend and not duplicate your code. In this case, we have several user types, which all have common properties of a user: email, createDate, lastLogin, and token, for example.

Because these properties are common to all users, we can put them all into a user class. The user class will serve as the base class that we can extend to our child classes. Your child classes will now have all the common properties without you having to declare them for each child class. As you can see, this is a much more efficient way to do things; it stops code duplication and allows for the consolidation of functionality.

First, let's go over some ground rules of inheritance in TypeScript:

TypeScript only supports inheritance in two ways: single-level and multi-level. Thus, in TypeScript, a child can inherit from a parent (single-level inheritance) or a child can inherit from another child (multi-level inheritance).

> **NOTE**
>
> They are other types of inheritance, but since Typescript does not support those patterns, this chapter will not address these types here.

Here, we have a diagram of the two types of inheritance that TypeScript supports – single-level and multi-level:

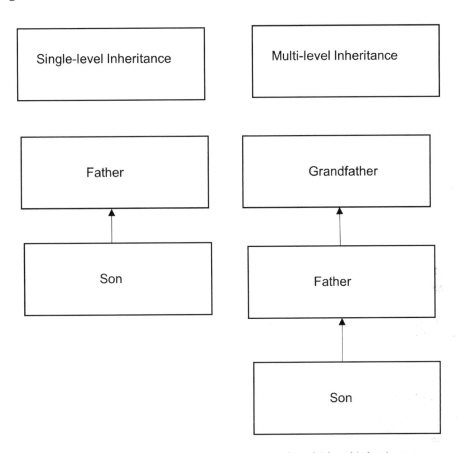

Figure 5.2: An example of single- and multi-level inheritance

Single-level inheritance occurs when a child class inherits directly from a parent class, as shown in the preceding diagram. The Son child class is derived from the Father parent class and has all its attributes. It can also have its own properties and functions that are unique to the child class. One of the goals of inheritance is to build on top of an existing base, therefore, just creating a duplicate of the class would be pointless. Multi-level inheritance works the same as single-level inheritance, except the child class inherits from another child class and not directly from the parent, as shown in the preceding diagram. In other words, single-level is derived directly from the base class, which has no parents, while a multi-level child class inherits from a derived class. As you can see, the Grandfather class is the base class and therefore has no parents. Father is derived from GrandFather, but Son, in this case, is derived from Father, making this example multi-level.

TypeScript makes use of the private and public keywords to allow you to hide code from a child class that is private and control how your class properties are accessed by a child class with getter and setter methods. You can override any method that is exposed by a parent class in the child that includes the constructor method by using the keyword super, which is a direct link to the parent class. super also allows you to access properties and methods of the parent class even if they are overridden in your child class.

To see how inheritance works in code, let's go back to our user example that we covered in the introduction to this section. The users of any given application have some common properties, email, createDate, lastLogin, and token, for example. We will use these common elements to build out a base user class:

Examples_Inheritance_1.ts

```
1  class UserOne {
2      email: string = "";
3      createDate: number = 0;
4      lastLogin: number = 0;
5      token: string = ""
6
7      setToken(token: string): void {
8          // set user token
9          this.token = token;
10     }
11     resetPassword(password: string):string {
12         // return string of new password
13         return password;
14     }
15 }
```

Link to the preceding example: https://packt.link/23ts2 .

Here is some information on the properties used in the base class. This will also help you understand why these properties are present in the base class:

- **email**: This property serves as a unique identifier.

- **createDate**: This property allows you to know when the user was added to the system.

- **lastLogin**: This property lets us know when the user was last active on the system.

- **token**: This property will validate user requests to the application's API.

- **setToken**: This property allows us to set and reset the token property; for example, the user logs out of the application and the token needs to be set to null.

- **resetPassword**: This property allows us to reset the current user's password.

We are also using the this keyword to access our class-level token in our **setToken** function. We have also provided a number of default values in our base class, such as setting an empty string for email and zero for **createDate**. This just makes it easier to create instances of the class as we do not need to provide values every time we initialize a class instance.

Now, let's move on to inheritance. We will now create a child class, **AdminUser**:

```
16 class AdminUser extends UserOne {
17     // pages admin has access to
18     adminPages: string [] = ["admin", "settings"];
19
20     // method that allows the admin to reset other users
21     resetUserPassword(email: string):string {
22         // return default user password
23         return "password123";
24     }
25 }
```

In order for us to create a child class, we must use the extends keyword followed by the parent class, as shown in the preceding snippet. The syntax structure is as follows: class keyword followed by the name of the child class, the extends keyword, and finally, the name of the parent class you would like to extend: class AdminUser extends UserOne.

Before we move on to some examples, let's list a few things we cannot do with class inheritance in TypeScript:

- You cannot use other types of inheritance other than single- and multi-level.

- If you declare a property or a method private, you cannot access it directly in your derived classes.

- You cannot override the constructor method of your base class unless you call **super** in your derived class's constructor.

Now, let's go back to our child class, **AdminUser**. Note that we have added some properties and methods unique to our child class. Unique to **AdminUser** are adminPages, which is a list of pages only the admin user has access to, and resetUserPassword, which takes an email address of a user and returns a default password:

> **NOTE**
>
> You can also reference directly the properties and methods of your parent class by using the **this** keyword in the child class, since **AdminUser** is now a combined class.

Now, consider the following snippet:

```
26 // create a instance of our child class
27 const adminUser: AdminUser = new AdminUser()
28
29 // create a string to hold our props
30 let propString = ''
31
32 // loop through your props and appends prop names to propString
33 for(let u in adminUser) {
34     propString += u + ','
35 }
```

In the preceding snippet, we create an instance of our child class, **AdminUser**. We also declare a string, **propString**, as an empty string. This string will hold a list of your class properties. Using a **for** loop, we loop over our class instance and append the properties to **propString**.

Now, console out an instance of our child class to verify that we have successfully inherited from our base class:

```
36 // console out the results
37 console.log(propString)
```

You should see the properties and methods of our child and parent classes printed on the console:

```
email,createDate,lastLogin,token,adminPages,constructor,
resetUserPassword,setToken,resetPassword,
```

The preceding output is the expected result. You now have a list of the combined properties of **UserOne** and **AdminUser**, showing that we have successfully extended our **UserOne** class to **AdminUser** or, in other words, we have shown that **AdminUser** inherits from **UserOne**.

Let's now take inheritance up one level by deriving a new class from the **AdminUser** class. Call the derived class **SuperAdmin**, because not all admins are created equal:

Examples_Inheritance_2.ts

```
class SuperAdmin extends AdminUser {
    superPages: string[] = ["super", "ultimate"]

    createAdminUser(adminUser: AdminUser ): AdminUser {
        return adminUser
    }
}
```

Link to the preceding example: https://packt.link/XcFR6.

As you can see from the preceding snippet, we are now extending the **AdminUser** class to create a **SuperAdmin** class. This means that we now have multi-level inheritance as our current class is inheriting from a derived class. We have also added a new property, **superPages**, and a method, **createAdmin**.

Multi-level inheritance is useful for building complexity while still keeping your code easy to manage.

Next, we are going to overload our **resetPassword** method in the **SuperAdmin** child class.

We want to create a new method for resetting passwords in our **SuperAdmin** class. We require a method that adds a hash to make the user password more secure as this will be the admin super user's password:

```
26 class SuperAdmin extends AdminUser {
27     superPages: string[] = ["super", "ultimate"]
28     readonly myHash: string
29
30     constructor() {
31         super()
32         this.myHash = '1234567'
33     }
34
35     createAdminUser(adminUser: AdminUser ): AdminUser {
36         return adminUser
37     }
38     resetPassword(password: string): string {
39         // add hash to password
40         return password + this.myHash;
41     }
42 }
```

The preceding code snippet creates a new method, **resetPassword**, and adds a new **myHash** property to our **SuperAdmin** class. We gave our new method the same name, **resetPassword**, as the **resetPassword** method in our grandfather class, **UserOne**. However, this new method returns a password appended with our hash property.

This is called method overriding because the methods have the same name and signature, meaning they take the same arguments. The method in the grandfather class is overridden and the new method will take precedence with instances of the **SuperAdmin** class.

This is useful when you need to add some functionality to a method in a child class but don't want to change the signature, as the new method does something similar but not exactly the same. Consumers of your code will be able to use the same method but get different outcomes based on which derived child class they invoke.

In the following snippet, we will console out the results of an instance of the **SuperAdmin** and **AdminUser** classes and the **resetPassword** method:

```
43 const superAdmin = new SuperAdmin()
44 const newAdmin = new AdminUser()
45 console.log( superAdmin.resetPassword('iampassword'))
46 console.log( newAdmin.resetPassword('iampassword'))
```

You will obtain the following output:

```
iampassword1234567
iampassword
```

As you can see from the output, we are calling the same method and getting a different output. This shows that we were able to successfully override the **resetPassword** method from our parent class, **UserOne**.

You can also add some access modifiers to our classes to show how they will affect our child classes:

```
class UserOne {
    email: string = "";
    createDate: number = 0;
    lastLogin: number = 0;
    private token: string = ""

    setToken(token: string): void {
        // set user token
        this.token = token;
    }
```

```
    resetPassword(password: string):string {
        // return string of new password
        return password;
}}
```

In the preceding snippet, we have added the **private** access modifier to the **token** property. Now, we can only access the **token** property through the **setToken** method, which is public, and all derived classes have access to the **setToken** method. This is useful in cases where you want to restrict which methods and properties to grant access to in your child classes. This is also useful in cases where you want to abstract functionality, thereby making interfacing with your code easier for consumers.

We want to make sure that every **AdminUser** class instance is initialized with an email address. Hence, we decide to add a constructor method to our **AdminUser** class to create an email address for our admin users whenever an **AdminUser** class is created.

However, we cannot just create a constructor as this is a child class, which means we already have a parent class with a constructor method and we cannot override a constructor method without invoking our base class's constructor method.

To invoke our base class's constructor method, we use **super()**, which is a direct reference to our base class's constructor method:

```
// adminUserTwo
class AdminUserTwo extends UserOne {
    // pages admin has access to
    constructor(email: string) {
        super()
        this.email = email;
    }

    adminPages: string [] = ["admin", "settings"];

    resetUserPassword():string {
        // return default user password
        return "password123";
    }
```

As you can see in the preceding snippet, we have a constructor method that takes an email address and sets the global email address. We also call the **super** method so that we can invoke the constructor method on our parent class.

Now, you can create an instance of our **AdminUserTwo** class and pass an email address when the instance is created. This is all transparent to the user of our **AdminUser** class:

```
const adminUserTwo = new AdminUserTwo('home@home.com');
```

Now that we have covered inheritance, we will put what we have learned to good use in the upcoming exercise.

EXERCISE 5.04: CREATING A BASE CLASS AND TWO EXTENDED CHILD CLASSES

Imagine that you are part of a development team working on a web application for a supermarket chain. You have the task of building a class to represent a user in the application. Because you are a good developer and are aware that you should not try to create one class for all use cases, you will build a base class with common attributes you think all users in your application should have and then extend that as required with child classes:

> **NOTE**
>
> The code file for this exercise can be found here: https://packt.link/hMd62.

1. Create a **User** class, as shown in the following code snippet:

```
class User {
    private userName: string;
    private token: string = ''
    readonly timeStamp: number = new Date().getTime()

    constructor(userName: string, token: string) {
        this.userName =  userName
        this.token = token
    }

    logOut():void {
        this.userName = ''
        this.token = ''
    }
```

```
    getUser() {
        return {
            userName: this.userName,
            token: this.token,
            createdAt: this.timeStamp
        }
    }

    protected renewToken (newToken: string) {
        this.token = newToken
    }}
```

The application requires all its users to have **username** and **token** upon creation of the user object, so we add those properties and they will be initialized in our constructor.

We also set them to **private** as we do not want child classes to access our properties directly. We also have a **timestamp** property that we will use to set a creation date for the user object. This is set to **readonly** as it is created when the class is instanced and we don't want it to be modified.

Different parts of your application will also need to access the properties of your user object. Therefore, we have added **getUser**, a method that returns your user properties. The **getUser** method will also allow derived or child classes to access private properties in an indirect way. The application allows the user to be logged in for a set period of time, after which the user token is expired. In order for a user to keep working in the application, we will need to renew their token, so we have added the **renewToken** method to allow for the setting of the user token property without giving direct access to properties.

2. Create a **Cashier** class derived from the **User** class:

```
class Cashier extends User {
    balance: number = 0
    float: number = 0

    start(balance: number, float: number): void {
        this.balance= balance
        this.float = float
    }
}
```

We now have a new user class, **Cashier**, derived from **User**, with some unique traits. A user of the **Cashier** type would need to function in our application. We do not, however, have access to all the properties of our parent class. You cannot access **userName** and **token** directly. You are able to access the **renewToken** method, but not through an instance of the **Cashier** class. However, you can call that method while building out the **Cashier** class as part of your user management for cashiers.

Why would we want to modify access in the child class as opposed to modifying a parent? This is because of encapsulation and standardization: we want to reduce the complexity of our code when consumed by others.

For example, you have been working on a library of useful functions. You want your coworkers to be able to use it, but they don't need to know the inner workings of your **User** class. They just need to be able to access the class using the exposed methods and properties. This allows you to guide the process even if you are not the person extending or implementing the code. A good example would be the **Date** class in JavaScript. You don't need to know how that works. You can simply instance it and use it as directed.

3. Create an **Inventory** class derived from **User**:

```
class Inventory extends User {
    products: string [] = []

    // override constructor method, add new prop
    constructor(userName: string, token: string, products: string[])
    {
        // call parent constructor method
        super(userName, token)
        // set new prop
        this.products = products
}}
```

Our new user type, **Inventory**, needs to be able to initialize products upon the declaration of a new inventory user, as this user will be dealing with products directly and should have some products in their user queue when the user logs in to the application.

In order to make that possible, we have overridden our parent class constructor method in our child class. Our constructor now takes a new argument, **products**, which is an array of the string type. This means that we have changed the number of arguments our constructor should take based on what we defined in our parent class. Whenever we override our constructor, we need to call **super**, which is a reference to our parent class.

As you can see, this allows us to access the parent constructor method, so we can now initialize **userName** and **token** and, in doing so, fulfill our child class's parent requirements. The main thing to take away from this is that all our code changes were made in the child class. Your new code for the **Inventory** class does not affect the other classes derived from **User**. You have extended and customized your code to deal with unique cases without having to write new code for this user case, saving you time and keeping your code base simple.

So far, we have derived two classes from our **User** class, which is single inheritance, as the child classes we created are directly derived from a base class. The next step involves multi-level inheritance.

4. Create a new derived class, **FloorWorker**:

```
class FloorWorker extends Inventory {
    floorStock: string [] = []

    CheckOut(id: number) {
        if(this.products.length >=0) {
            this.floorStock.push(
                this.products[id]
            )
        }
    }
}
```

This is multi-level inheritance. This class takes into account floor workers. These are users that deal with stocking shelves in the store, so they need to access products from the inventory. They also need to have a count of the products they have removed to stock the store shelves. They need to have access to the **User** class' properties as well as access to the **Products** array from the **Inventory** class.

In the following code snippet, we will instantiate our different user classes and console out the results of the work we have done so far.

5. Instantiate your basic user and console out the results:

```
const basicUser = new User('user1', '12345678ttt')
console.log(basicUser)
```

You will obtain the following output:

```
User {
    token: '12345678ttt',
    timeStamp: 1614074754797,
    userName: 'user1'
}
```

6. Instantiate the **Cashier** class user and console out the results:

```
const cashUser = new Cashier('user2', '12345678')
console.log(cashUser)
cashUser.start(10, 1.5)
console.log(cashUser)
```

You will obtain the following output:

```
Cashier {
    token: '12345678',
    timeStamp: 1614074754802,
    userName: 'user2',
    balance: 0,
    float: 0
}
Cashier {
    token: '12345678',
    timeStamp: 1614074754802,
```

```
  userName: 'user2',
  balance: 10,
  float: 1.5
```

7. Instantiate the **Inventory** class user and console out the results:

```
// init inventory
const iUser = new Inventory('user3', '123456789', [
    'orange', 'mango', 'playStation 2'
])
console.log(iUser)
```

You will obtain the following output:

```
Inventory {
  token: '123456789',
  timeStamp: 1614074754819,
  userName: 'user3',
  products: [ 'orange', 'mango', 'playStation 2' ]
}
```

8. Instantiate the **FloorWorker** class user and console out the results:

```
// FloorWorker
const fUser = new FloorWorker('user4', '12345678', [
    'orange', 'mango', 'playStation 2'
])
fUser.CheckOut(0)
console.log(fUser.products)
console.log(fUser.floorStock)
```

You will obtain the following output:

```
[ 'orange', 'mango', 'playStation 2' ]
[ 'orange' ]
```

> **NOTE**
>
> For *steps 5-8*, you can also instantiate and console out all your users belonging to the different classes at once, rather than individually, as shown in the exercise.

In this exercise, you created a base class, child classes, and worked on multi-level and single-level inheritance. You also made use of **super** and access modifiers.

EXERCISE 5.05: CREATING BASES AND EXTENDED CLASSES USING MULTI-LEVEL INHERITANCE

You are a developer working at a cell phone company and you are given the task of building a cell phone simulation application. The company manufactures two types of phone – a smartphone and a standard phone. The testing department wants to be able to showcase a number of functions of their phones and requires the ability to add more features to both phone types as the real devices are updated. After looking at the requirements, you come to the realization that you need the ability to model two types of phone and you also want to make it easy to update your code without doing a lot of refactoring and breaking other code that your phone models may use. You also know that both phones have a lot in common – they both have the basic functionality of communicating through voice and text data.

> **NOTE**
>
> The code file for this exercise can be found here: https://packt.link/pyqDK.

1. Create a **Phone** class that will serve as the base class for our child classes, as shown here:

```
class Phone {
powerButton: boolean;
mic: boolean;
speaker: boolean;
serialNumber: string;
powerOn: boolean = false;
restart: boolean = false;

constructor(
powerButton: boolean,
mic: boolean,
speaker: boolean,
serialNumber: string,
) {

this.powerButton = powerButton
```

```
this.mic = mic;
this.speaker = speaker;
this.serialNumber = serialNumber;
}


togglePower(): void {
this.powerOn ? this.powerOn = false : this.powerOn = true
}


reboot(): void {
this.restart = true
}
}
```

The **Phone** class is where we will store all the common elements of a phone. This will allow us to simplify our child classes to only deal with the elements unique to them.

2. Create a **Smart** class that extends the base or parent class created in *Step 1*:

```
class Smart extends Phone {
touchScreen: boolean = true;
fourG: boolean = true;

constructor(serial: string) {
super(true, true, true, serial)
}

playVideo(fileName: string): boolean {
return true
}
}
```

The **Smart** child class allows us to isolate all the methods and properties of a **Smart Phone** class.

3. Create a **Standard** class that extends the parent class created in *Step 1*, as shown here:

```
class Dumb extends Phone {
dialPad: boolean = true;
threeG: boolean = true;
```

```
constructor(serial: string) {
super(true, true, true, serial)
}


NumberToLetter(number: number): string {
const letter = ['a', 'b', 'c', 'd']
return letter[number]
}
}
```

Steps 2 and 3 deal with the creation of our child class, which allows us to meet our goals of being able to update our code without issues and keep our code clean and well maintained. Because we are planning well at this stage, if we need to add features to our **Smart** phone, we just need to update one child class. This is also true for the **Standard** phone class. Also, if we have a method or property that we need in both child classes, we only need to update the **Phone** parent class. With class inheritance, we work smart, not hard.

4. Create two instances of our child classes and initialize them:

```
const smartPhone = new Smart('12345678')
const standardPhone = new Standard('67890')
```

5. Console out and call the unique methods of our class instances to verify that our child classes are working as defined:

```
console.log(smartPhone.playVideo('videoOne'))
console.log(standardPhone.NumberToLetter(3))
```

You will obtain the following output:

```
true
d
```

if you revisit the respective class definitions of the **Smart** and **Standard** classes, you will be able to confirm that the preceding output is indeed evidence of the fact that the classes have worked as expected.

6. Display the child class instance to show that we have all the properties and methods of our parent class and child classes:

```
console.log(smartPhone)
console.log(standardPhone)
```

You will obtain the following output:

```
Smart {
  powerOn: false,
  restart: false,
  powerButton: true,
  mic: true,
  speaker: true,
  serialNumber: '12345678',
  touchScreen: true,
  fourG: true
}
Dumb {
  powerOn: false,
  restart: false,
  powerButton: true,
  mic: true,
  speaker: true,
  serialNumber: '67890',
  dialPad: true,
  threeG: true
}
```

For this preceding output, too, revisiting the respective class definitions of the **Smart** and **Dumb** classes should be proof enough that inheritance, as applied in this exercise, works correctly.

Now that you have an understanding of how inheritance works in TypeScript, we will test our skills in the form of the following activity.

ACTIVITY 5.02: CREATING A PROTOTYPE WEB APPLICATION FOR A VEHICLE SHOWROOM USING INHERITANCE

You are tasked with creating a web application for a vehicle showroom. You have decided to use your new skills in inheritance to build out the classes and child classes that will shape the vehicle objects we will require for our complete application. Note that the showroom has several types of vehicles. However, all these types will have some common properties. For example, all vehicles have wheels and a body. You can use this information to build your base class.

The following steps will help you to complete this activity:

> **NOTE**
>
> The code file for this exercise can be found here: https://packt.link/6Xp8H.

1. Create a parent class that will hold all common methods and properties for a base vehicle. Define a constructor method that allows you to initialize the base properties of this class and add a method that returns your properties as an object.

2. Add an access modifier to properties and class methods you want to control access to if necessary.

3. Derive two child classes from your parent class that are types of vehicles, for example, **Car** and **Truck**.

4. Override your constructor to add some unique properties to your child classes based on the type of vehicle.

5. Derive a class from one of the child classes created in *Step 3*, for example, **Suv**, which will have some of the properties a truck might have, so it would be logical to extend **Truck**.

6. Instantiate your child classes and seed them with data.

7. Console out our child class instance.

8. The expected output is as follows:

```
Car { name: 'blueBird', wheels: 4, bodyType: 'sedan', rideHeight: 14
}
Truck { name: 'blueBird', wheels: 4, bodyType: 'sedan', offRoad: true
}
Suv {
  name: 'xtrail',
  wheels: 4,
  bodyType: 'box',
  offRoad: true,
  roofRack: true,
  thirdRow: true
}
```

> **NOTE**
>
> The solution to this activity can be found on page 617.

SUMMARY

In this chapter, we covered interfaces in TypeScript. You learned how interfaces allow you to build contracts around your objects, classes, and methods. You also learned that interfaces are rules that outline how your code is implemented. This chapter covered how using interfaces makes your code easier to understand and is better supported by you and other developers when working in larger teams.

This chapter also taught you about inheritance, one of the core principles of object-oriented programing. You learned about the types of inheritance TypeScript supports and how you can use inheritance to build complexity in your code without making your code more complex. This chapter elucidated that stacking simple structures to make more complex ones is a good practice as it allows you to reuse code and not reinvent the wheel every time you need to build a class. This also lends itself to better code support as you will write only the code you need and have common parent classes that will remain constant throughout your application, thereby making mistakes and bugs easier to find.

You now have a good understanding of interfaces and inheritance, two building blocks you will make good use of as you move forward in this book and in web development using TypeScript.

The concepts you have covered here will make you a better developer overall as now you have the tools to write well-supported, clean, bug-free code.

In the next chapter, you will cover advanced types and will learn about type aliases, type literals, unions, and intersection types.

6

ADVANCED TYPES

OVERVIEW

This chapter introduces you to advanced types. You will start with the building blocks of advanced types – type alias, string, and number literals. This will allow you to gain a better understanding as you take on more complex concepts such as union types. You will also learn how you can combine types to build more complex types, such as intersections. Using advanced types, this chapter teaches you how to write code that is easier to understand for yourself and any others working with you or who are inheriting the project. By the end of this chapter, you will be able to build advanced types by combining primitive types, such as strings, numbers, and Booleans, with objects.

INTRODUCTION

In the previous chapter, we went over interfaces and inheritance. You saw how they allowed for the extension and modeling of your classes. Interfaces give your classes structure, and inheritance allows you to extend and build on your existing code.

As web applications become more complex, it is necessary to be able to model that complexity, and TypeScript makes that easy with advanced types. Advanced types allow you to model the complex data you will be working with as a modern web developer. You will be able to take primitive types and make more complex types from them, creating types that are conditional and flexible. This will allow you to write code that is easy to understand and therefore easier to work with. As a working developer, you may come across a dataset provided by an API that you need to integrate into your application. These datasets can be complex. For example, Cloud Firestore from Google is a document-based, real-time database that can have objects nested within objects. With advanced types, you can create a type that is an exact representation of the data coming from the API. This will provide much more context to your code, which, in turn, will make it easier to work with for you and your team. You will also be able to stack complexity by building simpler types and stacking them to make more complex types.

In this chapter, we will cover the building blocks of advanced types – type aliases and type literals. Once we learn how to build types, we will move on to more advanced concepts, including intersection, union, and index types. All these concepts will help you to learn how to use advanced types to add context and abstract complexity to code.

TYPE ALIASES

Type Aliases allow you to declare references to any type – advanced or primitive. Aliases make our code easier to read by allowing us to be less verbose. Aliases allow you, the developer, to declare your type once and reuse it throughout your application. This makes working with complex types easier and your code more readable and maintainable.

Let's say, for example, we are working on a social networking application and we needed to provide an administrator user type for users to manage the pages they created. Additionally, we also need to define a site administrator user. On a base level, they are both admins, and therefore the types would have some commonality between them. With a type alias, we could create an admin type as shown in *Figure 6.1*, with common properties an admin user would possess and build upon that admin when creating our site admin and user admin types. Aliases allow you to mask the complexity of your code, which will make it easier to understand. Here we have a diagram of an alias that assigns the **Admin** alias to an admin type, which is a complex **type** object. We also have an example of an alias, **One**, that is assigned to a type, **number**, which is a primitive type:

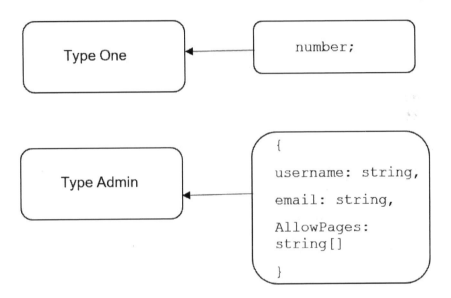

Figure 6.1: Alias assigning a complex admin type alias

Consider the following code snippet:

```
// primitive type assignment
type One = number;
```

In the preceding example, we have created an alias, **One**, that can be used as a type for any number, as it is assigned to the type number.

Now, consider the following code snippet:

```
// complex (object assignment)
type Admin = {
    username: string,
    email: string,
    userId: string,
    AllowedPages: string
};
```

Here, we have created an **Admin** alias, which we have assigned to an object that represents the common properties of a typical administrator, in the context of this example. As you can see, we have created a reference to a **type** object, which we can now use in our code instead of having to implement the object each time.

As you can see in the preceding diagram and code snippet, type aliases work in a similar way to variable assignments, except a reference is created for a primitive type and/or an object. This reference can then be used as a template for your data. This will allow you to take advantage of all the benefits of a strongly typed language, such as code completion and data validation.

Before we go into our first exercise on type aliases, we will look at some examples of primitive and complex assignments.

Let's say you are working on a class method that takes numbers as arguments, and only numbers. You want to make sure that when your method is used, only numbers are passed as arguments and the right error messages are shown to the user if any other type is passed.

First, we need to create a number type alias with the following syntax:

```
type OnlyNumbers = number;
```

The **type** keyword is followed by the alias, **OnlyNumbers**, and then the **number** type.

Now we can build a class with a method that only takes numbers as an argument and use the type alias to enforce our rule:

```
// instance of numbers only class
class NumbersOnly {
    count: number

    SetNumber(someNumber: OnlyNumbers) {
        this.count = someNumber
```

```
        }
}
```

Now, let's instance our class and pass some arguments to our method to see whether our code works.

For this example, let's try and assign a string as the argument type:

```
// class instance
const onlyNumbers = new NumbersOnly;


// method with incorrect arguments
onlyNumbers.SetNumber("15");
```

In the preceding code snippet, we have provided the wrong argument of the **string** type and this will result in a warning because our method, **SetNumber**, is expecting a number. Also, by providing your type aliases with meaningful names such as **onlyNumbers**, you can make your code easier to read and debug. For this example, the section of the code with the problem is highlighted, and when you hover over the error, you get a very helpful error message telling you what the issue is and how it can be resolved:

```
// class instance
const onlyNumbers = ne   Argument of type 'string' is not assignable to parameter
                         of type 'number'. ts(2345)

// method with incorre   View Problem (Alt+F8)    No quick fixes available
onlyNumbers.SetNumber("15");
```

Figure 6.2: Error message in VS Code

This is the case provided that you have the correct support from your IDE. If you don't have IDE support, you will be shown an error message at code compilation.

This is a simple use case, but as your applications become larger, some time has passed, or you are working in a large team, this kind of type security is vital to writing code that is free of mistakes.

Let's consider another example: Say you are working on an online store application and you need to use a product class that was not created by you. If the person who created the class made use of types and used descriptive names, it would be easier for you to work with that code.

Now, let's edit the first example with the correct argument type:

```
// method with correct arguments
onlyNumbers.SetNumber(15);
```

In the preceding code snippet, we have provided the correct argument type of **number** and your class method takes the argument with no issues.

Now, let's consider a complex alias assignment.

For example, we want to create a new function that takes a user object as a type argument. We could define the object as the function argument inline, as shown here:

```
// function and type definition
function badCode(user: {
    email: string,
    userName: string,
    token: string,
    lastLogin: number
}) {}
```

In the preceding snippet, the code creates a function that takes a user as an argument, but the type is defined in the function itself. While this would work, let's say you were using the object in a few places in your code, then, you would have to define this object each time. This is very inefficient and, as a good developer, you don't want to repeat code. This way of working will also lead to errors; it will make your code harder to work with and update as every instance of the **User** type will need to be changed throughout your code. Type aliases resolve this by allowing you to define your type once, as we will demonstrate in the following code snippet.

In much the same way as we have defined our primitive type, we have defined our **User** type. We use the **type** keyword, but now we have mapped to an object that is a template of our **User** type. We can now use the **User** alias, rather than having to redeclare the object every time we need to define the **User** type:

```
// object / complex type User
type User = {
    email: string,
    userName: string,
    token: string,
    lastLogin: number
};
```

As you can see, we have created a type with the alias **User**. This allows you to make a single reference to this object type and reuse it throughout your code. If we did not do this, we would have to reference the type directly.

Now you can build a new function using your **User** type:

```
// function with type alias
function goodCode(user: User){}
```

As you can see, this code is much less verbose and easy to understand. All your code regarding the **User** type is in one location, and when changes are made to the object, all aliases are updated. In the following exercise, you will implement what we have covered so far to build your own type alias.

EXERCISE 6.01: IMPLEMENTING A TYPE ALIAS

In this exercise, we will use our knowledge of types to build a function that creates products. Let's say, for example, you are working on a shopping application and when the inventory manager adds a product to the inventory, you need to push that product to your array of products. This exercise demonstrates a few ways in which type aliases can be useful by allowing you to define your **Product** model once and reuse it throughout your code.

Now, in an actual inventory management application, you might have a frontend page that allows a user to input the product name and supporting information manually. For the purpose of this exercise, let's assume the products you want to add are named **Product_0** through to **Product_5** and all have a price of 100, while the number of each of these products added to the inventory is 15.

This may not be truly reflective of an actual scenario in an inventory management application, but remember, our key goal is to use a type alias. So for now, a simple **for** loop to complete the aforementioned tasks will suffice:

> **NOTE**
>
> All files in this chapter can be executed by running **npx ts-node filename.ts** on the terminal. The code file for this exercise can be found here: https://packt.link/EAiHb.

1. Open VS Code and create a new file named **Exercise01.ts**.

2. Create a primitive type alias, **Count**, that is of the **number** type. **Count** will be used to keep track of the number of products:

```
//primitive type
type Count = number;
```

3. Create an object type alias, **Product**, that is of the **type** object. Re-use **Count** to define the count of the product. The **Product** type alias will be used to define every product we add to our inventory. The properties are common across all products:

```
// object type
type Product = {
    name: string,
    count: Count, //reuse Count
    price: number,
    amount:number,
}
```

4. Declare a **products** variable of the **Product** type array:

```
// product array
const products_list: Product[] = [];
```

In order for us to make use of the **Product** type, it was first assigned to a variable in the preceding code, and the **product_list** variable is an array of objects of the **Product** type.

5. Create a function that adds products to the array. Re-use the **Product** type alias to validate the argument input:

```
// add products to product array function
function makeProduct(p : Product ) {
    products_list.push(p); // add product to end of array
}
```

6. Use a **for** loop to create product objects of the **Product** type and add them to the **products** array:

```
// use a for loop to create 5 products
for (let index = 0; index < 5; index++) {
    let p : Product = {
        name: "Product"+"_"+`${index}`,
        count: index,
        price: 100,
        amount: 15
    }//make product
```

```
        makeProduct(p);
    }


    console.log(products_list);
```

7. Compile and run the program by executing **npx ts-node Exercise01. ts** in the correct directory in which this file is present. You should obtain the following output:

```
[
    { name: 'Product_0', count: 0, price: 100, amount: 15 },
    { name: 'Product_1', count: 1, price: 100, amount: 15 },
    { name: 'Product_2', count: 2, price: 100, amount: 15 },
    { name: 'Product_3', count: 3, price: 100, amount: 15 },
    { name: 'Product_4', count: 4, price: 100, amount: 15 }
]
```

In this exercise, you created two type aliases, which in turn created references to your actual types.

This allowed you to reduce complexity and make your code more readable, as now you can provide names that have additional context with descriptive names such as **Product** and **products_list**. If we were to write this code without the use of aliases, at every place where you used your aliases in the exercise, you would have to define the object or the type directly. This might not be much of an issue here with this simple function, but keep in mind how much more code you would need to build a class or a major project.

As we proceed to more complex type structures, this knowledge will become invaluable. We will continue to build on our knowledge in the next section as we cover type literals.

TYPE LITERALS

Type literals allow you to create a type based on a specific string or number. This, in itself, is not very useful, but as we move on to more complex types such as union types, their use will become apparent. Literals are straightforward, so we will not spend a lot of time on them but you will need to understand the concept of literals as we move into the next phase.

Let's start by creating our string and number literals.

We will begin with a string literal:

Example01.ts

```
1 // string literal
2 type Yes = "yes";
```

Link to the preceding example: https://packt.link/96IID.

The preceding code creates a **Yes** type that will take only a specific string, **"yes"**, as the input.

Similarly, we can create a number literal:

```
3 // number literal
4 type One = 1;
```

Here, we create a number literal type, **One**, that will only take **1** as the input.

The basic syntax as observed in the preceding examples is quite simple. We start with the **type** keyword, followed by the name (alias) of our new literal, and then the literal itself, as shown in the preceding syntax. We now have a type of the **yes** string and the number **1**.

Next, we will build a function that will make use of our new types:

```
5 // process my literal
6 function yesOne(yes: Yes, one: One ) {
7     console.log(yes, one);
8 }
```

We have cast our function arguments to our literal types, and because our types are literal, only the **"yes"** string or the number **1** will be accepted as arguments. Our function will not take other arguments. Let's say we passed **""** and **2** as arguments (**yesOne("", 2)**). You will notice the following warning in VS Code:

```
type One = 1;
// proc
functio    Argument of type '""' is not assignable to parameter of type
    con    '"yes"'. ts(2345)
}          View Problem (Alt+F8)    No quick fixes available
yesOne("", 2)
```

Figure 6.3: IDE warning when incorrect arguments are passed

Now, let's say we passed **"yes"** and **2** as arguments. Again, you will get the following warning:

```
type One = 1;
// process my literal
function yesOn   Argument of type '2' is not assignable to parameter of type
    console.lo   '1'. ts(2345)
}                View Problem (Alt+F8)    No quick fixes available
yesOne("yes", 2)
```

Figure 6.4: Errors displayed when a parameter that cannot be assigned is passed

The preceding are some examples of error messages you might expect if you provide the wrong arguments. The error messages are clear and tell you precisely what you need to do to resolve the error. As you can see, even though we are passing a string and a number, we still get a type error. This happens because these arguments are literal; they can only match themselves exactly.

Now, let's try and pass the correct arguments:

```
9 // function with the correct arguments
10 yesOne("yes", 1);
```

Once provided with the correct arguments, the function can be called without any issue, as shown in the following output:

```
yes 1
```

Before we move on to intersection types, let's quickly complete a simple exercise to cement our knowledge of string and number literals.

EXERCISE 6.02: TYPE LITERALS

Now that we have a better understanding of literals, let's go through a small exercise to reinforce what we have covered. Here we will create a function that takes a string literal and returns a number literal:

> **NOTE**
>
> The code file for this exercise can be found here: https://packt.link/hHgNa.

1. Open VS Code and create a new file named **Exercise02.ts**.

2. Create a string literal type, **No**, and assign the string **"no"** as the value. Also, create a number literal and assign 0 as the value:

```
type No = "no"
type Zero = 0
```

3. Build a function that takes the **"No"** literal and prints it to the console:

```
function onlyNo(no: No):Zero {
    return 0;
}
```

4. Console out the function call results:

```
console.log(
    onlyNo("no")
)
```

This will result in the following output:

```
0
```

Literals by themselves are not very useful, but when used in combination with more complex types, their usefulness will become apparent. For now, you need to understand how to create literals, so you can make use of them later in this chapter. In the next section, we move on to intersection types. All the work that we have completed so far will help as we make use of type aliases and literals.

INTERSECTION TYPES

Intersection Types allow you to combine types to form a new type with the properties of the combined types. This is useful in cases where you have an existing type that does not, by itself, address some data you need to define, but it can do so in combination with another existing type. This is similar to multi-class inheritance, as the child object can have more than one parent object that it derives its properties from.

Let's say you have a type **A** with a name and age property. You also have a type **B** with a height and weight property. In your application, you find that there is a need for a person type: you want to track the user's name, age, height, and weight. You can intersect type **A** and **B** to form a **Person** type. Why not just create a new type you ask? Well, this takes us back to wanting to be good coders and good coders stay DRY – Don't Repeat Yourself. Unless a type is truly unique in your application, you should reuse as much code as possible. Also, there is centralization.

If you need to make changes to any of the type code for **Person**, you just need to make the changes in **A** or **B**. This is also a bit limiting as there may be cases where type **A** is used by more than one object, and if you make changes, it will break the application. With intersection, you can simply create a type **C** with the changes and update your **Person** type. You can also merge types with common properties.

Consider a situation where you have a **name** property in **A** and also in **B**. When the types are intersected, you would now have just one **name** property; however, the merged properties must not only be the same in name, but should also be of the same type, otherwise the types will not merge and will result in errors.

If this is not clear, let's look at a property, **age**. This can be a number in one type and a string in another. The only way you could intersect these types would be to make the properties common, as either would need to be a string or number.

Imagine that as part of an e-commerce project, you are required to build a shopping cart object that derives its properties from a **Product** object and an **Order** object.

The following diagram shows the basic properties of each object and the properties of the new **Cart** object that is formed using the **Product** and **Order** objects:

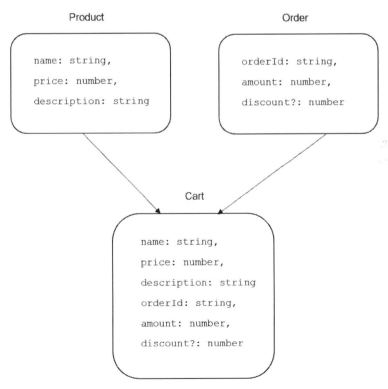

Figure 6.5: Diagram showing the properties of the Cart object

In the diagram, we have our parent objects, **Product** and **Order**, that combine to form a child object, **Cart**, with all the properties of its parent objects. Please note that we can have more than two parents in an intersection, but for the sake of this explanation, we will stick to two, as this will allow you to grasp the concept faster. In the upcoming example, we will walk through the process of creating our new **Cart** type in code and a basic use case.

Imagine you are working on the shopping application. You need to create an object to model the product data you will push to the cart for checking out. We already have a **Product** type for our product data. The **Product** type has most of what we need to display correct information pertaining to our products on the web page. However, we are missing a few things we require when checking a product out. We will address this not by creating a new type of product, but we will create an **Order** type with just the properties we need: **orderId**, **amount**, and **discount**, the last of which is optional as it will not always apply.

Here is the code for declaration of the **Product** type:

Example02.ts

```
1  // product type
2  type Product = {
3      name: string,
4      price: number,
5      description: string
6  }
7
8  // order type
9  type Order = {
10     orderId: string,
11     amount: number,
12     discount?: number
13 }
```

`Link to the preceding example:` https://packt.link/DZ7lz

In the preceding code snippet, we have created our parent types names **Product** and **Order**. Now we need to merge them. This will create the type we need to model our cart data:

```
14 // Alias Cart of Product intersect Order
15 type Cart = Product & Order;
```

We build our cart object by assigning an alias, **Cart**, to our **Product** and **Order** types and using **&** between our two types, as shown in the preceding snippet. We now have a new merged type, **Cart**, that we can use to model our cart data:

```
16 // cart of type Cart
17 const cart: Cart = {
18     name: "Mango",
19     price: 400,
20     orderId: "x123456",
21     amount: 4,
22     description: "big sweet, full of sugar !!!"
23 }
```

The preceding is an example of a cart object declared using the **Cart** type. As you can see, we have access to all our properties and can omit optional ones that may not always apply, such as **discount**.

If we do not provide all the required properties, the IDE gives a very helpful error message telling us just what we need to do in order to fix the issue:

```
// ord  Type '{ price: number; orderId: string; amount: number;
type O  description: string; }' is not assignable to type 'Cart'.
    or     Property 'name' is missing in type '{ price: number;
    am  orderId: string; amount: number; description: string; }' but
    di  required in type 'Product'. ts(2322)

}        example.ts(3, 5): 'name' is declared here.
// Ali
type C  const cart: Cart

// car  View Problem (Alt+F8)   No quick fixes available
const cart: Cart = {
    price: 400,
    orderId: "x123456",
    amount: 4,
    description: "big sweet, full of sugar !!!"
}
```

Figure 6.6: The error message displayed when missing required properties

Now, let's console out our new cart object: This will display the following output:

```
{
  name: 'Mango',
  price: 400,
  orderId: 'x123456',
  amount: 4,
  description: 'big, sweet, and full of sugar !!!'
}
```

In the next section, you will get some hands-on experience in terms of creating intersection types by performing an exercise in which you will build a prototype user management system.

EXERCISE 6.03: CREATING INTERSECTION TYPES

You are working on an e-commerce application; you have been assigned the task of building out the user management system. In the application requirements, the customer has listed the types of user profiles they expect will interact with the system. You will use type intersection to build out your user types. This will allow you to build simple types that can be combined to make more complex types and separate your concerns. This will result in code that is less error-prone and better supported. Here, we name the user types we will build and provide an overview of their functions:

- **Basic user**: This user will have the properties **_id**, **email**, and **token**.

- **Admin user**: This user will have the ability to access pages not accessible to a normal user. This user will have the properties **accessPages** and **lastLogin**. **accessPages** is a string array of pages that this user can access, while **lastLogin** will help us to log the activates of the Admin user.

- **Backup user**: This user has the job of backing up the system and the user properties of **lastBackUp** and **backUpLocation**. **lastBackUp** will let us know what time the system was last backed up, while **backUpLocation** will tell us where the backup files are stored.

- **superUser**: This user is an intersection of the Admin and User types. All users require the properties of a Basic user, but only Admin users require Admin properties. Here, we use type intersection to build the necessary properties we need.

- **BackUpUser**: This user is an intersection of the **Backup** user and **Basic** user types. Once again, we can incorporate into our basic user the necessary complexity this user type requires in order to function.

> **NOTE**
>
> The code file for this exercise can be found here: https://packt.link/FVvj5.

1. Open VS Code and create a new file named **Exercise03.ts**.

2. Create a basic **User** type:

```
// create user object type
type User = {
    _id: number;
    email: string;
    token: string;
}
```

This will be the type we will use as our base for the other user types in our application. Thus, it has all the common user properties that all users will require.

3. Create an **Admin** user type for users who need to perform the functions of an administrator:

```
// create an admin object type
type Admin = {
    accessPages: string[],
    lastLogin: Date
}
```

4. Create a **Backup** user type for users who are responsible for backing up the application data:

```
// create backupUser object type
type Backup = {
    lastBackUp: Date,
    backUpLocation: string
}
```

5. Using your **User** and **Admin** types, declare a **superuser** object of the **User** type at the **Admin** intersect. Add the required properties. In order to create a superuser, you will have to provide values for the properties of **User** and **Admin**, as shown in the following code block:

```
// combine user and admin to create the user object
const superUser: User & Admin = {
    _id: 1,
    email: 'rayon.hunte@gmail.com',
    token: '12345',
    accessPages: [
        'profile', 'adminConsole', 'userReset'
```

```
        ],
        lastLogin: new Date()
};
```

In an actual application, this code may be in a login function and the values returned might be from an API on login.

6. Build a **BackUpUser** type by assigning the alias **BackUpUser** to the intersection of **User** and **Backup**:

```
// create BackUpUser type
type BackUpUser = User & Backup
```

7. Declare a **backUpUser** object of the **BackUpUser** type and add the requisite properties:

```
// create backup user
const backUpUser: BackUpUser = {
    _id: 2,
    email: 'rayon.backup@gmail.com',
    token: '123456',
    lastBackUp: new Date(),
    backUpLocation: '~/backup'
};
```

8. Console out your **superUser** and **backupUser** objects:

```
// console out superUser props
console.log(superUser);

// console out backup user props
console.log(backUpUser);
```

This will print the following output:

```
{
  _id: 1,
  email: 'rayon.hunte@gmail.com',
  token: '12345',
  accessPages: [ 'profile', 'adminConsole', 'userReset' ],
  lastLogin: 2021-02-25T07:27:57.009Z
}
{
  _id: 2,
  email: 'rayon.backup@gmail.com',
```

```
    token: '123456',
    lastBackUp: 2021-02-25T07:27:57.009Z,
    backUpLocation: '~/backup'
}
```

In the preceding exercise, you built two user types using the **superUser** and **backupUser** intersections that are based on the **User**, **Admin**, and **Backup** types. The use of intersections allows you to keep your core user type simple and can therefore be used as a model for most of your user data. **Admin** and **Backup** are intersected with **User** only when it is necessary to model that specific user case. This is the separation of concerns. Now, any changes made to **User**, **Backup**, or **Admin** will be reflected in all child types. We will now take a look at union types, which is a type functionality. However, unlike intersections, union types provide an **OR** functionality when types are merged.

UNION TYPES

Union Types are similar to intersections as they are a combination of types to form a single type. Union types differ, however, in that they do not merge your types but provide **or** type functionality instead of an **and** type functionality, which was the case with intersection types. This works in a similar way to the ternary operator in JavaScript, where the types you are combining are separated by the | pipe. If this is confusing, it will all become clear as we move on to an example. We will also take a look at type guards, which is a pattern that will play a major role in the app use of union types. First, consider the following visual representation of a union type:

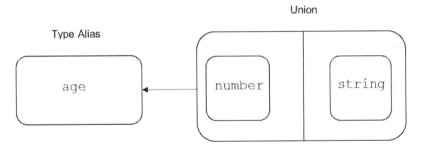

Figure 6.7: Illustration of a union type assignment

In the preceding diagram, we have a basic diagram of a union type assignment, where **Age** can be of the **number** or **string** datatypes. You can have union types with more than two options and non-primitive types. This gives you the option to write code that is more dynamic. In the upcoming example, we will extend our age example as mentioned previously and build a basic union type.

Let's say you're working on an application that needs to validate someone's age. You want to write one function that will process ages from a database that are stored as a number and ages from the web frontend that come in as a string. In a case such as this, you might be tempted to use **any** as a type. However, unions allow us to address this kind of scenario without creating a vector for errors by using **any**:

`Example03.ts`

```
1 // basic union type
2 type Age =  number | string;
```

Link to the preceding example: https://packt.link/EHziL.

First, we create a union type, **Age**, which can be of the **number** or **string** datatypes, as shown in the preceding syntax. We assign our **Age** alias to our types separated by a pipe, **|**. We could have more than two options, for example, **"number" | "string" | "object"**:

Now we create a function that will make use of the new type, **Age**, as shown in the preceding snippet:

```
3  function myAge(age: Age): Age {
4      if (typeof age === "number") {
5          return `my age is ${age} and this a number`;
6      } else if (typeof age === "string"){
7          return `my age is ${age} and this a string`;
8      } else {
9          return `incorrect type" ${typeof(age)}`;
10     }
11 }
```

The **myAge** function takes the **Age** type as an argument and returns a formatted string of the **Age** type using an **if** ...**else** loop. We are also making use of a type guard pattern, **typeof**, which allows you to check the type of your argument. This kind of type checking is necessary while using union types as your argument can be of several types, which, in the case of this preceding code snippet, is a string or a number. Each type will need to be processed with a different logic.

Union types can also be objects; however, in such a case, **typeof** will not be very useful as it will only return the type, which will always be **object**. To resolve such cases, you can check for any unique properties of your object and apply your logic in this way. We will see examples of this as we work through our exercise in the next section.

Now, let's get back to the example. To ensure that our functions are working as they should, we console out the results by calling them with different argument types (number and string):

```
console.log(myAge(45));
console.log(myAge("45"));
```

This will result in the following output:

```
my age is 45 and this a number
my age is 45 and this a string
```

Let's say that you passed an incorrect argument instead:

```
console.log(myAge(false));
```

You will see the following error message:

```
error TS2345: Argument of type 'boolean' is not assignable to parameter
of type 'Age'.
```

EXERCISE 6.04: UPDATING THE PRODUCTS INVENTORY USING AN API

In the following exercise, we will extend our inventory management example from *Exercise 03* by adding an API. This will allow remote users to add and update products in our inventory via an API **PUT** or **POST** request.

Since the processes of updating and adding a product are so similar, we will write one method to handle both requests and use a union type to allow our method to take both types and remain type safe. This will also mean that we can write less code and encapsulate all related code to the one method, which will make it easy for us or any other developer working on the application to find and resolve errors.

You could use the **any** type, but then your code would become type insecure, which could lead to bugs and unstable code:

> **NOTE**
>
> The code file for this exercise can be found here: https://packt.link/Qvx6D.

1. Open VS Code and create a new file named **Exercise04.ts**.

2. Create three types, **Product**, **Post**, and **Put**, along with the base objects you will require, as shown here:

```
type Product = {
    name: string,
    price: number,
    amount: number,
}

type Post = {
    header: string,
    method: string,
    product: Product
}

type Put = {
    header: string,
    method: string,
    product: Product,
    productId: number
}
```

We first create a product type that will help us to define what format the product data will take as part of a **Put** or **Post** request. We have also defined **Put** and **Post**, which differ slightly because a **Put** request will need to update a record that already exists. Note that **Put** has the property **productId**.

3. Create a union type, **SomeRequest**, which can be either the **Put** or **Post** type:

```
type SomeRequest =   Post | Put
```

The data being matched to the union type can be any of the types in the union. Note that unions do not combine types; they simply try to match the data to one of the types in the union, which gives you, the developer, more flexibility.

4. Create an instance of an array of the **Product** type:

```
const products: Product[] = [];
```

5. Build a handler function that processes a request of the **SomeRequest** type:

```
function ProcessRequest(request: SomeRequest ) {
    if ("productId" in request) { products.forEach(
            (p: Product, i: number) => {
                products[request.productId] = {
                    ...request.product
            };});
    } else {
        products.push(request.product);
    }}
```

This function will receive a request of the **Put** or **Post** type and add or update an attached product to the **products** array. In order to know whether it should update or add the function, it first checks whether the product has a **productId** argument. If it does, we will loop through the **Products** array until we find a matching **productId** argument. Then, we use the spread operator to update the product data with the data from the request. If the product does not have a **productId** argument, we then just use the **push** function attached to the array to add the new product to the array.

6. Declare **apple** and **mango** objects of the **Product** type, as shown here:

```
const apple: Product = {
    name: "apple",
    price: 12345,
    amount: 10
};
const mango: Product = {
    name: "mango",
    price: 66666,
    amount: 15
};
```

In a real API, the data would be provided by the user sending it via a request, but for the purposes of this exercise, we have hardcoded some data for you to work with.

7. Declare **postAppleRequest** and **putMangoRequest** objects of the **Post** and **Put** types:

```
const postAppleRequest : Post = {
    header: "zzzzz",
    method: 'new',
    product: apple,
};

const putMangoRequest : Put = {
    header:"ggggg",
    method: 'update',
    product: mango,
    productId: 2
};
```

In the preceding code, we have defined our **POST** and **PUT** objects. We have attached the product object as a payload of the request. Remember that the function is not checking the product object but the request type, which will tell the function whether it's **POST** or **PUT**.

8. Call the handler function and pass **postAppleRequest** and **putMangoRequest** as arguments, as shown in the following code snippet:

```
ProcessRequest(postAppleRequest);

ProcessRequest(putMangoRequest);
```

In a normal API, when the user makes a **PUT** or **POST** request, the **ProcessRequest** method would be called. We are, however, just simulating an API and making the calls ourselves.

9. Console out the results:

```
console.log(products)
```

You will see the following output:

```
[
  { name: 'apple', price: 12345, amount: 10 },
  <1 empty item>,
  { name: 'mango', price: 66666, amount: 15 }
]
```

In the preceding output, we can now see the products that we passed to our methods. This means that our simulated API code using unions works as intended.

Union types, such as intersection types, give you, the developer, more functionality and flexibility when building your applications. In the preceding exercise, we were able to write a function that takes a single argument of two different types and applies logic based on type checking patterns or type guards. In the next section, we will continue the theme of more code flexibility with index types.

INDEX TYPES

Index types allow us to create objects that have flexibility as regards the number of properties they may hold. Let's say you have a type that defines an error message, which can be more than one type, and you want the flexibility to add more types of messages over time. Because objects have a fixed number of properties, we would need to make changes to our message code whenever there was a new message type. Index types allow you to define a signature for your type using an interface, which gives you the ability to have a flexible number of properties. In the following example, we will expand on this in the code:

`Example04.ts`

```
1 interface ErrorMessage   {
2    // can only be string | number | symbol
3    [msg: number ]: string;
4    // you can add other properties once they are of the same type
5    apiId: number
6 }
```

Link to the preceding example: https://packt.link/IqpWH

First, we create our type signature, as shown in the preceding snippet. Here we have a property name and type, which is the index **[msg: number]** followed by the value type. The name of the **msg** argument can be anything, but as a good coder, you should provide a name that makes sense in the context of the type. Note that your index can only be a number, string, or symbol.

You can also add other properties to your index, but they must be the same type as the index, as shown in the preceding code snippet, **apiId: number**. Next, we make use of your type by casting it to **errorMessage**. We can now have an error message object with as many properties as we require. There is no need to modify the type as our list of messages grows. We maintain flexibility while keeping our code typed, thereby making it easy to scale and support:

```
7   // message object of Index type ErrorMessage
8   const errorMessage: ErrorMessage  = {
9       0: "system error",
10      1: "overload",
11      apiId: 12345
12  };
```

Now, we console out the new object just to make sure that everything works:

```
// console out object
console.log(
    errorMessage
);
```

You will get the following output once you run the file:

```
{ '0': 'system error', '1': 'overload', apiId: 12345 }
```

If we try to give a property name of an incorrect type, such as a string, we get the kind of error message you might expect:

```
interface ErrorMessage   {
    // can only be string | number | symbol
```

Type '{ some: string; 1: string; apiId: number; }' is not assignable to type 'ErrorMessage'.
  Object literal may only specify known properties, and ''some'' does not exist in type 'ErrorMessage'. ts(2322)

```
}
//
con View Problem (Alt+F8)    No quick fixes available

    'some': "system error",
    1: "overload",
    apiId: 12345
};
```

Figure 6.8: Output displaying the type error

You can, however, use strings that are numbers, for example, and the code will function as before and the output will be the same:

```
14 // message object of Index type ErrorMessage
15 const errorMessage: ErrorMessage  = {
16     '0': "system error",
17      1: "overload",
18    apiId: 12345 };
```

You may think that this will not work given that the value is a string, but it gets converted to a number literal. It will also work the other way around using a number literal that gets converted to a string. Next in our exercise, we will simulate the real-world usage of an index type, building a simple system to process error messages.

EXERCISE 6.05: DISPLAYING ERROR MESSAGES

In this exercise, we will build a system to process error messages. We will also reuse the **ErrorMessage** index type we created in our example. The code in this exercise is somewhat contrived but will serve to help you get a better understanding of index types:

> **NOTE**
>
> The code file for this exercise can be found here: https://packt.link/ZkApY.

1. Open VS Code and create a new file named **Exercise05.ts**.

2. Create the **ErrorMessage** type interface from our example if you have not already done so:

```
interface ErrorMessage  {
    // can only be string | number | symbol
    [msg: number ]: string;
    // you can add other properties once they are of the same type
    apiId: number
}
```

3. Build an **errorCodes** object as an **ErrorMessage** type, as shown here:

```
const errorMessage : ErrorMessage = {
    400:"bad request",
    401:"unauthorized",
    403:"forbidden",   apiId: 123456,
  };
```

4. Create an error code array as **errorCodes**, as shown here:

```
const errorCodes: number [] = [
    400,401,403
  ];
```

5. Loop through the **errorCodes** array and console out the error messages:

```
errorCodes.forEach(
    (code: number) =>   {
        console.log(
            errorMessage[code]
        );
    }
);
```

Once you run the file, you will obtain the following output:

```
bad request
unauthorized
forbidden
```

Index types allow you to have flexibility with your type definitions, as you can see in the preceding exercise. If you need to add new codes, you will not need to change your type definition; simply add the new code property to your **errorCode** object. Index types work here because even though the properties for the object are different, they all have the same basic makeup – a number property (key) followed by a string value.

Now that you have the building blocks for advanced types, you can work through the following activities. The activities will make use of all the skills you have acquired in this chapter.

ACTIVITY 6.01: INTERSECTION TYPE

Imagine that you are a developer working on a truck builder feature for a custom truck website. You will need to make it possible for customers that come to the site to build a variety of truck types. To that end, you need to build your own intersection type, **PickUptruck**, by combining two types, **Motor** and **Truck**. You can then use your new type, **PickUpTruck**, with a function that returns the type and validates its input with the **PickUpTruck** intersection type.

> **NOTE**
>
> The code file for this activity can be found here: https://packt.link/n4tfL.

Here are some steps that will help you to complete this activity:

1. Create a **Motor** type, which will house some common properties you may reuse on their own or in combination with other types to describe a vehicle object. You can use the following properties as a starting point: **color**, **doors**, **wheels**, and **fourWheelDrive**.

2. Create a **Truck** type with properties common to a truck, for example, **doubleCab** and **winch**.

3. Intersect the two types to create a **PickUpTruck** type.

4. Build a **TruckBuilder** function that returns our **PickUpTruck** type and also takes **PickUpTruck** as an argument.

5. Console out the function return.

6. Once you complete the activity, you should obtain the following output:

```
{
    color: 'red',
    doors: 4,
    doubleCab: true,
    wheels: 4,
    fourWheelDrive: true,
    winch: true
}
```

> **NOTE**
>
> The solution to this activity is presented on page 620.

ACTIVITY 6.02: UNION TYPE

A logistics company has asked you to develop a feature on their website that will allow customers to choose the way they would like their packages to be shipped – via land or air. You have decided to use union types to achieve this. You can build your own union type called **ComboPack**, which can be either the **LandPack** or **AirPack** type. You can add any properties to your package types that you think will be common to a package. Also, consider using one type literal to identify your package as air or land, and a label property that will be optional. You will then need to construct a class to process your packages. Your class should have a method to identify your package type that takes arguments of the **ComboPack** type and uses your literal property to identify the package type and add the correct label, **air cargo** or **land cargo**.

> **NOTE**
>
> The code file for this activity can be found here: https://packt.link/GQ2ZS.

Here are some steps that will help you to complete this activity:

1. Build a **LandPack** and an **AirPack** type. Make sure to have a literal to identify the package type.

2. Construct a union type, **ComboPack**, which can be **LandPack** or **AirPack**.

3. Make a **Shipping** class to process your packages. Make sure to use your literal to identify your package types and modify your package with the correct label for its type.

4. Create two package objects of the **AirPack** and **LandPack** types.

5. Instantiate your **Shipping** class, process your new objects, and console out the modified objects.

> **NOTE**
>
> The solution to this activity is presented on page 621.

ACTIVITY 6.03: INDEX TYPE

Now that you have done such a good job of incorporating the shipping option into the website, the company now needs you to add a feature that will allow their customers to track the status of their packages. It is important to the client that they have the ability to add new package statuses as the company grows, and as shipping methods change, they would like that flexibility.

Hence, you have decided to build an index type, **PackageStatus**, using an interface signature of the **status** property of the **string** type and a value of the **Boolean** type. You will then construct a **Package** type with some common package properties. You will also include a **packageStatus** property of the **PackageStatus** type. You will use **PackageStatus** to track three statuses of your package: **shipped**, **packed**, and **delivered**, set to **true** or **false**. You will then construct a class that takes an object of the **Package** type on initialization, contains a method that returns the **status** property, and a method that updates the **status** property, which takes **status** as a string and **Boolean** as a state.

The method that updates your package should also return your **packageStatus** property.

> **NOTE**
>
> The code file for this activity can be found here: https://packt.link/2LwHq.

Here are some steps that will help you to complete this activity:

1. Build your **PackageStatus** index type using an interface with a property of **status** of the **string** type and a value of the **Boolean** type.

2. Create a **Package** type that includes a property of the **PackageStatus** type and some common properties of a typical package.

3. Make a class to process your **Package** type that takes the **Package** type on initialization, has a method to return your **packageStatus** property, and a method that updates and returns the **packageStatus** property.

4. Create a **Package** object called **pack**.

5. Instantiate your **PackageProcess** class with your new **pack** object.

6. Console out your **pack** status.

7. Update your **pack** status and console out your new **pack** status.

   The expected output is as follows:

   ```
   { shipped: false, packed: true, delivered: true }
   { shipped: true, packed: true, delivered: true }
   ```

> **NOTE**
>
> The solution to this activity can be found page 623.

SUMMARY

In this chapter, we covered advanced types, which allow you to extend beyond your basic types. As applications become more complex and the frontend takes on more functionality, your data models will also become more complex. This chapter showed you how TypeScript advanced types give you the ability to implement strong typing, which will help you develop cleaner and more reliable applications. We covered the building blocks of advanced types – type aliases and literals, and we then moved on to intersection, union, and index types with some practical examples, exercises, and activities.

You now have the ability to create complex types that will allow you to build types for modern applications and write code that is well supported and scalable. Having reached this point, you now have the tools to take on web frameworks, such as Angular2 and React. You can even use TypeScript on the server side with Node.js. There is much more to advanced types and the topic is quite vast, complex, and abstract in its implementations. However, here in this chapter, you have been equipped with the skills you need to start building applications with advanced types.

7

DECORATORS

OVERVIEW

This chapter first establishes the motivation for decorators and then describes the various decorator types available in TypeScript. We'll take a look at how decorators are used and how they are customized to fit your specific needs. We'll also cover writing your own decorators. By the end of this chapter, you will be able to use decorators to alter the behavior of your code, and use decorator factories to customize the decorators that are being used. You will also learn how to create your own decorators, to be used by your code or that of others.

INTRODUCTION

In the previous chapters, you saw how to create types and classes and how to compose them into a proper class hierarchy using interfaces, inheritance, and composition.

Using the TypeScript type system, you can create some very elegant models of the domains of your applications. However, models do not live by themselves; they are part of a larger picture – they are part of an application. And classes need to be aware that they live in a larger world, with many other parts of the system running in tandem with them, with concerns that go beyond the scope of a given class.

Adding behaviors to or modifying classes to account for the preceding scenario is not always easy. And this is where decorators come to the rescue. Decorators are special declarations that can be added to class declarations, methods, and parameters.

In this chapter, we'll learn how you can use a technique called **decorators** to transparently add complicated and common behaviors to your classes, without getting your application logic all cluttered up with additional code.

Decorators are one of the features that are available and widely used in TypeScript but are not available in JavaScript. There is a proposal for decorators in JavaScript (https://github.com/tc39/proposal-decorators), but it's still not part of the standard. The decorators that you will use in TypeScript are closely modeled to function just like the proposal.

The TypeScript approach has its good and bad aspects. One good aspect is that once decorators become a standard feature in JavaScript, you can seamlessly transfer your decorating skill over to JavaScript, and the code that the TypeScript compiler (**tsc**) generates will be an even more idiomatic JavaScript. The bad thing is that until it becomes a standard feature, the proposal can and will change. That's why, by default, the usage of decorators is turned off in the compiler, and in order to use them, you need to pass in a flag, either as a command-line option or as part of your **tsconfig.json**. However, before you get into the details of how to do this, you first need to understand the concept of reflection, which will be explored in the following section.

REFLECTION

The concept of decorating your code is tightly coupled with a concept called **reflection**. In a nutshell, reflection is the capability of a certain piece of code to examine and be introspective about itself – in a sense, to do some navel-gazing. It means that a piece of code can have access to things such as the variables, functions, and classes defined inside it. Most languages provide us with some kind of reflection API that enables us to treat the code itself as if it was data, and since TypeScript is built upon JavaScript, it inherits the JavaScript reflection capabilities.

JavaScript does not have an extensive reflection API, but there is a proposal (https://tc39.es/ecma262/#sec-reflection) to add proper metadata (data about data) support to the language.

SETTING UP COMPILER OPTIONS

TypeScript's decorators use the aforementioned proposed feature, and in order to use them, you have to enable the TypeScript compiler (**tsc**) accordingly. As covered in the preface, there are two ways to do this. You can either add the necessary flags on the command line when you invoke **tsc** or you can configure the necessary options inside the **tsconfig.json** file.

There are two flags concerning decorators. The first one, **experimentalDecorators**, is needed to use decorators at all. If you have a file where you're using a decorator and try to compile it without specifying it, you get the following error:

```
tsc --target es2015 .\decorator-example.ts


decorator-example.ts:18:5 - error TS1219:
  Experimental support for decorators is a feature
  that is subject to change in a future release.
  Set the 'experimentalDecorators' option in your 'tsconfig' or
  'jsconfig' to remove this warning.
```

If you specify the flag, you can compile successfully:

```
tsc --experimentalDecorators --target es2015
   .\decorator-example.ts
```

In order to avoid specifying the flags all the time, add the following flags in the **tsconfig.json** file:

```
{
  "compilerOptions": {
    "target": "ES2015",
    "experimentalDecorators": true,
    "emitDecoratorMetadata": true,
  }
}
```

> **NOTE**
>
> Before you begin executing the examples, exercises, and activities, we suggest that you make sure the preceding complier options have been enabled in your **tsconfig.json** file. Alternatively, you can use the file provided here: https://packt.link/hoeVy.

IMPORTANCE OF DECORATORS

So, now you're ready to start decorating. But why would you want to do that? Let's run through a simple example that mimics the real-world scenarios you will be encountering later. Let's say that you are building a simple class that will encapsulate the score for a basketball game:

Example_Basketball.ts

```
1   interface Team {
2       score: number;
3       name: string;
4   }
5
6   class BasketBallGame {
7       private team1: Team;
8       private team2: Team;
9
10      constructor(teamName1: string, teamName2: string) {
11          this.team1 = { score: 0, name: teamName1 };
12          this.team2 = { score: 0, name: teamName2 };
13      }
14
15      getScore() {
```

```
16            return `${this.team1.score}:${this.team2.score}`;
17        }
18 }
19
20 const game = new BasketBallGame("LA Lakers", "Boston Celtics");
```

Link to the preceding example: https://packt.link/ORdNI.

Our class has two teams, each of which has a name and a numerical score. You're initializing your team in the class constructor, and you have a method that will provide the current score. However, you don't have a method that will update the score. Let's add one:

```
updateScore(byPoints: number, updateTeam1: boolean) {
    if (updateTeam1) {
        this.team1.score += byPoints;
    } else {
        this.team2.score += byPoints;
    }
}
```

This method accepts the number of points to add and a Boolean. If the Boolean is **true**, you're updating the first team's score, and if it's **false**, you're updating the second team's score. You can take your class for a spin, as here:

```
const game = new BasketBallGame("LA Lakers", "Boston Celtics");

game.updateScore(3, true);
game.updateScore(2, false);
game.updateScore(2, true);
game.updateScore(2, false);
game.updateScore(2, false);
game.updateScore(2, true);
game.updateScore(2, false);

console.log(game.getScore());
```

This code will show us that the Lakers are losing **7 : 8** against the Celtics (*Game 7 of the 2010 finals, if anyone wants to know*).

THE PROBLEM OF CROSS-CUTTING CONCERNS

So far so good, and your class is fully operational – as far as its own functionalities are concerned. However, as your class will be living within a whole application, you have other concerns as well. One of those concerns is authorization – will just anyone be able to update the score? Of course not, as the common use case is that you have a single person that is allowed to update the score and multiple people, maybe millions, that just watch the score change.

Let's add that concern to the code using a hypothetical function, **isAuthorized**, that will check whether the current user is actually authorized to change the score. You will call this function and if it returns **true**, we'll continue with the regular logic of the method. If it returns **false**, then we'll just issue an appropriate message. The code will look like this:

```
updateScore(byPoints: number, updateTeam1: boolean) {
    if (isAuthorized()) {
        if (updateTeam1) {
            this.team1.score += byPoints;
        } else {
            this.team2.score += byPoints;
        }
    } else {
        console.log("You're not authorized to change the score");
    }
}
```

Again, this will work nicely, albeit increasing the code size of your method from five lines of code to nine lines of code and adding some complexity. And, to be honest, the added lines are not really relevant to counting the score, but they had to be added in order to support authorization.

So, is that it? Of course not. Even if you know that somebody is authorized, it does not mean that your operator will be able to update the score whenever they want. The auditor will need detailed information of when and with what parameters the **updateScore** method was called. No problem, let's add that as well using a hypothetical function called **audit**. And you'll also need to add some verification for whether the **byPoints** parameter is a legal value (in basketball, you can only have 1-, 2-, or 3-point increments). And you could add some code that logs the performance of the method in order to have a trace of how long it takes to execute. So, your nice, clear, five-line method will become a 17-line monstrosity:

```
updateScore(byPoints: number, updateTeam1: boolean) {
    audit("updateScore", byPoints, updateTeam1);
    const start = Date.now();
    if (isAuthorized()) {
        if (validatePoints(byPoints)) {
            if (updateTeam1) {
                this.team1.score += byPoints;
            } else {
                this.team2.score += byPoints;
            }
        } else {
            console.log(`Invalid point value ${byPoints}`);
        }
    } else {
        console.log("You're not authorized to change the score");
    }
    const end = Date.now();
    logDuration("updateScore", start, end);
}
```

And inside all that complexity, you still have your simple and clear piece of logic that if the Boolean is **true**, will update the Lakers' score, and if it's **false**, will update the Celtics' score.

The important part here is that the added complexity does not come from your specific business model – the basketball game still works the same. All the added functionalities stem from the system in which the class lives. The basketball game, by itself, does not need authorization, or performance metrics, or auditing. But the scoreboard application does need all of those and more.

Note that all the added logic is already encapsulated within methods (**audit**, **isAuthorized**, **logDuration**), and the code that actually performs all the aforementioned operations is outside your method. The code you inserted into your function does the bare minimum – yet it still complicated your code.

In addition, authorization, performance metrics, and auditing will be needed in many places within your application, and in none of those places will that code be instrumental to the actual working of the code that is being authorized or measured or audited.

THE SOLUTION

Let's take a better look at one of the concerns from the previous section, the performance metric, that is, the duration measurement. This is something that is very important to an application, and to add it to any specific method, you need a few lines of code at the beginning and a few lines at the end of the method:

```
const start = Date.now();
// actual code of the method
const end = Date.now();
logDuration("updateScore", start, end);
```

We'll need to add this to each and every method you need to measure. It's very repetitive code, and each time you write it in, you're opening the possibility of doing it slightly wrong. Moreover, if you need to change it, that is, by adding a parameter to the **logDuration** method, you'll need to change hundreds, if not thousands, of call sites.

In order to avoid that kind of risk, what you can do is to wrap the actual code of the method inside some other function that will still call it. That function might look something like this:

```
function wrapWithDuration(method: Function) {
    const result = {
        [method.name]: function (this: any, ...args: any[]) {
            const start = Date.now();
            const result = method.apply(this, args);
            const end = Date.now();
            logDuration(method.name, start, end);
            return result;
        },
    };
    return result[method.name];
}
```

The **wrapWithDuration** function (whose details you can ignore for now) will take a method and return a function that has the following:

* The same **this** reference
* The same method name

- The same signature (parameters and return type)

- All the behavior that the original method has

- Extended behavior as it will measure the duration of the actual method

Since it will actually call the original method, when looking from outside, the new function is totally indistinguishable from the original. You have added some behavior while keeping everything that already was. Now, you can replace the original method with the new improved one.

What you will get with this approach is this: the original method won't know or care about the cross-cutting concerns of the application, instead focusing on its own business logic – the application can "upgrade" the method at runtime with one that has all the necessary business logic as well as all the required additions.

This kind of transparent "upgrade" is often termed a **decoration**, and the method that does the decorating is called a **decorator** method.

What has been shown here is just one form that a decoration can take. There can be as many solutions as there are developers, and none of them will be simple and straightforward. Some standards should be put in place, and the TypeScript design team decided to use the proposed JavaScript syntax.

The rest of the chapter will use that syntax, and you can ignore the solution given here.

DECORATORS AND DECORATOR FACTORIES

As we've seen so far, decorators are just special wrapping functions that add behavior to your regular methods, classes, and properties. What's special about them is how they can be used in TypeScript. TypeScript supports the following decorator types:

- **Class decorators**: These are attached to a class declaration.

- **Method decorators**: These are attached to a method declaration.

- **Accessor decorators**: These are attached to a declaration of an accessor of a property.

- **Property decorators**: These are attached to a property itself.

- **Parameter decorators**: These are attached to a single parameter in a method declaration.

And consequently, there are five different places where you can use decorators, so that means that there are five different kinds of special functions that can be used to decorate your code. All of them are shown in the following example:

```
@ClassDecorator
class SampleClass {

    @PropertyDecorator
    public sampleProperty:number = 0;

    private _sampleField: number = 0;

    @AccessorDecorator
    public get sampleField() { return this._sampleField; }

    @MethodDecorator
    public sampleMethod(@ParameterDecorator paramName: string) {}

}
```

The sample decorators are functions that are defined as follows:

```
function ClassDecorator (constructor: Function) {}

function AccessorDecorator (target: any, propertyName: string,
descriptor: PropertyDescriptor) {}

function MethodDecorator (target: any, propertyName: string, descriptor:
PropertyDescriptor) {}

function PropertyDecorator (target: any, propertyName: string) {}

function ParameterDecorator (target: any, propertyName: string,
parameterIndex: number) {}
```

DECORATOR SYNTAX

The syntax for adding a decorator to an item is that you have to use the special symbol @ followed by the name of the decorators. The decorator is placed before the code that it decorates, so in the preceding example, you have performed the following decorations:

- **@ClassDecorator** is immediately before the **SampleClass** class and is a class decorator.

- **@PropertyDecorator** is immediately before the **public sampleProperty** and is a property decorator.

- **@AccessorDecorator** is immediately before the **public get sampleField()** and is a **get** accessor decorator.

- **@MethodDecorator** is immediately before the **public sampleMethod()** and is a method decorator.

- **@ParameterDecorator** is immediately before **paramName: string** and is a parameter decorator.

While the decorators themselves are regular functions, it's conventional that the names use **PascalCase** instead of **lowerCamelCase**.

> **NOTE**
>
> For more information on **PascalCase** and **lowerCamelCase**, visit
> https://techterms.com/definition/camelcase and https://techterms.com/definition/pascalcase.

DECORATOR FACTORIES

You can see that you did not specify any parameters for the set of sample decorators in the previous section, yet the decorator function takes between one and three parameters. Those parameters are handled by TypeScript itself and are provided automatically when your code runs. This means that there is no way to configure your decorators directly, for example, by passing additional parameters.

Fortunately, you can use a construct called **decorator factories** to accomplish that. When decorating, when TypeScript encounters the @ symbol specifying a decorator, it will evaluate the expression that follows. So, instead of providing the name of a function that fits the special decorator requirements, you can provide an expression that will evaluate to such a function. In other words, decorator factories are simply higher-order functions that will return a decorator function.

For example, let's create a simple function that will take a message as a parameter and log a message to the console. The return value of that function, whose input parameters do not conform to the class decorator signature, will be another function, whose input parameters do conform to the class decorator signature. The resulting function will also simply log the message to the console as well. Consider the following code:

`Example_Decorator_Factory.ts`

```
1 function ClassDecoratorFactory(message: string) {
2     console.log(`${message} inside factory`);
3     return function (constructor: Function) {
4       console.log(`${message} inside decorator`);
5     };
6 }
```

Link to the preceding example: https://packt.link/M2lxp.

In essence, the **ClassDecoratorFactory** function is not a decorator, but its return value is. This means that you cannot use **ClassDecoratorFactory** as a decorator itself, but if you call it, for example, **ClassDecoratorFactory("Hi")**, that value will indeed be a decorator. You can use that to decorate a couple of classes using this syntax. The following example will help you understand this much better:

```
@ClassDecoratorFactory("Hi")
class DecoratedOne {}
```

```
@ClassDecoratorFactory("Hello")
class DecoratedTwo {}
```

Here, instead of using an expression such as @**ClassDecorator** as before, you use @**ClassDecoratorFactory("hi")** or @ **ClassDecoratorFactory("hello")**. Since the result of the execution of the **ClassDecoratorFactory** function is a class decorator, this is operational, and the decorators successfully decorate the code. You will see the following output when you run your code:

```
Hi inside factory
Hi inside decorator
Hello inside factory
Hello inside decorator
```

Note that most decorators that you will use and make will in essence be decorator factories, as it's extremely useful to add parameters when decorating. Most sources and even some documentation will not differentiate between the terms.

CLASS DECORATORS

A class decorator is a decorator function that is applied to the whole class. It can be used to observe, change, or replace wholesale a class definition. When a class decorator is called, it receives a single parameter – the constructor function of the calling class.

PROPERTY INJECTION

Property injection is one of the common scenarios that class decorations are used for. For example, let's say you're building a system that will model a school. You will have a class called **Teacher** that will have the properties and model the behavior of a teacher. The constructor for this class will take two parameters, an **id** number of the teacher, and the **name** of the teacher. This is how the class will look:

```
class Teacher {
    constructor (public id: number, public name: string) {}
    // other teacher specific code
}
```

Let's say we build the system and it's up and running. Everything is great, but after a while, it's time to update it.

We want to implement an access control system using tokens. Since the new system is not related to the teaching process, it is much better to add it without changing the code of the class itself, so you can use a decorator for this, and your decorator can inject an extra Boolean property to the prototype of the **Teacher** class. The **Teacher** class can be changed in the following way:

Example_PropertyInjection.ts

```
1 @Token
2 class Teacher {
3     // old teacher specific code
4 }
```

The **Token** decorator can be defined with the following:

```
5 function Token (constructor: Function) {
6     constructor.prototype.token = true;
7 }
```

Now, consider the following code, which creates instances of the class and prints a message:

```
8 const teacher = new Teacher(1, "John Smith");
9 console.log("Does the teacher have a token? ",teacher["token"]);
```

Running all this code will give the following result on the console:

```
Does the teacher have a token? true
```

Link to the preceding example: https://packt.link/asjvA.

In the injection scenario, you use the provided **constructor** parameter but do not return anything from your function. In this case, the class continues working as it did before. Usually, we'll be using the prototype of the constructor to add fields and properties to the object.

> **NOTE**
>
> For all exercises and activities in this chapter, before executing the code file, you need to install all dependencies using **npm i** in the target directory. Then, you can execute the file by running **npx ts-node 'filename'** in the target directory.

EXERCISE 7.01: CREATING A SIMPLE CLASS DECORATOR FACTORY

In this exercise, you will be creating a simple decorator factory for the **Token** decorator. Starting from the **Teacher** class code, we'll create a class called **Student** that will need to be decorated using the **Token** decorator. We'll extend the decorator to take a parameter, and decorate both classes using the created decorator factory.

The following steps will help you with the solution:

> **NOTE**
>
> Before you begin, make sure you have set up the correct compiler options as mentioned in the *Setting Up Compiler Options* section. The code file for this exercise can also be downloaded from https://packt.link/UpdO9. This repository contains two files: **school-token.start.ts** and **school-token.end.ts**. The former contains the code up to *step 6* of this exercise, and the latter contains the final code of the exercise.

1. Open Visual Studio Code, create a new file in a new directory (**Exercise01**), and save it as **school-token.ts**.

2. Enter the following code in **school-token.ts**:

```
@Token
class Teacher {
    constructor (public id: number, public name: string) {}
    // teacher specific code
}

function Token (constructor: Function) {
    constructor.prototype.token = true;
}



/////////////////////////////
const teacher = new Teacher(1, "John Smith");
console.log("Does the teacher have a token? ",teacher["token"]);
```

3. Execute the code, and notice that it outputs **true** to the console.

4. Add a **Student** class at the end of the file:

```
class Student {
    constructor (public id: number, public name: string) {}
    // student specific code
}
```

5. Add code that creates a student and tries to print its **token** property:

```
const student = new Student(101, "John Bender");
console.log("Does the student have a token? ",student["token"]);
```

6. Execute the code, and notice that it outputs **true** and **undefined** to the console.

7. Add the **Token** decorator to the **Student** class:

```
@Token
class Student {//...
```

8. Execute the code, and notice that it outputs **true** twice to the console.

9. Change the **Token** function to a factory function that takes a Boolean parameter:

```
function Token(hasToken: boolean) {
    return function (constructor: Function) {
        constructor.prototype.token = hasToken;
    }
}
```

10. Modify the **Teacher** class **Token** decorator to have a **true** Boolean parameter:

```
@Token(true)
class Teacher {//...
```

11. Modify the **Student** class **Token** decorator to have a **false** Boolean parameter:

```
@Token(false)
class Student {//...
```

12. Execute the code by running **npx ts-node school-token.ts** on the console, and notice that it outputs **true** and **false** to the console as shown:

```
Does the teacher have a token?   true
Does the student have a token?   false
```

In this exercise, you saw how to add a class decorator that adds a property to a decorated class. You then changed the decorator to use a factory and added two different parameters for two decorated classes. At the end, you verified that the injected properties exist on the decorated classes via the prototype chain and that they have the values you specified.

CONSTRUCTOR EXTENSION

Using property injection enabled you to add behaviors and data to the objects you decorate using their prototypes. That is OK, but sometimes you might want to add data to the constructed objects themselves. You can accomplish this with inheritance, but you can also wrap the inheritance with a decorator.

If you return a function from the decorator, that function will be used as a replacement constructor for the class. While this gives you the superpower to change the class completely, the main goal of this approach is to enable you to augment the class with some new behaviors or data, so let's use automatic inheritance to add properties to the class. A decorator that will add the **token** property not on the prototype but on the constructed objects themselves would look like this:

```
type Constructable = {new(...args: any[]):{}};

function Token(hasToken: boolean) {
    return function <T extends Constructable>(constructor: T) {
        return class extends constructor {
            token: boolean = hasToken;
        }
    }
}
```

The syntax for doing that looks a bit strange at first, as you are using a generic parameter to make sure that the class you return from your decorator will still be compatible with the constructor that was passed as a parameter. Aside from the syntax, the important part to remember is that the code **token: boolean = hasToken;** will be executed in addition to the regular constructor.

EXERCISE 7.02: USING A CONSTRUCTOR EXTENSION DECORATOR

In this exercise, you will be creating a constructor extension decorator factory for the **Token** decorator. Starting from the **Teacher** class code, we'll add a token factory called **Token** that will augment the class by adding a **token** Boolean property. We'll create an object of the provided class and verify that the object indeed has its own **token** property. The following steps will help you with the solution:

> ### NOTE
>
> Before you begin, make sure you have set up the correct compiler options as mentioned in the *Setting Up Compiler Options* section. The code file for this exercise can also be downloaded from https://packt.link/DhVfC. This repository contains two files: **school-token.start.ts** and **school-token.end.ts**. The former contains the code up to *step 3* of this exercise, and the latter contains the final code of the exercise.

1. Open Visual Studio Code, create a new file in a new directory (**Exercise02**), and save it as **school-token.ts**.

2. Enter the following code in **school-token.ts**:

```
class Teacher {
    constructor (public id: number, public name: string) {}
    // teacher specific code
}

/////////////////////////////
const teacher = new Teacher(1, "John Smith");
console.log("Do you have a token:", teacher["token"]);
console.log("Do you have a token property: ", teacher.
hasOwnProperty("token"));
```

3. Execute the code, and notice that it outputs **undefined** and **false** to the console:

```
Do we have a token: undefined
Do we have a token property:   false
```

4. Add a **Token** function at the end of the file:

```
type Constructable = {new(...args: any[]):{}};

function Token(hasToken: boolean) {
    return function <T extends Constructable>(constructor: T) {
        return class extends constructor {
            token: boolean = hasToken;
        }
    }
}
```

5. Decorate the **Teacher** class using the **Token** decorator factory:

```
@Token(true)
class Teacher {
```

6. Execute the code, and notice that it outputs **true** twice to the console:

```
Do we have a token: true
Do we have a token property:   true
```

In this exercise, you saw how to change the provided class constructor to run custom code while instantiating an object. You used that to inject a property on the constructed object itself, and then you verified that the injected properties exist on objects of the decorated class and that they have the value you specified.

CONSTRUCTOR WRAPPING

Another common scenario for class decorators is the need to just run some code when an instance of a class is being created, for example, to add some logging when an instance of a class is created. You do not need or want to change the class behavior in any way, but you do want to be able to somehow piggyback on the process. This means that you need to execute some code whenever a class constructor is being run – you don't need to change the existing constructor.

In this case, the solution is to have the decorator function return a new constructor that executes the new code needed by the decorator itself as well as the original constructor. For example, if you want to write some text to the console each time you instantiate a decorated class, you can use this decorator:

Example_ConstructorWrapping.ts

```
1   type Constructable = { new (...args: any[]): {} };
2
3   function WrapConstructor(message: string) {
4       return function <T extends Constructable>(constructor: T) {
5           const wrappedConstructor: any = function (...args: any[]) {
6               console.log(`Decorating ${message}`);
7               const result = new constructor(...args);
8               console.log(`Decorated ${message}`);
9               return result;
10          };
11          wrappedConstructor.prototype = constructor.prototype;
12          return wrappedConstructor;
13      };
14  }
```

Link to the preceding example: https://packt.link/kgAme.

This decorator factory will generate a decorator using a provided message. Since you're returning a new constructor, you have to use a generic parameter to make sure that the constructor you return from your decorator will still be compatible with the constructor that was passed as a parameter. You can create a new **wrappedConstructor** function within which you can both call custom code (the **Decorating** and **Decorated** messages) and actually create the object by calling **new** on the original constructor, passing in the original arguments.

You should note the following here: it's possible to add custom code both pre- and post-creation of the object. In the preceding example, the **Decorating** message will be printed to the console before the object is created, while the **Decorated** message will be printed to the console after the creation is finished.

Another very important thing is that this kind of wrapping breaks the prototype chain of the original object. If the object you decorate thus uses any properties or methods that were available through the prototype chain, they would be missing, changing the behavior of the decorated class. Since that is exactly the opposite of what you wanted to achieve with constructor wrapping, you need to reset the chain. That is done by setting the **prototype** property of the newly created wrapper function to the prototype of the original constructor.

So, let's use a decorator on a client class, like this:

```
@WrapConstructor("decorator")
class Teacher {
    constructor(public id: number, public name: string) {
        console.log("Constructing a teacher class instance");
    }
}
```

Next, you can create an object of the **Teacher** class:

```
const teacher = new Teacher(1, "John");
```

When you run the file, you will see the following written to the console:

```
Decorating decorator
Constructing a teacher class instance
Decorated decorator
```

EXERCISE 7.03: CREATING A LOGGING DECORATOR FOR A CLASS

In this exercise, you'll be creating a constructor wrapping decorator factory for the **LogClass** decorator. Starting from the **Teacher** class code, you'll add a decorator factory called **LogClass** that will wrap the class constructor with some logging code. You'll create an object of the provided class and verify that the logging methods are actually called. The following steps will help you with the solution:

> **NOTE**
>
> Before you begin, make sure you have set up the correct compiler options as mentioned in the *Setting Up Compiler Options section*. The code file for this exercise can also be downloaded from https://packt.link/vBLMg.

1. Open Visual Studio Code, create a new file in a new directory (**Exercise03**), and save it as **teacher-logging.ts**.

2. Enter the following code in **teacher-logging.ts**:

```
class Teacher {
    constructor(public id: number, public name: string) {
        console.log("Constructing a teacher");
    }
}
```

```
    }
    /////////////////////////
    const teacher = new Teacher(1, "John Smith");
```

3. Execute the code, and notice that it outputs **Constructing a teacher** to the console.

4. Next, create the decorator. First, you need to add the **Constructable** type definition:

```
    type Constructable = { new (...args: any[]): {} };
```

5. Now, add a definition of your decorator factory:

```
    function LogClass(message: string) {
        return function <T extends Constructable>(constructor: T) {
            return constructor;
        };
    }
```

In the preceding code, the constructor takes in a string parameter and returns a decorator function. The decorator function itself will initially just return the original, unchanged constructor of the decorated class.

6. Decorate the **Teacher** class using the **LogClass** decorator with an appropriate message parameter:

```
    @LogClass("Teacher decorator")
    class Teacher {
        constructor(public id: number, public name: string) {
            console.log("Constructing a teacher");
        }
    }
```

7. Execute the code, and notice that there are no changes to the behavior.

8. Now, add a logger object to your application:

```
    const logger = {
        info: (message: string) => {
            console.log(`[INFO]: ${message}`);
        },
    };
```

In actual production-grade code implementation, you might log to a database, a file, a third-party service, and so on. In the preceding step, you are simply logging to the console.

9. Next, use the **logger** object to add a wrapping constructor to your decorator:

```
return function <T extends Constructable>(constructor: T) {
    const loggingConstructor: any = function(...args: any[]){
        logger.info(message);
        return new constructor(...args);
    }
    loggingConstructor.prototype = constructor.prototype;
    return loggingConstructor;
};
```

10. Execute the code and verify that you get a logging message to the console:

```
[INFO]: Teacher decorator
Constructing a teacher
```

11. Construct a few more objects and verify that the constructor runs each time an object is created:

```
for (let index = 0; index < 10; index++) {
    const teacher = new Teacher(index +1, "LouAnne Johnson");
}
```

You'll see the following output when you execute the file:

```
[INFO]: Teacher decorator
Constructing a teacher
[INFO]: Teacher decorator
Constructing a teacher
[INFO]: Teacher decorator
Constructing a teacher
[INFO]: Teacher decorator
Constructing a teacher
[INFO]: Teacher decorator
Constructing a teacher
[INFO]: Teacher decorator
Constructing a teacher
[INFO]: Teacher decorator
Constructing a teacher
```

In this exercise, you saw how to wrap the provided class constructor so that it can run custom code, but without changing the construction of the objects. Through wrapping, you added logging capabilities to a class that did not have any. You constructed objects of that class and verified that the logging functionality was operational.

METHOD AND ACCESSOR DECORATORS

A method decorator is a decorator function that is applied to a single method of a class. In a method decorator, you can observe, modify, or outright replace a method definition with one provided by the decorator. When a method decorator is called, it receives three parameters: **target**, **propertyKey**, and **descriptor**:

- **target**: Since methods can be both instance methods (defined on instances of the class) and static methods (defined on the class itself), **target** can be two different things. For instance methods, it's the prototype of the class. For static methods, it's the constructor function of the class. Usually, you type this parameter as **any**.

- **propertyKey**: This is the name of the method you're decorating.

- **descriptor**: This is the property descriptor of the method you're decorating. The **PropertyDescriptor** interface is defined with this:

```
interface PropertyDescriptor {
    configurable?: boolean;
    enumerable?: boolean;
    value?: any;
    writable?: boolean;
    get?(): any;
    set?(v: any): void;
}
```

This interface defines the value of an object property, as well as the property's properties (whether the property is configurable, enumerable, and writable). We'll also be using a typed version of this interface, **TypedPropertyDescriptor**, which is defined as shown:

```
interface TypedPropertyDescriptor<T> {
    enumerable?: boolean;
    configurable?: boolean;
    writable?: boolean;
```

```
    value?: T;
    get?: () => T;
    set?: (value: T) => void;
}
```

Note that, in JavaScript, and subsequently TypeScript, property accessors are just special methods that manage access to a property. Everything that is applicable to decorating methods is also applicable to decorating accessors. Any accessor specifics will be covered separately.

If you set up a decorator on a method, we'll be getting the **PropertyDescriptor** instance of the method itself, and the **value** property of the descriptor will give us access to its body. If you set up a decorator on an accessor, we'll be getting the **PropertyDescriptor** instance of the corresponding property, with its **get** and **set** properties respectively set to the getter and setter accessors. This means that if you're decorating property accessors, you don't have to separately decorate the getter and the setter, as any decoration of one is a decoration on the other. In fact, TypeScript will issue the following error if you do so:

```
TS1207: Decorators cannot be applied to multiple get/set accessors of the
same name.
```

The method decorators do not have to return a value, as most of the time you can do the desired actions by modifying the property descriptor. If you do return a value, however, that value will replace the originally provided property descriptor.

DECORATORS ON INSTANCE FUNCTIONS

As described in the preceding section, any function that takes the **target**, **propertyKey**, and **descriptor** parameters can be used to decorate methods and property accessors. So, let's have a function that will simply log the **target**, **propertyKey**, and **descriptor** parameters to the console:

Example_Decorators_Instance_Functions.ts

```
1 function DecorateMethod(target: any, propertyName: string,
2 descriptor: PropertyDescriptor) {
3     console.log("Target is:", target);
4     console.log("Property name is:", propertyName);
5     console.log("Descriptor is:", descriptor);
6 }
```

Link to the preceding example: https://packt.link/gle5U.

You can use this function to decorate a class' methods. This is an extremely simple decorator, but you can use it to investigate the usage of method decorators.

Let's start with a simple class:

```
class Teacher {
    constructor (public name: string){}

    private _title: string = "";

    public get title() {
        return this._title;
    }

    public set title(value: string) {
        this._title = value;
    }

    public teach() {
        console.log(`${this.name} is teaching`)
    }
}
```

The class has a constructor, a method called **teach**, and a **title** property with a defined getter and setter. The accessors simply pass through control to the **_title** private field. You can add the decorator to the **teach** methods using the following code:

```
@DecorateMethod
public teach() {
    // ....
```

When you run your code (no need to instantiate the class), you'll get the following output on the console:

```
Target is: {}
Property name is: teach
Descriptor is: {
    value: [Function: teach],
    writable: true,
    enumerable: false,
    configurable: true
}
```

Consider the following snippets in which you apply the decorator to the setter or getter (either one will work fine, but not both):

```
@DecorateMethod
public get title() {
    // ....
```

Or:

```
@DecorateMethod
public set title(value: string) {
    // ....
```

You will get the following output when you run the code using either of the preceding suggestions:

```
Target is: {}
Property name is: title
Descriptor is: {
    get: [Function: get title],
    set: [Function: set title],
    enumerable: false,
    configurable: true
}
```

Note that you cannot add a method decorator on the constructor itself, as you will get an error:

```
TS1206: Decorators are not valid here.
```

If you need to change the behavior of the constructor, you should use class decorators.

EXERCISE 7.04: CREATING A DECORATOR THAT MARKS A FUNCTION ENUMERABLE

In this exercise, you will create a decorator that will be able to change the **enumerable** state of the methods and accessors that it decorates. You will use this decorator to set the **enumerable** state of some functions in a class that you'll write, and finally, you'll verify that when you enumerate the properties of the object instance, you get the modified methods as well.

> **NOTE**
>
> Before you begin, make sure you have set up the correct compiler options as mentioned in the *Setting Up Compiler Options* section. The code file for this exercise can also be downloaded from https://packt.link/1nAff. This repository contains two files: **teacher-enumerating.start.ts** and **teacher-enumerating.end.ts**. The former contains the code up to *step 5* of this exercise, and the latter contains the final code of the exercise.

1. Open Visual Studio Code, create a new file in a new directory (**Exercise04**), and save it as **teacher-enumerating.ts**.

2. Enter the following code in **teacher-enumerating.ts**:

```
class Teacher {
    constructor (public name: string){}

    private _title: string = "";

    public get title() {
        return this._title;
    }

    public set title(value: string) {
        this._title = value;
    }

    public teach() {
        console.log(`${this.name} is teaching`)
    }
}
```

3. Write code that will instantiate an object of this class:

```
const teacher = new Teacher("John Smith");
```

4. Write code that will enumerate all the keys in the created object:

```
for (const key in teacher) {
    console.log(key);
}
```

5. Execute the file and verify that the only keys that are displayed on the console are **name** and **_title**.

6. Add a decorator factory that takes a Boolean parameter and generates a method decorator that will set the **enumerable** status to the provided parameter:

```
function Enumerable(value: boolean) {
    return function (target: any, propertyName: string, descriptor:
PropertyDescriptor) {
        descriptor.enumerable = value;
    }
};
```

7. Use the decorator to decorate the **title** getter or setter accessors and the **teach** method:

```
    @Enumerable(true)
    public get title() {
        return this._title;
    }

    public set title(value: string) {
        this._title = value;
    }

    @Enumerable(true)
    public teach() {
        console.log(`${this.name} is teaching`)
    }
```

8. Rerun the code and verify that the **title** and **teach** properties are being enumerated:

```
name
_title
title
teach
```

In this exercise, you saw how to add a create a method decorator factory and how to apply it to an instance method or an instance property accessor. You learned how to make a property enumerable, and you used that knowledge to set the **enumerable** state of the functions of a class. Finally, you enumerated all the properties of a class.

DECORATORS ON STATIC FUNCTIONS

Just like with instance methods, decorators can be used with static methods as well. You add a static method to your **Teacher** class like this:

Example_Decorator_StaticFunctions.ts

```
1 class Teacher {
2     //.....
3
4     public static showUsage() {
5         console.log("This is the Teacher class")
6     }
7     //.....
```

Link to the preceding example https://packt.link/Ckuct.

We are allowed to use method decorators on the static methods as well. So, you can add the **DecorateMethod** decorator using the following code:

```
@DecorateMethod
public static showUsage() {
    //......
```

When you run the code, you will get output similar to this:

```
Target is: [Function: Teacher]
Property name is: showUsage
Descriptor is: {
  value: [Function: showUsage],
  writable: true,
  enumerable: false,
  configurable: true
}
```

The principal difference with the instance methods is the **target** parameter. Instance methods and accessors are generated on the class prototype, and consequently, when using a method/accessor decorator, you receive the class prototype as a **target** parameter. Static methods and accessors are generated on the class variable itself, and consequently, when using a method/accessor decorator, you receive the class variable in the guise of the constructor function as a **target** parameter.

Note that this is the exact same object that you're getting as a class decorator parameter. You can even use it in much the same way. However, in method decorators, the focus should be on the actual property we've decorated. It is considered a bad practice to manipulate the constructor inside a non-class decorator.

METHOD WRAPPING DECORATORS

The most common usage of method decorators is to use it to wrap the original method, adding some custom cross-cutting code. Examples would be adding some general error handling or adding automatic logging capabilities.

In order to do that, you need to change the function that is being called. You can do that using the **value** property of method property descriptors, and by using the **get** and **set** properties of the property accessor descriptors.

EXERCISE 7.05: CREATING A LOGGING DECORATOR FOR A METHOD

In this exercise, you'll be creating a decorator that will log each time a decorated method or accessor is called. You will use this decorator to add logging to the **Teacher** class and you'll verify that each time you use the decorated methods and property accessors, you get an appropriate log entry:

> **NOTE**
>
> Before you begin, make sure you have set up the correct compiler options as mentioned in the *Setting Up Compiler Options* section. The code file for this exercise can also be downloaded from https://packt.link/rmEZi.

1. Open Visual Studio Code, create a new file in a new directory (**Exercise05**), and save it as **teacher-logging.ts**.

2. Enter the following code in **teacher-logging.ts**:

```
class Teacher {
    constructor (public name: string){}

    private _title: string = "";

    public get title() {
        return this._title;
    }
}
```

```
        public set title(value: string) {
            this._title = value;
        }

        public teach() {
            console.log(`${this.name} is teaching`)
        }
    }

    ////////////////
    const teacher = new Teacher("John Smith");
    teacher.teach(); // we're invoking the teach method
    teacher.title = "Mr." // we're invoking the title setter
    console.log(`${teacher.title} ${teacher.name}`); // we're invoking
    the title getter
```

3. Execute the code, and notice that it outputs **John Smith is teaching** and **Mr. John Smith** to the console.

4. Create a method decorator factory that can wrap any method, getter or setter, with a logging statement. It will take a string parameter and return a decorator function. Initially, you won't make any changes to the property descriptor:

```
function LogMethod(message: string) {
    return function (target: any, propertyName: string, descriptor:
    PropertyDescriptor) {
    };
}
```

5. Decorate the **teach** method and the **title** get accessor using the **LogMethod** decorator with an appropriate message parameter:

```
    @LogMethod("Title property")
    public get title() {
    //...

    @LogMethod("Teach method")
    public teach() {
    //...
```

6. Execute the code, and notice that there are no changes to the behavior.

7. Now, add a **logger** object to your application:

```
const logger = {
    info: (message: string) => {
        console.log(`[INFO]: ${message}`);
    },
};
```

In an actual production-grade implementation, you might log to a database, a file, a third-party service, and so on. In the preceding step, you are simply logging to the console.

8. Add code to the decorator factory that will wrap the property descriptors, **value**, **get**, and **set** properties (if they are present):

```
function LogMethod(message: string) {
    return function (target: any, propertyName: string, descriptor:
PropertyDescriptor) {
        if (descriptor.value) {
            const original = descriptor.value;
            descriptor.value = function (...args: any[]) {
                logger.info(`${message}: Method ${propertyName}
invoked`);
                // we're passing in the original arguments to the
method
                return original.apply(this, args);
            }
        }
        if (descriptor.get) {
            const original = descriptor.get;
            descriptor.get = function () {
                logger.info(`${message}: Getter for ${propertyName}
invoked`);
                // getter accessors do not take parameters
                return original.apply(this, []);
            }
        }
        if (descriptor.set) {
            const original = descriptor.set;
            descriptor.set = function (value: any) {
                logger.info(`${message}: Setter for ${propertyName}
invoked`);
```

```
                        // setter accessors take a single parameter, i.e. the
        value to be set
                        return original.apply(this, [value]);
                }
            }
        }
    }
```

9. Execute the code and verify that you get logging messages to the console when you call the method as well as when you use the **title** property:

```
[INFO]: Teach method: Method teach invoked
John Smith is teaching
[INFO]: Title property: Setter for title invoked
[INFO]: Title property: Getter for title invoked
Mr. John Smith
```

In this exercise, you saw how to wrap the provided definitions of methods and property accessors class in such a way that you could run custom code on every invocation without changing the behavior of the functions themselves. You used that to add logging capabilities to functions that did not have any. You constructed objects of that class and verified that the logging functionality is operational.

ACTIVITY 7.01: CREATING DECORATORS FOR CALL COUNTING

As a developer of a backend service for a website, you are tasked with creating a solution that will enable the operations department to have clear auditing on the behavior of the service. For that, the app is required to have a tally of all class instantiations and method invocations.

In this activity, you're going to create class and method decorators that can be used to count class instantiations and method invocations. You will create a class that contains data about a person and use the decorators to count how many such objects were created and how many times each method was called. After you have constructed several objects and used their properties, take a look at the values of the counters.

The aim of this activity is to demonstrate the uses of class and method decorators in order to address a cross-cutting concern of your application, without changing the functionality of the given class. You should have a detailed statistic of the life cycles of your objects, without adding any complexity to the business logic.

The following steps should help you with the solution:

> **NOTE**
>
> Before you begin, make sure you have set up the correct compiler options as mentioned in the *Setting Up Compiler Options* section. The code file for this activity can also be downloaded from https://packt.link/UK49t.

1. Create a class called **Person** with public properties named **firstName**, **lastName**, and **birthday**.

2. Add a constructor that initializes the properties via the constructor parameters.

3. Add a private field called **_title** and expose it via a getter and setter as a property called **title**.

4. Add a method called **getFullName** that will return the full name of a person.

5. Add a method called **getAge** that will return the current age of the person (by subtracting the birthday from the current year).

6. Create a global object called **count** and initialize it to the empty object. This will be your state variable, where you store the counts for every instantiation and invocation.

7. Create a constructor wrapping decorator factory called **CountClass** that will take a string parameter called **counterName**. We'll use that parameter as a key into the **count** object.

8. Inside the wrapping code, increase the **count** object's property defined in the **counterName** parameter by 1.

9. Don't forget to set the prototype chain of the wrapped constructor.

10. Create a method wrapping decorator factory called **CountMethod** that will take a string parameter called **counterName**.

11. Add checks for whether the **descriptor** parameter has **value**, **get**, and **set** properties. You need to cover both the cases where this decorator is used as an accessor and as a method decorator.

12. In each respective branch, add code that wraps the method.

13. Inside the wrapping code, increase the **count** object's property defined in the **counterName** parameter by 1.

14. Decorate the class using the **CountClass** decorator, with a **person** parameter.

15. Decorate **getFullName**, **getAge**, and the **title** property getter with the **CountMethod** decorator, using the **person-full-name**, **person-age**, and **person-title** parameters, respectively. Note that you need to decorate only one of the property accessors.

16. Write code outside the class that will instantiate three **person** objects.

17. Write code that will call the **getFullName** and **getAge** methods on the objects

18. Write code that will check whether the **title** property is empty and set it to something if it is.

19. Write code that will log the **count** object to the console in order to see if your decorators are running correctly.

The expected output is as follows:

```
{
    person: 3,
    "person-full-name": 3,
    "person-age": 3,
    "person-title": 6
}
```

This activity demonstrates the power of using decorators to extend and augment the capabilities of your classes without polluting the code. You were able to inject custom code execution into your objects, without changing any of the underlying business logic.

> **NOTE**
>
> The solution to the activity can be found on page 625.

USING METADATA IN DECORATORS

So far, you've been decorating classes and methods. These are basically pieces of code that get executed, and you have been able to change and augment the code that got executed. But your code consists not only of "active," live code, but of other definitions as well – in particular, your classes have fields, and your methods have parameters. In the activity before this section, you were able to detect whenever the `title` property was accessed because you had a method that was getting the value, and a method that was setting the value – so you piggybacked your code to the already existing "active" code. But how do you decorate the "passive" parts of your program? You cannot attach code that runs when your "passive" code gets executed, because frankly there's nothing to execute in `public firstName: string`. It's a simple definition.

You cannot attach any code that gets executed for your "passive code," but what you can do using decorators is add some data to some global object regarding the decorated "passive" piece of code. In *Activity 7.01: Creating Decorators for Call Counting*, you defined a global `count` object and used that in your decorators to keep track of the executions. That approach works, but it requires creating a global variable, which is bad in most cases. It would be much cleaner if you were able to define some kind of properties on the methods and classes themselves. But, on the other hand, you don't want to add too many properties that are available alongside the business logic code – the possibility of incidental error is too high. What you need is to be able to somehow add metadata to your classes and methods.

Fortunately, this is a common problem and there is a proposal to add proper metadata support to JavaScript. In the meantime, there is a polyfill library called **reflect-metadata** that can be used.

> **NOTE**
>
> For more information on the `reflect-metadata` library, visit https://www.npmjs.com/package/reflect-metadata.

What this library does, in essence, is attach a special property to your classes that gives us a place to store, retrieve, and work with metadata about your class.

In TypeScript, in order to use this feature, you have to specify an additional compiler flag, either via the command line or via **tsconfig.json**. That is the **emitDecoratorMetadata** flag, which needs to be set to **true** in order to work with the metadata methods.

REFLECT OBJECT

The API of the **reflect-metadata** library is straightforward, and mostly you can focus on the following methods:

- **Reflect.defineMetadata**: Defines a piece of metadata on a class or a method

- **Reflect.hasMetadata**: Returns a Boolean indicating whether a certain piece of metadata is present

- **Reflect.getMetadata**: Returns the actual piece of metadata, if present

Consider the following code:

```
class Teacher {
    constructor (public name: string){}

    private _title: string = "";

    public get title() {
        return this._title;
    }

    public set title(value: string) {
        this._title = value;
    }

    public teach() {
        console.log(`${this.name} is teaching`)
    }
}
```

Here you have a class called **Teacher** that has a simple private field, **_title**, which has **get** and **set** accessor methods for a property called **title**, and a method called **teach** that logs to the console that the teacher is, in fact, teaching.

You can define a metadata key called **call-count** on the **Teacher** class and set its value to **0** by executing the following call to **defineMetadata**:

```
Reflect.defineMetadata("call-count", 0, Teacher);
```

If you want to add a metadata key called **call-count**, not on the **Teacher** class itself but on the **teach** method, you could do so with the following call to **defineMetadata**:

```
Reflect.defineMetadata("call-count", 10, Teacher, "teach");
```

This will define a metadata key called **call-count** on the **Teacher** class' **teach** property and set its value to **10**. You can retrieve these values using the following commands:

```
Reflect.getMetadata("call-count", Teacher); // will return 0
Reflect.getMetadata("call-count", Teacher, "teach"); // will return 10
```

In essence, you can create a method that will register a call of a method with the following code:

```
function increaseCallCount(target: any, propertyKey: string) {
    if (Reflect.hasMetadata("call-count", target)) {
        const value = Reflect.getMetadata("call-count", target,
propertyKey);
        Reflect.defineMetadata("call-count", value+1, target, propertyKey)
    } else {
        Reflect.defineMetadata("call-count", 1, target, propertyKey)
    }
}
```

This code will first call the **hasMetadata** method, to check whether you have already defined a value for the **call-count** metadata. If that is **true**, the **hasMetadata** method will call **getMetadata** to get the current value and then call **defineMetadata** to re-define the metadata property with an increased (**value+1**) value. If you did not have such a metadata property, the **defineMetadata** method will define it with a value of 1.

When called with **increaseCallCount(Teacher, "teach")** ;, it will successfully increase the call count of the **teach** method of the **Teacher** class. The metadata added to the class will in no way hinder the behaviors that the class already has, so any code that is being executed won't be affected.

EXERCISE 7.06: ADDING METADATA TO METHODS VIA DECORATORS

In this exercise, we'll create a simple class and apply some metadata for describing its methods. After you have done this, you will write a function that given a class, will display its available descriptions:

> **NOTE**
>
> Before you begin, make sure you have set up the correct compiler options as mentioned in the *Setting Up Compiler Options* section. The code file for this exercise can also be downloaded from https://packt.link/JG4F8.

1. Open Visual Studio Code, create a new file in a new directory (**Exercise06**), and save it as **calculator-metadata.ts**.

2. Enter the following code in **calculator-metadata.ts**:

```
class Calculator {
    constructor (public first: number, public second: number) {}

    public add() {
        return this.first + this.second;
    }

    public subtract() {
        return this.first - this.second;
    }

    public multiply() {
        return this.first / this.second;
    }

    public divide() {
        return this.first / this.second;
    }
}
```

3. Next, add metadata descriptions for the class and some of its methods:

```
Reflect.defineMetadata("description", "A class that offers common
operations over two numbers", Calculator);
Reflect.defineMetadata("description", "Returns the result of adding two
numbers", Calculator, "add");
Reflect.defineMetadata("description", "Returns the result of
subtracting two numbers", Calculator, "subtract");
Reflect.defineMetadata("description", "Returns the result of dividing
two numbers", Calculator, "divide");
```

4. Define a function that when given a class will reflect upon it and extract and display the class' **description** metadata:

```
function showDescriptions (target: any) {
    if (Reflect.hasMetadata("description", target)) {
        const classDescription = Reflect.getMetadata("description",
target);
        console.log(`${target.name}: ${classDescription}`);
    }
}
```

5. Call the function using **showDescriptions(Calculator)**; and verify that it will display the following output:

```
Calculator: A class that offers common operations over two numbers
```

In order to get a list of all methods of a class, we'll have to use the **Object.getOwnPropertyNames** function. Additionally, since the methods are actually defined on the prototype of the class, the correct line that gets all methods names of a class is **const methodNames = Object.getOwnPropertyNames(target.prototype)**;.

6. Next, loop over the returned array and check each method for a description. The **showDescription** function will now have the following format:

```
function showDescriptions (target: any) {
    if (Reflect.hasMetadata("description", target)) {
        const classDescription = Reflect.getMetadata("description",
target);
        console.log(`${target.name}: ${classDescription}`);
        const methodNames = Object.getOwnPropertyNames(target.
prototype);
        for (const methodName of methodNames) {
            if (Reflect.hasMetadata("description", target,
methodName)) {
                const description = Reflect.getMetadata("description",
target, methodName);
```

```
                    console.log(`  ${methodName}: ${description}`);
        }
      }
    }
  }
```

7. Call the function again and verify that it will display the following output:

```
Calculator: A class that offers common operations over two numbers
   add: Returns the result of adding two numbers
   subtract: Returns the result of subtracting two numbers
   divide: Returns the result of dividing two numbers
```

Note that you're not displaying anything for the **multiply** method, as you did not add any metadata for it.

In this exercise, you learned how to add metadata to classes and methods and how to check its existence and, if present, to retrieve it. You also managed to get a list of all the methods of a given class.

PROPERTY DECORATORS

A property decorator is a decorator function that is applied to a single property of a class. Unlike in a method or class decorators, you cannot modify or replace the property definition, but you can indeed observe it.

> **NOTE**
>
> Since you receive the constructor function in the decorator, this is not strictly true. You could change the code of the class, but it's extremely inadvisable.

When a property decorator is called, it receives two parameters: **target** and **propertyKey**:

*   **target**: Since properties can be both instance properties (defined on instances of the class) and static properties (defined on the class itself), **target** can be two different things. For instance properties, it's the prototype of the class. For static properties, it's the constructor function of the class. Usually, you would type this parameter as **any**.

*   **propertyKey**: This is the name of the property you're decorating.

In contrast to the method decorators, you're not receiving a property descriptor parameter, because, plainly, there isn't one available. Also, because you do not return any code that can be replaced, the return value of a property decorator is ignored.

For example, you can define a simple property decorator factory that just logs a message to the console to notify that the property is actually decorated:

Example_PropertyDecorators.ts

```
1 function DecorateProperty(message: string) {
2     return function (target: any, propertyKey: string) {
3         console.log(`Decorated
4 ${target.constructor.name}.${propertyKey} with '${message}'`);
5     }
6 }
```

Link to the preceding example: https://packt.link/HkkNi.

Consider the following class definitions:

```
class Teacher {

    public id: number;

    public name: string;

    constructor(id: number, name: string) {
        this.id = id;
        this.name = name;
    }

}
```

You can annotate the **id** and **name** properties using the following code:

```
@DecorateProperty("ID")
public id: number;


@DecorateProperty("NAME")
public name: string;
```

If you now execute the code (we don't need to call anything; it will be called by the TypeScript engine), you obtain the following output:

```
Decorated Teacher.id with 'ID'
Decorated Teacher.name with 'NAME'
```

Note that you did not create any objects of the teacher class, or call any methods. The decorators executed when the class was defined. Since property decorators are passive, usually you'll use them to feed some kind of data into some mechanism that will use it. One of the common approaches is to combine the passive decorators with one or several active decorators, that is, class and method decorators.

> **NOTE**
>
> This is the case in Angular, for example, where the passive @`Input` and @ `Output` decorators are combined with the active @`Component` decorator.

Another common use case is to have an additional mechanism that will get the data provided by the decorators and use it. For example, you can have the decorators recording some metadata, and then have another function that reads and uses that metadata.

EXERCISE 7.07: CREATING AND USING A PROPERTY DECORATOR

In this exercise, you'll create a simple property decorator factory that will provide each property with a description. After you have done this, you will write a function that given a class will display its available descriptions:

> **NOTE**
>
> Before you begin, make sure you have set up the correct compiler options as mentioned in the *Setting Up Compiler Options* section. The code file for this exercise can also be downloaded from https://packt.link/1WU6d.

1. Open Visual Studio Code, create a new file in a new directory (**Exercise07**), and save it as **teacher-properties.ts**.

2. Enter the following code in **teacher-properties.ts**:

```
class Teacher {

    public id: number;

    public name: string;

    constructor(id: number, name: string) {
```

```
        this.id = id;
        this.name = name;
    }
}
```

3. Add a decorator factory that takes a string parameter and generates a property decorator that will add a metadata **description** field to the class for the given property:

```
function Description(message: string) {
    return function (target: any, propertyKey: string) {
        Reflect.defineMetadata("description", message, target,
propertyKey)
    }
}
```

4. Next, annotate the properties of the **Teacher** class using the description:

```
    @Description("This is the id of the teacher")
    public id: number;


    @Description("This is the name of the teacher")
    public name: string;
```

5. Define a function that, when given an object, will reflect upon it and extract and display the **description** metadata for the object's properties:

```
function showDescriptions (target: any) {
    for (const key in target) {
        if (Reflect.hasMetadata("description", target, key)) {
            const description = Reflect.getMetadata("description",
target, key);
            console.log(`   ${key}: ${description}`);
        }
    }
}
```

6. Create an object of the **Teacher** class:

```
const teacher = new Teacher(1, "John Smith");
```

7. Pass that object to the **showDescriptions** function:

```
showDescriptions(teacher);
```

8. Execute the code and verify that the descriptions are displayed:

```
id: This is the id of the teacher
name: This is the name of the teacher
```

In this exercise, you learned how to add metadata to properties using property decorators and how to use property decorators to add quick basic documentation to your classes.

PARAMETER DECORATORS

A parameter decorator is a decorator function that is applied to a single parameter of a function call. Just like property decorators, parameter decorators are passive, that is, they can be used only to observe values, but not to inject and execute code. The return value of a parameter decorator is similarly ignored. As a consequence, parameter decorators are almost exclusively used in conjunction with other, active decorators.

When a parameter decorator is called, it receives three parameters: **target**, **propertyKey**, and **parameterIndex**:

- **target**: The behavior for this parameter is identical to the decorators on the corresponding method. There is an exception if the parameter is on a class' constructor, but that is explained shortly.

- **propertyKey**: This is the name of the method whose parameter you're decorating (the constructor exception is explained shortly).

- **parameterIndex**: This is the ordinal index of the parameter in the function's parameter list (starting with zero for the first parameter).

So, let's have a function that will simply log the **target**, **propertyKey**, and **parameterIndex** parameters to the console:

`Example_ParameterDecorators.ts`

```
1 function DecorateParam(target: any, propertyName: string,
2 parameterIndex: number) {
3     console.log("Target is:", target);
4     console.log("Property name is:", propertyName);
5     console.log("Index is:", parameterIndex);
6 }
```

Link to the preceding example: https://packt.link/5vuL2.

You can use this function to decorate a function's parameters and can investigate the usage of parameter decorators. Let's start with a simple class:

```
class Teacher {

    public id: number;

    public name: string;

    constructor(id: number, name: string) {
        this.id = id;
        this.name = name;
    }

    public getFullName(title: string, suffix: string) {
        return `${title} ${this.name}, ${suffix}`
    }
}
```

The class has a constructor that takes two parameters, **id** and **name**, and a method called **getFullName**, which takes two parameters, **title** and **suffix**. Say you add your decorator to the first parameter of the **getFullName** methods, using this:

```
    public getFullName(@DecorateParam title: string, suffix: string) {
        // ....
```

If you run your code (no need to instantiate the class), you'll get the following output on the console:

```
Target is: Teacher {}
Property name is: getFullName
Index is: 0
```

We can also apply parameter decorators to the parameters of the constructor function itself. Say you decorate the second constructor parameter, like this:

```
    constructor(id: number, @DecorateParam name: string) {
        // ....
```

You will get the following output when you run the code:

```
Target is: [Function: Teacher]
Property name is: undefined
Index is: 1
```

Note that in this case, the target is not the prototype of the class, but the class constructor itself. Also, when decorating constructor parameters, the name of the property is **undefined**.

EXERCISE 7.08: CREATING AND USING A PARAMETER DECORATOR

In this exercise, you will create a parameter decorator that will indicate that a certain parameter is required; that is, it should not have an empty value. You will also create a validation decorator for the method, so that the validation can actually take place. We'll create a class that uses the decorators, and you will try to call the method with both valid and invalid values:

> **NOTE**
>
> Before you begin, make sure you have set up the correct compiler options as mentioned in the *Setting Up Compiler Options* section. The code file for this exercise can also be downloaded from https://packt.link/Hf3fv.

1. Open Visual Studio Code, create a new file in a new directory (**Exercise08**), and save it as **teacher-parameters.ts**.

2. Enter the following code in **teacher-parameters.ts**:

```
class Teacher {

    public id: number;

    public name: string;

    constructor(id: number, name: string) {
        this.id = id;
        this.name = name;
    }

    public getFullName(title: string, suffix: string) {
        return `${title} ${this.name}, ${suffix}`
    }
}
```

3. Create a parameter decorator called **Required** that will add the index of the parameter to the **required** metadata field to the class for the given property:

```
function Required(target: any, propertyKey: string, parameterIndex:
number) {
    if (Reflect.hasMetadata("required", target, propertyKey)) {
        const existing = Reflect.getMetadata("required", target,
propertyKey) as number[];
        Reflect.defineMetadata("required", existing.
concat(parameterIndex), target, propertyKey);
    } else {
        Reflect.defineMetadata("required", [parameterIndex], target,
propertyKey)
    }
}
```

Here, if the metadata already exists, that means that there is another required parameter. If so, you load it and concatenate your **parameterIndex**. If there is no previous metadata, you define it with an array consisting of your **parameterIndex**.

4. Next, create a method decorator that will wrap the original method and check all required parameters *before* calling the original method:

```
function Validate(target: any, propertyKey:string, descriptor:
PropertyDescriptor) {
    const original = descriptor.value;
    descriptor.value = function (...args: any[]) {
        // validate parameters
        if (Reflect.hasMetadata("required", target, propertyKey)) {
            const requiredParams = Reflect.getMetadata("required",
target, propertyKey) as number[];
            for (const required of requiredParams) {
                if (!args[required]) {
                    throw Error(`The parameter at position
${required} is required`)
                }
            }
        }
        return original.apply(this, args);
    }
}
```

If any of your required parameters has a falsy value, instead of executing the original method, your decorator will throw an error.

5. After that, annotate the **title** parameter of the **getFullName** method with the **Required** decorator and the method itself with the **Validate** decorator:

```
@Validate
public getFullName(@Required title: string, suffix: string) {
    // ....
```

6. Create an object of the **Teacher** class:

```
const teacher = new Teacher(1, "John Smith");
```

7. Try to call the **getFullName** method with an empty string as the first parameter:

```
try {
    console.log(teacher.getFullName("", "Esq"));
} catch (e) {
    console.log(e.message);
}
```

8. Execute the code and verify that the error message is displayed instead:

```
The parameter at position 0 is required
```

In this exercise, you covered how to create parameter decorators and how to use them to add metadata. You also orchestrated the usage of the same metadata into another decorator, and build a basic validation system.

APPLICATION OF MULTIPLE DECORATORS ON A SINGLE TARGET

It is often necessary to apply more than one decorator on a single target. And as decorators can (and do) change the code that actually gets executed, it's important to have an understanding of how different decorators play together.

Basically, decorators are functions, and you're using them to compose your targets. This means that, in essence, decorators will be applied and executed bottom-up, with the decorator that's closest to the target going first and providing the result for the second decorators, and so on. This is similar to functional composition; that is, when we're trying to calculate **f(g(x))**, first the **g** function will be called, and then the **f** function will be called.

There is a small catch when using decorator factories, though. The composition rule only applies to the decorators themselves – and decorator factories are not decorators per se. They are functions that need to be executed in order to return a decorator. This means that they are executed in source code order, that is, top-down. Imagine that you have two decorator factories:

Example_MultipleDecorators.ts

```
1 function First () {
2     console.log("Generating first decorator")
3     return function (constructor: Function) {
4         console.log("Applying first decorator")
5     }
6 }
```

Link to the preceding example https://packt.link/jMhDj.

Second decorator factory:

```
7  function Second () {
8      console.log("Generating second decorator")
9      return function (constructor: Function) {
10         console.log("Applying second decorator")
11     }
12 }
```

Now imagine that they are applied on a single target:

```
13 @First()
14 @Second()
15 class Target {}
```

The generation process will generate the first decorator before the second, but in the application process, the second will be applied, and then the first:

```
Generating first decorator
Generating second decorator
Applying second decorator
Applying first decorator
```

ACTIVITY 7.02: USING DECORATORS TO APPLY CROSS-CUTTING CONCERNS

In this activity, we're going full circle to the basketball game example (**Example_ Basketball.ts**). You are tasked with adding all the necessary cross-cutting concerns, such as authentication, performance metrics, auditing, and validation to the **Example_Basketball.ts** file in a maintainable manner.

You can begin the activity with the code that you already have in the **Example_ Basketball.ts**. First, take stock of the elements that are already present in the file:

- The interface that describes the team.

- The class for the game itself. You have a constructor that creates the team objects given the team names. You also have a **getScore** function that displayed the score and a simple **updateScore** method that updates the score of the game, taking the scoring team and the score value as parameters.

Now you need to add the cross-cutting concerns as mentioned previously without changing the code of the class itself, only by using decorators.

Earlier in **Example_Basketball.ts**, you had to completely subsume the business logic of keeping score under the code that was needed to address everything else (such as authorization, auditing, metrics, and so on). Now apply all the decorator skills that are needed so that the application runs properly but still has a crisp and clear codebase.

> **NOTE**
>
> The code file for this activity can also be downloaded from
> https://packt.link/7KfCx.

The following steps should help you with the solution:

1. Create the code for the **BasketBallGame** class.

2. Create a class decorator factory called **Authenticate** that will take a **permission** parameter and return a class decorator with constructor wrapping. The class decorator should load the **permissions** metadata property (array of **strings**), then check if the passed parameter is an element of the array. If the passed parameter is not an element of the array, the class decorator should throw an error, and if it's present, it should continue with the class creation.

3. Define a metadata property of the **BasketballGame** class called **permissions** with the value **["canUpdateScore"]**.

4. Apply the class decorator factory on the **BasketballGame** class with a parameter value of **canUpdateScore**.

5. Create a method decorator called **MeasureDuration** that will use method wrapping to start a timer before the method body is executed and stop it after it's done. It should calculate the duration and push it to a metadata property called **durations** for the method.

6. Apply the **MeasureDuration** method decorator on the **updateScore** method.

7. Create a method decorator factory called **Audit** that will take a **message** parameter and return a method decorator. The method decorator should use method wrapping to get the arguments and the return value of the method. After the successful execution of the original method, it should display the audit log to the console.

8. Apply the **Audit** method decorator factory on the **updateScore** method, with a parameter value of **Updated score**.

9. Create a parameter decorator called **OneTwoThree** that will add the decorated parameter in the **one-two-three** metadata property.

10. Create a method decorator called **Validate** that will use method wrapping to load all values for the **one-two-three** metadata property, and for all marked parameters check their value. If the value is **1**, **2**, or **3**, it should continue the execution of the original method. If not, it should stop the execution with an error.

11. Apply the **OneTwoThree** decorator to the **byPoints** parameter of **updateScore** and apply the **Validate** decorator to the **updateScore** method:

```
Create a game object, and update its score a few times. The console
should reflect the applications of all decoratorsas shown:
[AUDIT] Updated score (updateScore) called with arguments:
[AUDIT] [ 3, true ]
[AUDIT] and returned result:
[AUDIT] undefined
//…
[AUDIT] Updated score (updateScore) called with arguments:
[AUDIT] [ 2, true ]
```

```
[AUDIT] and returned result:
[AUDIT] undefined
[AUDIT] Updated score (updateScore) called with arguments:
[AUDIT] [ 2, false ]
[AUDIT] and returned result:
[AUDIT] undefined
7:8
```

> **NOTE**
>
> For ease of presentation, only a section of the expected output is shown here. The solution to this activity can be found on page 629.

In this activity, you are leveraging decoration to quickly and efficiently implement complicated cross-cutting concerns. When you have successfully completed the activity, you will have implemented multiple kinds of decorators, according to the needs of the application, and thus will have widened the functionalities of your code without sacrificing clarity and readability.

SUMMARY

In this chapter, you looked at a technique called **decorating** that is natively supported in TypeScript. The chapter first established the motivation for the use of decorators and then looked at the multiple types of decorators in TypeScript (class, method, accessor, property, and parameter decorators), along with examining the possibilities of each. You learned how to swap or change the complete constructor of a class with a class decorator, how to wrap a single method or property accessor with a method decorator, and how to enrich the available metadata using property and parameter decorators.

The chapter also discussed the differences between active and passive decorators, which boil down to a difference between code and definition. You implemented several common variants of each of the decorator types and demonstrated how different decorator types can nicely complement each other. This chapter should help you easily manage the usage and creation of decorators both from third-party libraries such as Angular and from decorator factories created by yourself. In the next chapter, we will begin our foray into dependency injection in TypeScript.

8

DEPENDENCY INJECTION IN TYPESCRIPT

OVERVIEW

This chapter introduces you to **Dependency Injection** (**DI**) in TypeScript. It demonstrates how to implement the DI design pattern. You will also see some common use cases for the DI pattern, including ones from libraries such as Angular and Nest.js. This chapter will teach you how to build a simple Angular application that uses DI. You will also learn some basics of InversifyJS and how to use it in your TypeScript applications. By the end of this chapter, you will be able to build a calculator application that utilizes DI using InversifyJS.

INTRODUCTION

A design pattern is a general, repeatable way to solve a commonly recurring problem in software design. It is not just code that you can paste and use in your own code, but a guideline to writing code. It is usually not tied to any specific language, so a given pattern can be transformed from language to language, with its implementation changed to match the desired language and environment.

Design patterns can usually be used in many different situations and help you solve a lot of different problems. For example, if you want to make sure you only have one active connection to a database, you may want to use the Singleton design pattern, which basically ensures that only a single instance of something exists, or if you want to write an ORM tool (an object-relational mapping tool, for abstracting away a database) that allows the use of multiple databases, you may want to use the Adapter design pattern, which allows the ORM tool to talk to multiple types of database drivers using a "common language."

Using design patterns can speed up development, since they are battle-tested through decades of prior usages, in a variety of problems. Furthermore, if working in a team, it is easier to explain a solution to a given problem compared with conventional methods. Design patterns serve as a sort of "common language."

Note that when beginning to learn the concepts of design patterns, it may be difficult to wrap your head around them, and you may find it harder to solve problems with them than without them. This is because it's not straightforward to spot when a specific design pattern fits a given problem, especially when you don't have experience using it, or don't understand either the pattern or the problem completely. There are also some patterns that are commonly easier to understand than others (for example, the Singleton pattern is easier to understand than the Adapter pattern).

Furthermore, if you're just beginning to use a design pattern, its usefulness may not be apparent until further down the project lifetime, where you might actually want to add features that you may have not initially thought of or even just fix bugs. Lastly, it's important to note that not every problem can be solved using a design pattern, and using the wrong one may entail more issues than it solves. Also, not every problem requires a design pattern – you can add as many patterns as you want to a "Hello World" program, but their usefulness will be doubtful. So, it's important to take a step back and see whether using it really fits the problem you're trying to solve.

THE DI DESIGN PATTERN

DI is a technique whereby one object supplies the dependencies of another object. A dependency of an object is *anything* required in order to perform its operation in the application. Before diving into an explanation of what DI is, let's try to understand the fundamental element in the preceding definition with an example.

Let's say we have two classes:

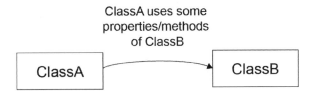

Figure 8.1: A simple class dependency

As shown in the preceding diagram, Class A uses some properties/methods of Class B. Thus, we can say that **ClassB** is a dependency of **ClassA**.

Let's look at a more real-world example (albeit simplified). Most websites, whether social media websites, government websites for disbursal of services, or e-commerce platforms, require a user to register in order to use the services offered by the website. Imagine you are developing one such website. You require a **UserRegistrationService** class to gather user details, save them in a database, a file, or any other repository, and then send an email to the user informing them of a successful registration.

Your website's method for handling the registration process would therefore probably look something like this:

```
class UserRegistrationService {
    registerUser(email: string, password: string) {
        // TODO: process registration
        // TODO: send registration success email

    }
}
```

This service has two primary responsibilities – saving the user's details to persistent storage and sending them an email. For now, you are not concerned with whether the details are stored in a database, SaaS, or a file. In the same vein, you are not concerned if the registration email is automated or done manually. Thus, we just want to get *some* **UserRepository**, and *some* **EmailService**, as shown here:

```typescript
interface User {
    email: string;
    password: string;
}


interface UserRepository {
    save(user: User): Promise<User>;
}


interface EmailService {
    sendEmail(to: string, subject: string, body?: string): Promise<void>;
}
```

As mentioned, we don't care about their implementation, or even creating them; we want someone else to do that, so our implementation of **UserRegistrationService** could look something like this:

```typescript
class UserRegistrationService {
    constructor(
        private userRepository: UserRepository,
        private emailService: EmailService
    ) {}

    async registerUser(email: string, password: string){
        await this.userRepository.save({
            email,
            password,
        });

        await this.emailService.
sendEmail(email, 'Welcome to my website!');
    }
}
```

Note that we don't know what the actual implementation behind **UserRepository** or **EmailService** is; we just know their structure.

Now, if we change how users are saved, for example, deciding to migrate from a file to a MySQL database, or if we change our email provider from Mailchimp to SendGrid, the **UserRegistrationService** class stays intact and should still function as before as long as any implementation thereof conforms to the same **UserRepository** and **EmailService** interfaces (for example, have the same structure – same method signatures, with the same parameters, and so on) and provide the same functionality as described previously.

For example, in the following code snippets, notice both the file-based and the MySQL-based implementations, implement **UserRepository**, which is the only thing that **UserRegistrationService** is aware of.

The file-based implementation is as follows:

```
// FileUserRepository.ts
import * as fs from 'fs';

class FileUserRepository implements UserRepository {
  save(user: User): Promise<User> {
    return new Promise((resolve, reject) => {
      fs.appendFile('users.txt', JSON.stringify(user), err => {
        if (err) return reject(err);

        resolve(user);
      });
    });
  }
}
```

The MySQL-based implementation is as follows:

```
// MySqlUserRepository.ts
import mysql from 'mysql';

class MySqlUserRepository implements UserRepository {
  connection = mysql.createConnection({
    // connection details
  });

  save(user: User): Promise<User> {
    return new Promise((resolve, reject) => {
      return this.connection.query(
```

```
      `INSERT INTO users (email, password)
      VALUES (?, ?)`,
      [user.email, user.password],
      (err, data) => {
        if (err) return reject(err);

        resolve(data);
      }
    );
  });
  }
}
```

To put it simply, DI allows us to separate the *what* from the *how*. The dependent class only needs to know *how* to interact with *a user repository* – by calling a method called **save**, with a single parameter of the **User** type), as well as with *an email sender* – by calling a method called **sendEmail** that takes in two parameters; a *to* email address, of the **string** type, a second parameter for the email's subject, also of the **string** type, and an optional third parameter for the email's body (also of the **string** type).

Then, these services can handle the *what should (actually) be done* portion – saving the user's details to a file, to a MySQL database, or an entirely different thing, and then sending the email automatically using an SaaS service, queuing them for manual sending later, or anything else.

Going back to the dependency chart, in this example, the dependencies are as follows:

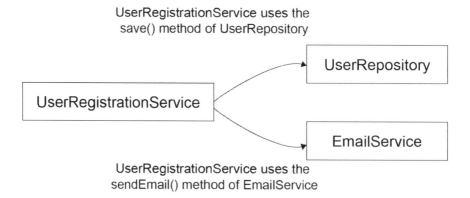

Figure 8.2: UserRegistrationService dependencies

Another benefit of having used DI here is that it simplifies testing our implementations separately from their dependencies. For example, when testing the **registerUser** method of **UserRegistrationService**, we only want to test the **registerUser** method; we don't care about how its dependencies behave in production (we will test these separately). We can just mock them with any implementation while testing to have them behave how we want. Remember that the whole point of DI is that we don't care about what the dependencies do and how they do it, as long as they conform to the agreed-upon interface – **UserRepository** and **EmailService** in this case. Here is how we would test the **registerUser** method in code:

```
interface User {
  email: string;
  password: string;
}

test('User registration', async () => {
  const mockUserRepository: UserRepository = {
    async save(user: User) {
      return user;
    },
  };

  const mockEmailService: EmailService = {
    async sendEmail(to: string, subject: string, body?: string) {},
  };

  const userRegistrationService = new UserRegistrationService(
    mockUserRepository,
    mockEmailService
  );

  await userRegistrationService.registerUser(
    'example@domain.com',
    'super-secret-password'
  );
```

```
  expect(mockUserRepository.save).toHaveBeenCalled();
  expect(mockEmailService.sendEmail).toHaveBeenCalled();
  // ...
});
```

Even though the preceding examples only demonstrate classes, dependencies can be of any type – classes, functions, plain objects, and even simple constants (depending on the language and specific implementation).

For example, if **UserRegistrationService** were to require a constant value, for example, a salt to hash the user's password with, it would be provided in the constructor, too, as another argument, as shown here:

```
import * as bcrypt from 'bcrypt';

class UserRegistrationService {
  constructor(
    private userRepository: UserRepository,
    private emailService: EmailService,
    private passwordHashSalt: string
  ) {}

  async registerUser(email: string, password: string) {
    const hashedPassword = await bcrypt.hash(password, this.passwordHashSalt);

    await this.userRepository.save({
      email,
      password: hashedPassword,
    });

    await this.emailService.sendEmail(email, 'Welcome to my website!');
  }
}
```

> **NOTE**
>
> The following sections will be using decorators, covered in *Chapter 7. Decorators*. Please make sure that you have read and understood them before continuing, as decorators are an essential part of how all DI libraries covered next are built on.

Another concept related to DI is **Inversion of Control (IoC)**, a programming principle in which the control flow is inverted, as the name suggests. While DI's concern is to decouple dependencies via abstractions (such as our **UserRepository** abstraction over the **MySqlUserRepository** implementation), in IoC, the concern is to let the consumer decide what should be done by the component/library. For example, in our implementation of **UserRegistrationService** above, we used IoC, since we allow how the user's details are sent, as well as how an email is sent by the consumer, to be specified. In the application's case, it could decide whether it wanted to use **FileUserRepository** or **MySqlUserRepository**, and in the test code we decided that both of them should do nothing. This was also decided at the consumer (test code) level.

To summarize, DI concerns itself with letting a class know about abstractions over implementations, while IoC's concerns revolve around letting the consumer decide about the implementation(s) that should be used.

Some popular frameworks, both in the frontend as well as the backend, have embraced DI as a core part of their framework – the most popular ones are Angular in frontend development and Nest.js in the backend. DI allows applications built on top of these frameworks to be very robust and flexible, especially in large applications due to the nature of DI, which allows the creation of classes (and other dependencies) to be separated from their usage.

DI IN ANGULAR

Another actual real-world example of DI can be found in the Angular framework – a modern framework for building frontend applications using TypeScript. Angular has its own implementation for a DI library. Furthermore, the Angular framework itself, as well as apps built on it, heavily relies on this DI implementation.

Let's take a look at a simple Angular app and see how DI makes it straightforward to build an easy-to-maintain, scalable application.

An Angular app is made up of several **NgModule**, each of which is usually a logical part of an app – this can be a feature, a UI components library, or anything else. Each **NgModule** can have two types of "things:"

1. Declarations (**Component** and **Directive**)

2. Providers (usually **Service**)

Declarations are what constitute the UI of the app, things such as the **WelcomeMessageComponent** class (shown in the following snippet), which takes in **name** as an input (using the @**Input** decorator, which is kind of like passing in parameters to a function or a constructor of a class, just with components), and displays it in an HTML **h1** tag (an HTML tag to display a main header):

```
import { Component, Input } from '@angular/core';

@Component({
    selector: 'welcome-message',
    template: `
        <h1>Welcome {{ name }}!</h1>
    `,
})
export class WelcomeMessageComponent {
    @Input() name: string;
}
```

The preceding code will yield the following output:

Welcome John!

Figure 8.3: Displayed output of rendering WelcomeMessageComponent with "John" passed in to the name input

Providers are usually services, which hold the main logic of the app and are usually used for anything that's not specifically related to the UI.

For example, you could have a **UsersService** class that handles fetching a list of users from a backend, as shown here:

```
import { Injectable } from '@angular/core';
import { Observable, of } from 'rxjs';

export interface User {
    name: string;
}

@Injectable()
export class UsersService {
```

```
    getUsers(): Observable<User[]> {
        return of([
            { name: 'Alice' },
            { name: 'Bob' },
            { name: 'Charlie' }
        ]);
    }
}
```

The preceding code has a **UsersService** class that has a single method –
getUsers(), which returns a static array of **User** objects. Note that we wrap our
static array with **of()**, which takes a static value and wraps it in an **Observable**, so
we can later change the behavior of this method to asynchronously return data (for
example, from a remote endpoint, as we'll see next).

> **NOTE**
> An observable is an asynchronous stream of data, basically allowing data
> to be passed between "publishers" and "subscribers." This data can be a
> one-time operation, such as with an HTTP call, can have multiple emits (for
> example, emit an increasing number from 1 through 10, in sequence, every
> 1 second), or can even be infinite (for example, emitting an event every time
> the user clicks a specific button). It is part of the Observer pattern.

We would then use **UsersService** in our **UsersList** component, which displays
the users in a list, as shown here:

```
import { Component } from "@angular/core";
import { Observable } from "rxjs";
import { UsersService, User } from "./users.service";

@Component({
    selector: 'users-list',
    template: `
        <ul>
            <li *ngFor="let user of (users$ | async)">
                {{ user.name }}
            </li>
```

```
    </ul>
  `
})
export class UsersListComponent {
  readonly users$: Observable<User[]>;

  constructor(private usersService: UsersService) {
    this.users$ = usersService.getUsers();
  }
}
```

Here, we create a simple component, **UsersListComponent**, that displays a list of users, which it gets from **UsersService** that's *injected* into it at creation time by the Angular DI.

Once the service is injected, we call **getUsers()** and store the returned **Observable** in a **users$** member so we can later access it from the template, which utilizes the **async** pipe to tell Angular to subscribe to the **Observable** and update the template when its underlying value changes:

- Alice
- Bob
- Charlie

Figure 8.4: The output from running the app

We won't dive into Angular's template engine or change detection mechanisms – those are two big topics in themselves – but you can refer to the Angular documentation for more information on that. Instead, let's focus on what's going on with regard to DI – notice that we asked for a **UsersService** object in the **UsersListComponents** constructor; we didn't specify that we wanted to get a specific instance of the service and so on, just that we want one. This is very powerful, since this offloads the logic of how and where this service is instantiated to a dedicated place (the **NgModule**) and opens up a lot of possibilities. We could test the component more easily (by providing a fake **UsersService**), or even just replace the **UsersService** implementation at runtime with another one.

Angular providers can also require other providers; for example, we could have a generic HTTP client service that knows how to make HTTP calls, and then inject that into our **UsersService**, which can focus on more high-level details such as the endpoint, which it needs to use in order to fetch the users. In fact, Angular has such an HTTP service built in, called **HttpClient**. You can use it and fix the mock implementation we had for the users with a real one, utilizing DI further as shown here:

```typescript
import { Injectable } from '@angular/core';
import { HttpClient } from '@angular/common/http';
import { Observable } from 'rxjs';

export interface User {
    name: string;
}

@Injectable()
export class UsersService {
    constructor(private httpClient: HttpClient) {}

    getUsers(): Observable<User[]> {
        return this.httpClient.get<User[]>('/api/users');
    }
}
```

Here, we ask for an **HttpClient** and use its **get()** method to make a **GET** request to the **/api/users** endpoint in our site, which should return an array of **User** objects – that is, objects with a property called **name**, with a **string** type.

This replaces the mock implementation we had earlier with a more real-world use case by calling an external endpoint instead of returning a static list of users.

Again, notice that we just asked for an **HttpClient** interface again. We don't care about how it's implemented (this could involve using **XMLHttpRequest**, **fetch**, or even another underlying library), as long as it conforms to the **HttpClient** interface.

You may have noticed that the path that we request from **HttpClient** is a relative one. This works if our backend is on the same domain as our frontend (for example, https://example.com is our website and https://example.com/api/users would return the users). However, if we want to move our backend to a different server, this will break our website. In the next exercise, we will fix this, using Angular's DI mechanism and by adding **HttpInterceptor**.

HttpInterceptor is an interface Angular provides that we can implement in order to "hook," or even change network requests, either on their way out (the request), or on their way back (the response), before any other consumer "sees" the response. This will work wherever **HttpClient** is used in the application, without requiring any more code modifications in other services that use **HttpClient**.

> **NOTE**
>
> The example discussed in this section is the basis of our next exercise.

EXERCISE 8.01: ADDING HTTPINTERCEPTOR TO AN ANGULAR APP

In this exercise, we'll add **HttpInterceptor** to our existing Angular application, which we built in the preceding section, to allow our backend service to sit on a different domain from our frontend application. This allows the two applications to be separated completely, and very easily, without requiring any extra changes in the rest of the application. Here are the steps to complete this exercise:

> **NOTE**
>
> Before you begin, make sure you run **npm install** in the **exercise-starter** directory. The code files for this exercise can be found here: https://packt.link/avWRA. This repository contains two folders, **exercise-starter** and **exercise-solution**. The former contains the template files that you can use to code along with this exercise, whereas the latter contains the final code of this exercise for your reference.

1. Start by cloning the application we have written so far in this section. This can be found at https://packt.link/JAgZ7.

2. Create a class, **ApiHttpInterceptor**, in a new file, **api-http. interceptor.ts**, and save the file in the **exercise-starter/src/ app/interceptors/** folder. This file implements the **HttpInterceptor** interface (imported from **@angular/common/http**). Be sure to mark it with the **@Injectable** decorator so that Angular knows it's a service that can be used in DI:

```
import { HttpEvent, HttpHandler, HttpInterceptor, HttpRequest } from
'@angular/common/http';
import { Injectable } from '@angular/core';
import { Observable } from 'rxjs';


@Injectable()
export class ApiHttpInterceptor implements HttpInterceptor {
  intercept(req: HttpRequest<any>, next: HttpHandler):
Observable<HttpEvent<any>> {
    throw new Error('Method not implemented.');
  }
}
```

Angular will call the **intercept()** method of **ApiHttpInterceptor** when a request is made by any **HttpClient**. We get the request (**req**) and **HttpHandler** (**next**), which we need to call when we're finished to let Angular call any other **HttpInterceptor** in the chain.

3. Update the code to change the URL path:

```
import { HttpEvent, HttpHandler, HttpInterceptor, HttpRequest } from
"@angular/common/http";
import { Injectable } from "@angular/core";
import { Observable } from "rxjs";


@Injectable()
export class ApiHttpInterceptor implements HttpInterceptor {
    intercept(req: HttpRequest<any>, next: HttpHandler):
Observable<HttpEvent<any>> {
    if (!req.url.startsWith('/api/')) {
      return next.handle(req);
    }

    const relativeUrl = req.url.replace('/api/', '');
    const newRequest = req.clone({
```

```
url: `https://jsonplaceholder.typicode.com/${relativeUrl}`
    });

    return next.handle(newRequest);
  }
}
```

The preceding code checks the URL path. For each request, if it's issued to a relative path, starting with **/api**, the code changes it. It does so by looking at the **url** property of **HttpRequest**. If the URL doesn't start with **/api**, you don't need to do anything, just call **next.handle()** with the original request. Otherwise, clone the original request with a new URL, and then call **next.handle()** with the new request. This is the request that will actually be sent out. We're using https://jsonplaceholder.typicode.com here, a free service that has some predefined endpoints we can use to get data from, for testing purposes. In an actual application, this would be your backend service's endpoint.

Lastly, we also need to register this interceptor in our **AppModule** so that it can know what interceptors to inject into **HttpClient**. We do this by adding **ApiHttpInterceptor**, which we created as a provider, and we tell Angular to use it when looking for **HTTP_INTERCEPTORS** – this is the DI symbol that Angular uses when it asks for all the interceptors it needs to use when making a network request via the **HttpClient** service.

4. Open the **app.module.ts** file present in the **exercise-starter/src/app** folder and update it with the code given here:

```
import { HttpClientModule, HTTP_INTERCEPTORS } from '@angular/common/
http';
import { NgModule } from '@angular/core';
import { BrowserModule } from '@angular/platform-browser';
import { AppComponent } from './app.component';
import { ApiHttpInterceptor } from './interceptors/api-http.
interceptor';
import { UsersListComponent } from './users-list.component';
import { UsersService } from './users.service';
import { WelcomeMessageComponent } from './welcome-message.
component';

@NgModule({
  imports: [BrowserModule, HttpClientModule],
  declarations: [AppComponent, WelcomeMessageComponent,
UsersListComponent],
  providers: [UsersService, { provide: HTTP_INTERCEPTORS, useClass:
ApiHttpInterceptor, multi: true }],
```

```
    bootstrap: [AppComponent],
})
export class AppModule { }
```

Since we want Angular to know about our interceptor, we add it to the **HTTP_ INTERCEPTORS** list (notice the bold line).

5. Run the new app by running **npm start -- --open** in the **exercise-starter** directory. Your default browser should open up at **http:// localhost:4200**, and you should see a list of 10 users:

- Leanne Graham
- Ervin Howell
- Clementine Bauch
- Patricia Lebsack
- Chelsey Dietrich
- Mrs. Dennis Schulist
- Kurtis Weissnat
- Nicholas Runolfsdottir V
- Glenna Reichert
- Clementina DuBuque

Figure 8.5: Output of the exercise

If you open the DevTools, you should see only one request to the **users** endpoint, which is for https://jsonplaceholder.typicode.com/users (and not http:// localhost:4200/users):

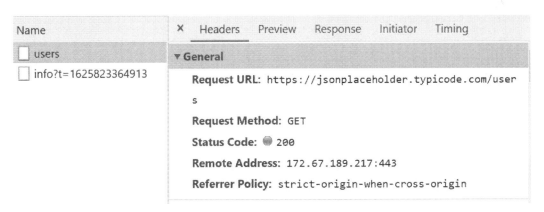

Figure 8.6: Requests to the users endpoint

Notice that our **UsersService** didn't change at all here (and you can imagine the benefits if we had dozens of services like it), but it is still working as expected from its point of view.

All the code explained in this section and the exercise is just some examples of how DI comes into play in Angular. However, there is much more. You can register any value as a dependency to be injected (not just classes). You can control the instantiation of the providers to be Singletons for the entire app, creating a new instance for every **NgModule** or even for every **Component** instance. You can also create them using some more complex logic via factories and more. You have just scratched the surface of the very powerful DI library that Angular offers.

DI IN NEST.JS

Another framework to look at, also heavily inspired by Angular's architecture, is Nest.js, which also heavily utilizes DI. Nest.js is a framework for building backend applications using Node.js and TypeScript. Like Angular, Nest.js also has **Modules** (equivalent to Angular's **NgModule**), and **Providers**. It also has **Controller**, which handles incoming requests from clients and returns responses. These are similar to Angular's components – both are what the consumers see. In Angular, **Component** and **Directive** make up the UI, and in Nest.js, **Controller** makes up the API to be consumed.

We won't dive into Nest.js' architecture, but here's a small example of a couple of things that it leverages DI for:

```typescript
import { Controller, Get, Param } from '@nestjs/common';
import { HelloService } from './hello.service';

@Controller('hello')
export class HelloController {
  constructor(private helloService: HelloService) {}

  @Get(':username')
  async getByUsername(@Param('username') username: string) {
    const message = await this.helloService.getHello(username);

    return { message };
  }
}
```

This is a simple "Hello World" controller, which, for a **GET** request to **/hello/foo**, will return **{ message: "Hello foo" }**. A controller is a container for endpoints under a given prefix (so in this case, any request that starts with **"/hello"** will end up going to this controller), and the @**Get** decorator around the **getByUserName()** function tells Nest.js to call that method when a **GET** method is performed to the given path (the paths of the individual methods/decorators are concatenated to those of the controller) – **"/hello/:username"** in this case (anything starting with a **:** is a placeholder for dynamic content. In this case, **:username** is the placeholder, and we can get it by using the **Param** decorator, giving it the placeholder's name).

Notice that we get **HelloService** in the constructor, similar to Angular, via DI. We also get the username param from the **Param** decorator, which also leverages DI behind the scenes to get the current **Request** object. Lastly, the framework is responsible for creating both **HelloService** and **HelloController** for us; we don't need to do so ourselves. This, like in Angular, makes testing **HelloController** easy, since you can just fake **HelloService** in your tests with a mock implementation to either assert or modify the behavior of the controller. This is a very simple example, but you can imagine **HelloService** replaced with something like an authentication service, or an ORM tool for accessing the database.

In the next section, we'll cover InversifyJS – an IoC container for TypeScript (and JavaScript) applications. Unlike Angular, which is only for the frontend, or Nest.js, which is only for the backend, and which are both frameworks that dictate what your application's architecture will be (at least at some level), InversifyJS is a generic library that only does IoC and allows you to use DI in any application.

INVERSIFYJS

InversifyJS is an implementation of an IoC container (inversion of control, which DI is part of) for TypeScript (and JavaScript) applications. It is one of many implementations and, as we've seen above, some frameworks come with their own DI solution, such as Angular or Nest.js.

> **NOTE**
>
> Other alternatives to InversifyJS for general-purpose projects include **TypeDI** and **TSyringe**, as well as **typescript-ioc**.

The basic idea in InversifyJS, as in most other implementations for an IoC container, is to have one place that defines all the concrete implementations of functionality, and the rest of the app only depends on abstractions (for example, interfaces). This greatly reduces coupling, and changing one implementation to another doesn't affect the entire app or require lots of code changes.

> **NOTE**
>
> Coupling is about how tightly integrated/dependent two components (usually classes) are, in the sense that if we change one of them, how likely is the other to break without applicable changes to it too? The more tightly integrated/connected two components are to one another, the more coupled they are, and vice versa.
>
> Ideally, changing one class should not require changes in others. In such cases, the classes are considered decoupled (or loosely coupled).

To make InversifyJS work, we first need to add a **polyfill** for **reflect-metadata**, which allows libraries to perform runtime reflection on objects to get their types in a more powerful manner than the (currently) built-in **typeof** and **instanceof** operators.

In addition, since InverisfyJS works through decorators, you need to enable them by setting **experimentalDecorators** and **emitDecoratorMetadata** to **true** in your project's **tsconfig.json** file (note the **bold** lines):

```
{
    "compilerOptions": {
        "target": "es5",
        "lib": ["es6", "dom"],
        "types": ["reflect-metadata"],
        "module": "commonjs",
        "moduleResolution": "node",
        "experimentalDecorators": true,
        "emitDecoratorMetadata": true
    }
}
```

> **NOTE**
>
> There are additional requirements in order for InversifyJS to work, but all modern browsers and Node.js versions should be able to use it without further polyfills. For more details, visit the following link: https://github.com/inversify/InversifyJS/blob/master/wiki/environment.md.

Just as with Angular and Nest.js' DI containers (**NgModule** and **Module**, respectively), InversifyJS also needs to know how to resolve dependencies. This is generally configured in a single place, usually in a file named **inversify.config.ts** in the root of the project.

> **NOTE**
>
> This is the recommendation, but this file can be placed anywhere and named anything, or split into multiple files; for example, for separating the registration of classes of different features or domains, similar to **NgModules** in Angular or **Modules** in Nest.js.

This file should be the only place in the application where there is coupling. The rest of the app should only be dependent on abstractions.

These abstractions will usually be interfaces, but you can also depend on a specific implementation, or a **class** (which can then be injected with a compatible subclass).

In addition, since interfaces in TypeScript only exist at compile time (see *Chapter 7, Inheritance and Interfaces*), InversifyJS also requires a runtime abstraction token to know what to resolve.

EXERCISE 8.02: "HELLO WORLD" USING INVERSIFYJS

In this exercise, we'll create a simple "hello world" application using InversifyJS. We'll implement all the basic building blocks for a typical use case. Perform the following steps to implement this exercise:

> **NOTE**
>
> The code files for this exercise can be found at https://packt.link/bXSTd.

1. First, create the abstraction for our logger using an **interface** in a new file called **logger.interface.ts** in the **src** folder. This is what consumers will reference later:

```
export interface Logger {
    log(message: string): void;
}
```

2. Next, create a concrete implementation for **Logger**. This implementation is what the consumers of the code will get injected with when they require **Logger** later on:

```
import { injectable } from "inversify";
import { Logger } from "./logger.interface";
@injectable()
export class ConsoleLogger implements Logger {
    log(message: string) {
        console.log(message);
    }
}
```

Note that **ConsoleLogger** implements **Logger**. This ensures that we write a compatible implementation to what our consumers expect, and that they don't break at runtime. In addition, the **@injectable** decorator is used to indicate to InversifyJS that this implementation can be used *as a dependency*, and also that it can be injected to *other dependencies*. This is how we make InversifyJS aware that **ConsoleLogger** is something that it should be aware of.

3. Create a new file called **types.ts** in the **src** folder. Then, define an injection token that consumers can rely on later to ask InversifyJS to inject whatever implementation is behind it at runtime:

```
export const TYPES = {
    Logger: Symbol.for("Logger"),
};
```

In this exercise, we'll stick with the recommended approach of creating a **TYPES** object that resolves to a **Symbol** for each type (using an injection token is required in most DI libraries in TypeScript, since interfaces don't exist at runtime, so InversifyJS can't rely on them).

> **NOTE**
>
> If your target environment doesn't support **symbols**, you can instead use a plain string. Just ensure that you don't have the same string registered for multiple types.

4. Create a new file called **ioc.config.ts** in the **src** folder. Then, configure the IoC container using the following code:

```
import { Container } from "inversify";
import { ConsoleLogger } from "./console-logger";
import { Logger } from "./logger.interface";
import { TYPES } from "./types";
export const container = new Container();
container.bind<Logger>(TYPES.Logger).to(ConsoleLogger);
```

This is what ties all three things (**console-logger**, **logger.interface**, and **types**) together:

5. Create a consumer for the logger in a new file called **main.ts** in the **src** folder. Notice that we use the **@inject** decorator to tell InversifyJS that we want the **Logger** type:

```
import "reflect-metadata";

import { inject, injectable } from "inversify";
import { container } from "./ioc.config";
import { Logger } from "./logger.interface";
```

```
import { TYPES } from "./types";

@injectable()
class Main {
    constructor(@inject(TYPES.Logger) private logger: Logger) {}

    run() {
        this.logger.log('Hello from InversifyJS!');
    }
}

// Run the app:
const main = container.resolve(Main);
main.run();
```

> **NOTE**
>
> The interface type annotation is just for TypeScript to be able to type check the `logger` instance, but since interfaces only exist at compile time, this is irrelevant for runtime, in which the argument passed to `@inject` is what matters.

6. Now, run the app by executing **npm start** in the parent directory. You should get the following output on your console:

```
Hello from InversifyJS!
```

Of course, for such a simple example, it would have been better to just have a single line as follows:

```
console.log('Running');
```

However, in more complex applications, and even simple ones, DI can help, especially if the application is expected to be actively maintained, with the addition of features and the fixing of bugs happening all the time.

In the next activity, you will be tasked with creating a more complex app to demonstrate how DI can help us develop applications while keeping best practices in mind to make the app easy to maintain.

ACTIVITY 8.01: DI-BASED CALCULATOR

As a TypeScript developer, you are tasked with creating a calculator. Like any calculator, you need your app to do the four basic math operations of addition (+), subtraction (-), multiplication (*), and division (/).

> **NOTE**
>
> To keep things simple and focused solely on DI, you won't be adding support for additional operators (for example, power (^)), or support the order of operations, so your calculator will just walk through the expression from left to right and perform the relevant operation. For example, the expression (**13+5*3−7** will result in **47** and not the mathematically correct **21**).

To complete this activity, you will have to implement InversifyJS and utilize IoC to provide the math operators that the calculator can operate on.

You can start with the starter project and build it up by following the high-level steps provided here. This activity will challenge the skills that you have developed not only in this chapter but also in preceding ones. Hence, feel free to glance at the solution to debug any issues you may have with your implementation or code.

> **NOTE**
>
> This activity is based on the last section, on InversifyJS, so be sure you understand it fully before moving on to this one. You can find both the activity starter and solution at https://packt.link/Pt3Vq. The **activity-starter** folder contains the template files you can use to code along with this activity. The **activity-solution** folder contains the files representing the solution of this activity.

Perform the following steps to implement this activity:

1. You will have to start off by creating the basic building block of your calculator – an operator defined via an interface.

2. Then, create operators for addition, subtraction, multiplication, and division.

   For the preceding two steps, note that you need to create the requisite abstract interface and injection token.

3. Implement a calculator class that uses these operators via InversifyJS. This file represents your main app. You might need to map all expression parts and parse them. For this, you can refer to the **maths.ts** file placed in the **src/utils** folder, which creates and exports two such functions – **tryParseNumberString** and **tryParseOperatorSymbol**.

4. Configure the IoC container (present in the **src/ioc.config.ts** file) so that **Calculator** can receive **AddOperator**, **SubtractOperator**, and so on when it asks for **TYPES.AddOperator**, for example. You can simplify the **ioc.config.ts** file further by using barrels. The code for this can be found in the **operator/index.ts** file. You can use the code in the aforementioned file to configure and then simplify your IoC container.

5. Create the **main.ts** file that will kick-start your calculator.

   After solving the preceding steps, the expected output should look like the following:

```
result is 150
```

6. **Bonus Steps:**

   As a bonus, let's say that you want some reporting on the operations performed in the calculator. You can add logging (console- and file-based) easily without too many changes:

7. For console-based logging, you need to add a logger via DI that the calculator will write to on every expression evaluation. You can follow the given sequence to do so. First, you need to define the **Logger** interface. Then, create the console-based implementation of **Logger**. Next, create an injection token for it and register it in our container. Then, use the logger in the code for the main calculator app.

8. Now, let's say we want to replace our console-based logger with a file-based one, which will persist across runs so that we can track the calculator's evaluation history.

9. To do this, you first need to create a **FileLogger** class that implements **Logger** in a new file in the **src/logger** folder. Then, you need to make a single-line change in the **ioc.config.ts** file, which you used for console-based logging.

For console-based logging, use this command:

```
container.bind<Logger>(TYPES.Logger).to(ConsoleLogger);
```

For file-based logging, use this command:

```
container.bind<Logger>(TYPES.Logger).to(FileLogger);
```

However, note that you will have to correctly import all **Logger** interfaces across all files.

The output for the console-based logger is as follows:

```
[LOG] Calculated result of expression:13*10+20 is 150
```

The output for the file-based logger is as follows:

```
Activity01 > activity-solution > src > tmp >  ☰ calculator.log
   1     [LOG]: Calculated result of expression:13*10+20 is 150
```

Figure 8.7: Final output of the file-based logger in activity-starter/src/tmp/calculator.log, after changing the app to use it

---

NOTE

The solution to this activity can be found on page 636.

The solution to this activity (**activity-solution**) also includes unit tests for everything, so you can see how easy testing is when IoC is used as well as check that your own implementation passes the tests. In addition, **activity-solution** also includes a file that creates a **ConfigurationService** to supply **FileLogger** with a dynamic **loggerPath**, with implementations for an in-memory one, or an environment variables-based one.

There is a lot more ground to cover on InversifyJS. However, this chapter serves as a good start. We encourage you to take a look at the official documentation to learn more about what it can offer and to see further examples, including factories, container modules, and middlewares. However, these topics are beyond the scope of this chapter.

SUMMARY

This chapter equipped you first with the fundamentals of DI in TypeScript by explaining how you can implement the DI design pattern and by taking you through a number of use cases. You also learned how to build a basic Angular app using DI.

This chapter also introduced some basics of InversifyJS and explained how to use it in your applications. You have seen how easy it is to add or change dependencies without breaking the code for other consumers, along with the power of IoC and DI to replace one implementation with another in a very simple manner, for all consumers.

Of course, there's a lot more to this topic in general than this chapter covered. However, this chapter serves as a good start in getting up and running with DI in TypeScript. In the next chapter, you will learn about generics in TypeScript.

9

GENERICS AND CONDITIONAL TYPES

OVERVIEW

This chapter introduces generics and conditional types. This chapter first teaches you about what generics are, and some basic generics usage in different contexts – interfaces, classes, functions, and so on. Next, you'll learn about generic constraints, and how to make your code more type-safe while using generics, to avoid errors at runtime. Lastly, you'll learn about conditional types and how they make generics even more powerful by introducing type-level *logic* at compile time.

By the end of this chapter, you will be able to apply generics to real-world use cases.

INTRODUCTION

In the previous chapter, we saw how we can use dependency injection in TypeScript. In this chapter, we'll cover two of the more advanced features that TypeScript's type system offers, useful mostly in advanced applications or when building libraries – generics and conditional types.

TypeScript includes a very strong type system that covers a lot of use cases and advanced types. In earlier chapters, we saw some of the more basic ways in which you can utilize the type system while building applications.

Generics are one of the building blocks of many languages, such as Java, C#, Rust, and of course TypeScript, and they aim to allow developers to write dynamic and reuseable *generic* pieces of code with types that are *unknown* when writing the code but will be specified later, when using these generic pieces of code. In other words, generics are a sort of "placeholder" when the concrete type isn't known at the time of creating an application.

For example, if you want to write a generic *List* data structure, the implementation is the same for whatever type of item it may store, but the actual type of item is *unknown* when writing the *List* class. We can then use generics as a sort of a "placeholder" type when writing it, and the user of the *List* class will specify it when they know the concrete type it'll use, thereby filling in this "placeholder."

Conditional types allow us to bring *logic* into TypeScript's type system, which will be checked at *compile time*. This means that our types can be safer, and we can make code stricter, and move some of our logic from runtime to compile time, which means that less code needs to run on the server or in the user's browser. Additionally, conditional types allow us to write more complex types, with more complex relations between them.

For example, if we want to remove some options from a string literal union, we can use the **Extract** type to only take some of them:

```
type Only FooAndBar = Extract<"foo" | "bar" | "baz", "foo" | "bar">;  //
"foo" | "bar"
```

While not restricted to usage with generic types, conditional types are usually used in these cases, since you want to write some logic on a type unknown and ahead of time, because otherwise, you could write it explicitly yourself.

In this chapter, we'll explore both generics and conditional types and see how they can make your code more robust, resilient to changes, and offer a better developer experience when used externally.

GENERICS

As mentioned, generics help us write code that has types that are unknown when writing it but will be known later on, when someone uses the code. They allow us to put "placeholders" where concrete types would've been used otherwise, and for these placeholders to be filled in later, by the user of our code. Generics allow us to write a code once, and use it for multiple **types**, without losing type-safety along the way, or even increasing the type-safety in comparison to what we can achieve without it.

Let's see how generics help us with typing things more correctly, starting with a very basic function—**identity**:

```
// identity.ts
function identity(x: number): number {
    return x;
}
```

The **identity** function takes in a **number**, **x**, and just returns **x**. Now, let's say we want the same functionality for strings too:

```
// identityString.ts
function identityString(x: string) {
    return x;
}
```

Since type information is just for compile time, the two functions are the exact same in the compiled JavaScript output:

```
// identity.js
function identity(x) {
    return x;
}
```

```
// identityString.js
function identityString(x) {
    return x;
}
```

Since the output JavaScript code is the same and given that TypeScript only adds types on top of existing JavaScript, there's a way to type this existing **identity** function such that it'll support both use cases. We can type **identity** in multiple ways – the most simple way is to type **x** as **any**. However, this means we lose type-safety inside the function, not to mention in the **return** type:

```
function identity(x: any): any {
    return x;
}


const result = identity('foo');
result.toFixed();
```

This is probably not what we want. Since **result** is of type **any**, TypeScript cannot know that **result.toFixed()** in the preceding code will throw an error at runtime (since strings don't have a **toFixed()** method):

```
⊗ ▶ Uncaught TypeError: result.toFixed is not a function
        at eval (eval at <anonymous> (main-3.js:1239), <anonymous>:6:8)
        at main-3.js:1239
```

Figure 9.1: Running this code results in a TypeError at runtime

Instead, we can leverage generics – we'll type **x** as a generic type **T**, and return the same type from the function. Consider the following code:

```
function identity<T>(x: T): T {
    return x;
}
```

In TypeScript, generics are written using angled brackets, and a placeholder type name between them. In the preceding code, **T** is generic and serves as a "placeholder." Now if we update the code with the following details, we will get a compile-time error as shown here (red underline):

```
5    const stringResult = identity('foo');
6    const numberResult = identity(2);
7    stringResult.toFixed();
8    numberResult.toFixed();
```

Figure 9.2: Compile-time error due to generics being used

> **NOTE**
>
> The placeholder type name can be anything, and its name is only useful for the developer using the code – so try to give generic types useful names that have meaning in the context they're used in.

Note that we only have a single function (identity) implementation that can be used with both strings and numbers. TypeScript also knows the return type automatically and can provide useful errors at compile time. Moreover, we can pass any other type to the **identity** function, without the need to modify it at all.

> **NOTE**
>
> We didn't even have to tell TypeScript what the type of the generic is when calling **identity()**. TypeScript can usually infer the type of the generic(s) itself from the arguments.
>
> Usually, having to manually specify the type of the generic when calling a function is a code smell (a sign that the underlying code might contain a bigger problem), when it can be inferred from the arguments (though there are exceptions to this).

Generics come in all sorts of forms—from functions like we just saw, to interfaces, types, and classes. They all behave the same, just in their own scope—so function generics are only applicable for that function, while class generics are for that class's instance, and can also be used inside its methods/properties. In the next sections, we'll explore each of these types of generics.

GENERIC INTERFACES

Generic interfaces are interfaces that have some additional type, not previously known to the author of the interface, "attached" to them. This additional type gives "context" to the interface and allows better type-safety when using it.

In fact, if you've used TypeScript in the past, you've probably already interacted with generics, maybe without even realizing it. They are at play everywhere—just take a look at this basic line of code:

```
const arr = [1, 2, 3];
```

If you hover over **arr**, you'll see it's of type **number[]**:

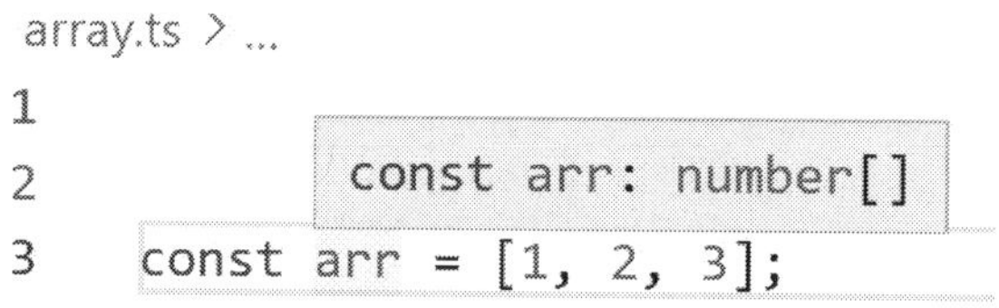

```
array.ts > ...
1
2           const arr: number[]
3    const arr = [1, 2, 3];
```

Figure 9.3: The type of arr is inferred to be number[]

number[] is just a shorter syntax for **Array<number>** —generics at play again.

In arrays, generics are used for the type of elements that the array holds. Without generics, **Array** would have to be typed with **any** all over the place or have a separate **interface** for every type possible (including non-built-in ones, so that's out of the question).

Let's take a look at the **Array<T>** interface definition:

TS lib.es5.d.ts ✕

```
1205    interface Array<T> {
1206      /**
1207       * Gets or sets the length of the array
1208       */
1209      length: number;
1210      /**
1211       * Returns a string representation of
1212       */
1213      toString(): string;
1214      /**
1215       * Returns a string representation of
1216       */
1217      toLocaleString(): string;
1218      /**
1219       * Removes the last element from an arra
1220       */
1221      pop(): T | undefined;
1222      /**
1223       * Appends new elements to an array, and
1224       * @param items New elements of the Arra
1225       */
1226      push(...items: T[]): number;
1227      /**
1228       * Combines two or more arrays.
1229       * @param items Additional items to add
1230       */
1231      concat(...items: ConcatArray<T>[]): T[];
```

Figure 9.4: Some of the Array<T> interface, where generics are heavily used

As you can see, the **pop, push**, and **concat** methods all use the **T** generic type to know what they return, or what they can accept as arguments. This is why the following code doesn't compile:

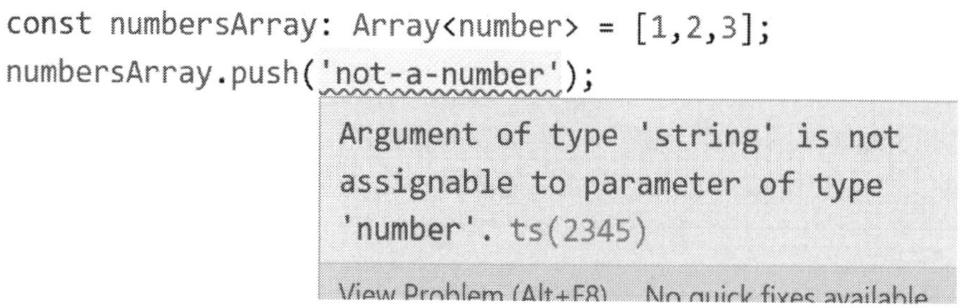

```
const numbersArray: Array<number> = [1,2,3];
numbersArray.push('not-a-number');
```

> Argument of type 'string' is not
> assignable to parameter of type
> 'number'. ts(2345)
>
> View Problem (Alt+F8)   No quick fixes available

Figure 9.5: An error when trying to push an incompatible type to an array with a specific generic type

This is also how TypeScript can infer the type of the **value** in the callback for **map**, **filter**, and **forEach**:

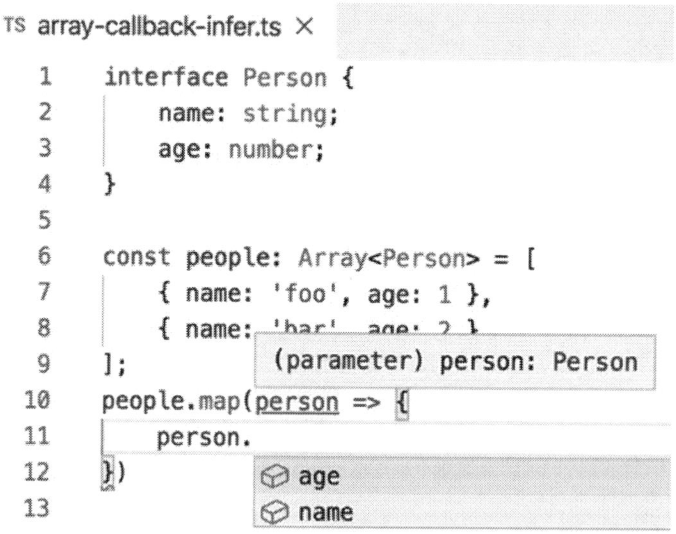

```
TS array-callback-infer.ts ×
1    interface Person {
2        name: string;
3        age: number;
4    }
5
6    const people: Array<Person> = [
7        { name: 'foo', age: 1 },
8        { name: 'bar', age: 2 }
9    ];                      (parameter) person: Person
10   people.map(person => {
11       person.
12   })              ⊘ age
13                   ⊘ name
```

Figure 9.6: Type inference when using the map method of `Array`

GENERIC TYPES

Generics can be used on plain types, for example, to create a **Dictionary<V>** type, and also to describe a map between strings of any values of type **V**, which is unknown ahead of time, and therefore *generic*:

```
type Dictionary<V> = Record<string, V>;
```

There are more use cases for generic types, but mostly you'll either be using them together with generic constraints (explained later in this chapter) or describing them with interfaces (though mostly anything that an **interface** can do, a **type** can as well).

GENERIC CLASSES

Generics are also very useful for classes. As we've seen earlier in the chapter, the built-in **Array** class uses generics. These generics are specified at the class's definition and apply to that instance of the class. Properties and methods of the class can then utilize that generic type for their own definitions.

For example, let's create a simple **Box<T>** class that holds a value of any type **T** and allows retrieving it later:

```
class Box<T>  {
    private _value: T;

    constructor(value: T) {
        this._value = value
    }

    get value(): T {
        return this.value;
    }

}
```

The **_value** property, the **constructor**, and the **value** getter use the **T** generic type from the class's definition for their own types. This type could also be used for other methods in this class if there were any.

Additionally, methods of the class can add their own generics, which will only apply to that method's scope – for example, if we wanted to add a **map** method to the **Box** class, we could type it like so:

```
class Box<T>  {
    ...

    map<U>(mapper: (value: T) => U): U {
        return mapper(this.value)
    }
}
```

The **U** generic type can be used inside the **map** method declaration, as well as within its implementation, but it cannot be used in other class members (like the **value** getter from earlier), unlike **T** – which is scoped to the entire class.

EXERCISE 9.01: GENERIC SET CLASS

In this exercise, we'll create a **Set<T>** class that implements that **Set** data structure – a data structure that can hold items, without a specific order, and without duplications, using generics.

Follow these steps to implement this exercise:

> **NOTE**
>
> The code file for this exercise can be found here: https://packt.link/R336a.

1. Start by creating a **Set** class that has a generic **T** type. This type will be the type of the items in the set:

```
class Set<T> {
}
```

2. Next, let's add a constructor that takes some optional initial values. These will need to be an array with items of type **T**, to match our **Set** items:

```
class Set<T> {
  private items: T[];

  constructor(initialItems: T[] = []) {
```

```
      this.items = initialItems;
  }
}
```

We use default parameters to initialize **initialItems** with an empty array if we haven't been supplied with one – this makes this parameter optional, while still making it convenient to work with inside our constructor implementation.

3. Let's add the **size** getter, which returns the size of the set. This will simply be our **items** length:

```
class Set<T> {
  private items: T[];

  //...

  get size(): number {
    return this.items.length;
  }
}
```

4. Next, let's add a **has** method, which checks whether a given item is already in the set:

```
class Set<T> {
  private items: T[];

  //...

  has(item: T): boolean {
    return this.items.includes(item);
  }
}
```

Notice that we use the **T** type in the **has** definition – we can use it since it's in the scope of the class, where **T** was declared.

5. Lastly, we also need a way to add and remove items from our set – let's add those:

```
class Set<T> {
  ...

  add(item: T): void {
```

```
        if (!this.has(item)) {
           this.items.push(item);
        }
     }


     remove(item: T): void {
       const itemIndex = this.items.indexOf(item);
       if (itemIndex >= 0) {
          this.items.splice(itemIndex, 1);
       }
     }
   }
```

For the **add** method, we first check whether the given **item** already exists, and if not, add it.

For the **remove** method, we look for the index of the given item. If it exists, we remove it from the array.

6.   Now, write the following two lines of code:

```
const set = new Set <number>([1,2,3]);
set.add(1) // works - since 1 is a number
set.add('hello') //Error - since 'hello' is not a number
```

On your IDE, you will see the following:

```
   }
 }                   Argument of type 'string' is not assignable to parameter of
 const se            type 'number'. ts(2345)
 set.add(            View Problem (Alt+F8)   No quick fixes available
 set.add('hello') //Error - since 'hello' is not a number
```

Figure 9.7: Type-safety in the Set class because of generics

We can see how the **Set** class can be used, and how it keeps itself type-safe, not allowing items of multiple types to be mixed together in the same class, for instance, in the following *step 7*.

7. Lastly, if you go back to the **Set** class implementation, you'll notice that the type of **items** within the class is **T[]**, so if we tried to add an item that TypeScript doesn't know is of type **T** to the **items** array, we'd get an error:

```
has(item: T): boolea  Argument of type '"some-string"' is not assignable to parameter of type
    return this.item  'T'.
}                        '"some-string"' is assignable to the constraint of type 'T', but 'T'
                      could be instantiated with a different subtype of constraint '{}'. (2345)
add(item: T): void {  Peek Problem    No quick fixes available
    this.items.push('some-string')
```

Figure 9.8: Type-safety in the Set class because of generics

This is expected, since **T** can be of any type, and not just a string – as we saw in the preceding example where we created a **Set<number>** – a set that can only hold numbers.

GENERIC FUNCTIONS

We've already briefly seen generic functions at the beginning of this chapter with the **identity<T>()** function. But let's look at a more real-world, more useful use case—say you want to write a wrapper around **fetch()** for fetching JSON data, such that users won't have to call **.json()** on the response. Consider the following code:

```
interface FetchResponse {
    status: number;
    headers: Headers;
    data: any;
}

async function fetchJson(url: string): Promise<FetchResponse> {
    const response = await fetch(url);

    return {
      headers: response.headers,
      status: response.status,
      data: await response.json(),
    };
}
```

Here, we use the browser's **fetch** function to make a **GET** call to the given **url** and then return an object with the main parts of the response – the **headers**, the status code (**status**), and the body, after parsing it as JSON (**data**).

> **NOTE**
>
> **fetch()** is not part of ECMAScript and is therefore not part of the language. It's available natively in all modern browsers and can be used in Node.js via packages such as **node-fetch**, **isomorphic-fetch**, and others.

The **json()** method returns **Promise<any>**. This means that the following code *may* throw at runtime, if the returned object doesn't have a **title** property, or it isn't of type **string**:

```
    const { data } = await fetchJson('https://jsonplaceholder.typicode.
com/todos/1');
    console.log(data.title.toUpperCase()); // does data have a title
property? What type is it?..
```

It would be useful if a consumer calling the **fetchJson** function could know what the type of **data** is. For that, we could add a generic type to the **fetchJson** function, which we'd also need to indicate in the return type somehow – that's where **interface** and **type** generics come in again. Consider the following code of **fetchJson.ts**:

```
// fetchJson.ts
interface FetchResponse<T> {
    status: number;
    headers: Headers;
    data: T;
}

async function fetchJson<T>(url: string): Promise<FetchResponse<T>> {
    const response = await fetch(url);

    return {
        headers: response.headers,
```

```
        status: response.status,
        data: await response.json(),
    };
}
```

This is very similar to the first declaration of **fetchJson** seen previously. Actually, the resulting JavaScript is exactly the same. However, this declaration now uses generics to allow the users of the function to specify the return type expected from making the **GET** call.

Now consider the code of **usage.ts**:

```
// usage.ts
(async () => {
    interface Todo {
        userId: number;
        id: number;
        title: string;
        completed: boolean;
    }
    const { data } = await fetchJson<Todo>('https://jsonplaceholder.
typicode.com/todos/1');

    console.log(data.title); // ✔ title is of type 'string'
    console.log(data.doesntExist); // ✘ 'doesntExist' doesn't compile
})();
```

Here, we allow the user to pass in a **T** generic type to **fetchJson<T>()**, which the function declaration later passes to the **FetchResponse<T>** interface, tying things together.

> **NOTE**
>
> Just like interfaces, generics only exist at compile time. So, anything you write there is as safe as you make the compiler understand it to be. For example, if you were to type **Todo** differently, or pass a different type, then the actual result – there is no guard built into TypeScript to verify it at runtime (without user/library code – see user type guard in *Chapter 5, Inheritance and Interfaces*).

Note that in the preceding example, the **T** generic is a *convenience generic*—it's only there for the user's convenience—it's only used once, and doesn't offer any more type-safety than a simple type assertion would:

```
const response = await fetchJson('https://jsonplaceholder.typicode.com/
todos/1');
const todo = response.data as Todo;
```

Note that generics, just like variables, have scopes, and you can define generics at multiple levels, letting the user provide them as needed. For example, notice how we use the **T** generic type that's declared in the **map** function, in our inner function (in line 2 in the following snippet):

```
function map<T, U>(fn: (item: T) => U) {
    return (items: T[]) => {
        return items.map(fn);
    };
}


const multiplier = map((x: number) => x * 2);
const multiplied = multiplier([1, 2, 3]); // returns: [2, 4, 6]
```

This applies to things such as interfaces and classes too. In the **Array<T>** interface, the **map** function takes an additional generic to be used as the output type, as can be seen in the **Array<T>** interface declaration in TypeScript:

```
interface Array<T> {
    // ...
    map<U>(callbackfn: (value: T, index: number, array: T[]) => U,
thisArg?: any): U[];
    // ...
}
```

Consider the following screenshot:

```
7    const arr: Array<number> = [1, 2, 3];
8    const strArr = arr.map(n => n.toString());
9
            (method) Array<number>.map<string>(callbackfn: (value: number, index: nu
            mber, array: number[]) => string, thisArg?: any): string[] (+1 overload)
```

Figure 9.9: The map method of Array<T> has a return type inferred based
on the type returned from callbackfn

Once we add the code shown above, again, we don't need to explicitly tell TypeScript that **U** is **string** – it can *infer* it from the return type of the callback function (though we could explicitly pass it if we wanted to). The **map** method of **Array<T>** has a return type inferred based on the type returned from **callbackfn**. It's inferred to **string[]** in this case.

GENERIC CONSTRAINTS

Sometimes you want to define a generic to be constrained to some subset of types. At the beginning of this chapter, we looked at the **identity** function – there it was easy and made sense to support *any* type. But what about typing a **getLength** function – which only makes sense for arrays and strings. It doesn't make sense to accept just *any* type – what would the output of **getLength(true)** be? In order to constrain the type of values our function can accept, we can use generic constraints. Consider the following code:

```
function getLength<T extends any[] | string>(x: T): number {
    return x.length;
}
```

This definition *constrains* the given **T** type to be a subtype of either **any[]** (an array of anything – **string[]**, **number[]**, or any **Foo[]** would all be valid types) or a **string**. If we pass an invalid type, we get a compilation error as you can see here:

```
5   getLength([1, 2, 3]); //    returns 3
6   getLength('Hello world'); //    returns 11
7   getLength(123); // ✗ Error: Argument of type '123' is not assignable to parameter of type 'string | any[]'
8   getLength(true); // ✗ Error: Argument of type 'true' is not assignable to parameter of type 'string | any[]'
9   getLength({}) // ✗ Error: Argument of type '{}' is not assignable to parameter of type 'string | any[]'
10
```

Figure 9.10: Compile-time errors are given for invalid types when passed
to the getLength function

There are many use cases for generic constraints, and more often than not you'll want to set some of these in place when using generics, since when writing the code, you probably assume some underlying type for it. Additionally, putting generic constraints lets TypeScript narrow the possible type of the generic type, and gives you better suggestions and type-checking.

For example, in a more real-world scenario, we might have some functions that return us plain dates while others return an epoch. We want to always work with dates, so we can create a function, **toDate**, that accepts these types and normalizes a **Date** function from them:

```
function toDate<T extends Date | number>(value: T) {
    if (value instanceof Date) {
        return value;
    }

    return new Date(value);
}
```

Here, we first check if the given value is a date. If so, we can just return it. Otherwise, we create a new **Date** function with the **value** and return that.

Generic constraints are especially powerful for creating higher-order functions, where typing the incoming function can be very hard, and keeping type-safety is a big benefit for code maintainability. In the next exercise, we'll see more uses for generic constraints in a real-world application and cases where it brings better typing to our code.

> **NOTE**
>
> Higher-order functions are functions that either take in another function as an argument or return a function. We'll explore these more in *Chapter 12, Guide to Promises in TypeScript*.

EXERCISE 9.02: THE GENERIC MEMOIZE FUNCTION

In this exercise, we'll create a **memoize** function that, using generics, will be completely type-safe—it takes in a function and returns a function of the same type.

> **NOTE**
>
> Memoization is a way to optimize performance, by reducing the number of times something is done. A memorization function is a higher-order function that caches the results of the inner function passed to it.

Follow these steps to implement this exercise:

> **NOTE**
>
> The code files for this exercise can be found here: https://packt.link/zUx6H.

1. Start by implementing the naïve function definition. We'll add types later:

```
function memoize(fn: Function, keyGetter?: (args: any[]) => string) {
    // TODO: we'll implement the function in the next steps
}
```

memoize takes in a function, **fn**, to memoize, as well as an optional **keyGetter** to serialize the arguments to a key, used for later lookups.

2. Next, let's implement the function itself:

```
function memoize(fn: Function, keyGetter?: (args: any[]) => string) {
    const cache: Record<string, any> = {};

    return (...args: any[]) => {
        const key = (keyGetter || JSON.stringify)(args);

        if (!(key in cache)) {
            cache[key] = fn(...args);
        }

        return cache[key];
    };
}
```

In the **memoize** function, we create an empty **cache** dictionary – the keys are the serialized arguments, and the values are the results of running the **fn** function on those arguments.

We then return a function that, given some arguments, **args** will check to see if the results for running **fn** with them have already been cached. If they haven't, we run **fn** with these arguments and cache the result. Lastly, we return the value we have stored in the cache, which is either a past calculation or the one we just ran and cached.

3. To test this out, we'll write an "expensive" function with one that loops for 10 seconds before adding two numbers:

```
function expensiveCalculation(a: number, b: number) {
    const timeout = 10000;
    const start = Date.now();
    while (Date.now() <= start + timeout);

    return a + b;
}
```

> **NOTE**
>
> Since memoization is meant to reduce the number of calls, it is usually effective in functions that take a long time to run – to illustrate this, we made **expensiveCalculation**, a function that takes a needlessly long time to run (10 seconds).

4. Next's let's **memoize** it:

```
const memoizedExpensiveCalculation = memoize(expensiveCalculation);
```

Notice that the memoized version is not type-safe. It does verify that we give it a **function**, but the returned value is a very loosely typed function, which may fail at runtime or have unexpected behavior if not typed correctly – you can pass in any number of arguments to it, with any type, and it will compile fine, even though at runtime the function expects to only be called with two arguments, both of which should be of type **number**.

Here we are memoizing with the following:

```
expensiveCalculation("not-a-number", 1);
memoizedExpensiveCalculation("not-a-number", 1);
```

5. On your IDE, hover over the preceding two line of code. You will notice the following:

```
57         const memoizedExpensiveCalculation: (...args: any[]) => any
58    const memoizedExpensiveCalculation = memoize(expensiveCalculation);
59
60    expensiveCalculation('not-a-number', 1); // 🐛 Argument of type '"not-a-number"' is not assignable to parameter of type 'number'.
61    memoizedExpensiveCalculation('not-a-number', 1); // ✗ compiles without errors, when it shouldn't.
```

Figure 9.11: Message on the IDE

As can be seen in the preceding screenshot, the memoized version of **expensiveCalculation** is not type-safe – it allows passing in a string as the first parameter, when it should only accept a number.

6. Go back to the top of the file and then add generic constraints and make our **memoize** function more type-safe. First, we need to define a couple of helper types:

```
type AnyFunction = (...args: any[]) => any;
type KeyGetter<Fn extends AnyFunction> = (...args: Parameters<Fn>) =>
string;
```

The first type, **AnyFunction**, describes a function that takes any number of arguments and returns anything. The second type, **KeyGetter**, describes a function that takes in the parameters of the generically constrained function **Fn** and returns a string. Notice that we constrain **Fn** to be of type **AnyFunction**. This ensures that we get a function, and allows us to use the built-in **Parameters<T>** type, which takes in a type of a function and returns the parameters it takes.

7. Next, make our **memoize** function definition more type-safe using the two types we just defined – typing both arguments in a better way:

```
function memoize<Fn extends AnyFunction>(fn: Fn, keyGetter?:
KeyGetter<Fn>) {
```

Again, we constrain **Fn** to be of type **AnyFunction** to ensure we get a function, as we did before, as well as to be able to use the specific function type later, for our return type.

Now we have a more type-safe function, since **keyGetter** is now type-safe but it still doesn't return a typed function back.

8. Let's fix that by also making the implementation more type-safe:

```
function memoize<Fn extends AnyFunction>(fn: Fn, keyGetter?:
KeyGetter<Fn>) {
    const cache: Record<string, ReturnType<Fn>> = {};

    return (...args: Parameters<Fn>) => {
        const key = (keyGetter || JSON.stringify)(args);

        if (!(key in cache)) {
            cache[key] = fn(...args);
```

```
        }

        return cache[key];
    };
}
```

We use **ReturnType<Fn>** for the values of our cache instead of **any**. **ReturnType<T>** is another built-in type that types in a type of a function and returns the return type of that function. We also use the **Parameters<T>** type again here, to describe the function we're returning from **memoize**.

9. Hover your mouse over **memoizedExpensiveCalculation('not-a-number')**. Now, our **memoize** implementation is completely type-safe, and the code that didn't cause a compile-time error in *step 4* now runs correctly:

```
const memoizedExpensiveCalculation: (a: number, b: number) => number  a-number"' is not assignab
memoizedExpensiveCalculation("not-a-number", 1); // ✖ compiles without errors, when it shouldn't
```

Figure 9.12: The type of memoizedExpensiveCalculation is the same as the original expensiveCalculation function

This exercise demonstrates how generics can be used in functions and types, and how they integrate with one another. Using generics here is what allows the **memoize** function to be completely type-safe, so there is less chance of our code hitting errors during runtime.

GENERIC DEFAULTS

Sometimes, you want to *allow* for generics, but not *require* them – you want to give some sensible defaults, but allow overriding them as needed. For example, consider the following definition of an **Identifiable** interface:

```
interface Identifiable<Id extends string | number = number> {
    id: Id;
}
```

This can be used by other interfaces like so:

```
interface Person extends Identifiable<number> {
    name: string;
    age: number;
}

interface Car extends Identifiable<string> {
    make: string;
```

```
}
```

```
declare const p: Person; // typeof p.id === 'number'
declare const c: Car; // typeof c.id === 'string';
```

The current implementation requires every implementer of the **Identifiable**
interface to specify the type of **Id** it has. But maybe we want to give some default,
so you only have to specify it if you don't want that default type. Consider the
following code:

```
interface Identifiable<Id extends string | number = number> {
    id: Id;
}
```

Notice the **bolded** code change. We give the **Id** generic type a default type of
number, which simplifies the code for the implementors of this interface:

```
interface Person extends Identifiable {
    name: string;
    age: number;
}
```

```
interface Car extends Identifiable<string> {
    make: string;
}
```

Note that now **Person** doesn't have to specify the type of **Id**, and the code is
equivalent to before.

Another, more real-world, scenario is with React components—each React
component *may* have props and *may* have state, both of which you can specify when
declaring a component (by extending React's **Component** type), but it doesn't have to
have either, so there's a default **{ }** given to the generic type of both:

```
// Base component for plain JS classes
// tslint:disable-next-line:no-empty-interface
interface Component<P = {}, S = {}, SS = any> ex
```

Figure 9.13: Partial snippet from the @**types/react** package

This makes React components have no props and no state by default, but these can
be specified if they need either of them.

CONDITIONAL TYPES

Conditional types were introduced in TypeScript 2.8 and allow complex type expressions, some of which drive some of the built-in types we saw earlier. These are really powerful, since they allow us to write *logic* inside our types. The syntax for this is **T extends U ? X : Y**. This is very similar to the regular JavaScript ternary operator, which allows for inline conditions, the only difference in the syntax is that you have to use the **extends** keyword and that this check is done at compile time and *not* runtime.

This allows us to write a **NonNullable<T>** type:

```
type NonNullable<T> = T extends null | undefined ? never : T;
```

This is already built into the language, but it's driven by the same code you could write in your app.

This means that you can check whether a type is nullable at compile time and change the type signature or inference based on that. An example use case for this would be an **isNonNullable** function. Consider the following code:

```
function isNonNullable<T>(x: T): x is NonNullable<T> {
    return x !== null && x !== undefined;
}
```

The preceding code together with the **filter** method of **Array** can allow you to filter for relevant items. For example, consider the following definition of an array with items of mixed types:

```
}
```
```
const arr: (number | null | undefined)[]
```
```
const arr = [1, 2, null, 3, undefined, 4];
```

Figure 9.14: The type of arr is an array, where each element is either number, null, or undefined

When we call **arr.filter(isNonNullable)**, we can get a properly typed array:

```
4
5    const   const nonNullableArr: number[]    4];
6    const nonNullableArr = arr.filter(isNonNullable);
```

Figure 9.15: The type of nonNullalbeArr is inferred to be number[]

Lastly, another addition to TypeScript in 2.8 was the **infer** keyword, which allows you to get help from the compiler in *inferring* the type of something, from another type.

Here's a simple example:

```
type ArrayItem<T extends any[]> = T extends Array<infer U> ? U : never;
```

Here, we want to get the inner type of an array (for example, for an array of type **Person[]**, you want to get **Person**). So we check if the passed generic type **T** **extends Array<infer U>** the **infer** keyword suggests to the compiler that the compiler should try to understand what the type is, and assign that to **U**, which we then use as the return value from this conditional type.

> **NOTE**
>
> This specific example type was also possible in previous versions via **type ArrayItem<T extends any[]> = T[number]**.

Another very useful example that was not previously possible outside of arrays was to "unbox" a type. For example, given the **Promise<Foo>** type, we want to get the **Foo** type back. This is now possible with the **infer** keyword.

Similarly to the last example, where we extracted the array inner type, we can use the same technique for any other generic type that "boxes" another type:

```
type PromiseValueType<T> = T extends Promise<any> ? T : never;
```

This will yield the following type information on the IDE:

```
type PromiseValueType<T> = T extends Promise<any> ? T : never;
interface Person {
    name: string;
    age: number;
}

type PromisedPerson = Promise<Person>;
    type UnpromisedPerson = Promise<Person>
type UnpromisedPerson = PromiseValueType<PromisedPerson>;
```

Figure 9.16: The type of UnpromisedPerson is Person

In the next activity, we'll take a look at a more real-world use case for conditional types, as well as usage of the **infer** keyword.

ACTIVITY 9.01: CREATING A DEEPPARTIAL<T> TYPE

In this activity, we'll be using concepts learned in this chapter—generics, conditional types, and the **infer** keyword—to create a **DeepPartial<T>** type. This type is like the built-in **Partial<T>** type. But we will work recursively and make every property in the object optional, recursively.

This will allow you to correctly type variables and so on so that all of their properties, at any level, can be optional. For example, a **REST** server will serve resources, and allow modifying them using a **PATCH** request, which should get a partial structure of the original resource, to modify.

> **NOTE**
>
> The code file for this activity can be found here: https://packt.link/YQUex.

To create this type, we'll need to deal with a few cases:

1. Primitives – strings, numbers, and other primitives, in addition to dates, are not something we can apply **Partial** to. So **DeepPartial<string> === string**.

2. For constructs like objects, **Array**, **Set**, and **Map**, we want to "reach into" the construct and apply **DeepPartial** to their values.

3. For everything else, we want to just apply **Partial**.

Perform the following steps to implement this activity:

1. Create a **PartialPrimitive** type.

2. Define a basic **DeepPartial<T>** type that can handle primitives and objects at the top level.

3. Add support for arrays by defining a **DeepPartialArray<T>** type and add handling for it in our **DeepPartial<T>** type.

4. Add support for sets by defining a **DeepPartialSet<T>** type and add handling for it in our **DeepPartial<T>** type.

5. Add support for maps by defining a **DeepPartialMap<T>** type and add handling for it in our **DeepPartial<T>** type.

6. Add support for plain objects, by applying the **?** property modifier on each of their properties, and passing their values wrapped in **DeepReadonly**.

> **NOTE**
>
> The solution to this activity can be found on page 650.

SUMMARY

This chapter got you started with the basics of generics and conditional types. We learned about generics in a lot of different use cases, why they are useful, as well as some extensions to their basic usage – generic defaults and conditional types. We performed a couple of exercises to show how you can include generics in your code to make it type-safe and avoid errors at runtime.

Generics are useful in all kinds of applications, both frontend and backend, and are used everywhere, but especially so in libraries, where a lot of the time, you want to expose an API that leverages the applications' types, which you might not know ahead of time.

In the next chapter, you'll learn about asynchronous development, some of which you encountered briefly in this chapter when typing external APIs.

10

EVENT LOOP AND ASYNCHRONOUS BEHAVIOR

OVERVIEW

In this chapter, you'll investigate how a web page actually works within the browser, with a special focus on how, when, and why the browser executes the JavaScript code we provide. You'll dive deep into the intricacies of the event loop and see how we can manage it. Lastly, you'll learn about the tools that TypeScript offers you. By the end of this chapter, you will be able to better manage the asynchronous nature of the execution.

INTRODUCTION

In the previous chapter, you learned the fundamentals of generics and conditional types. This chapter introduces you to event loops and asynchronous behavior. However, before you proceed with learning these topics, let's have a look at a hypothetical scenario to really understand how synchronous and asynchronous executions work.

Imagine a small bank that has a single teller. His name is Tom, and he's serving clients all day. Since it's a small bank and there are few clients, there's no queue. So, when a client comes in, they get Tom's undivided attention. The client provides all the necessary paperwork, and Tom processes it. If the process needs some kind of outside input, such as from a credit bureau or the bank's back-office department, Tom submits the request, and he and the client wait for the response together. They might chat a bit, and when the response comes, Tom resumes his work. If a document needs to be printed, Tom sends it to the printer that's right on his desk, and they wait and chat. When the printing is done, Tom resumes his work. Once the work is completed, the bank has another satisfied client, and Tom continues with his day. If somebody comes while Tom is serving a client (which happens seldom), they wait until Tom is completely done with the previous client, and only then do they begin their process. Even if Tom is waiting on an external response, the other client will have to wait their turn, while Tom idly chats with the current client.

Tom effectively works synchronously and sequentially. There are lots of benefits of this approach to working, namely, Tom (and his bosses) can always tell whether he is serving a client or not, he always knows who his current client is, and he can completely forget all the data about the client as soon as the client leaves, knowing that they have been serviced completely. There are no issues with mixing up documents from different clients. Any problems are easy to diagnose and easy to fix. And since the queue never gets crowded, this setup works to everyone's satisfaction.

So far, so good. But what happens when the bank suddenly gets more clients? As more and more clients arrive, we get a long queue, and everyone is waiting, while Tom chats with the current client, waiting on a response from the credit bureau. Tom's boss is, understandably, not happy with the situation. The current system does not scale – at all. So, he wants to change the system somehow, to be able to serve more clients. How can he do that? You will look at a couple of solutions in the following section.

THE MULTI-THREADED APPROACH

Basically, there are two different approaches. One is to have multiple Toms. So, every single teller will still work in the exact same simple and synchronous way as before – we just have lots of them. Of course, the boss will need to have some kind of organization to know which teller is available and which is working, whether there are separate queues for each teller, or a single large queue, along with some kind of distribution mechanism (that is, a system where a number is assigned to each customer). The boss might also get one of those big office printers, instead of having one printer per teller, and have some kind of rule in order to not mix up the print jobs. The organization will be complex, but the task of every single teller will be straightforward.

By now, you know we're not really discussing banks. This is the usual approach for server-side processing. Grossly simplified, the server process will have multiple sub-processes (called threads) that will work in parallel, and the main process will orchestrate everything. Each thread will execute synchronously, with a well-defined beginning, middle, and end. Since servers are usually machines with lots of resources, with heavy loads, this approach makes sense. It can accommodate low or high loads nicely, and the code that processes each request can be relatively simple and easy to debug. It even makes sense to have the thread wait for some external resource (a file from the file system, or data from the network or database), since we can always spin up new threads if we have more requests. This is not the case with real live tellers. We cannot just clone a new one if more clients come. The kind of waiting done by the threads (or by Tom) is usually referred to as *busy waiting*. The thread is not doing anything, but it's not available for any work, since it's busy doing something – it's busy waiting. Just like Tom was actually busy chatting with the client while waiting for a response from the credit bureau.

We have a system that can be massively parallel and concurrent, but still, each part of it is run synchronously. The benefit of this approach is that we can serve many, many clients at the same time. One obvious downside is the cost, both in hardware and in complexity. While we managed to keep the client processing simple, we'll need a huge infrastructure that takes care of everything else – adding tellers, removing tellers, queueing customers, managing access to the office printer, and similar tasks.

This will use all the available resources of the bank (or the server), but that is fine, since that's the whole point – to serve clients, as many and as fast as possible, and nothing else.

However, there is another approach – asynchronous execution.

THE ASYNCHRONOUS EXECUTION APPROACH

The other approach, the one taken by the web and, by extension, JavaScript and TypeScript, is to use just a single thread – so Tom is still on his own. But, instead of Tom idly chatting with a waiting client, he could do something else. If a situation arises where he needs some verification from the back office, he just writes down what he was doing and how far he got on a piece of paper, gives that paper to the client, and sends them to the back of the queue. Tom is now ready to start serving the next client in line. If that client does not need external resources, they are processed completely and are free to leave. If they need something else that Tom needs to wait for, they too are sent to the back of the line. And so on, and so forth. This way, if Tom has any clients at all, he's processing their requests. He's never busy waiting, instead, he's busy working. If a client needs to wait for a response, they do so separately from Tom. The only time Tom is idle is when he has no clients at all.

The benefit of this approach is fairly obvious – before, Tom spent a lot of his time chatting, now he is working all the time (of course, this benefit is from Tom's boss' point of view – Tom liked the small talk). An additional benefit is that we know our resource consumption up front. If we only have one teller, we know the square footage that we will need for the office. However, there are some downsides as well. The most important downside is that our clients now have to know our process quite intimately. They will need to understand how to queue and requeue, how to continue working from where they left off, and so on. Tom's work also got a lot more complicated. He needs to know how to pause the processing of a client, how to continue, how to behave if an external response is not received, and so on. This model of working is usually called asynchronous and concurrent. Doing his job, Tom will jump between multiple clients at the same time. More than one client will have their process started but not finished. And there's no way for a client to estimate how long it will take to process their task once it is started – it depends on how many other clients Tom processes at the same time.

From the early days, this model made much more sense for the web. For starters, web applications are processed on the device of the client. We should not make any technical assumptions about it – as we cannot be sure about the kind of device that the client might be using. In essence, a web page is a guest on the client's device – and it should behave properly. For example, using up all of a device's resources to show what amounts to a fancy animation is not proper behavior at all. Another important issue is security. If we think of web pages as applications that contain some code, we're basically executing someone's code on our machine whenever we enter a web address in the browser's address bar.

The browser needs to make sure that the code on the page, even if it's malicious, is restricted in what it can do to our machine. The web would not have been as popular as it is today if visiting a website could make your computer explode.

So, since the browser cannot know in advance which pages it will be used for, it was decided that each web page will only get access to a single thread. Also, for security reasons, each web page will get a separate thread, so a running web page cannot meddle in the execution of other pages that may execute at the same time (with features such as web workers and Chrome applications, these restrictions are somewhat loosened, but in principle, they still apply).

There is simply no way for a web page to spawn enough threads to swarm the system, or for a web page to get the data from another web page. And, since a web page needs to do lots of things at once, using the synchronous and sequential approach was out of the question. That is why all the JavaScript execution environments completely embraced the asynchronous, concurrent approach. This was done to such an extent that some common synchronization techniques are, intentionally, just not available in JavaScript.

For example, lots of other languages have a "wait some time" primitive, or a library function that does that. For example, in the C# programming language, we can have this code:

```
Console.WriteLine("We will wait 10 s");
Thread.Sleep(10000);
Console.WriteLine("... 10 seconds later");
Thread.Sleep(15000);
Console.WriteLine("... 15 more seconds later");
```

This code will write some text to the console, and 10 seconds later, write some more text. During the 25 seconds of the wait, the thread this executes on will be completely non-responsive, but the code written is simple and linear – easily understood, easily changeable, and easily debuggable. JavaScript simply does not have such a synchronous primitive, but it has an asynchronous variant in the **setTimeout** function. The simplest equivalent code would be the following:

```
console.log("We will wait 10 s");
setTimeout(() => {
    console.log("... 10 seconds later");
    setTimeout(() => {
        console.log("... 15 more seconds later");
    }, 15000);
}, 10000);
```

It's obvious that this code is much more complex than the C# equivalent, but the advantage that we get is that this code is non-blocking. In the 25 total seconds that this code is executing, our web page can do everything it needs to do. It can respond to events, the images can load and display, we can resize the window, scroll the text – basically, the application will resume the normal and expected functionalities.

Note that while it's possible to block the JavaScript execution with some special synchronous code, it's not easy to do it. When it does actually happen, the browser can detect that it did happen and terminate the offending page:

Figure 10.1: Unresponsive page

EXECUTING JAVASCRIPT

When a JavaScript execution environment, such as a node or a browser loads a JavaScript file, it parses it and then runs it. All the functions that are defined in a JavaScript file are registered, and all the code that is not in a function is executed. The order of the execution is according to the code's position in the file. So, consider a file having the following code:

```
console.log("First");
console.log("Second");
```

The console will always display this:

```
First
Second
```

The order of the output cannot be changed, without changing the code itself. This is because the line with **First** will be executed completely – always – and then, and only then, will the line with **Second** begin to execute. This approach is synchronous because the execution is synchronized by the environment. We are guaranteed that the second line will not start executing, until and unless the line above it is completely done. But what happens if the line calls some function? Let's take a look at the following piece of code:

```javascript
function sayHello(name){
    console.log(`Hello ${name}`);
}

function first(){
    second();
}

function second(){
    third();
}

function third(){
    sayHello("Bob");
}

first();
```

When the code is parsed, the environment will detect that we have four functions – **first**, **second**, **third**, and **sayHello**. It will also execute the line of code that is not inside a function (**first();**), and that will start the execution of the **first** function. But that function, while it's executing, calls the **second** function. The runtime will then suspend the running of the **first** function, remember where it was, and begin with the execution of the **second** function. This function, in turn, calls the **third** function. The same thing happens again – the runtime starts executing the **third** function, remembering that once that function is done, it should resume with the execution of the **second** function, and that once **second** is done, it should resume with the execution of the **first** function.

The structure the runtime uses to remember which function is active, and which are waiting, is called a **stack**, specifically, *the call stack*.

> **NOTE**
>
> The term "stack" is used in the sense of a stack of dishes, or a stack of pancakes. We can only add to the top, and we can only remove from the top.

The executing functions are put one on top of the other, and the topmost function is the one being actively executed, as shown in the following representation:

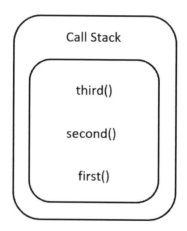

Figure 10.2: Stack

In the example, the **third** function will call the **sayHello** function, which will in turn call the **log** function of the **console** object. Once the **log** function finishes executing, the stack will start unwinding. That means that once a certain function finishes executing, it will be removed from the stack, and the function below it will be able to resume executing. So, once the **sayHello** function finishes executing, the **third** function will resume and finish in turn. This will trigger the continuation of the **second** function, and when that function is done as well, the **first** function will continue, and eventually finish. When the **first** function finishes executing, the stack will become empty – and the runtime will stop executing code.

It's worth noting that all of this execution is done strictly synchronously and deterministically. We can deduce the exact order and number of function calls just from looking at the code. We can also use common debugging tools such as breakpoints and stack traces.

EXERCISE 10.01: STACKING FUNCTIONS

In this exercise, we'll define few simple functions that call each other. Each of the functions will log to the console when it starts executing and when it's about to finish executing. We will analyze when and in what order the output is mapped to the console:

> **NOTE**
>
> The code files for this exercise can be found at https://packt.link/X7QZQ.

1. Create a new file, **stack.ts**.

2. In **stack.ts**, define three functions called **inner**, **middle**, and **outer**. None of them need to have parameters or return types:

```
function inner () {
}

function middle () {
}

function outer () {
}
```

3. In the body of the **inner** function, add a single **log** statement, indented by four spaces:

```
function inner () {
    console.log("    Inside inner function");
}
```

4. In the body of the **middle** function, add a call to the **inner** function. Before and after the call, add a **log** statement, indented by two spaces:

```
function middle () {
    console.log("  Starting middle function");
    inner();
    console.log("  Finishing middle function");
}
```

5. In the body of the **outer** function, add a call to the **middle** function. Before and after the call, add a **log** statement:

```
function outer () {
    console.log("Starting outer function");
    middle();
    console.log("Finishing outer function");
}
```

6. After the function declaration, create a call only to the **outer** function:

```
outer();
```

7. Save the file, and compile it with the following command:

```
tsc stack.ts
```

8. Verify that the compilation ended successfully and that there is a **stack.js** file generated in the same folder. Execute it in the **node** environment with this command:

```
node stack.js
```

You will see the output looks like this:

```
Starting outer function
  Starting middle function
    Inside inner function
  Finishing middle function
Finishing outer function
```

The output shows which function started executing first (**outer**), as that is the first message displayed. It can also be noted that the **middle** function finished executing after the **inner** function was already finished, but before the **outer** function was finished.

BROWSERS AND JAVASCRIPT

When a web page is requested by the user, the browser needs to do lots of things. We won't go into the details of each of them, but we'll take a look at how it handles our code.

First of all, the browser sends the request to the server and receives an HTML file as a response. Within that HTML file, there are embedded links to resources that are needed for the page, such as images, stylesheets, and JavaScript code. The browser then downloads those as well and applies them to the downloaded HTML. Images are displayed, elements are styled, and JavaScript files are parsed and run.

The order in which the code is executed is according to the file's order in the HTML, then according to the code's position in the file. But when are the functions called? Let's say we have the following code in our file:

```
function sayHello() {
    console.log("Hello");
}


sayHello();
```

First, the **sayHello** function is registered, and then when it's called later, the function actually executes and writes **Hello** to the console. Take a look at the following code now:

```
function sayHello() {
    console.log("Hello");
}

function sayHi() {
    console.log("Hi");
}


sayHello();
sayHi();
sayHello();
```

When the file with the preceding code is processed, it will register that it has two functions, **sayHello** and **sayHi**. Then it will detect that it has three invocations, that is, there are three tasks that need to be processed. The environment has something that is called the **task queue**, where it will put all the functions that need to be executed, one by one. So, our code will be transformed into three tasks. Then, the environment will check if the stack is actually empty, and if it is, it will take the first task off the queue and start executing it. The stack will grow and shrink depending on the execution of the code of the first task, and eventually, when the first task is finished, it will be empty. So, after the first task is executed, the situation will be as follows:

1. The execution stack will be empty.

2. The task queue will contain two tasks.

3. The first task will be completely done.

Once the stack is empty, the next task is dequeued and executed, and so on, until both the task queue and the stack are empty, and all the code is executed. Again, this whole process is done synchronously, in a specified order.

EVENTS IN THE BROWSER

Now, take a look at a different example:

```
function sayHello() {
    console.log("Hello");
}


document.addEventListener("click", sayHello);
```

If you have this code in a JavaScript file that is loaded by the browser, you can see that the **sayHello** function is registered but not executed. However, if you click anywhere on the page, you will see that the **Hello** string appears on the console, meaning the **sayHello** function got executed. If you click multiple times, you'll get multiple instances of **"Hello"** on the console. And this code did not invoke the **sayHello** function even once; you don't have the **sayHello()** invocation in the code at all.

What happened is, you *registered* our function as an event listener. Consider that you don't call our function at all, but the browser's environment will call it for us, whenever a certain event occurs – in this case, the `click` event on the whole `document`. And since those events are generated by the user, we cannot know if and when our code will execute. Event listeners are the principal way that our code can communicate with the page that it's on, and they are called asynchronously – you don't know when or if the function will be invoked, nor how many times it will be invoked.

What the browser does, when an event occurs, is to look up its own internal table of registered event handlers. In our case, if a `click` event occurs anywhere on the `document` (that's the whole web page), the browser will see that you have registered the `sayHello` function to respond to it. That function will not be executed directly – instead, the browser will place an invocation of the function in the task queue. After that, the regular behavior explained previously takes effect. If the queue and stack are empty, the event handler will begin executing immediately. Otherwise, our handler will wait for its turn.

This is another core effect of asynchronous behavior – we simply cannot guarantee that the event handler will execute immediately. It might be the case that it does, but there is no way to know if the queue and stack are empty at a specific moment. If they are, we'll get immediate execution, but if they're not, we'll have to wait our turn.

ENVIRONMENT APIS

Most of our interaction with the browser will be done in the same pattern – you will define a function, and pass that function as a parameter to some browser API. When and if that function will actually be scheduled for execution will depend on the particulars of that API. In the previous case, you used the event handler API, `addEventListener`, which takes two parameters, the name of an event, and the code that will be scheduled when that event happens.

> **NOTE**
>
> You can get a list of different possible events at
> https://developer.mozilla.org/en-US/docs/Web/Events.

In the rest of this chapter, you will use two other APIs as well, the environment's method to defer some code for later execution (**setTimeout**) and the ability to call on external resources (popularly called AJAX). There are two different AJAX implementations that we will be working with, the original **XMLHttpRequest** implementation, and the more modern and flexible **fetch** implementation.

SETTIMEOUT

As mentioned previously, the environment offers no possibility to pause the execution of JavaScript for a certain amount of time. However, the need to execute some code after some set amount of time has passed arises quite often. So, instead of pausing the execution, we get to do something different that has the same outcome. We get to schedule a piece of code to get executed after an amount of time has passed. To do that we use the **setTimeout** function. This function takes two parameters: A function that will need to be executed, and the time, in milliseconds, it should defer the execution of that function by:

```
setTimeout(function() {
    console.log("After one second");
}, 1000);
```

Here it means that the anonymous function that is passed as a parameter will be executed after 1,000 milliseconds, that is, one second.

EXERCISE 10.02: EXPLORING SETTIMEOUT

In this exercise, you'll use the **setTimeout** environment API call to investigate how asynchronous execution behaves and what it does:

> **NOTE**
>
> The code files for this exercise can be found at https://packt.link/W0mlS.

1. Create a new file, **delays-1.ts**.

2. In **delays-1.ts**, log some text at the beginning of the file:

```
console.log("Printed immediately");
```

3. Add two calls to the **setTimeout** function:

```
setTimeout(function() {
    console.log("Printed after one second");
}, 1000);

setTimeout(function() {
    console.log("Printed after two second");
}, 2000);
```

Here, instead of creating a function and giving it to the **setTimeout** function using its name, we have used an anonymous function that we have created in-place. We can also use arrow functions instead of functions defined with the **function** keyword.

4. Save the file, and compile it with the following command:

```
tsc delays-1.ts
```

5. Verify that the compilation ended successfully and that there is a **delays-1.js** file generated in the same folder. Execute it in the **node** environment with this command:

```
node delays-1.js
```

You will see the output looks like this:

```
Printed immediately
Printed after one second
Printed after two second
```

The second and third lines of the output should not appear immediately, but after 1 and 2 seconds respectively.

6. In the **delays-1.ts** file, switch the two calls to the **setTimeout** function:

```
console.log("Printed immediately");

setTimeout(function() {
    console.log("Printed after two second");
}, 2000);

setTimeout(function() {
    console.log("Printed after one second");
}, 1000);
```

7. Compile and run the code again, and verify that the output behaves identically. Even if the former **setTimeout** was executed first, its **function** parameter is not scheduled to run until 2 seconds have passed.

8. In the **delays-1.ts** file, move the initial **console.log** to the bottom:

```
setTimeout(function() {
    console.log("Printed after two second");
}, 2000);

setTimeout(function() {
    console.log("Printed after one second");
}, 1000);

console.log("Printed immediately");
```

9. Compile and run the code again, and verify that the output behaves identically. This illustrates one of the most common problems with code that behaves asynchronously. Even though the line was at the bottom of our file, it was executed first. It's much harder to mentally trace code that does not follow the top-down paradigm we're used to.

10. Create a new file, **delays-2.ts**.

11. In **delays-2.ts**, add a single call to the **setTimeout** function, and set its delay time to **0**. This will mean that our code needs to wait 0 milliseconds in order to execute:

```
setTimeout(function() {
    console.log("#1 Printed immediately?");
}, 0);
```

12. Add a **console.log** statement after the call to **setTimeout**:

```
console.log("#2 Printed immediately.");
```

13. Save the file, and compile it with the following command:

```
tsc delays-2.ts
```

14. Verify that the compilation ended successfully and that there is a **delays-2.js** file generated in the same folder. Execute it in the **node** environment with this command:

```
node delays-2.js
```

You will see the output looks like this:

```
#2 Printed immediately.
#1 Printed immediately?;
```

Well, that looks unexpected. Both lines appear basically immediately, but the one that was in the **setTimeout** block, and was first in the code, came after the line at the bottom of the script. And we explicitly told **setTimeout** not to wait, that is, to wait 0 milliseconds before the code got executed.

To understand what happened, we need to go back to the call queue. When the file was loaded, the environment detected that we had two tasks that needed to be done, the call to **setTimeout** and the bottom call to **console.log** (#2). So, those two tasks were put into the task queue. Since the stack was empty at that time, the **setTimeout** call started executing, and #2 was left in the task queue. The environment saw that it has a zero delay, so immediately took the function (#1), and put it *at the end* of the task queue, after #2. So, after the **setTimeout** call was done, we were left with two **console.log** tasks in the queue, with #2 being the first, and #1 being the second.

They got executed sequentially, and on our console, we got #2 first, and #1 second.

AJAX (ASYNCHRONOUS JAVASCRIPT AND XML)

In the early days of the web, it was not possible to get data from a server once the page was loaded. That was a huge inconvenience for developing dynamic web pages, and it was solved by the introduction of an object called **XMLHttpRequest**. This object enabled developers to get data from a server after the initial page load – and since loading data from a server means using an external resource, it had to be done in an asynchronous manner (even if it has XML right in the name, currently, it will mostly be used for JSON data). To use this object, you'll need to instantiate it and use a few of its properties.

To illustrate its usage, we'll try to get data about William Shakespeare from the Open Library project. The URL that we'll use to retrieve that information is https://openlibrary. org/authors/OL9388A.json, and the access method that we will use is **GET**, as we will only be getting data.

The data received is of a specific format, defined by Open Library, so you'll start by creating an interface for the data that you will actually use. You'll display only an image of the Bard (received as an array of photo IDs), and the name, so you can define the interface like this:

```
interface OpenLibraryAuthor {
  personal_name: string;
  photos: number[];
}
```

Next, create the **XMLHttpRequest** object, and assign it to a variable called **xhr**:

```
const xhr = new XMLHttpRequest();
```

Now you need to **open** a connection to our URL:

```
const url = "https://openlibrary.org/authors/OL9388A.json";
xhr.open("GET", url);
```

This call doesn't actually send anything, but it prepares the system for accessing the external resource. Lastly, you need to actually send the request, using the **send** method:

```
xhr.send();
```

Since the request is asynchronous, this call will execute and finish immediately. In order to actually process the data once this request is done, you need to add something to this object – a callback. That is a function that will not be executed by us, but by the **xhr** object, once some event happens. This object has several events, such as **onreadystatechange**, **onload**, **onerror**, **ontimeout**, and you can set different functions to react to different events, but in this case, you will just use the **onload** event. Create a function that will get the data from the response and show it on the web page where our script is running:

```
const showData = () => {
  if (xhr.status != 200) {
    console.log(`An error occured ${xhr.status}: ${xhr.statusText}`);
  } else {
    const response: OpenLibraryAuthor = JSON.parse(xhr.response);
    const body = document.getElementsByTagName("body")[0];

    const image = document.createElement("img");
```

```
    image.src = `http://covers.openlibrary.org/a/id/${response.
photos[0]}-M.jpg`;
    body.appendChild(image);

    const name = document.createElement("h1");
    name.innerHTML = response.personal_name;
    body.appendChild(name);
  }
};
```

In this method, you will be using some properties of the **xhr** variable that was defined previously, such as **status**, which gives us the HTTP status code of the request, or **response**, which gives us the actual response. If we just call the **showData** method by ourselves, we'll most likely get empty fields or an error, as the response will not have finished. So, we need to give this function to the **xhr** object, and it will use it to call the **showData** back:

```
xhr.onload = showData;
```

Save this code as **shakespeare.ts**, compile it, and add it to an HTML page using the following:

```
<script src="shakespeare.js"></script>
```

You will get a result similar to the following:

Figure 10.3: Retrieved image of William Shakespeare

ACTIVITY 10.01: MOVIE BROWSER USING XHR AND CALLBACKS

As a TypeScript developer, you have been tasked with creating a simple page to view movie data. The web page will be simple, with a text input field and a button. When you enter the name of a movie in the search input field and press the button, general information about the movie will be displayed on the web page, along with some images relevant to the movie.

You can use *The Movie Database* (https://www.themoviedb.org/) as a source of general data, specifically its API. You need to issue AJAX requests using **XmlHttpRequest**, and use the data the site provides to format your own object. When using an API the data will rarely, if ever, be in the format we actually need. This means that you will need to use several API requests to get our data, and piecemeal construct our object. A common TypeScript approach to this issue is to use two sets of interfaces – one that exactly matches the format of the API, and one that matches the data that you use in your application. In this activity, you need to use the **Api** suffix to denote those interfaces that match the API format.

Another important thing to note is that this particular API does not allow completely open access. You'll need to register for an API key and then send it in each API request. In the setup code for this activity, three functions (**getSearchUrl**, **getMovieUrl**, **getPeopleUrl**) will be provided that will generate the correct URLs for the needed API requests, once the **apiKey** variable is set to the value you will receive from The Movie Database. Also provided will be the base HTML, styling, as well as the code used to actually display the data – all that is missing is the data itself.

Those resources are listed here:

- **display.ts** – A TypeScript file that houses the **showResult** and **clearResults** methods, which you will call to display a movie and clear the screen, respectively.

- **interfaces.ts** – A TypeScript file that contains the interfaces that you will use. All interfaces that have an **Api** suffix are objects that you will receive from The Movie Database API, and the rest (**Movie** and **Character**) will be used to display the data.

- **script.ts** – A TypeScript file that has some boilerplate code that will start the application. The **search** function is here, and that function will be the main focus of this activity.

- **index.html** – An HTML file that has the basic markup for our web page.

- **styles.css** – A style sheet file that is used to style the results.

The following steps should help you with the solution:

1. In the **script.ts** file, locate the **search** function and verify that it takes a single string parameter and that its body is empty.

2. Construct a new **XMLHttpRequest** object.

3. Construct a new string for the search result URL using the **getSearchUrl** method.

4. Call the **open** and **send** methods of the **xhr** object.

5. Add an event handler for the **xhr** object's **onload** event. Take the response and parse it as a JSON object. Store the result in a variable of the **SearchResultApi** interface. This data will have the results of our search in a **results** field. If you get no results, this means that our search failed.

6. If the search returned no results, call the **clearResults** method.

7. If the search returned some results, just take the first one and store it in a variable, ignoring the other ones.

8. Inside the **onload** handler, in the successful search branch, create a new **XMLHttpRequest** object.

9. Construct a new string for the search result URL using the **getMovieUrl** method.

10. Call the **open** and **send** method of the constructed **xhr** object.

11. Add an event handler for the **xhr** objects's **onload** event. Take the response, and parse it as a JSON object. Store the result in a variable of the **MovieResultApi** interface. This response will have the general data for our movie, specifically, everything except the people who were involved in the movie. You will need to have another call to the API to get the data about the people.

12. Inside the **onload** handler, in the successful search branch, create a new **XMLHttpRequest** object.

13. Construct a new string for the search result URL using the **getPeopleUrl** method.

14. Call the **open** and **send** method of the constructed **xhr** object.

15. Add an event handler for the **xhr** object's **onload** event. Take the response, and parse it as a JSON object. Store the result in a variable of the **PeopleResultApi** interface. This response will have data about the people who were involved in the movie.

16. Now you actually have all the data you need, so you can create your own object inside the people **onload** handler, which is inside the movie **onload** handler, which is inside the search **onload** handler.

17. The people data has **cast** and **crew** properties. You'll only take the first six cast members, so first sort the **cast** property according to the **order** property of the cast members. Then slice off the first six cast members into a new array.

18. Transform the cast data (which is **CastResultApi** objects) into our own **Character** objects. You need to map the **character** field of **CastResultApi** to the **name** field of **Character**, the **name** field to the **actor** name, and the **profile_path** field to the **image** property.

19. From the **crew** property of the people data, you'll only need the director and the writer. Since there can be multiple directors and writers, you'll get the names of all directors and writers and concatenate them, respectively. For the directors, from the **crew** property, filter the people who have a **department** of **Directing** and a **job** of **Director**. For those objects, take the **name** property, and **join** it together with an **&** in between.

20. For the writers, from the **crew** property, filter the people who have a **department** of **Writing** and a **job** of **Writer**. For those objects, take the **name** property, and **join** it together with an **&** in between.

21. Create a new **Movie** object (using object literal syntax). Fill in all the properties of the **Movie** object using the data from the movie and people responses you prepared so far.

22. Call the **showResults** function with the movie you constructed.

23. In your parent directory (**Activity01** in this case), install dependencies with **npm i**.

24. Compile the program using **tsc ./script.ts ./interfaces.ts ./display.ts**.

25. Verify that the compilation ended successfully.

26. Open **index.html** using the browser of your choice.

You should see the following in your browser:

Figure 10.4: The final web page

> **NOTE**
>
> The solution to this activity can be found on page 654.

We will improve this application further in *Activity 10.02, Movie Browser using fetch and Promises,* and *Activity 10.03, Movie Browser using fetch and async/await.* However, before we do that, you need to learn about Promises and **async/await** in TypeScript.

PROMISES

Using callbacks for asynchronous development gets the job done – and that is great. However, in many applications, our code needs to use external or asynchronous resources all the time. So, very quickly, we'll get to a situation where inside our callback, there is another asynchronous call, which requires a callback inside the callback, which in turn needs a callback on its own....

It was (and in some cases, it still is) not uncommon to be a dozen levels deep inside the callback hole.

EXERCISE 10.03: COUNTING TO FIVE

In this exercise, we'll create a function that, when executed, will output the English words one through five. Each word will appear on the screen 1 second after the last word was displayed:

> **NOTE**
>
> The code files for this exercise can be found at https://packt.link/zD7TT.

1. Create a new file, **counting-1.ts**.

2. In **counting-1.ts**, add an array with the English number names up to and including five:

```
const numbers = ["One", "Two", "Three", "Four", "Five"];
```

3. Add a single call to the **setTimeout** function, and print out the first number after a second:

```
setTimeout(function() {
    console.log(numbers[0]);
}, 1000);
```

4. Save the file, and compile it with the following command:

```
tsc counting-1.ts
```

5. Verify that the compilation ended successfully and that there is a **counting-1. js** file generated in the same folder. Execute it in the **node** environment with this command:

```
node counting-1.js
```

You will see the output looks like this:

```
One
```

The line should appear 1 second after the application was run.

6. In the **counting-1.ts** file, inside the **setTimeout** function, below **console.log**, add another, nested, call to the **setTimeout** function:

```
setTimeout(function() {
    console.log(numbers[0]);
    setTimeout(function() {
        console.log(numbers[1]);
    }, 1000);
}, 1000);
```

7. Compile and run the code again, and verify that the output has an extra line, displayed 1 second after the first:

```
One
Two
```

8. In the **counting-1.ts** file, inside the nested **setTimeout** function, above **console.log**, add another nested call to the **setTimeout** function:

```
setTimeout(function() {
    console.log(numbers[0]);
    setTimeout(function() {
        setTimeout(function() {
            console.log(numbers[2]);
        }, 1000);
        console.log(numbers[1]);
    }, 1000);
}, 1000);
```

9. In the innermost **setTimeout** function, below **console.log**, add yet another nested call to **setTimeout**, and repeat the process for the fifth number as well. The code should look like this:

```
setTimeout(function() {
    console.log(numbers[0]);
    setTimeout(function() {
        setTimeout(function() {
            console.log(numbers[2]);
            setTimeout(function() {
```

```
            console.log(numbers[3]);
            setTimeout(function() {
                console.log(numbers[4]);
            }, 1000);
        }, 1000);
    }, 1000);
    console.log(numbers[1]);
}, 1000);
}, 1000);
```

10. Compile and run the code again, and verify that the output appears in the correct order as shown:

```
One
Two
Three
Four
Five
```

In this simple example, we implemented a simple functionality – counting to five. But as you can already see, the code is becoming extremely messy. Just imagine if we needed to count to 20 instead of 5. That would be a downright unmaintainable mess. While there are ways to make this specific code look a bit better and more maintainable, in general, that's not the case. The use of callbacks is intrinsically connected with messy and hard-to-read code. And messy and hard-to-read code is the best place for bugs to hide, so callbacks do have a reputation of being the cause of difficult-to-diagnose bugs.

An additional problem with callbacks is that there cannot be a unified API across different objects. For example, we needed to explicitly know that in order to receive data using the **xhr** object, we need to call the **send** method and add a callback for the **onload** event. And we needed to know that in order to check whether the request was successful or not, we have to check the **status** property of the **xhr** object.

WHAT ARE PROMISES?

Fortunately, we can promise you that there is a better way. That way was initially done by third-party libraries, but it has proven to be so useful and so widely adopted that it was included in the JavaScript language itself. The logic behind this solution is rather simple. Each asynchronous call is basically a promise that, sometime in the future, some task will be done and some result will be acquired. As with promises in real life, we can have three different states for a promise:

- A promise might not be resolved yet. This means that we need to wait some more time before we get a result. In TypeScript, we call these promises "pending."

- A promise might be resolved negatively – the one who promised broke the promise. In TypeScript, we call these promises "rejected" and usually we get some kind of an error as a result.

- A promise might be resolved positively – the one who promised fulfilled the promise. In TypeScript, we call these promises "resolved" and we get a value out of them – the actual result.

And since promises are objects themselves, this means that promises can be assigned to variables, returned from functions, passed as arguments into functions, and lots of other things we're able to do with regular objects.

Another great feature of promises is that it is relatively easy to write a promisified wrapper around an existing callback-based function. Let's try to promisify the Shakespeare example. We'll start by taking a look at the **showData** function. This function needs to do a lot of things, and those things are sometimes not connected to one another. It needs to both process the **xhr** variable to extract the data, and it needs to know what to do with that data. So, if the API we're using changes, we'll need to change our function. If the structure of our web page changes, that is, if we need to display a **div** instead of an **h1** element, we'll need to change our function. If we need to use the author data for something else, we'll also need to change our function. Basically, if anything needs to happen to the response, it needs to happen then and there. We have no way to somehow defer that decision to another piece of code. This creates unnecessary coupling inside our code, which makes it harder to maintain.

Let's change that. We can create a new function that will return a promise, which will provide the data about the author. It will have no idea what that data will be used for:

```
const getShakespeareData = () => {
  const result = new Promise<OpenLibraryAuthor>((resolve, reject) => {
    const xhr = new XMLHttpRequest();
    const url = "https://openlibrary.org/authors/OL9388A.json";
    xhr.open("GET", url);
    xhr.send();

    xhr.onload = () => {
      if (xhr.status != 200) {
        reject({
          error: xhr.status,
```

```
                    message: xhr.statusText
            })
        } else {
            const response: OpenLibraryAuthor = JSON.parse(xhr.response);
            resolve(response);
        }
    }
  });
  return result;
};
```

This function returns a **Promise** object, which was created using the **Promise** constructor. This constructor takes a single argument, which is a function. That function takes two arguments as well (also functions), which are by convention called **resolve** and **reject**. You can see that the function inside the constructor just creates an **xhr** object, calls its **open** and **send** methods, sets its **onload** property, and returns. So, basically, nothing gets done, except that the request is fired off.

A promise thus created will be in the pending state. And the promise stays in this state until one of the **resolve** or **reject** functions is called inside the body. If the **reject** function is called, it will transition to a rejected state, and we'll be able to use the **catch** method of the **Promise** object to handle the error, and if the **resolve** function is called, it will transition to the resolved state, and we'll be able to use the **then** method of the **Promise** object.

One thing that we should note is that this method does nothing that is UI-related. It does not print any errors on the console or change any DOM elements. It simply promises us that it will get us an **OpenLibraryAuthor** object. Now, we're free to use this object however we want:

```
getShakespeareData()
  .then(author => {
    const body = document.getElementsByTagName("body")[0];

    const image = document.createElement("img");
    image.src = `http://covers.openlibrary.org/a/id/${author.
photos[0]}-M.jpg`;
    body.appendChild(image);

    const name = document.createElement("h1");
    name.innerHTML = author.personal_name;
    body.appendChild(name);
  })
```

```
.catch(error => {
  console.log(`An error occured ${error.error}: ${error.message}`);
})
```

In this piece of code, we call the **getShakespeareData** data function, and then on its result, we're calling two methods, **then** and **catch**. The **then** method only executes if the promise is in the resolved state and it takes in a function that will get the result. The **catch** method only executes if the promise is in the rejected state, and it will get the error as an argument to its function.

One important note for the **then** and **catch** methods – they also return promises. This means that **Promise** objects are chainable, so instead of going in depth, as we did with callbacks, we can go in length, so to say. To illustrate that point, let's count to five once again.

> **NOTE**
>
> A more comprehensive discussion of Promises will be presented in *Chapter 12, Guide to Promises in TypeScript*.

EXERCISE 10.04: COUNTING TO FIVE WITH PROMISES

In this exercise, we'll create a function that, when executed, will output the English words one through five. Each word will appear on the screen 1 second after the last one was displayed:

> **NOTE**
>
> The code files for this exercise can be found at https://packt.link/nlge8.

1. Create a new file, **counting-2.ts**.

2. In **counting-2.ts**, add an array with the English number names up to and including five:

```
const numbers = ["One", "Two", "Three", "Four", "Five"];
```

3. Add a promisified wrapper of the **setTimeout** function. This wrapper will only execute when the given timeout expires:

```
const delay = (ms: number) => {
    const result = new Promise<void>((resolve, reject) => {
        setTimeout(() => {
            resolve();
        }, ms)
    });
    return result;
}
```

Since our promise will not return any meaningful result, instead just resolving after a given amount of milliseconds, we have provided **void** as its type.

4. Call the **delay** method with a parameter of **1000**, and after its resolution, print out the first number:

```
delay(1000)
.then(() => console.log(numbers[0]))
```

5. Save the file, and compile it with the following command:

```
tsc counting-2.ts
```

6. Verify that the compilation ended successfully and that there is a **counting-2. js** file generated in the same folder. Execute it in the **node** environment with this command:

```
node counting-2.js
```

You will see the output looks like this:

```
One
```

The line should appear 1 second after the application was run.

7. In the **counting-2.ts** file, after the **then** line, add another **then** line. Inside it, call the **delay** method again, with a timeout of 1 second:

```
delay(1000)
.then(() => console.log(numbers[0]))
.then(() => delay(1000))
```

We can do this because the result of the **then** method is **Promise**, which has its own **then** method.

8. After the last **then** line, add another **then** line, inside which you print out the second number:

```
delay(1000)
.then(() => console.log(numbers[0]))
.then(() => delay(1000))
.then(() => console.log(numbers[1]))
```

9. Compile and run the code again, and verify that the output has an extra line, displayed 1 second after the first.

10. In the **counting-2.ts** file, add two more **then** lines for the third, fourth, and fifth numbers as well. The code should look like this:

```
delay(1000)
.then(() => console.log(numbers[0]))
.then(() => delay(1000))
.then(() => console.log(numbers[1]))
.then(() => delay(1000))
.then(() => console.log(numbers[2]))
.then(() => delay(1000))
.then(() => console.log(numbers[3]))
.then(() => delay(1000))
.then(() => console.log(numbers[4]))
```

11. Compile and run the code again, and verify that the output appears in the correct order.

    Let's compare this code with the code of the previous exercise. It's not the cleanest code, but its function is relatively obvious. We can see how we could expand this code to count to 20. And the major benefit here is that this code, while asynchronous, is still sequential. We can reason about it, and the lines that are at the top will execute before the lines at the bottom. Furthermore, since we have objects now, we can even refactor this code into an even simpler and more extensible format – we can use a **for** loop.

12. In the **counting-2.ts** file, remove the lines starting with **delay(1000)** until the end of the file. Add a line that will define a resolved promise:

```
let promise = Promise.resolve();
```

13. Add a **for** loop that, for each number of the **numbers** array, will add to the **promise** chain a delay of 1 second, and print the number:

```
for (const number of numbers) {
    promise = promise
        .then(() => delay(1000))
        .then(() => console.log(number))
};}
```

14. Compile and run the code again, and verify that the output appears in the correct order as shown:

```
One
Two
Three
Four
Five
```

ACTIVITY 10.02: MOVIE BROWSER USING FETCH AND PROMISES

In this activity, we will be repeating the previous activity. The major difference is that, instead of using **XMLHttpRequest** and its **onload** method, we'll be using the **fetch** web API. In contrast to the **XMLHttpRequest** class, the **fetch** web API returns a **Promise** object, so instead of nesting our callbacks to have multiple API calls, we can have a chain of promise resolutions that will be far easier to understand.

The activity has the same files and resources as the previous activity.

The following steps should help you with the solution:

1. In the **script.ts** file, locate the **search** function and verify that it takes a single string parameter and that its body is empty.

2. Above the **search** function, create a helper function called **getJsonData**. This function will use the **fetch** API to get data from an endpoint and format it as JSON. It should take a single string called **url** as a parameter, and it should return a **Promise**.

3. In the body of the **getJsonData** function, add code that calls the **fetch** function with the **url** parameter, and **then** call the **json** method on the returned response.

4. In the **search** method, construct a new string for the search result URL using the **getSearchUrl** method.

5. Call the **getJsonData** function with the **searchUrl** as a parameter.

6. Add a **then** handler to the promise returned from **getJsonData**. The handler takes a single parameter of the type **SearchResultApi**.

7. In the body of the handler, check whether we have any results and if we don't, throw an error. If we do have results, return the first item. Note that the handler returns an object with **id** and **title** properties, but the **then** method actually returns a **Promise** of that data. This means that after the handler, we can chain other **then** calls.

8. Add another **then** call to the previous handler. This handler will take a **movieResult** parameter that contains the **id** and **title** of the movie. Use the **id** property to call the **getMovieUrl** and **getPeopleUrl** methods to, respectively, get the correct URLs for the movie details and for the cast and crew.

9. After getting the URLs, call the **getJsonData** function with both, and assign the resulting values to variables. Note that the **getJsonData(movieUrl)** call will return a **Promise** of **MovieResultApi**, and **getJsonData(peopleUrl)** will return a **Promise** of **PeopleResultApi**. Assign those result values to variables called **dataPromise** and **peoplePromise**.

10. Call the static **Promise.all** method with **dataPromise** and **peoplePromise** as parameters. This will create another promise based on those two values, and this promise will be resolved successfully if and only if both (that is, all) promises that are contained within resolve successfully. Its return value will be a **Promise** of an array of results.

11. Return the promise generated by the **Promise.all** call from the handler.

12. Add another **then** handler to the chain. This handler will take the array returned from **Promise.all** as a single parameter.

13. Deconstruct the parameter into two variables. The first element of the array should be the **movieData** variable of type **MovieResultApi**, and the second element of the array should be the **peopleData** variable of type **PeopleResultApi**.

14. The people data has **cast** and **crew** properties. We'll only take the first six cast members, so first sort the **cast** property according to the **order** property of the cast members. Then slice off the first six cast members into a new array.

15. Transform the cast data (which is **CastResultApi** objects) into your own **Character** objects. We need to map the **character** field of **CastResultApi** to the **name** field of **Character**, the **name** field to the **actor** name, and the **profile_path** field to the **image** property.

16. From the **crew** property of the people data, we'll only need the director and the writer. Since there can be multiple directors and writers, we'll get the names of all directors and writers and concatenate them, respectively. For the directors, from the **crew** property, filter the people who have a **department** of **Directing** and a **job** of **Director**. For those objects, take the **name** property, and **join** it together with an **&** in between.

17. For the writers, from the **crew** property, filter the people who have a **department** of **Writing** and a **job** of **Writer**. For those objects, take the **name** property, and **join** it together with an **&** in between.

18. Create a new **Movie** object (using object literal syntax). Fill in all the properties of the **Movie** object using the data from the movie and people responses we've prepared so far.

19. Return the **Movie** object from the handler.

20. Note that we did not do any UI interactions in our code. We just received a string, did some promise calls, and returned a value. The UI work can now be done in UI-oriented code. In this case, that's in the **click** event handler of the **search** button. We should simply add a **then** handler to the **search** call that will call the **showResults** method, and a **catch** handler that will call the **clearResults** method.

Although we used **fetch** and promises in this activity, and our code is now much more efficient but complex, the basic function of the website will be the same and you should see an output similar to the previous activity.

> **NOTE**
>
> The code files for this activity can be found at https://packt.link/leDTF.
> The solution to this activity can be found on page 658.

ASYNC/AWAIT

Promises solved the problem of callbacks quite nicely. However, often, they carry with them lots of unneeded fluff. We need to write lots of **then** calls, and we need to be careful not to forget to close any parentheses.

The next step is to add a piece of syntactic sugar to our TypeScript skills. Unlike the other things in this chapter, this feature originated in TypeScript, and was later adopted in JavaScript as well. I'm talking about the **async/await** keywords. These are two separate keywords, but they are always used together, so the whole feature became known as **async/await**.

What we do is we can add the **async** modifier to a certain function, and then, in that function, we can use the **await** modifier to execute promises easily. Let's go once more to our Shakespearean example, and let's wrap the code we used to call **getShakespeareData** inside another function, simply called **run**:

```
function run() {
    getShakespeareData()
    .then(author => {
        const body = document.getElementsByTagName("body")[0];

        const image = document.createElement("img");
        image.src = `http://covers.openlibrary.org/a/id/${author.
photos[0]}-M.jpg`;
        body.appendChild(image);

        const name = document.createElement("h1");
        name.innerHTML = author.personal_name;
        body.appendChild(name);
    })
    .catch(error => {
        console.log(`An error occured ${error.error}: ${error.message}`);
    })
}

run();
```

This code is functionally equivalent to the code we had previously. But now, we have a function that we can mark as an **async** function, like this:

```
async function run() {
```

Now, we're allowed to just get the result of a promise and put it inside of a variable. So, the whole **then** invocation will become this:

```
const author = await getShakespeareData();
const body = document.getElementsByTagName("body")[0];

const image = document.createElement("img");
image.src = `http://covers.openlibrary.org/a/id/${author.photos[0]}-M.jpg`;
body.appendChild(image);

const name = document.createElement("h1");
name.innerHTML = author.personal_name;
body.appendChild(name);
```

You can see that we don't have any wrapping function calls anymore. The **catch** invocation can be replaced with a simple **try/catch** construct, and the final version of the **run** function will look like this:

```
async function run () {
  try {
    const author = await getShakespeareData();
    const body = document.getElementsByTagName("body")[0];

    const image = document.createElement("img");
    image.src = `http://covers.openlibrary.org/a/id/${author.photos[0]}-M.jpg`;
    body.appendChild(image);

    const name = document.createElement("h1");
    name.innerHTML = author.personal_name;
    body.appendChild(name);
  } catch (error) {
    console.log(`An error occured ${error.error}: ${error.message}`);
  }
}
```

You will notice that the amount of code that is deeply nested is drastically reduced. Now we can look at the code, and have a good idea of what it does, just from a quick glance. This is still the same, deeply asynchronous code, the only difference is that it looks almost synchronous and definitely sequential.

EXERCISE 10.05: COUNTING TO FIVE WITH ASYNC AND AWAIT

In this exercise, we'll create a function that, when executed, will output the English words one through five. Each word will appear on the screen 1 second after the last one was displayed:

> **NOTE**
>
> The code files for this exercise can be found at https://packt.link/TaH6b.

1. Create a new file, **counting-3.ts**.

2. In **counting-3.ts**, add an array with the English number names up to and including five:

```
const numbers = ["One", "Two", "Three", "Four", "Five"];
```

3. Add a promisified wrapper of the **setTimeout** function. This wrapper will only execute when the given timeout expires:

```
const delay = (ms: number) => {
    const result = new Promise<void>((resolve, reject) => {
        setTimeout(() => {
            resolve();
        }, ms)
    });
    return result;
}
```

Since our promise will not return any meaningful results, instead of just resolving after a given number of milliseconds, we have provided **void** as its type.

4. Create an empty **async** function called **countNumbers** and execute it on the last line of the file:

```
async function countNumbers() {

}

countNumbers();
```

5. Inside the **countNumbers** function, await the **delay** method with a parameter of **1000**, and after its resolution, print out the first number:

```
async function countNumbers() {
    await delay(1000);
    console.log(numbers[0]);
}
```

6. Save the file, and compile it with the following command:

```
tsc counting-3.ts
```

7. Verify that the compilation ended successfully and that there is a **counting-3. js** file generated in the same folder. Execute it in the **node** environment with this command:

```
node counting-3.js
```

You will see the output looks like this:

```
One
```

The line should appear 1 second after the application was run.

8. In the **counting-3.ts** file, after the **console.log** line, add two more lines for the rest of the numbers as well. The code should look like this:

```
async function countNumbers() {
    await delay(1000);
    console.log(numbers[0]);
    await delay(1000);
    console.log(numbers[1]);
    await delay(1000);
    console.log(numbers[2]);
    await delay(1000);
    console.log(numbers[3]);
    await delay(1000);
    console.log(numbers[4]);
}
```

9. Compile and run the code again, and verify that the output appears in the correct order.

   Since the code is completely identical for all the numbers, it's trivial to replace it with a **for** loop.

10. In the **counting-3.ts** file, remove the body of the **countNumbers** function, and replace it with a **for** loop that, for each number of the **numbers** array, will **await** a delay of a second, and then print the number:

```
for (const number of numbers) {
    await delay(1000);
    console.log(number);
};
```

11. Compile and run the code again, and verify that the output appears in the correct order:

```
One
Two
Three
Four
Five
```

ACTIVITY 10.03: MOVIE BROWSER USING FETCH AND ASYNC/AWAIT

In this activity, we will be improving on the previous activity. The major difference is that instead of using the **then** method of the **Promises** class, we'll use the **await** keyword to do that for us magically. Instead of a chain of **then** calls, we'll just have code that looks completely regular, with some **await** statements peppered throughout.

The activity has the same files and resources as the previous activity.

The following steps should help you with the solution:

1. In the **script.ts** file, locate the **search** function and verify that it takes a single string parameter and that its body is empty. Note that this function is now marked with the **async** keywords, which allows us to use the **await** operator.

2. Above the **search** function, create a helper function called **getJsonData**. This function will use the **fetch** API to get data from an endpoint and format it as JSON. It should take a single string called **url** as a parameter, and it should return a promise.

3. In the body of the **getJsonData** function, add code that calls the **fetch** function with the **url** parameter, and **then** call the **json** method on the returned response.

4. In the **search** method, construct a new string for the search result URL using the **getSearchUrl** method.

5. Call the **getJsonData** function with **searchUrl** as a parameter, and **await** the result. Place the result into the **SearchResultApi** variable.

6. Check whether we have any results and if we don't, throw an error. If we do have results, set the first item of the **result** property into a variable called **movieResult**. This object will contain the **id** and **title** properties of the movie.

7. Use the **id** property to call the **getMovieUrl** and **getPeopleUrl** methods to, respectively, get the correct URLs for the movie details and for the cast and crew.

8. After getting the URLs, call the **getJsonData** function with both, and assign the resulting values to variables. Note that the **getJsonData(movieUrl)** call will return a promise of **MovieResultApi**, and **getJsonData(peopleUrl)** will return a promise of **PeopleResultApi**. Assign those result values to variables called **dataPromise** and **peoplePromise**.

9. Call the static **Promise.all** method with **dataPromise** and **peoplePromise** as parameters. This will create another promise based on those two values, and this promise will be resolved successfully if and only if both (that is, all) promises that are contained within resolve successfully. Its return value will be a promise of an array of results. **await** this promise, and place its result into a variable of type **array**.

10. Deconstruct that array into two variables. The first element of the array should be the **movieData** variable of type **MovieResultApi**, and the second element of the array should be the **peopleData** variable of type **PeopleResultApi**.

11. The people data has **cast** and **crew** properties. We'll only take the first six cast members, so first sort the **cast** property according to the **order** property of the cast members. Then slice off the first six cast members into a new array.

12. Transform the cast data (which is **CastResultApi** objects) into our own **Character** objects. We need to map the **character** field of **CastResultApi** to the **name** field of **Character**, the **name** field to the **actor** name, and the **profile_path** field to the **image** property.

13. From the **crew** property of the people data, we'll only need the director and the writer. Since there can be multiple directors and writers, we'll get the names of all directors and writers and concatenate them, respectively. For the directors, from the **crew** property, filter the people who have a **department** of **Directing** and a **job** of **Director**. For those objects, take the **name** property, and **join** it together with an **&** in between.

14. For the writers, from the **crew** property, filter the people who have a **department** of **Writing** and a **job** of **Writer**. For those objects, take the **name** property, and **join** it together with an **&** in between.

15. Create a new **Movie** object (using object literal syntax). Fill in all the properties of the **Movie** object using the data from the movie and people responses we've prepared so far.

16. Return the **Movie** object from the function.

17. Note that we did not do any UI interactions in our code. We just received a string, did some promise calls, and returned a value. The UI work can now be done in UI-oriented code. In this case, that's in the **click** event handler of the **search** button. We should simply add a **then** handler to the **search** call that will call the **showResults** method, and a **catch** handler that will call the **clearResults** method.

Although we used **fetch** and **async/await** in this activity, and our code is now just as efficient but less complex compared with the previous activity, the basic function of the website will be the same and you should see an output similar to the previous activity.

> **NOTE**
>
> The code files for this activity can be found at https://packt.link/fExtR.
> The solution to this activity can be found on page 662.

SUMMARY

In this chapter, we looked at the execution model that is used on the web, and how we can use it to actually execute code. We glanced at the surface of the intricacies of asynchronous development – and how we can use it to load data from external resources. We showed the problems that arise when we get too deep into the hole of callbacks and managed to exit it using promises. Finally, we were able to await our asynchronous code, and have the best of both words – code that looks like it's synchronous, but that executes asynchronously.

We also tested the skills developed in the chapter by creating a movie data viewer browser, first using XHR and callbacks, and then improved it progressively using `fetch` and promises, and then using `fetch` and `async/await`.

The next chapter will teach you about higher-order functions and callbacks.

11

HIGHER-ORDER FUNCTIONS AND CALLBACKS

OVERVIEW

This chapter introduces higher-order functions and callbacks in TypeScript. You will first understand what higher-order functions are, why they are useful, and how to type them correctly in TypeScript. Then, the chapter will teach you about what callbacks are, why they are used, and in what situations. You will also learn about why callbacks are so widely used, especially in Node.js.

Additionally, the chapter will provide you with a basic introduction to the event loop. Not only will you learn about "callback hell," but also how you can avoid it. By the end of this chapter, you will be able to create a well-typed higher-order `pipe` function.

INTRODUCTION

You have already covered the use of functions in TypeScript in *Chapter 3, Functions*. This chapter will introduce you to higher-order functions in TypeScript. Hitherto, with all the functions that you have used in this book, you either passed parameters or arguments into them. However, JavaScript and, by extension, TypeScript, has many ways of composing and writing code. In this chapter, we'll explore one such pattern – higher-order functions/callbacks (hereinafter called HOCs) are functions that either take in another function as an argument or return a function (or both).

Additionally, this chapter also explores the concept of callbacks. Callbacks are required in Node.js, as well as in other JavaScript runtimes, since the language is single-threaded and runs in an event loop, and so, in order to not hold up the main thread, we let other code run, and when needed it will call our code back. This chapter will also touch upon "callback hell" and equip you with the skills needed to avoid it.

INTRODUCTION TO HOCS – EXAMPLES

HOCs are frequently used in JavaScript, and especially in Node.js, where even the simplest backend server application contains it. Here is an example:

```
const http = require("http");

http.createServer((req, res) => {
  res.write("Hello World");
  res.end();
}).listen(3000, () => {
  console.log("🚀 running on port 3000");
});
```

Notice that the **createServer** function takes in a request listener *function*, which will be used to handle any incoming requests. This function will take in two arguments, **req** and **res** – the request object and the response object, respectively:

```
declare module "http" {
  // ...

  type RequestListener = (req: IncomingMessage, res: ServerResponse) => void;

  function createServer(requestListener?: RequestListener): Server;

  // ...
}
```

Figure 11.1: Part of the http module in Node.js describing the callback structure of RequestListener

In addition, the **listen** method also takes in an optional function that will run when the server is ready to listen for requests.

Both **createServer** and **listen** are HOCs because they take in functions as arguments. These argument functions are usually called *callbacks*, since this is how our code can get "called back" (notified) when something happens, and, if needed, handle it appropriately. In the preceding example, the HTTP server needs to know how to handle incoming requests, so it calls our given **requestListener** function, which provides the logic for that. Later, the **listen** function wants to let us know when it's ready to accept requests, and it calls our given callback when it is.

Another example is the **setTimeout** function, which takes in another *function* as an argument to call later – after the timeout has passed:

```
setTimeout(() => {
    console.log('5 seconds have passed');
}, 5000);
function setTimeout(callback: (...args: any[]) => void, ms: number,
...args: any[]): NodeJS.Timeout;
```

Another example of an HOC that does not take a callback function is the **memoize** function. This takes in a function to **memoize** as an argument and returns a function with the same signature:

```
function memoize<Fn extends AnyFunction>(fn: Fn, keyGetter?:
KeyGetter<Fn>): Fn;
```

> **NOTE**
>
> The `memoize` function takes in a function and returns a function with the same type signature; however, the returned function caches the results of the original function. This is usually useful for expensive functions that take a long time to run and return the same output for the same arguments. *Chapter 9*, *Generics and Conditional Types*, *Exercise 9.01*, implements such a `memoize` function.

In the following sections, we'll explore both kinds of HOCs in more detail and see how we can avoid some of the pitfalls they introduce.

HIGHER-ORDER FUNCTIONS

Higher-order functions are regular functions that follow at least one of these two principles:

1. They take one or more functions as arguments.

2. They return a function as a result.

For example, let's say we want to write a **greet** function:

Example01.ts

```
1 function greet(name: string) {
2   console.log(`Hello ${name}`);
3 }
4
5 greet('John');
```
Link to the preceding example: https://packt.link/GCFjN

The following is the output:

```
Hello John
```

This is a fine function, but it's very limited – what if each person has a favorite greeting? Consider the following example:

Example02.ts

```
1 const favoriteGreetings: Record<string, string> = {
2    John: 'Hey',
3    Jane: 'Hello',
4    Doug: 'Howdy',
5    Sally: 'Hey there',
6 };
```

Link to this example: https://packt.link/CXBrV

We could put that inside the **greet** function:

```
function greet(name: string) {
   const greeting = favoriteGreetings[name] || 'Hello';
   console.log(`${greeting} ${name}`);
}


greet('John');
```

The following is the output:

```
Hey John
```

But that means that the **greet** function is no longer reusable by itself since, if we were to take it, we'd also need to bring along the **favoriteGreetings** mapping with it. Instead, we could pass it in as a parameter:

Example03.ts

```
1 function greet(name: string, mapper: Record<string, string>) {
2    const greeting = mapper[name] || 'Hello';
3    console.log(`${greeting} ${name}`);
4 }
5
6 greet('John', favoriteGreetings); // prints 'Hey John'
7 greet('Doug', favoriteGreetings); // prints 'Howdy Doug'
```

Link to this example: https://packt.link/bG0p7

The following is the output:

```
Hey John
Howdy Doug
```

This works, but it's very cumbersome to pass in the **favoriteGreetings** object in every call.

We can improve on this by making the **greet** function accept a function that will serve as a more generic solution to the favorite-greeting issue – it will accept the name and return the greeting to use:

Example04.ts

```
1  function greet(name: string, getGreeting: (name: string) => string) {
2    const greeting = getGreeting(name);
3    console.log(`${greeting} ${name}`);
4  }
5
6  function getGreeting(name: string) {
7    const greeting = favoriteGreetings[name];
8    return greeting || 'Hello';
9  }
10
11 greet('John', getGreeting); // prints 'Hey John'
12 greet('Doug', getGreeting); // prints 'Howdy Doug'
```

Link to this example: https://packt.link/uRe2r

The following is the output:

```
Hey John
Howdy Doug
```

This may feel the same as our previous solution, which took the mapper object as an argument, but passing in a function is much more powerful. We can do a lot more with a function than with a static object. For example, we could base the greeting on the time of day:

Example05.ts

```
1   function getGreeting(name: string) {
2     const hours = new Date().getHours();
3     if (hours < 12) {
4       return 'Good morning';
5     }
6
7     if (hours === 12) {
8       return 'Good noon';
9     }
10
11    if (hours < 18) {
12      return 'Good afternoon';
13    }
14
```

```
15  return 'Good night';
16  }
17
18  greet('John', getGreeting); // prints 'Good morning John' if it's morning
19  greet('Doug', getGreeting); // prints 'Good morning Doug' if it's morning
```

Link to this example: https://packt.link/xSYDF

An example output would be as follows:

```
Good afternoon John
Good afternoon Doug
```

We could even go further and make the function return a random greeting, get it from a remote server, and a lot more, something which we couldn't do without passing in a function to the **greet** function.

By making **greet** accept a function, we opened up endless possibilities, while keeping **greet** reusable.

This is great, but passing in the **getGreeting** function in each call still feels cumbersome. We can change this by changing the **greet** function to both accept a function, and return a function. Let's take a look at how that appears:

Example06.ts

```
1 function greet(getGreeting: (name: string) => string) {
2   return function(name: string) {
3     const greeting = getGreeting(name);
4     console.log(`${greeting} ${name}`);
5   };
6 }
```

Link to this example: https://packt.link/8nHeD

You'll notice that the logic stays the same as in the previous solution, but we split up the function to first take in the **getGreeting** function, and then return another function that takes in the **name** argument. This allows us to call **greet** like so:

```
const greetWithTime = greet(getGreeting);
greetWithTime('John'); // prints 'Good morning John' if it's morning
greetWithTime('Doug'); // prints 'Good morning Doug' if it's morning
```

Splitting greet in this way allows us even more flexibility – since we now only need the **getGreeting** function once we can inline it, if it doesn't make sense to use it elsewhere:

```
8   const greetWithTime = greet(function(name: string) {
9     const hours = new Date().getHours();
10    if (hours < 12) {
11      return 'Good morning';
12    }
13
14    if (hours === 12) {
15      return 'Good noon';
16    }
17
18    if (hours < 18) {
19      return 'Good afternoon';
20    }
21
22    return 'Good night';
23 });
```

We could also use it to greet an array of people (names), using the **forEach** method of **Array**:

```
const names = ['John', 'Jane', 'Doug', 'Sally'];
names.forEach(greetWithTime);
```

The following is the output:

```
Good afternoon John
Good afternoon Jane
Good afternoon Doug
Good afternoon Sally
```

Higher-order functions, especially ones that accept other functions, are very widespread and useful, especially for manipulating datasets. We've even used them in previous chapters. For instance, the **map**, **filter**, **reduce**, and **forEach** methods of **Array** accept functions as arguments.

EXERCISE 11.01: ORCHESTRATING DATA FILTERING AND MANIPULATION USING HIGHER-ORDER FUNCTIONS

In this exercise, we get a list of students and want to get the average score of the students who graduated in 2010. This exercise will make use of higher-order functions to complete this task.

The list of students is given in the following form:

```
interface Student {
  id: number;
  firstName: string;
  lastName: string;
  graduationYear: number;
  score: number;
}

const students: Student[] = [
  { id: 1, firstName: 'Carma', lastName: 'Atwel', graduationYear: 2010,
score: 88 },
  { id: 2, firstName: 'Shaun', lastName: 'Knoller', graduationYear: 2011,
score: 84 },
  // ...
];
```

> **NOTE**
>
> You can refer to the following starter file to get the code for student interface: https://packt.link/6Jmeu.

Perform the following steps to implement this exercise:

1. Create a function, **getAverageScore**, that will accept a **Student[]** argument, and return a **number**:

```
function getAverageScoreOf2010Students(students: Student[]): number {
   // TODO: implement
}
```

2. First, we want to get *only those students who graduated in 2010*. We can use the array's **filter** method for that – a higher-order function that accepts a predicate, a function that accepts an item from the array and returns **true** or **false**, depending on whether the item should be included in the result. **filter** returns a new array comprising some of the original array items, depending on the predicate. The length of the new array is smaller or equal to the length of the original array.

3. Update your function with the following code:

```
function getAverageScoreOf2010Students(students: Student[]): number {
   const relevantStudents = students.filter(student => student.
graduationYear === 2010);
}
```

Next, we only care about the score of each student. We can use the array's **map** method for that – a higher-order function that accepts a mapping function, a function that accepts an item from the array and returns a new, transformed value (of a type of your choosing) for each item. **map** returns a new array comprising the transformed items.

4. Use the **map** method as shown:

```
function getAverageScoreOf2010Students(students: Student[]): number {
    const relevantStudents = students.filter(student => student.
graduationYear === 2010);
    const relevantStudentsScores = relevantStudents.map(student =>
student.score);
}
```

Lastly, we want to get the average from the array of scores. We can use the array's **reduce** method for that – a higher-order function that accepts a reducer function and an initial value.

5. Update the function with the **reduce** method as shown:

```
function getAverageScoreOf2010Students(students: Student[]): number {
    const relevantStudents = students.filter(student => student.
graduationYear === 2010);
    const relevantStudentsScores = relevantStudents.map(student =>
student.score);
    const relevantStudentsTotalScore = relevantStudentsScores.
reduce((acc, item) => acc + item, 0);

    return relevantStudentsTotalScore / relevantStudentsScores.length;
}
```

The reducer function accepts the accumulator and the current value and returns an accumulator. **reduce** iterates over the items in the array, calling the reducer function in each iteration with the current item and the previously returned accumulator (or the initial value, for the first run). Finally, it returns the resulting accumulator, after iterating through the entire array. In this case, we want to average out the numbers in the array, so our reducer function will sum all the items, which we'll then divide by the number of female students. We can then call the function with any dataset and get the average score.

6. Run the file using **npx ts-node**. You should see the following output on your console:

```
The average score of students who graduated in 2010 is: 78.5
```

> **NOTE**
>
> In this exercise, we could also extract each function given to **filter**, **map**, and **reduce** into a named, non-inlined function, if it made sense to use it outside of this context; for example, if we wanted to test the filtering logic outside of **getAverageScoreOf2010Students**.

CALLBACKS

Callbacks are functions that we pass into other functions, which, in turn, will be invoked when they are needed. For example, in the client, if you want to listen to clicks on a specific DOM element, you attach an event handler via **addEventListener**. The function you pass in is then called when clicks on that element occur:

```
const btnElement = document.querySelector<HTMLButtonElement>('.
my-button');

function handleButtonClick(event: MouseEvent) {
  console.log('.my-button was clicked!');
}


btnElement.addEventListener('click', handleButtonClick);
```

In this example, **handleButtonClick** is a *callback function* given to **addEventListener**. It will be called whenever someone clicks the **.my-button** element.

> **NOTE**
>
> You can also inline the **handleButtonClick** function, but you won't be able to call **removeEventListener** later, which is required in certain cases, to avoid memory leaks.

On the server, callbacks are widely used. Even the most basic request handler in Node.js' **http** module requires a callback function to be passed:

```
import http from 'http';

function requestHandler(req: http.IncomingMessage, res: http.
ServerResponse) {
  res.write('Hello from request handler');
  res.end();
}


http
  .createServer(requestHandler)
  .listen(3000);
```

In this example, **requestHandler** is a callback function given to **createServer**. It will be called whenever a request reaches the server, and this is where we define what we want to do with it, and how we want to respond.

THE EVENT LOOP

Since JavaScript is single-threaded, callbacks are required to keep the main thread free – the basic idea is that you give the engine a function to call when something happens, where you can handle it, and then return the control to whatever other code needs to run.

> **NOTE**
>
> In more recent versions of browsers and Node.js, you can create threads via *Web Workers* on the browser or via *Worker Threads* in Node.js. However, these are usually saved for CPU-intensive tasks, and they are not as easy to use as callbacks or other alternatives are (for example, Promises – explored in more detail in *Chapter 13, Async Await in TypeScript*).

To illustrate this, let's look at a version of some JavaScript code where there are no callbacks, and we want to create a simple server that greets the users by their name:

```
// server.ts

function logWithTime(message: string) {
  console.log(`[${new Date().toISOString()}]: ${message}`);
}

http
  .createServer((req, res) => {
    logWithTime(`START: ${req.url}`);

    const name = req.url!.split('/')[1]!;
    const greeting = fetchGreeting(name);

    res.write(greeting);
    res.end();
```

```
    logWithTime(`END: ${req.url}`);
  })
  .listen(3000);
```

`fetchGreeting` is faking a network operation, which is done synchronously to illustrate the issue:

```
function fetchGreeting(name: string) {
  const now = Date.now();
  const fakeRequestTime = 5000;

  logWithTime(`START: fetchGreeting for user: ${name}`);

  while (Date.now() < now + fakeRequestTime);

  logWithTime(`END: fetchGreeting for user: ${name}`);

  return `Hello ${name}`;
}
```

In a more real-world example, **`fetchGreening`** could be replaced by a call to get the user's data from the database.

If we run the server and try to request a few greetings simultaneously, you'll notice that they each wait for the previous request to complete before starting requesting the data for the current one. We can simulate a few concurrent requests by calling fetch multiple times, without waiting for the previous request to finish first:

```
// client.ts
fetch('http://localhost:3000/john');
fetch('http://localhost:3000/jane');
```

The output you'll see on the server's console is this:

```
[2019-11-30T17:01:20.065Z]: START: /john
[2019-11-30T17:01:20.066Z]: START: fetchGreeting for user: john
[2019-11-30T17:01:25.066Z]: END: fetchGreeting for user: john
[2019-11-30T17:01:25.067Z]: END: /john
[2019-11-30T17:01:25.071Z]: START: /jane
[2019-11-30T17:01:25.071Z]: START: fetchGreeting for user: jane
[2019-11-30T17:01:30.071Z]: END: fetchGreeting for user: jane
[2019-11-30T17:01:30.071Z]: END: /jane
```

Figure 11.2: Output of running the sync server while making multiple requests simultaneously

As you can see, Jane had to wait for John's request to finish (5 seconds in this case) before the server even started handling her request. The total time to greet both users was 10 seconds. Can you imagine what would happen in a real server, serving hundreds or more requests at the same time?

Let's see how callbacks solve this.

We first change **fetchGreeting** to use callback APIs – **setTimeout** in this case serves the same purpose as the **while** loop from before, while not holding up the main thread:

```
function fetchGreeting(name: string, cb: (greeting: string) => void) {
  const fakeRequestTime = 5000;

  logWithTime(`START: fetchGreeting for user: ${name}`);

  setTimeout(() => {
    logWithTime(`fetched greeting for user: ${name}`);

    cb(`Hello ${name}`);
  }, fakeRequestTime);

  logWithTime(`END: fetchGreeting for user: ${name}`);
}
```

Then, change the request handler to use the new implementation:

```typescript
// server.ts
http
  .createServer((req, res) => {
    logWithTime(`START: ${req.url}`);

    const name = req.url!.split('/')[1]!;

    fetchGreeting(name, greeting => {
      logWithTime(`START: callback for ${name}`);
      res.write(greeting);
      res.end();
      logWithTime(`END: callback for ${name}`);
    });

    logWithTime(`END: ${req.url}`);
  })
  .listen(3000);
```

And run the client code again. This results in the following output:

```
[2019-11-30T17:04:30.526Z]: START: /john
[2019-11-30T17:04:30.527Z]: START: fetchGreeting for user: john
[2019-11-30T17:04:30.527Z]: END: fetchGreeting for user: john
[2019-11-30T17:04:30.527Z]: END: /john
[2019-11-30T17:04:30.528Z]: START: /jane
[2019-11-30T17:04:30.528Z]: START: fetchGreeting for user: jane
[2019-11-30T17:04:30.528Z]: END: fetchGreeting for user: jane
[2019-11-30T17:04:30.528Z]: END: /jane
[2019-11-30T17:04:35.534Z]: fetched greeting for user: john
[2019-11-30T17:04:35.534Z]: START: callback for john
[2019-11-30T17:04:35.536Z]: END: callback for john
[2019-11-30T17:04:35.538Z]: fetched greeting for user: jane
[2019-11-30T17:04:35.538Z]: START: callback for jane
[2019-11-30T17:04:35.538Z]: END: callback for jane
```

Figure 11.3: Output of running the async server while making
multiple requests simultaneously

As you can see, the server started handing John's request first, since that's the first one to arrive, but then immediately switched to handling Jane's request while waiting for John's greeting to be ready. When John's greeting was ready 5 seconds later, the server sent the greeting back, and then waited for Jane's greeting to be ready a few milliseconds later and sent that to her.

To conclude, the *same flow* as before now took 5 seconds to respond to *both users* instead of the 10 seconds from before. In addition, most of that time was spent idle – waiting to receive more requests to handle. This is instead of the flow prior to the callbacks, where the server was stuck and wasn't able to answer any requests for the majority of the time.

CALLBACKS IN NODE.JS

Since callbacks are very common in Node.js, and especially since the whole ecosystem relies on using external packages for a lot of things, there is a standard callback API structure for any async function:

1. The callback function will be the last parameter.

2. The callback function will take **err** as the first parameter, which may be **null** (or **undefined**), and the response data as the second parameter.

Further parameters are also allowed, but these two are mandatory. This results in a predictable structure for handling callbacks, illustrated by the following example for reading a file from the filesystem:

```
import fs from "fs";

fs.readFile("some-file", (err, file) => {
  if (err) {
    // handle error...
    return;
  }

  // handle file...
});
```

CALLBACK HELL

Unfortunately, code that uses callbacks can make it very hard to follow, understand, and reason about very quickly. Every async operation requires another callback level, and if you want to run multiple async operations consecutively, you have to nest these callbacks.

For example, let's say we want to build a social network, which has an endpoint where you can ask for a given user's friends, based on their username. Getting this list of friends requires multiple operations, each requiring an async operation that depends on the result of the previous one:

1. Get the requested user's ID from the database (given their username).

2. Get the privacy settings of the user to make sure they allow others to view their list of friends.

3. Get the user's friends (from an external service or otherwise).

Here is some example code for how this could be done, using callbacks. We're using **express** here to set up a basic server, listening on port **3000**. The server can accept a **GET** request to **/:username/friends** (where **:username** will be replaced with the actual requested username). After accepting the request, we get the ID of the user from the database, then get the user privacy preferences using the user's ID (this can be in an external service, or otherwise) to check that they allow others to view their friends' list, then get the user's friends, and finally return the result:

```
import express from 'express';
import request from 'request';
import sqlite from 'sqlite3';

const db = new sqlite.Database('db.sql', err => {
  if (err) {
    console.error('Error opening database:', err.message);
  }
});

const app = express();

app.get('/:username/friends', (req, res) => {
  const username = req.params.username;

  db.get(
```

```
      `SELECT id
      FROM users
      WHERE username = username`,
      [username],
      (err, row) => {
        if (err) {
          return res.status(500).end();
        }

        getUserPrivacyPreferences(row.id, (err, privacyPreferences) => {
          if (err) {
            return res.status(500).end();
          }

          if (!privacyPreferences.canOthersViewFriends) {
            return res.status(403).end();
          }

          getFriends(row.id, (err, friends) => {
            if (err) {
              return res.status(500).end();
            }

            return res
              .status(200)
              .send({ friends })
              .end();
          });
        });
      }
    );
  });

app.get('*', (req, res) => {
  res.sendFile('index.html');
});

app.listen(3000);
```

Also note that in each callback, we got an **err** parameter and had to check whether it was true, and bail early if it wasn't accompanied by an appropriate error code.

The preceding example is not unrealistic, and a lot of cases require more levels than this to get all the data they need in order to perform a task. And so, this "callback hell" becomes more apparent, and harder to understand and reason about very quickly, since, as discussed previously, a lot of APIs in Node.js work with callbacks, due to the nature of how JavaScript works, as explained in the event loop section.

AVOIDING CALLBACK HELL

There are quite a few solutions to the callback hell problem. We'll take a look at the most prominent ones, demonstrating how the preceding code snippet would look in each variation:

1. Extract the callback functions to function declarations at the file level and then use them – this means you only have one level of functions with business logic, and the callback hell functions become a lot shorter.

2. Use a higher-order function to chain the callbacks, meaning only a single level of callbacks in practice.

3. Use promises, when can be chained together, as explained in *Chapter 13, Async Await in TypeScript*.

4. Use **async/await** (which is syntactic sugar on top of **Promise**), as explained in *Chapter 13, Async Await in TypeScript*.

SPLITTING THE CALLBACK HANDLERS INTO FUNCTION DECLARATIONS AT THE FILE LEVEL

The simplest way to simplify callback hell is to extract some of the callbacks into their own top-level functions and let each one call the next in the logical chain.

Our main endpoint handler will call the **get** of **db** as before, but then just call **handleDatabaseResponse** with the response, leaving it to handle any errors, and so on. This is why we also pass in the response object to the function, in case it needs to return the data, or an error, to the user:

```
app.get('/:username/friends', (req, res) => {
  const username = req.params.username;

  db.get(
    `SELECT id
    FROM users
```

```
    WHERE username = username`,
    [username],
    (err, row) => {
      handleDatabaseResponse(res, err, row);

    }
  );
});
```

The **handleDatabaseResponse** function will perform the same logic as before, but now pass the handling of the **getUserPrivacyPreferences** response to **handleGetUserPrivacyPreferences**:

```
function handleDatabaseResponse(res: express.Response, err: any, row: {
id: string }) {
  if (err) {
    return res.status(500).end();

  }


  getUserPrivacyPreferences(row.id, (err, privacyPreferences) => {
    handleGetUserPrivacyPreferences(res, row.id, err,
privacyPreferences);
  });
}
```

handleGetUserPrivacyPreferences will again perform the same logic as before, and pass the handling of the **getFriends** response to **handleGetFriends**:

```
function handleGetUserPrivacyPreferences(
  res: express.Response,
  userId: string,
  err: any,
  privacyPreferences: PrivacyPreferences
) {
  if (err) {
    return res.status(500).end();

  }


  if (!privacyPreferences.canOthersViewFriends) {
    return res.status(403).end();
```

```
    }

    getFriends(userId, (err, friends) => handleGetFriends(res, err,
friends));
}
```

And finally, **handleGetFriends** will return the data to the user via the response:

```
function handleGetFriends(res: express.Response, err: any, friends:
any[]) {
  if (err) {
    return res.status(500).end();
  }

  return res
    .status(200)
    .send({ friends })
    .end();
}
```

Now we only have a single nesting level, and no more callback hell.

The main trade-off here is that while the code is less nested, it is split among multiple functions and may be harder to follow, especially when debugging or skimming through it to understand what's going on at a high level.

CHAINING CALLBACKS

There are libraries to help us eliminate the callback hell problem by chaining the callbacks to one another – artificially removing nesting levels from our code. One of the popular ones is async.js (https://github.com/caolan/async), which exposes a few functions to compose callback functions, such as **parallel**, **series**, and **waterfall**. In our preceding code example, we could use the **waterfall** function to chain the callbacks to happen one after the other:

1. We implement an array of functions, and a final handler. **async** will then call our functions, one by one, when we call the callback in each function, as demonstrated here:

```
...

import async from 'async';

...
```

```typescript
type CallbackFn = <T extends any[]>(err: any, ...data: T) => void;

class ServerError extends Error {
  constructor(public readonly statusCode: number, message?: string) {
    super(message);
  }
}

app.get('/:username/friends', (req, res) => {
  const username = req.params.username;
```

2. Get the user ID from the database:

```typescript
async.waterfall(
  [
    // 1. Get the user id from the database
    (cb: CallbackFn) => {
      db.get(
        `SELECT id
          FROM users
          WHERE username = username`,
        [username],
        (err, row) => {
          if (err) {
            return cb(err);
          }

          return cb(null, row);
        }
      );
    },
```

3. Get the user's privacy settings:

```
(row: { id: string }, cb: CallbackFn) => {
  getUserPrivacyPreferences(row.id, (err, privacyPreferences)
=> {
    if (err) {
      return cb(err);
    }


    return cb(null, privacyPreferences, row.id);
  });
},
```

4. Check that the user privacy settings allow others to view their friends:

```
(privacyPreferences: PrivacyPreferences, userId: string, cb:
CallbackFn) => {
    if (!privacyPreferences.canOthersViewFriends) {
      return cb(new ServerError(403, "User doesn't allow others
to view their friends"));
    }

    return cb(null, userId);
},
```

5. Get the user's friends:

```
(userId: string, cb: CallbackFn) => {
  getFriends(userId, (err, friends) => {
    if (err) {
      return cb(err);
    }


    return cb(null, friends);
  });
},
],
```

6. Finally, handle any errors that occurred, or the data that was returned from the last callback:

```
(error, friends) => {
  if (error) {
    if (error instanceof ServerError) {
      return res
```

```
          .status(error.statusCode)
          .send({ message: error.message })
          .end();
      }

      return res.status(500).end();
    }

    return res
      .status(200)
      .send({ friends })
      .end();
    }
  );
});
```

Now the code is much easier to follow – we only have one error handler that's tied down to the response object, and we follow the code from top to bottom, with not much nesting in between, at least not due to callbacks.

PROMISES

Promises allow you to essentially flatten the callback tree by doing something similar to async.js' waterfall, but it's more seamless, built into the language itself, and also allows promises to be "squashed."

We won't go into too much detail here – refer to *Chapter 13, Async Await in TypeScript* for an in-depth explanation of promises, but the preceding code, using promises, would look like this:

```
...

app.get('/:username/friends', (req, res) => {
  const username = req.params.username;

  promisify<string, string[], { id: string }>(db.get)(
    `SELECT id
  FROM users
  WHERE username = username`,
    [username]
  )
    .then(row => {
```

```
      return getUserPrivacyPreferences(row.id).then(privacyPreferences =>
{
        if (!privacyPreferences.canOthersViewFriends) {
          throw new ServerError(403, "User doesn't allow others to view
their friends");
        }

        return row.id;
      });
    })
    .then(userId => {
      return getFriends(userId);
    })
    .then(friends => {
      return res
        .status(200)
        .send({ friends })
        .end();
    })
    .catch(error => {
      if (error instanceof ServerError) {
        return res
          .status(error.statusCode)
          .send({ message: error.message })
          .end();
      }

      return res.status(500).end();
    });
});
```

ASYNC/AWAIT

Async/await builds upon promises and provides further syntactic sugar on top of them in order to make promises look and read like synchronous code, even though, behind the scenes, it's still async. You can get a more in-depth explanation of them in *Chapter 13, Async Await in TypeScript*, but the preceding code that used promises is equivalent to the following code that uses async/await:

```
...

app.get('/:username/friends', async (req, res) => {
```

```
  const username = req.params.username;

  try {
    const row = await promisify<string, string[], { id: string }>(db.get)
(
      `SELECT id
       FROM users
       WHERE username = username`,
      [username]
    );

    const privacyPreferences = await getUserPrivacyPreferences(row.id);
    if (!privacyPreferences.canOthersViewFriends) {
      throw new ServerError(403, "User doesn't allow others to view their
friends");
    }

    const friends = await getFriends(row.id);

    return res
      .status(200)
      .send({ friends })
      .end();
  } catch (error) {
    if (error instanceof ServerError) {
      return res
        .status(error.statusCode)
        .send({ message: error.message })
        .end();
    }

    return res.status(500).end();
  }
});
```

ACTIVITY 11.01: HIGHER-ORDER PIPE FUNCTION

In this activity, you are tasked with implementing a **pipe** function – a higher-order function that accepts other functions, as well as a value, and composes them – returning a function that accepts the arguments of the first function in the composition, runs it through the functions – feeding each function with the output of the previous one (and the first function with the initial value), and returns the result of the last function.

Such functions exist in utility libraries such as Ramda (https://ramdajs.com/docs/#pipe), and with variations in other libraries such as Lodash (https://lodash.com/docs#chain) and RxJS (https://rxjs.dev/api/index/function/pipe).

> **NOTE**
>
> You can find both the activity starter file and solution at
> https://packt.link/CQLfx.

Perform the following steps to implement this activity:

1. Create a **pipe** function that accepts functions as arguments and composes them, from left to right.

2. Make sure that the return type of the returned functional is correct – it should accept arguments of type **T**, **T** being the arguments of the first function in the chain, and return type **R**, **R** being the return type of the last function in the chain.

   Note that due to a current TypeScript limitation, you have to manually type this for the number of arguments you want to support.

3. Your **pipe** function should be callable in multiple ways – supporting composition of up to five functions, and will only support composing functions with a single argument, for simplicity.

   Here is the structure of the **pipe** function that you can use:

```
const func = pipe(
  (x: string) => x.toUpperCase(),
  x => [x, x].join(','),
  x => x.length,
  x => x.toString(),
```

```
    x => Number(x),
  );

    console.log('result is:', func('hello'));
```

After solving the preceding steps, the expected output for this code is presented here:

```
result is: 11
```

Bonus: As a challenge, try expanding the **pipe** function to support the composition of more functions, or more arguments.

> **NOTE**
>
> The solution to this activity can be found on page 666.

SUMMARY

In this chapter, we introduced two key concepts in TypeScript – higher-order functions and callbacks. The chapter first defined HOCs and illustrated this concept with a number of examples. You also orchestrated data filtering and manipulation using higher-order functions. Finally, you also tested your skills by creating a higher-order pipe function.

With regard to callbacks, the chapter first introduced the definition of callbacks with a few generic examples, along with examples relating to callbacks in Node.js. You also saw how you can easily fall into callback hell and how you can avoid it. Although there are several additional steps that you need to take in order to master higher-order functions and callback, this chapter got you started on the journey. The next chapter deals with another important concept in TypeScript – promises.

12

GUIDE TO PROMISES IN TYPESCRIPT

OVERVIEW

This chapter explores asynchronous programming in TypeScript using promises and discusses uses for asynchronous programming and how it is implemented in single-threaded JavaScript with the event loop. By the end of the chapter, you should have a solid understanding of how promises work and how TypeScript can enhance them. You will also be able to build a promise-based app using the concepts taught in this chapter.

INTRODUCTION

In the previous chapter, we learned about asynchronous programming using callbacks. With this knowledge, we can manage concurrent requests and write non-blocking code that allows our applications to render web pages faster or serve concurrent requests on a Node.js server.

In this chapter, we will learn how promises allow us to write more readable, concise code to better manage asynchronous processes and forever escape deep callback nesting, sometimes known as "callback hell." We will explore the evolution of the **Promise** object and how it eventually became part of the JavaScript language. We'll look at different transpilation targets for TypeScript and how TypeScript can enhance promises and allow developers to leverage generics to infer return types.

We will work on some practical exercises, such as managing multiple API requests from a website and managing concurrency in Node.js. We will use the Node.js FileSystem API to perform asynchronous operations on files and see how powerful asynchronous programming can be.

THE EVOLUTION OF AND MOTIVATION FOR PROMISES

As we've learned, a callback is a function that is given as an argument to another function, in effect saying, "do this when you are done." This capability has been in JavaScript since its inception in 1995 and can work very well, but as the complexity of JavaScript applications grew through the 2000s, developers found callback patterns and nesting in particular to be too messy and unreadable, giving rise to complaints about "callback hell" as shown in the following example:

```
doSomething(function (err, data) {
  if(err) {
    console.error(err);
  } else {
    request(data.url, function (err, response) {
      if(err) {
        console.error(err);
      } else {
        doSomethingElse(response, function (err, data) {
          if(err) {
            console.error(err);
          } else {
```

```
            // ...and so it goes!
        }
    })
  }
})
}
});
```

In addition to making code more readable and concise, promises have advantages beyond callbacks in that promises are objects that contain the state of the resolving asynchronous function. This means that a promise can be stored and either queried for the current state or called via its **then()** or **catch()** methods at any time to obtain the resolved state of the promise. We'll discuss those methods later in this chapter, but it's worth calling out at the beginning here that promises are more than syntactic sugar. They open up entirely new programming paradigms in which event handling logic can be decoupled from the event itself, just by storing the event in a promise.

Promises are not unique to JavaScript but were first proposed as a computer programming concept in the 1970s.

> **NOTE**
>
> For more information, refer to Friedman, Daniel; David Wise (1976). *The Impact of Applicative Programming on Multiprocessing.* International Conference on Parallel Processing. pp. 263–272.

As web frameworks gained popularity, proposals for promises started to appear in 2009 and libraries such as jQuery started implementing promise-like objects in 2011.

> **NOTE**
>
> For more information, refer to the following: https://groups.google.com/g/commonjs/c/6T9z75fohDk and https://api.jquery.com/category/version/1.5/

It wasn't long before Node.js started to have some promise libraries as well. Google's AngularJS bundled the Q library. All of these libraries wrapped callbacks in a higher-level API that appealed to developers and helped them to write cleaner and more readable code.

In 2012, promises were proposed as an official specification in order to standardize the API. The specification was accepted in 2015 and has since been implemented in all major browsers as well as Node.js.

> **NOTE**
>
> For more details, refer to http://www.ecma-international.org/ecma-262/6.0/#sec-promise-constructor.

"Promisification," the ability to wrap an existing asynchronous function in a promise, was added to many libraries and became part of the **util** package in the standard Node.js library as of version 8.0 (released in 2017).

TypeScript, as a superset of JavaScript, will always support native language features such as promises; however, TypeScript does not provide polyfills, so if the target environment doesn't support native promises, a library is required.

Most JavaScript runtimes (such as a web browser or Node.js server) are single-threaded execution environments. That means the main JavaScript process will only do one thing at a time. Thanks to the event loop, the runtime will seem like it's capable of doing many things at once as long as we write non-blocking code. The event loop recognizes asynchronous events and can turn to other tasks while it waits for those events to resolve.

Consider the example of a web page that needs to call an API to load data into a table. If that API call were blocking, then that would mean the page render couldn't complete until the data loaded. Our user would have to stare at a blank page until all the data loaded and page elements rendered. But because of the event loop, we can register a listener that allows rendering of the website to continue and then load the table when our data is finally returned. This is visualized in the following figure:

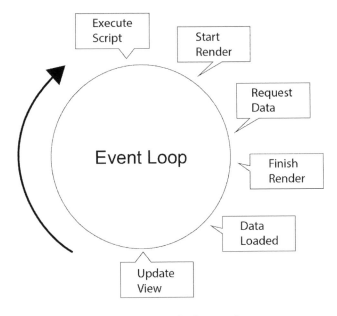

Figure 12.1: A typical event loop

This can be implemented using callbacks or promises. The event loop is what makes this possible. Node.js works similarly, but now we may be responding to requests from a multitude of clients. In this simple example, three different requests are being made:

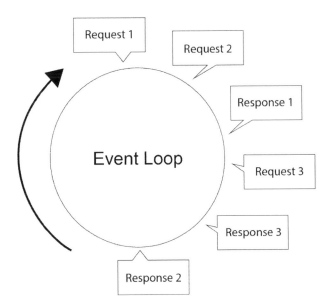

Figure 12.2: Multiple requests

The API is not blocking so additional requests can come in even when the initial one has not been served. The requests are served in the order the work is completed.

ANATOMY OF A PROMISE

A promise is a JavaScript object that can exist in three states: *pending, fulfilled*, or *rejected*. Although promises can be instantly fulfilled or rejected, it is most typical for a promise to be created in a pending state and then resolved to be fulfilled or rejected as an operation succeeds or fails. Promises are chainable and implement several convenience methods that we'll go into.

To understand the states of a promise better, it's important to know that the states of a promise cannot be queried. As a programmer, we do not check the state of the promise and take action based on that state. Rather we provide a function callback that will be invoked when the promise reaches that state. For example, we make an HTTP request to our backend server and get a promise in response. Now we have set up our event and we merely need to tell the promise what to do next and how to handle any errors. Examples of this will follow.

THE PROMISE CALLBACK

A promise can be instantiated using the **new** keyword and **Promise** constructor. When instantiated in this way, **Promise** expects a callback argument that contains the actual work to be done. The callback has two arguments of its own, **resolve** and **reject**. These arguments can be called explicitly to either resolve or reject the promise. For example, we can create a promise that resolves after 100 ms like this:

```
new Promise<void>((resolve, reject) => {
  setTimeout(() => resolve(), 100);
});
```

We could also create a promise that rejects after 100 ms:

```
new Promise<void>((resolve, reject) => {
  setTimeout(() => reject(), 100);
});
```

THEN AND CATCH

Promises can be chained into callback functions of their own using **then** and **catch**. The callback function given to **then** will fire only once the promise is fulfilled and the callback function given to **catch** will only fire if the promise is rejected. Most libraries that return promises will automatically call **resolve** and **reject**, so we only need to provide **then** and **catch**. Here's an example using the Fetch API:

```
fetch("https://my-server.com/my-resource")
   .then(value => console.log(value))
   .catch(error => console.error(error));
```

This code will make a call to our backend server and log out the result. If the call fails, it'll log that too.

If this were a real application, we might have a couple of functions, **showData** and **handleError**, that could manage what our application does with the response from the server. In that case, the use of **fetch** would likely be something like this:

```
fetch("https://my-server.com/my-resource")
   .then(data => showData(data))
   .catch(error => handleError(error));
```

Using promises like this shows how we can decouple our asynchronous processes from business logic and display elements.

PENDING STATE

A pending promise is one that has yet to complete its work. It's simple to create a promise that is forever stuck in a pending state:

```
const pendingPromise = new Promise((resolve, reject) => {});

console.log(pendingPromise);
```

This promise will never do anything as neither **resolve** nor **reject** are ever called. The promise will remain in a pending state. If we execute this code, it'll print out **Promise { <pending> }**. As noted above, we do not query the state of a promise but rather provide a callback for the eventual resolution of a promise. The sample code above contains a promise that can never be resolved and as such could be seen as invalid code. There is no use case for promises that cannot resolve.

FULFILLED STATE

We can create a promise that is fulfilled immediately:

```
const fulfilledPromise = new Promise(resolve => {
  resolve("fulfilled!");
});


console.log(fulfilledPromise);
```

This will log out **Promise { 'fulfilled!' }**.

Unlike the pending state, creating a promise that resolves immediately has a few more practical use cases. The primary use of an immediately resolved promise would be when working with an API that expects a promise.

REJECTED STATE

We can create a promise that is fulfilled immediately:

```
const rejectedPromise = new Promise((resolve, reject) => {
  reject("rejected!");
});


console.log(rejectedPromise);
```

This will log out **Promise { <rejected> 'rejected!' }** and then throw an unhandled promise rejection warning. Rejected promises always need to be caught. Failure to catch a promise rejection may cause our program to crash!

As with the fulfilled state, the primary use case for immediately rejecting a promise would be for writing a good unit test, but there may be secondary use cases in which some process throws an error during an asynchronous workflow and it may make sense to return a rejected promise. This circumstance would be most likely when working with a third-party library where the API isn't quite to our liking and we need to wrap it with something more in line with the rest of our application architecture.

CHAINING

One of the main advantages of promises over callbacks is the ability to chain promises together. Consider a function that waits 1 second, generates a random number between 0 and 99, and adds it to the previous result. There are better ways to write recursive functions, but this is meant to simulate a website making several calls to a backend:

Example01.ts

```
1   const getTheValue = async (val: number, cb: Function) => {
2     setTimeout(() => {
3       const number = Math.floor(Math.random() * 100) + val;
4       console.log(`The value is ${number}`);
5       cb(number);
6     }, 1000);
7   };
8
9   getTheValue(0, (output: number) => {
10     getTheValue(output, (output: number) => {
11       getTheValue(output, (output: number) => {
12         getTheValue(output, (output: number) => {
13           getTheValue(output, (output: number) => {
14             getTheValue(output, (output: number) => {
15               getTheValue(output, (output: number) => {
16                 getTheValue(output, (output: number) => {
17                   getTheValue(output, (output: number) => {
18                     getTheValue(output, () => {});
19                   });
20                 });
21               });
22             });
23           });
24         });
25       });
26     });
27   });
```

Link to the example: https://packt.link/VHZJc

A sample output of this program is the following:

```
The value is 49
The value is 133
The value is 206
The value is 302
The value is 395
The value is 444
The value is 469
The value is 485
The value is 528
The value is 615
```

Each time we call **getTheValue**, we wait 1 second, then generate a random number and add it to the value we passed in. In a real-world scenario, we can think of this as a program that completes several asynchronous tasks, using the output from the last one as input to the next.

> **NOTE**
>
> As the starting point of the program is a random number, your output would be different from the one presented above.

Everything in the previous program works correctly; however, the callback nesting isn't very nice to look at and could be challenging to maintain or debug. The next exercise will teach you how you can write more readable and maintainable code using promises.

EXERCISE 12.01: CHAINING PROMISES

In this exercise, we will refactor the preceding example and chain promises to eliminate nesting and make the code more readable:

> **NOTE**
>
> The code file for this exercise can be found here: https://packt.link/IO8Pz.

1. Write the following program, which refactors the previous example using promises:

```
const getTheValue = async (val: number): Promise<number> => {
  return new Promise(resolve => {
    setTimeout(() => {
      const number = Math.floor(Math.random() * 100) + val;
      console.log(`The value is ${number}`);
      resolve(number);
    }, 1000);
  });
};

getTheValue(0)
  .then((result: number) => getTheValue(result))
  .then((result: number) => getTheValue(result))
  .then((result: number) => getTheValue(result))
  .then((result: number) => getTheValue(result))
  .then((result: number) => getTheValue(result))
  .then((result: number) => getTheValue(result))
  .then((result: number) => getTheValue(result))
  .then((result: number) => getTheValue(result))
  .then((result: number) => getTheValue(result));
```

The nesting is gone and the code is a lot more readable. Our **getTheValue** function now returns a promise instead of using a callback. Because it returns a promise, we can call **.then()** on the promise, which can be chained into another promise call.

2. Run the program. The chain of promises will resolve each in turn and we'll get similar output to the previous program:

```
The value is 50
The value is 140
The value is 203
The value is 234
The value is 255
The value is 300
The value is 355
The value is 395
The value is 432
The value is 451
```

Note that you will get an output that is different from the one shown above because the program uses a random number as the starting point.

Chaining can also be a big help when it comes to error conditions. If my **getTheValue** function rejects the promise, I'm able to catch the error by chaining a single **catch** to the end of the chain:

Example02.ts

```
1   const getTheValue = async (val: number): Promise<number> => {
2     return new Promise((resolve, reject) => {
3       setTimeout(() => {
4         const number = Math.floor(Math.random() * 100) + val;
5         if (number % 10 === 0) {
6           reject("Bad modulus!");
7         } else {
8           console.log(`The value is ${number}`);
9           resolve(number);
10        }
11      }, 1000);
12    });
13  };
14
15  getTheValue(0)
16    .then((result: number) => getTheValue(result))
17    .then((result: number) => getTheValue(result))
18    .then((result: number) => getTheValue(result))
19    .then((result: number) => getTheValue(result))
20    .then((result: number) => getTheValue(result))
21    .then((result: number) => getTheValue(result))
22    .then((result: number) => getTheValue(result))
23    .then((result: number) => getTheValue(result))
24    .then((result: number) => getTheValue(result))
25    .catch(err => console.error(err));
```

Link to the example: https://packt.link/sBTgk

We are introducing a 10% chance (the chance our number when divided by 10 will have a remainder of 0) of throwing an error on each iteration. On average, our program will fail more often than it executes successfully now:

```
The value is 25
The value is 63
The value is 111
Bad modulus!
```

FINALLY

In addition to **then** and `catch` methods, the **Promise** object also exposes a `finally` method. This is a callback function that will be called regardless of whether an error is thrown or caught. It's great for logging, closing a database connection, or simply cleaning up resources, regardless of how the promise is eventually resolved.

We can add a `finally` callback to the above promise:

Example03.ts

```
1   const getTheValue = async (val: number) => {
2     return new Promise<number>((resolve, reject) => {
3       setTimeout(() => {
4         const number = Math.floor(Math.random() * 100) + val;
5         if (number % 10 === 0) {
6           reject("Bad modulus!");
7         } else {
8           console.log(`The value is ${number}`);
9           resolve(number);
10        }
11      }, 1000);
12    });
13  };
14
15  getTheValue(0)
16    .then(result => getTheValue(result))
17    .then(result => getTheValue(result))
18    .then(result => getTheValue(result))
19    .then(result => getTheValue(result))
20    .then(result => getTheValue(result))
21    .then(result => getTheValue(result))
22    .then(result => getTheValue(result))
23    .then(result => getTheValue(result))
24    .then(result => getTheValue(result))
25    .catch(err => console.error(err))
26    .finally(() => console.log("We are done!"));
```

`Link to the example:` https://packt.link/izqwS

Now **"We are done!"** will be logged regardless of whether or not we trip the **"Bad modulus!"** error condition:

```
The value is 69
The value is 99
Bad modulus!
We are done!
```

PROMISE.ALL

Promise.all is one of the most useful utility methods that **Promise** has to offer. Even code written with async/await syntax (see *Chapter 13, Async/Await*) can make good use of **Promise.all**. This method takes an iterable (likely an array) of promises as an argument and resolves all of them. Let's see how we can change our example promise using **Promise.all**:

Example04.ts

```
1   const getTheValue = async (val: number = 0) => {
2     return new Promise<number>((resolve, reject) => {
3       setTimeout(() => {
4         const number = Math.floor(Math.random() * 100) + val;
5         if (number % 10 === 0) {
6           reject("Bad modulus!");
7         } else {
8           console.log(`The value is ${number}`);
9           resolve(number);
10        }
11      }, 1000);
12    });
13  };
14
15  Promise.all([
16    getTheValue(),
17    getTheValue(),
18    getTheValue(),
19    getTheValue(),
20    getTheValue(),
21    getTheValue(),
22    getTheValue(),
23    getTheValue(),
24    getTheValue(),
25    getTheValue()
26  ])
27    .then(values =>
28      console.log(
29        `The total is ${values.reduce((prev, current) => prev + current, 0)}`
30      )
31    )
32    .catch(err => console.error(err))
33    .finally(() => console.log("We are done!"));
```

Link to the example: https://packt.link/8pzx4

The output should be similar to the ones obtained for the preceding examples. In this example, we call the same function 10 times, but imagine these are 10 different API calls we need to reach and then sum the total. Each call takes approximately 1 second. If we chain a series of promises, this operation will take just over 10 seconds. By using **Promise.all**, we are able to run those operations in parallel and now it takes only 1 second to complete the function.

Promise.all is useful any time you can run two or more asynchronous processes in parallel. It can be useful for persisting data to multiple database tables, letting multiple independent components render in a web browser independently, or making multiple HTTP requests. A good example of making multiple HTTP requests in parallel would be a service that monitors the uptime and ping duration of other services. There's no reason such an operation would need to be synchronous and **Promise.all** lets us wait on several web requests within the same process.

EXERCISE 12.02: RECURSIVE PROMISE.ALL

In this exercise, instead of repeating the same function call 10 times, let's optimize the programs from the previous examples to be more DRY (don't repeat yourself). We can load up an array of promises and then use **Promise.all** to resolve all the promises in parallel and use **catch** and **finally** to resolve errors and ensure we return some output:

> **NOTE**
>
> The code file for this exercise can also be found here:
> https://packt.link/KNpqx.

1. The following code will be our starting place for this refactor:

```
const getTheValue = async (val: number = 0) => {
  return new Promise<number>((resolve, reject) => {
    setTimeout(() => {
      const number = Math.floor(Math.random() * 100) + val;
      if (number % 10 === 0) {
        reject('Bad modulus!');
      } else {
        console.log(`The value is ${number}`);
        resolve(number);
      }
    }, 1000);
  });
};

Promise.all([
  getTheValue(),
  getTheValue(),
```

```
      getTheValue(),
      getTheValue(),
      getTheValue(),
      getTheValue(),
      getTheValue(),
      getTheValue(),
      getTheValue(),
      getTheValue(),
])
    .then((values) =>
      console.log(
         `The total is ${values.reduce((prev, current) => prev +
current, 0)}`
      )
    )
    .catch((err) => console.error(err))
    .finally(() => console.log('We are done!'));
```

In order to catch errors and make the program recursive, we'll need to wrap **Promise.all** in a function. Recursion is a pattern in which the same function can be called multiple times within the same execution.

2. To add the recursion, create a new function and make the **Promise.all** statement the body of that function. Then call the function:

```
const doIt = () => {
  Promise.all([
    getTheValue(),
    getTheValue(),
    getTheValue(),
    getTheValue(),
    getTheValue(),
    getTheValue(),
    getTheValue(),
    getTheValue(),
    getTheValue(),
    getTheValue(),
])
    .then((values) =>
        console.log(
           `The total is ${values.reduce((prev, current) => prev +
current, 0)}`
        )
```

```
    )
    .catch((err) => console.error(err))
    .finally(() => console.log('We are done!'));
```

We can use some functional programming techniques to, rather than having an array in which **getTheValue()** is repeated 10 times, programmatically construct an array of 10 elements, all of which are that function call. Doing this won't change how our program operates, but it will make it a bit nicer to work with.

3. Update the code given in the preceding step with the following:

```
Promise.all(
Array(10)
    .fill(null)
    .map(() => getTheValue())
)
```

The logic here is that **Array(10)** creates a new array of 10 elements, **fill(null)** will initialize the array, then **map** will remap the array elements to be the **getTheValue()** function call.

Th above code actually calls the function and returns the pending promise to the array that is already wrapped in **Promise.all**.

Now we want to use recursion in the case of an error. We will change our **catch()** callback from simply logging the error to starting the process over again. In this case, our business rule is we want the entire set of calculations to complete and we will restart if there is an error. The code to do this is very easy as **catch()** expects a function as its callback so we can just pass our **doIt** function back to it again.

4. Pass the **doIt** function back to **catch()**:

```
    .catch(doIt)
```

Note that we do not invoke the callback function here. We want to pass a function and it will be invoked in the case of an error.

5. We will now want to clean up our error messages a little so we can have a clean run:

```typescript
const getTheValue = async (val: number = 0) => {
  return new Promise<number>((resolve, reject) => {
    setTimeout(() => {
      const number = Math.floor(Math.random() * 100) + val;
      if (number % 10 === 0) {
        reject('Bad modulus!');
      } else {
        // console.log(`The value is ${number}`);
        resolve(number);
      }
    }, 1000);
  });
};


let loopCount = 0;

const doIt = () => {
  Promise.all(
    Array(10)
      .fill(null)
      .map(() => getTheValue())
  )
    .then((values) =>
      console.log(
        `The total is ${values.reduce((prev, current) => prev +
current, 0)}`
      )
    )
    .catch(doIt)
    .finally(() => console.log(`completed loop ${++loopCount}`));
};


doIt();
```

When we run the program, we'll see a few iterations of the program looping. The output may be something like this:

```
completed loop 1
The total is 438
completed loop 2
```

Note that depending on the number of iterations, you might get an output different from the one shown above.

PROMISE.ALLSETTLED

This method is a variation on **Promise.all**, which is ideal for when it's acceptable for some of our promises to resolve successfully and some of them to be rejected. Let's see how it's different from **Promise.all**:

```
const getTheValue = async (val: number = 0) => {
  return new Promise<number>((resolve, reject) => {
    setTimeout(() => {
      const number = Math.floor(Math.random() * 100) + val;
      // Arbitrary error condition - if the random number is divisible by
10.
      if (number % 10 === 0) {
        reject("Bad modulus!");
      } else {
        console.log(`The value is ${number}`);
        resolve(number);
      }
    }, 1000);
  });
};


const generateTheNumber = (iterations: number): void => {
  Promise.allSettled(
    // Produces an array of `iterations` length with the pending promises
of `getTheValue()`.
    Array(iterations)
      .fill(null)
      .map(() => getTheValue())
  )
    .then((settledResults) => {
      // Map all the results into the failed, succeeded and total values.
      const results = settledResults.reduce(
```

```
        (prev, current) => {
          return current.status === "fulfilled"
            ? {
                ...prev,
                succeeded: prev.succeeded + 1,
                total: prev.total + current.value,
              }
            : { ...prev, failed: prev.failed + 1 };
        },
        {
          failed: 0,
          succeeded: 0,
          total: 0,
        }
      );
      console.log(results);
    })
    .finally(() => console.log("We are done!"));
};

generateTheNumber(10);
```

The program will generate output like this:

```
current { status: 'fulfilled', value: 85 }
current { status: 'fulfilled', value: 25 }
current { status: 'fulfilled', value: 11 }
current { status: 'fulfilled', value: 43 }
current { status: 'rejected', reason: 'Bad modulus!' }
current { status: 'fulfilled', value: 41 }
current { status: 'fulfilled', value: 81 }
current { status: 'rejected', reason: 'Bad modulus!' }
current { status: 'rejected', reason: 'Bad modulus!' }
current { status: 'fulfilled', value: 7 }
{ failed: 3, succeeded: 7, total: 293 }
We are done!
```

We've made a couple of enhancements here. For one thing, we are now passing the array size into **generateTheNumber**, which can give a bit more flavor or variation to our program. The main improvement now is the use of **Promise.allSettled**. Now, **Promise.allSettled** allows us to have a mix of successes and failures, unlike **Promise.all**, which will call the **then()** method if all the promises resolve successfully or call the **catch()** method if any of them fail. The output of **Promise.allSettled** could look something like this:

```
settledResults [
    { status: 'fulfilled', value: 85 },
    { status: 'fulfilled', value: 25 },
    { status: 'fulfilled', value: 11 },
    { status: 'fulfilled', value: 43 },
    { status: 'rejected', reason: 'Bad modulus!' },
    { status: 'fulfilled', value: 41 },
    { status: 'fulfilled', value: 81 },
    { status: 'rejected', reason: 'Bad modulus!' },
    { status: 'rejected', reason: 'Bad modulus!' },
    { status: 'fulfilled', value: 7 }
]
```

Each of the resolved promises will have a status containing the string **'fulfilled'** if the promise resolved successfully or **'rejected'** if there was an error. Fulfilled promises will have a **value** property containing the value the promise resolved to and rejected promises will have a **reason** property containing the error.

In the example given, we are totaling the rejected promises and summing the values of the fulfilled promises, then returning that as a new object. To perform this operation, we use the built-in array function **reduce()**. Now, **reduce()** will iterate over each element of an array and collect transformed results in an accumulator, which is returned by the function. **MapReduce** functions are common in functional programming paradigms.

Note that **Promise.allSettled** is a fairly recent addition to ECMAScript, having landed in Node.js 12.9. In order to use it, you'll need to set your **compilerOptions** target to **es2020** or **esnext** in your **tsconfig.json** file. Most modern browsers support this method, but it's a good idea to verify support before using this recent feature.

EXERCISE 12.03: PROMISE.ALLSETTLED

We've seen an example of using **Promise.allSettled** to produce a mixed result of fulfilled and rejected promises. Now let's combine **Promise.allSettled** and **Promise.all** to aggregate multiple results of our runs of **getTheValue()**:

> **NOTE**
>
> The code file for this exercise can also be found here:
> https://packt.link/D8jIQ.

1. Start with the code from the example above. We are going to want to call **generateTheNumber()** three times. Once we have all the results, we can sort them to print out the highest and lowest results. We can use the same **Array().fill().map()** technique described above to create a new array of **generateTheNumber()** calls:

```
Promise.all(
  Array(3)
    .fill(null)
    .map(() => generateTheNumber(10))
);
```

2. Now that we can resolve three separate calls, we need to manage the output. First, we can log out the results to see what we need to do next:

```
Promise.all(
  Array(3)
    .fill(null)
    .map(() => generateTheNumber(10))
).then((result) => console.log(result));
```

We log out **[undefined, undefined, undefined]**. That's not what we wanted. The reason for this is **generateTheNumber** doesn't actually return its promise – it didn't need to in the prior example.

3. We can fix that by adding a **return** statement and removing the **void** return type. We also need our callback function to return the results instead of simply logging them out. All these changes would help a program like this integrate into a larger application:

```
const generateTheNumber = (iterations: number) => {
  return Promise.allSettled(
```

```
    Array(iterations)
      .fill(null)
      .map(() => getTheValue())
  )
    .then((settledResults) => {
      const results = settledResults.reduce(
        (prev, current) => {
          return current.status === 'fulfilled'
            ? {
                ...prev,
                succeeded: prev.succeeded + 1,
                total: prev.total + current.value,
              }
            : { ...prev, failed: prev.failed + 1 };
        },
        {
          failed: 0,
          succeeded: 0,
          total: 0,
        }
      );
      return results;
    })
    .finally(() => console.log('Iteration done!'));
};
```

With that done we can get our output.

```
[
  { failed: 0, succeeded: 10, total: 443 },
  { failed: 1, succeeded: 9, total: 424 },
  { failed: 2, succeeded: 8, total: 413 },
]
```

4. The last step to complete this exercise is we only want to output the highest and lowest totals. To accomplish this, we can use the **Array.map()** function to extract only the totals from the output and the **Array.sort()** function to order the above output from lowest to highest, then print the totals from the first and last entries:

```
const totals = results.map((r) => r.total).sort();
console.log(`The highest total is ${totals[totals.length - 1]}.`);
console.log(`The lowest total is ${totals[0]}.`);
```

You might get an output similar to the following:

```
The value is 62
The value is 77
The value is 75
The value is 61
The value is 61
The value is 61
The value is 15
The value is 83
The value is 4
The value is 23
Iteration done!
.

.

.

The highest total is 522.
The lowest total is 401.
```

Note that only a section of the actual output is displayed for ease of presentation.

This exercise showed us how we can filter and sort the results of many promises and create data structures that accurately reflect the state of our application.

PROMISE.ANY

At the other end of the spectrum from **Promise.allSettled** lies **Promise.any**. This method takes an iterable (or array) of promises, but instead of settling all of them, it will resolve to the value of the first promise that resolves successfully. **Promise.any** is so new it has yet to be implemented in every browser and at the time of writing is not available in the LTS version of Node.js. You should check compatibility and availability before using it.

PROMISE.RACE

`Promise.race` has been around for some time and is similar to `Promise.any`.
Now, `Promise.race` again takes an iterable of promises and executes them all. The
first promise that resolves or rejects will resolve or reject the race. This is in contrast
to `Promise.any` in that if the first promise in `Promise.any` rejects, the other
promises still have an opportunity to resolve successfully:

```
const oneSecond = new Promise((_resolve, reject) => {
  setTimeout(() => reject("Too slow!"), 1000);
});

const upToTwoSeconds = new Promise(resolve => {
  setTimeout(() => resolve("Made it!"), Math.random() * 2000);
});
Promise.race([oneSecond, upToTwoSeconds])
  .then(result => console.log(result))
  .catch(err => console.error(err));
```

In this example, one promise always rejects in 1 second while the other resolves at a
random interval between 0 and 2 seconds. If the **oneSecond** promise wins the race,
the entire promise is rejected. If **upToTwoSeconds** takes less than a second, then
the promise resolves successfully with the message **"Made It!"**.

A practical example of using `Promise.race` might be a timeout and fallback feature
where if the primary web service can't respond within an expected amount of time,
the application either switches to a secondary source for data or exhibits some other
behavior. Or perhaps we want to deal with a slow render issue in a web browser
where if a screen paint hasn't finished in the expected amount of time, we switch to a
simpler view. There are lots of cases where `Promise.race` can ease the complexity
of handling asynchronous operations in TypeScript.

ENHANCING PROMISES WITH TYPES

The example we're working with so far specifies the type of input to the promise, but we have to provide a type for the result in each step of the chain. That's because TypeScript doesn't know what the promise may resolve to so we have to tell it what kind of type we're getting as the result.

In other words, we're missing out on one of TypeScript's most powerful features: *type inference*. Type inference is the ability for TypeScript to know what the type of something should be without having to be told. A very simple example of type inference would be the following:

```
const hello = "hello";
```

No type is specified. This is because TypeScript understands that the variable **hello** is being assigned a string and cannot be reassigned. If we try to pass this variable as an argument to a function that expects another type, we will get a compilation error, even though we never specified the type. Let's apply type inference to promises.

First, let's look at the type definition for the **Promise** object:

```
new <T>(executor: (resolve: (value?: T | PromiseLike<T>) => void, reject:
(reason?: any) => void) => void): Promise<T>;
```

T is what's known as a generic. It means any type can be specified to take the place of **T**. Let's say we define a promise like this:

```
new Promise(resolve => {
  resolve("This resolves!");
});
```

What we're doing here is stating the **resolve** argument will resolve to an unknown type. The receiving code will need to provide a type for it. This can be improved by adding a type value for **T**:

```
new Promise<string>(resolve => {
  resolve("This resolves!");
});
```

Now the promise constructor resolves to a type of **Promise<string>**. When the promise becomes fulfilled, it is expected to return a type of **string**.

Let's examine an example where casting the return type of a promise becomes important:

```
const getPromise = async () => new Promise(resolve => resolve(Math.
ceil(Math.random() * 100)));
const printResult = (result: number) => console.log(result);
getPromise().then(result => printResult(result));
```

If you put this example into an IDE such as VS Code, you'll see that you have a type error on the **result** parameter given to **printResult**. The type that the promise returned by **getPromise** is unknown but **printResult** expects **number**. We can fix this problem by providing a type to the promise when we declare it:

```
const getPromise = async () => new Promise<number>(resolve =>
resolve(Math.ceil(Math.random() * 100)));
const printResult = (result: number) => console.log(result);
getPromise().then(result => printResult(result));
```

We have added **<number>** immediately after our promise declaration and TypeScript knows this promise is expected to resolve to a number. This type-checking will also be applied to the resolution of our promise. For example, if we tried to resolve to a value of **"Hello!"**, we'd get another type error now that our promise is expected to return a number.

EXERCISE 12.04: ASYNCHRONOUS RENDERING

In this exercise, we'll create a simple website with synchronous rendering and refactor it so the rendering is asynchronous:

> **NOTE**
>
> The code file for this exercise can also be found here:
> https://packt.link/q8rka.

1. Clone the project from GitHub (https://packt.link/q8rka) to begin. Then, install dependencies:

```
npm i
```

We just installed TypeScript into our project as well as **http-server**, which is a simple Node.js HTTP server that will allow us to run our website on localhost.

Now we'll add a few files to get the project started.

2. In the root of your project, create a file called **index.html** and add the following lines to it:

```html
<html>
  <head>
    <title>The TypeScript Workshop - Exercise 12.03</title>
    <link href="styles.css" rel="stylesheet"></link>
  </head>
  <body>
    <div id="my-data"></div>
  </body>
  <script type="module" src="data-loader.js"></script>
</html>
```

3. Next, optionally add a stylesheet as the default styles are quite an eyesore. Bring your own or use something simple like this:

```css
body {
  font-family: Arial, Helvetica, sans-serif;
  font-size: 12px;
}


input {
  width: 200;
}
```

4. Add a file called **data.json** to represent the data we are fetching from a remote server:

```json
{ "message": "Hello Promise!" }
```

5. One more to go. Let's add a TypeScript file called **data-loader.ts**:

```typescript
const updateUI = (message: any): void => {
  const item = document.getElementById("my-data");
  if (item) {
    item.innerText = `Here is your data: ${message}`;
  }
};


const message = fetch("http://localhost:8080/data.json");
updateUI(message);
```

That's all you need to run a local service with a TypeScript web application! Later in the book, we'll see some more robust solutions, but for now, this will let us focus on the TypeScript without too many bells or whistles around.

6. To see our application, we'll need to transpile the TypeScript and start the local server. For the best experience, we'll need two separate Command Prompt windows. In one of them, we'll type a command to transpile the TypeScript and watch for changes:

```
npx tsc -w data-loader.ts
```

7. And in the other window, we'll start our server with a flag to avoid caching so we can see our changes right away:

```
npx http-server . -c-1
```

8. If we navigate to **http://localhost:8080**, we'll see our application load and receive this message:

```
"Here is your data: [object Promise]".
```

Something hasn't worked correctly. What we want to see is **"Here is your data: Hello Promise!"**. If we go and look at the TypeScript code, we'll see this line:

```
const message = fetch("http://localhost:8080/data.json");
```

This isn't working correctly. **fetch** is an asynchronous request. We are just seeing the unresolved promise and printing it to the screen.

Another warning sign is the use of **any** in the **updateUI** function. Why is the **any** type being used there when it should be a string? That's because TypeScript won't allow us to use a string. TypeScript knows we're calling **updateUI** with an unresolved promise and so we'll get a type error if we try to treat that as a string type. New developers sometimes think they are fixing a problem by using **any**, but more often than not they will be ignoring valid errors.

In order to get this code to work correctly, you will need to refactor it so that the promise **fetch** returns is resolved. When it works correctly, **fetch** returns a response object that exposes a **data** method that also returns a promise, so you will need to resolve two promises in order to display the data on your page.

> **NOTE**
>
> The fetch library is a web API for browsers that is a great improvement on the original **XMLHttpRequest** specification. It retains all the power of **XMLHttpRequest** but the API is much more ergonomic and as such is used by many web applications, rather than installing a third-party client library. **fetch** is not implemented in Node.js natively but there are some libraries that provide the same functionality. We'll take a look at those later in the chapter.

LIBRARIES AND NATIVE PROMISES — THIRD-PARTY LIBRARIES, Q, AND BLUEBIRD

As stated previously, promises became part of the ECMAScript standard in 2015. Up until that point, developers used libraries such as Q or Bluebird to fill the gap in the language. While many developers choose to use native promises, these libraries remain quite popular with weekly downloads still growing. That said, we should carefully consider whether it's a good idea to depend on a third-party library over a native language feature. Unless one of these libraries provides some critical functionality that we can't do without, we should prefer native features over third-party libraries. Third-party libraries can introduce bugs, complexity, and security vulnerabilities and require extra effort to maintain. This isn't an indictment against open source.

Open source projects (such as TypeScript) are an essential part of today's developer ecosystem. That said, it's still a good idea to carefully choose our dependencies and make sure they are well-maintained libraries that are not redundant with native features.

It's also worth noting that the APIs of third-party libraries may differ from the native language feature. For example, the Q library borrows a deferred object from the jQuery implementation:

```
import * as Q from "q";

const deferred = Q.defer();
deferred.resolve(123);

deferred.promise.then(val => console.log(val));
```

This written in a native promise is more like the examples we've seen so far:

```
const p = new Promise<number>((resolve, reject) => {
   resolve(123);
});

p.then(val => console.log(val));
```

There's nothing inherently wrong with the Q implementation here, but it's non-standard and this may make our code less readable to other developers or prevent us from learning standard best practices.

Bluebird is more similar to the native promise. In fact, it could be used as a polyfill.

POLYFILLING PROMISES

TypeScript will transpile code, but it will *not* polyfill native language features that are not present in your target environment. This is critical to understand to avoid frustration and mysterious bugs. What TypeScript will do for us is allow us to specify the target environment. Let's look at a simple example.

Consider the following **tsconfig.json** file:

```
{
  "compilerOptions": {
    "target": "es6",
    "module": "commonjs",
    "outDir": "./public",
    "strict": true,
    "esModuleInterop": true,
    "forceConsistentCasingInFileNames": true
  }
}
```

Now consider this module in **promise.ts**:

```
const p = new Promise<number>((resolve, reject) => {
  resolve(123);
});


p.then(val => console.log(val));
```

Our code will transpile fine. We enter **npx tsc** and the transpiled JavaScript output looks very much like our TypeScript code. The only difference is the type has been removed:

```
const p = new Promise((resolve, reject) => {
    resolve(123);
});
p.then(val => console.log(val));
```

However, consider if we change the target to **es5**:

```
{
  "compilerOptions": {
    "target": "es5",
    "module": "commonjs",
    "outDir": "./public",
    "strict": true,
    "esModuleInterop": true,
    "forceConsistentCasingInFileNames": true
  }
}
```

Now the project will no longer build:

```
% npx tsc
src/promise.ts:1:15 - error TS2585: 'Promise' only refers to a type, but
is being used as a value here. Do you need to change your target library?
Try changing the `lib` compiler option to es2015 or later.


1 const p = new Promise<number>((resolve, reject) => {
                ~~~~~~~


Found 1 error.
```

TypeScript even warns me that I might want to fix my target. Note that **"es2015"** and **"es6"** are the same thing (as are **"es2016"** and **"es7"**, and so on). This is a somewhat confusing convention that we simply need to get used to.

This will be fine if I can build my project for an **es6+** environment (such as a current version of Node.js or any modern browser), but if I need to support a legacy browser or a very old version of Node.js, then "fixing" this by setting the compilation target higher will only result in a broken application. We'll need to use a polyfill.

In this case, Bluebird can be a really good choice as it has an API very similar to native promises. In fact, all I will need to do is **npm install bluebird** and then import the library into my module. The Bluebird library does not include typings so to have full IDE support, you'd need to also **install @types/bluebird** as a **devDependency**:

```
import { Promise } from "bluebird";

const p = new Promise<number>(resolve => {
   resolve(123);
});


p.then(val => console.log(val));
```

My transpiled code will now run in a very early version of Node.js, such as version 0.10 (released in 2013).

Note that Bluebird is designed to be a full-featured **Promise** library. If I'm just looking for a polyfill, I might prefer to use something like **es6-promise**. Its use is exactly the same. I **npm install es6-promise** and then import the **Promise** class into my module:

```
import { Promise } from "es6-promise";

const p = new Promise<number>(resolve => {
   resolve(123);
});

p.then(val => console.log(val));
```

If you want to try this yourself, be aware that modern versions of TypeScript won't even run on Node.js 0.10! You'll have to transpile your code in a recent version (such as Node.js 12) and then switch to Node.js 0.10 to execute the code. To do this, it's a good idea to use a version manager such as **nvm** or **n**.

This is actually a great example of the power of TypeScript. We can write and build our code on a modern version but target a legacy runtime. Setting the compilation target will make sure we build code that is suitable for that runtime.

PROMISIFY

Promisification is the practice of taking an asynchronous function that expects a callback and turning it into a promise. This is essentially a convenience utility that allows you to always write in promises instead of having to use the callbacks of a legacy API. It can be really helpful to promisify legacy APIs so that all our code can use promises uniformly and be easy to read. But it's more than just a convenience to convert callbacks into promises. Some modern APIs will only accept promises as parameters. If we could only work on some code with callbacks, we would have to wrap the callback asynchronous code with promises manually. Promisification saves us the trouble and potentially many lines of code.

Let's work through an example of *promisifying* a function that expects a callback. We have a few options to choose from. Bluebird again provides this functionality with **Promise.promisify**. This time, we'll try a polyfill, **es6-promisify**. Let's start with a function that expects a callback:

```
const asyncAdder = (n1: number, n2: number, cb: Function) => {
  let err: Error;
  if (n1 === n2) {
    cb(Error("Use doubler instead!"));
  } else {
    cb(null, n1 + n2);
  }
};


asyncAdder(3, 4, (err: Error, sum: number) => {
  if (err) {
    throw err;
  }
  console.log(sum);
});
```

Functions that can be promisified follow a convention where the first argument into the callback is an error object. If the error is null or undefined, then the function is considered to have been invoked successfully. Here, I am calling **asyncAdder**, giving it two numbers and a callback function. My callback understands that **asyncAdder** will have an error in the first argument position if an error was thrown or the sum of the two numbers in the second argument position if it was successful. By adhering to this pattern, the function can be promisified. First, we **npm install es6-promisify** and then we import the module:

```
import { promisify } from "es6-promisify";

const asyncAdder = (n1: number, n2: number, cb: Function) => {
  let err: Error;
  if (n1 === n2) {
    cb(Error("Use doubler instead!"));
  } else {
    cb(null, n1 + n2);
  }
};

const promiseAdder = promisify(asyncAdder);

promiseAdder(3, 4)
  .then((val: number) => console.log(val))
  .catch((err: Error) => console.log(err));
```

We use the **promisify** import to wrap our function and now we can work exclusively with promises.

Bluebird gives us exactly the same functionality:

```
import { promisify } from "bluebird";

const asyncAdder = (n1: number, n2: number, cb: Function) => {
  if (n1 === n2) {
    cb(Error("Use doubler instead!"));
  } else {
    cb(null, n1 + n2);
  }
};
```

```
const promiseAdder = promisify(asyncAdder);

promiseAdder(3, 4)
  .then((val: number) => console.log(val))
  .catch((err: Error) => console.log(err));
```

NODE.JS UTIL.PROMISIFY

Node.js introduced its own version of **promisify** as a native feature in version 8 (2017). Instead of using **es6-promise** or Bluebird, if we are targeting a Node.js 8+ environment, we can leverage the **util** package. Note that since we are writing TypeScript, we will need to add the @**types/node** dependency to take advantage of this package. Otherwise, TypeScript will not understand our import. We'll run **npm install -D @types/node**. The **-D** flag will install the type as a **devDependency**, which means it can be excluded from production builds:

```
import { promisify } from "util";

const asyncAdder = (n1: number, n2: number, cb: Function) => {
  let err: Error;
  if (n1 === n2) {
    cb(Error("Use doubler instead!"));
  } else {
    cb(null, n1 + n2);
  }
};

const promiseAdder = promisify(asyncAdder);

promiseAdder(3, 4)
  .then((val: number) => console.log(val))
  .catch((err: Error) => console.log(err));
```

Obviously, if we want our code to run in a browser, this won't work and we should use one of the other libraries, such as Bluebird, to enable this functionality.

ASYNCHRONOUS FILESYSTEM

As of Node.js 10 (released 2018), the FileSystem API (**fs**) comes with promisified async versions of all the functions as well as blocking synchronous versions of them. Let's look at the same operation with all three alternatives.

FS.READFILE

Many Node.js developers have worked with this API. This method will read a file, taking the file path as the first argument and a callback as the second argument. The callback will receive one or two arguments, an error (should one occur) as the first argument and a data buffer object as the second argument, should the read be successful:

```
import { readFile } from "fs";
import { resolve } from "path";


const filePath = resolve(__dirname, "text.txt");

readFile(filePath, (err, data) => {
  if (err) {
    throw err;
  }
  console.log(data.toString());
});
```

We read the file and log out the contents asynchronously. Anyone who has worked with the Node.js **fs** library in the past has probably seen code that looks like this. The code is non-blocking, which means even if the file is very large and the read is very slow, it won't prevent the application from performing other operations in the meantime. There's nothing wrong with this code other than it's not as concise and modern as we might like.

In the example above, we're reading the file and logging to the console – not very useful, but in a real-world scenario, we might be reading a config file on startup, handling the documents of clients, or managing the lifecycle of web assets. There are many reasons you might need to access the local filesystem in a Node.js application.

FS.READFILESYNC

The **fs** library also exposes a fully synchronous API, meaning its operations are blocking and the event loop won't progress until these operations are complete. Such blocking operations are more often used with command-line utilities where taking full advantage of the event loop isn't a priority and instead, simple, clean code is the priority. With this API, we can write some nice, concise code like this:

```
import { readFileSync } from "fs";
import { resolve } from "path";
```

```
const filePath = resolve(__dirname, "text.txt");

console.log(readFileSync(filePath).toString());
```

It could be tempting to write code like this and call it a day, but **readFileSync** is a blocking operation so we must beware. The main execution thread will actually be paused until this work is complete. This may still be appropriate for a command-line utility, but it could be a real disaster to put code like this in a web API.

THE FS PROMISES API

The **fs** library exposes the promises API, which can give us the best of both worlds, asynchronous execution and concise code:

```
import { promises } from "fs";
import { resolve } from "path";

const filePath = resolve(__dirname, "text.txt");

promises.readFile(filePath).then(file => console.log(file.toString()));
```

Using the promises API lets us write nearly as concise code as the synchronous version, but now we are fully asynchronous, making the code suitable for a high-throughput web application or any other process where a blocking operation would be unacceptable.

EXERCISE 12.05: THE FS PROMISES API

In this exercise, you will use the **fs** promises API to concatenate two files into one. Whenever possible, make your code DRY (don't repeat yourself) by using functions. You'll need to use **readFile** and **writeFile**. The only dependencies needed for this program are **ts-node** (for execution), **typescript**, and @ **types/node** so we have the types for the built-in **fs** and **path** libraries in Node.js:

> **NOTE**
>
> The code file for this exercise can also be found here:
> https://packt.link/M3MH3.

1. Using the file in the GitHub repo as a basis for this exercise, navigate to the exercise directory and type **npm i** to install these dependencies.

2. We are going to want to read two separate files using **readFile** and then use **writeFile** to write our output text file. The sample project already has two text files with some simple text. Feel free to add your own files and text.

3. This project could be completed using **readFileSync** and **writeFileSync**. That code would look something like this:

```
import { readFileSync, writeFileSync } from "fs";
import { resolve } from "path";


const file1 = readFileSync(resolve(__dirname, 'file1.txt'));
const file2 = readFileSync(resolve(__dirname, 'file2.txt'));


writeFileSync(resolve(__dirname, 'output.txt'), [file1, file2].
join('\n'));
```

The **resolve** function from the path library resolves paths on your filesystem and is often used alongside the **fs** library, as depicted above. Both these libraries are part of the Node.js standard library so we need only install typings, not the libraries themselves.

4. We can execute this program with **npx ts-node file-concat.ts**. This will produce a file called **output.txt**, which contains this text:

```
Text in file 1.

Text in file 2.
```

So this works without promises. And this is probably fine for a command-line utility executed by a single user on a single workstation. However, if this kind of code were put into a web server, we might start to see some blocking issues. Synchronous filesystem calls are *blocking* and block the event loop. Doing this in a production application can cause latency or failure.

5. We could solve this problem using **readFile** and **writeFile**, which are both asynchronous functions that take callbacks, but then we'd need to nest the second **readFile** inside the first. The code would look like this:

```
import { readFile, writeFile } from 'fs';
import { resolve } from 'path';


readFile(resolve(__dirname, 'file1.txt'), (err, file1) => {
  if (err) throw err;
    readFile(resolve(__dirname, 'file1.txt'), (err, file2) => {
```

```
      if (err) throw err;
      writeFile(
        resolve(__dirname, 'output.txt'),
        [file1, file2].join('\n'),
        (err) => {
          if (err) throw err;
        }
      );
    });
  });
```

We are now clear of blocking issues, but the code is looking quite ugly. It's not hard to imagine another developer failing to understand the intent of this code and introducing a bug. Additionally, by putting the second **readFile** as a callback in the first, we are making the function slower than it needs to be. In a perfect world, those calls can be made in parallel. To do that, we can leverage the promises API.

6.   The best way to do things in parallel with promises is **Promise.all**. We can wrap our two **readFile** calls in a single **Promise.all**. To do that, we need to promisify **readFile**. Lucky for us, the **fs** library comes with a helper that will do that for us. Instead of importing **readFile**, we import promises from **fs** and call the **readFile** method on that object:

```
import { promises } from 'fs';
import { resolve } from 'path';

Promise.all([
  promises.readFile(resolve(__dirname, 'file1.txt')),
  promises.readFile(resolve(__dirname, 'file2.txt')),
]);
```

7.   These two reads will now run asynchronously in parallel. Now we can handle the output and use the same **array.join** function from the earlier example along with **promises.writeFile**:

```
import { promises } from 'fs';
import { resolve } from 'path';

Promise.all([
  promises.readFile(resolve(__dirname, 'file1.txt')),
  promises.readFile(resolve(__dirname, 'file2.txt')),
```

```
]).then((files) => {
    promises.writeFile(resolve(__dirname, 'output.txt'), files.
join('\n'));
});
```

8. This code is looking quite a lot cleaner than the nested code above. When we execute it with **npx ts-node file-concat.ts**, we get the expected output of **output.txt** containing the concatenated text:

```
Text in file 1.

Text in file 2.
```

Now that we have this working, we can certainly imagine much more complicated programs manipulating other types of files, such as a PDF merge function as a web service. Though some of the internals would be a lot more challenging to implement, the principles would be the same.

WORKING WITH DATABASES

It is very common for Node.js applications to work with a backend database such as **mysql** or **postgres**. It is critical that queries against a database be made asynchronously. Production-grade Node.js web services may serve thousands of requests per second. If it were necessary to pause the main execution thread for queries made synchronously against a database, these services just wouldn't scale at all. Asynchronous execution is critical to making this work.

The process of negotiating a database connection, sending a SQL string, and parsing the response is complicated and not a native feature of Node.js and so we will almost always use a third-party library to manage this. These libraries are guaranteed to implement some kind of callback or promise pattern and we'll see it throughout their documentation and examples. Depending on the library you choose, you may have to implement a callback pattern, you may get to work with promises, or you may be presented with **async/await** (see *Chapter 13 Async/Await*). You may even get a choice of any of these as it's definitely possible to provide all of the above as options.

For these examples, we'll use **sqlite**. Now, **sqlite** is a nice library that implements a fairly standard SQL syntax and can operate against a static file as a database or even run in memory. We will use the in-memory option. This means that there is nothing that needs to be done to set up our database. But we will have to run a few scripts to create a table or two and populate it on startup. It would be fairly simple to adapt these exercises to work with **mysql**, **postgres**, or even **mongodb**. All of these databases can be installed on your workstation or run in a Docker container for local development.

For the first example, let's look at **sqlite3**. This library has an asynchronous API. Unlike more permanent and robust databases such as **mysql** or **postgres**, some **sqlite** client libraries are actually synchronous, but we won't be looking at those as they aren't very useful for demonstrating how promises work. So **sqlite3** implements an asynchronous API, but it works entirely with callbacks. Here is an example of creating an in-memory database, adding a table, adding a row to that table, and then querying back the row we added:

```
import { Database } from "sqlite3";

const db = new Database(":memory:", err => {
  if (err) {
    console.error(err);
    return db.close();
  }
  db.run("CREATE TABLE promise (id int, desc char);", err => {
    if (err) {
      console.error(err);
      return db.close();
    }
    db.run(
      "INSERT INTO promise VALUES (1, 'I will always lint my code.');",
      () => {
        db.all("SELECT * FROM promise;", (err, rows) => {
          if (err) {
            console.error(err);
            return db.close();
          }
          console.log(rows);
          db.close(err => {
            if (err) {
              return console.error(err);
            }
          });
        });
      }
    );
  });
});
```

This is exactly what developers mean when they complain about "callback hell." Again, this code executes perfectly well, but it is needlessly verbose, becomes deeply nested, and repeats itself, especially in the error-handling department. Of course, the code could be improved by adding abstractions and chaining together methods, but that doesn't change the fact that callbacks aren't a very modern way to think about writing Node.js code.

Since all of these callbacks follow the pattern of expecting the first argument to be an error object, we could promisify **sqlite3**, but as is often the case, somebody has already done this work for us and provided a library called simply **sqlite** that mimics the exact API of **sqlite3**, but implements a promise API.

I can rewrite the same code using this library and the result is a good deal more pleasing:

```
import { open } from "sqlite";
import * as sqlite from "sqlite3";


open({ driver: sqlite.Database, filename: ":memory:" }).then((db) => {
return db
    .run("CREATE TABLE promise (id int, desc char);")
    .then(() => {
      return db.run(
        "INSERT INTO promise VALUES (1, 'I will always lint my code.');"
      );
    })
    .then(() => {
      return db.all("SELECT * FROM promise;");
    })
    .then(rows => {
      console.log(rows);
    })
    .catch(err => console.error(err))
    .finally(() => db.close());
});
```

We've dropped nearly half of the lines of code and it's not nested as deeply. This still could be improved, but it's much cleaner now. Best of all, we have a single **catch** block followed by **finally**, to make sure the database connection is closed at the end.

DEVELOPING WITH REST

In the next exercise, we'll build a RESTful API. REST is a very common standard for web traffic. Most websites and web APIs operate using REST. It stands for Representational State Transfer and defines concepts such as operations (sometimes called "methods" or even "verbs") such as **GET**, **DELETE**, **POST**, **PUT**, and **PATCH** and resources (the "path" or "noun"). The full scope of REST is beyond this book.

Developers working on RESTful APIs frequently find it useful to work with some sort of REST client. The REST client can be configured to make different kinds of requests and display the responses. Requests can be saved and run again in the future. Some REST clients allow the creation of scenarios or test suites.

Postman is a popular and free REST client. If you don't already have a REST client you're comfortable working with, try downloading Postman at https://www.postman.com/downloads/ before the next exercise. Once you've installed Postman, check its documentation (https://learning.postman.com/docs/getting-started/sending-the-first-request/) and get ready for the next exercise.

EXERCISE 12.06: IMPLEMENTING A RESTFUL API BACKED BY SQLITE

In this exercise, you will create a REST API backed by **sqlite**. In this project, you will implement all CRUD (create, read, update, and delete) operations in the **sqlite** database and we will expose the corresponding REST verbs (**POST**, **GET**, **PUT**, and **DELETE**) from our web server:

> **NOTE**
>
> The code file for this exercise can also be found here:
> https://packt.link/rIX7G.

1. To get started, clone the project from GitHub and change to the directory for this exercise.

2. Install the dependencies:

```
npm i
```

This will install typings for Node.js, as well as **ts-node** and **typescript** as development dependencies while **sqlite** and **sqlite3** are regular dependencies. All of these dependencies are already specified in the project's **package.json** file. Some of the dependencies, such as @**types/node**, **ts-node**, and **typescript**, are specified as **devDependencies** and others are regular dependencies. For the purpose of this exercise, the distinction is not going to matter but it's a common practice to run application builds so that only the necessary dependencies are part of the production build, thus the separation. The way to run this kind of build is **npm install --production** if you only wish to install the production dependencies or **npm prune --production** if you've already installed your **devDependencies** and wish to remove them.

3. Now let's create a file to hold our **sqlite** database. Add a file in the root of your project called **db.ts**. We'll go with an object-oriented approach for the database and create a singleton object to represent our database and access patterns. One reason for doing this is we are going to want to maintain the state of whether or not the database has been initialized. Calling open on an in-memory **sqlite** database will destroy the database and create another one immediately, thus we only want to open the database connection if it isn't already open:

```
import { Database } from "sqlite";
import sqlite from "sqlite3";

export interface PromiseModel {
  id: number;
  desc: string;
}

export class PromiseDB {
  private db: Database;
  private initialized = false;
  constructor() {
    this.db = new Database({
      driver: sqlite.Database,
      filename: ":memory:",
    });
  }
}
```

It's always a good idea to create a class or interface to describe our entity, so here we have created **PromiseModel**. It will be useful to other parts of our application to be able to understand the properties our entity has as well as their types, since the database will only return untyped query results. We export the interface so that it can be used by other modules.

4. Our database is an object with a constructor that will have a private member representing the actual database connection and a Boolean value to track whether the database has been initialized. Let's add a method for initialization:

```
initialize = () => {
  if (this.initialized) {
    return Promise.resolve(true);
  }
  return this.db
    .open()
    .then(() =>
      this.db
        .run("CREATE TABLE promise (id INTEGER PRIMARY KEY, desc
CHAR);")
        .then(() => (this.initialized = true))
    );
};
```

First, we check to see if we've already initialized the database. If so, we're done and we resolve the promise. If not, we call **open**, then once that promise has resolved, run our table creation SQL, and then finally update the state of the database so that we don't accidentally re-initialize it.

We could try to initialize the database in the constructor. The problem with that approach is that constructors do not resolve promises before returning. Constructor functions may call methods that return promises, but they will not resolve the promise. It's usually cleaner to create the singleton object and then invoke the initialization promise separately. For more information about singleton classes, see *Chapter 8, Dependency Injection in TypeScript*.

5. Now let's add some methods. This will be pretty simple since our table only has two columns:

```
create = (payload: PromiseModel) =>
  this.db.run("INSERT INTO promise (desc) VALUES (?);", payload.
desc);
```

This method takes an object of type **PromiseModel** as an argument, sends a prepared statement (a parameterized SQL statement that is safe from SQL injection attacks), and then returns **RunResult**, which contains some metadata about the operation that took place. Since the **sqlite** library ships with typings, we're able to infer the return type without needing to specify it. The return type in this case is **Promise<ISqlite.RunResult<sqlite.Statement>>**. We could paste all of that into our code, but it's much cleaner the way it is. Remember, if a good type can be inferred, it's best to just let TypeScript do the heavy lifting.

6. In addition to the **create** method, we will want **delete**, **getAll**, **getOne**, and **update** methods. The **delete** method is very straightforward:

```
delete = (id: number) => this.db.run("DELETE FROM promise WHERE id
= ?", id);
```

7. Since we're calling **db.run** again, we're again returning that **RunResult** type. Let's see what it looks like to return some of your own data:

```
getAll = () => this.db.all<PromiseModel[]>("SELECT * FROM
promise;");

getOne = (id: number) =>
    this.db.get<PromiseModel>("SELECT * FROM promise WHERE id = ?",
id);
```

These methods use type parameters to specify the expected return types. If the type parameters were omitted, these methods would return **any** types, which wouldn't be very helpful to the other parts of our application.

8. Last of all is the **update** method. This one will use our **PromiseModel** again to type check the input:

```
update = (payload: PromiseModel) =>
  this.db.run(
    "UPDATE promise SET desc = ? where id = ?",
    payload.desc,
    payload.id
  );
```

9. The final code for the class looks like this:

```typescript
import { Database } from "sqlite";
import sqlite from "sqlite3";

export interface PromiseModel {
  id: number;
  desc: string;
}

export class PromiseDB {
  private db: Database;
  private initialized = false;
  constructor() {
    this.db = new Database({
      driver: sqlite.Database,
      filename: ":memory:",
    });
  }

  initialize = () => {
    if (this.initialized) {
      return Promise.resolve(true);
    }
    return this.db
      .open()
      .then(() =>
        this.db
          .run("CREATE TABLE promise (id INTEGER PRIMARY KEY, desc
CHAR);")
          .then(() => (this.initialized = true))
      );
  };

  create = (payload: PromiseModel) =>
    this.db.run("INSERT INTO promise (desc) VALUES (?);", payload.
desc);

  delete = (id: number) => this.db.run("DELETE FROM promise WHERE id
= ?", id);

  getAll = () => this.db.all<PromiseModel[]>("SELECT * FROM
```

```
promise;");

  getOne = (id: number) =>
    this.db.get<PromiseModel>("SELECT * FROM promise WHERE id = ?",
id);

  update = (payload: PromiseModel) =>
    this.db.run(
      "UPDATE promise SET desc = ? where id = ?",
      payload.desc,
      payload.id
    );
}
```

The next step is to build an HTTP server implementing a RESTful interface. Many Node.js developers use frameworks such as Express.js, Fastify, or NestJS, but for this exercise, we're just going to build a basic HTTP server. It won't have all the niceties of those frameworks, but it'll help us focus on asynchronous programming.

10. To create our server, we'll create a class called **App** and expose an instance of it. Create a file called **app.ts** and declare the class:

```
import { createServer, IncomingMessage, Server, ServerResponse } from
"http";

import { PromiseDB } from "./db";

class App {
  public db: PromiseDB;
  private server: Server;
  constructor(private port: number) {
    this.db = new PromiseDB();
    this.server = createServer(this.requestHandler);
  }
}

export const app = new App(3000);
```

11. Our **App** class takes an argument of the port number we'll run our server on. The class will maintain the state of the running server as well as the database connection. Like our **PromiseDB** class, the constructor needs to be supplemented by an **initialize** method to handle the asynchronous setup:

```
initialize = () => {
  return Promise.all([
    this.db.initialize(),
    new Promise((resolve) => this.server.listen(this.port, () =>
resolve(true))),
  ]).then(() => console.log("Application is ready!"));
};
```

This method uses **Promise.all** so that we can initialize our database and server in parallel. When both are ready, it'll log a message letting us know the application is ready to handle requests. We are calling the **initialize** method on the **PromiseDB** instance that we've exposed to our **App** class. Unfortunately, **server.listen** doesn't return a promise but instead implements a fairly primitive API that requires a callback so we are wrapping it in our own promise. It's tempting to want to wrap **server.listen** in **util.promisify**, but even that won't work because **util.promisify** expects the callback function to expect the first argument to be an error object and the **server.listen** callback doesn't take any arguments. Sometimes, despite our best efforts, we just have to use a callback, but we can usually wrap them with promises.

12. We're also going to need to add a **requestHandler** method. **createServer** is a method exposed by the **http** module in Node.js. It takes an argument that should be a function to handle requests and supply a response. Again, the API for the **http** module is fairly low-level:

```
requestHandler = (req: IncomingMessage, res: ServerResponse) => {
  res.setHeader("Access-Control-Allow-Origin", "*");
  res.setHeader("Access-Control-Allow-Headers", "*");
  res.setHeader(
    "Access-Control-Allow-Methods",
    "DELETE, GET, OPTIONS, POST, PUT"
  );
  if (req.method === "OPTIONS") {
    return res.end();
  }
  const urlParts = req.url?.split("/") ?? "/";
  switch (urlParts[1]) {
```

```
        case "promise":
          return promiseRouter(req, res);
        default:
          return this.handleError(res, 404, "Not Found.");
    }
  };
```

We want our application to direct all traffic on the **/promise** resource to our promises API. This will allow us to add more resources (maybe **/admin** or **/users**) later on. The request handler's job is to see if we have requested the **/promise** route and then direct traffic to that specific router. Since we haven't defined any other resources, we'll return a 404 if we request any other route.

Note that we are handling the **OPTIONS** HTTP verb differently than any other. If we get a request with that verb, we set the **"Access-Control-Allow-Origin"** header and return a successful response. This is for development convenience. The topic of CORS is beyond the scope of this book, and readers are encouraged to learn more about it before implementing it in a production environment.

13. That error handler needs a definition, so let's add one:

```
  handleError = (
    res: ServerResponse,
    statusCode = 500,
    message = "Internal Server Error."
  ) => res.writeHead(statusCode).end(message);
```

This is a nice one-liner that by default will throw a 500 status code **Internal Server Error**, but can take optional parameters to return any error code or message. Our default handler sets the status code to 404 and provides the message **"Not Found"**.

14. We add a call to **initialize** at the end and we're good to go. Let's take another look at the **App** class:

```
import { createServer, IncomingMessage, Server, ServerResponse } from
"http";

import { PromiseDB } from "./db";
import { promiseRouter } from "./router";

class App {
  public db: PromiseDB;
```

```typescript
  private server: Server;

  constructor(private port: number) {
    this.db = new PromiseDB();
    this.server = createServer(this.requestHandler);
  }

  initialize = () => {
    return Promise.all([
      this.db.initialize(),
      new Promise((resolve) => this.server.listen(this.port, () =>
resolve(true))),
    ]).then(() => console.log("Application is ready!"));
  };

  handleError = (
    res: ServerResponse,
    statusCode = 500,
    message = "Internal Server Error."
  ) => res.writeHead(statusCode).end(message);

  requestHandler = (req: IncomingMessage, res: ServerResponse) => {
    res.setHeader("Access-Control-Allow-Origin", "*");
    res.setHeader("Access-Control-Allow-Headers", "*");
    res.setHeader(
      "Access-Control-Allow-Methods",
      "DELETE, GET, OPTIONS, POST, PUT"
    );
    if (req.method === "OPTIONS") {
      return res.end();
    }
    const urlParts = req.url?.split("/") ?? "/";
    switch (urlParts[1]) {
      case "promise":
        return promiseRouter(req, res);
      default:
        return this.handleError(res, 404, "Not Found.");
    }
  };
}
```

```
export const app = new App(3000);

app.initialize();
```

If you've implemented all this in code, you're probably still getting an error on **promiseRouter**. That's because we haven't written that yet.

15. Add a **router.ts** file to your project. This will be the last part we need to build this simple API. A more complicated application would hopefully include a more sophisticated directory structure and most likely be based on a leading framework such as Express.js or NestJS.

    Unlike our database and server modules, the router is stateless. It does not need to be initialized and does not track any variables. We could still create a class for our router, but let's instead use a functional programming style. There's really no right or wrong way to do this. Instead of using classes for our database and server, we could likewise use a functional style.

    We're going to work on creating several handlers, tie them together with a router based on HTTP verbs, and also create a body parser. Let's start with the body parser.

16. Readers who have some experience with the Express.js framework may have used its powerful **bodyParser** module. It's normally a good idea to use an off-the-shelf solution for something like that, but in this exercise, you will write your own in order to get a closer look at how we can take the request or **IncomingMessage** object as a stream and convert it into a typed object:

```
const parseBody = (req: IncomingMessage): Promise<PromiseModel> => {
  return new Promise((resolve, reject) => {
    let body = "";
    req.on("data", (chunk) => (body += chunk));
    req.on("end", () => {
      try {
        resolve(JSON.parse(body));
      } catch (e) {
        reject(e);
      }
    });
  });
};
```

The data stream is again a fairly low-level API that we must wrap in a promise. The stream is event-based, as are a lot of the Node.js APIs. In this case, we are listening for two separate events, **data** and **end**. Each time we get a **data** event, we add data to the **body** string. When we receive the **end** event, we can finally resolve our promise. Since the data is a string at this point and we want an object, we will use **JSON.parse** to parse the object. **JSON.parse** must be wrapped with **try/catch** to catch any parsing errors.

By default, **JSON.parse** returns an **any** type. This type is too broad to be of any use in checking our application for type correctness. Fortunately, we can add proper type checking by setting the return type of **parseBody** to **Promise<PromiseModel>**. This will narrow the type of the object returned by **JSON.parse** to **PromiseModel** and the rest of our application can expect that type to have been parsed. Note that this is a compile-time check and does not guarantee the correct data has come from a third-party source such as an end user. It is advisable to combine type checks with validators or type guards to ensure consistency. When in doubt, employ good error handling.

17. Now that you have a good method for parsing the request body, let's add one to handle the create action:

```
const handleCreate = (req: IncomingMessage, res: ServerResponse) =>
  parseBody(req)
    .then((body) => app.db.create(body).then(() => res.end()))
    .catch((err) => app.handleError(res, 500, err.message));
```

18. This function parses the body of the request, attempts to insert it into our database, and then responds with a default 200 response if the operation was successful. Note that the chained catch at the end will catch any errors that occur in the promise. If our body parsing fails, the error will be caught here, even though it's placed after **db.create** in the chain.

19. Now let's handle the delete action:

```
const handleDelete = (requestParam: number, res: ServerResponse) =>
  app.db
    .delete(requestParam)
    .then(() => res.end())
    .catch((err) => app.handleError(res, 500, err.message));
```

The HTTP **DELETE** verb does not use a body. Instead, we will take the ID of the row we want to delete from the URL. We'll see how that routing works in a moment.

20. The **GET** operations need to return some data and will use **JSON.stringify** to serialize their response objects to send them to a client:

```
const handleGetAll = (res: ServerResponse) =>
  app.db
    .getAll()
    .then((data) => res.end(JSON.stringify(data)))
    .catch((err) => app.handleError(res, 500, err.message));

const handleGetOne = (requestParam: number, res: ServerResponse) =>
  app.db
    .getOne(requestParam)
    .then((data) => res.end(JSON.stringify(data)))
    .catch((err) => app.handleError(res, 500, err.message));
```

21. The update action looks similar to delete:

```
const handleUpdate = (req: IncomingMessage, res: ServerResponse) =>
  parseBody(req)
    .then((body) => app.db.update(body).then(() => res.end()))
    .catch((err) => app.handleError(res, 500, err.message));
```

22. Finally, we just need a router. Your router will need to make a decision based on the HTTP verb used as well as any request parameter that may refer to the ID of the row we want to interact with. We will also set the **Content-Type** header to **application/json** for all responses. Then we simply need to delegate to the correct handler:

```
export const promiseRouter = (req: IncomingMessage, res:
ServerResponse) => {
  const urlParts = req.url?.split("/") ?? "/";
  const requestParam = urlParts[2];
  res.setHeader("Content-Type", "application/json");
  switch (req.method) {
    case "DELETE":
      if (requestParam) {
```

```
          return handleDelete(Number.parseInt(requestParam), res);
      }
    case "GET":
      if (requestParam) {
        return handleGetOne(Number.parseInt(requestParam), res);
      }
      return handleGetAll(res);
    case "POST":
      return handleCreate(req, res);
    case "PUT":
      return handleUpdate(req, res);
    default:
      app.handleError(res, 404, "Not Found.");
  }
};
```

23. Now it's time to try our application. We installed **ts-node** earlier. This library allows us to transpile and run our TypeScript program in a single step. It is not necessarily recommended to use **ts-node** in production, but it makes for a very handy development tool. Let's try it now:

```
npx ts-node app.ts
```

You should see the following on your console:

```
Application is ready!
```

This implies that your application is ready to start receiving requests. If not, you may have a typo somewhere. Let's try it out. You can either use a REST client or curl. This exercise uses Postman

24. If you make a **GET** request to `http://localhost:3000/promise`, you will get an empty array ([]) back:

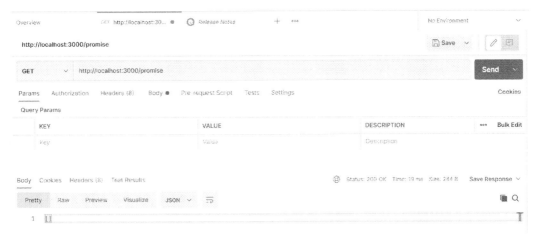

Figure 12.3: Initial GET request

This is because we haven't created any records yet.

25. Try a **POST** with the payload `{"desc":"Always lint your code"}`:

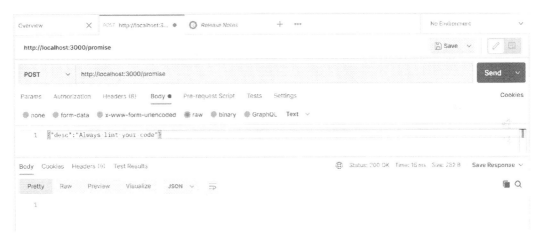

Figure 12.4: POST data

26. Now the **GET** request returns `[{"id":1,"desc":"Always lint your code"}]`:

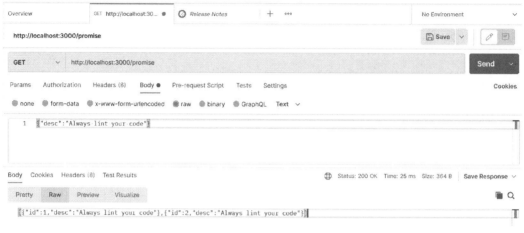

Figure 12.5: Use GET to retrieve data

27. If you do a request to `http://localhost:3000/promise/1`, you will get a single object back:

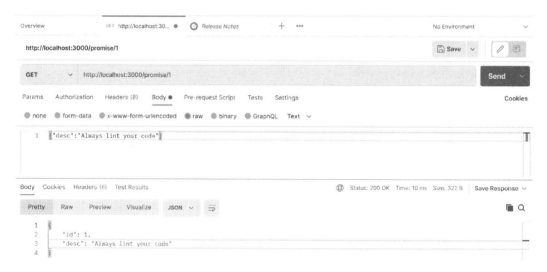

Figure 12.6: Single object

28. If you request **http://localhost:3000/promise/2**, you will get nothing:

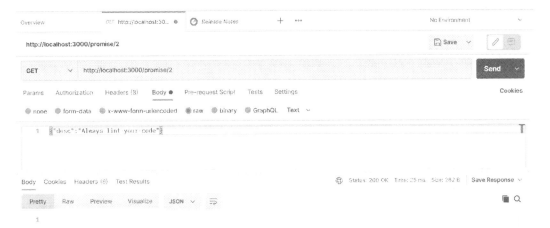

Figure 12.7: No items found

29. If you request **http://localhost:3000/something-else**, you will get a 404 response:

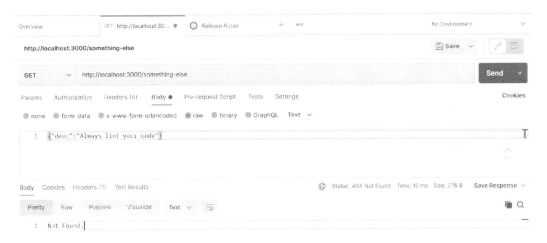

Figure 12.8: 404 response

Looks like things are working. Experiment with the different HTTP verbs. Try giving invalid input and see how the error handling works. We'll use this API in the next section.

PUTTING IT ALL TOGETHER — BUILDING A PROMISE APP

We've learned techniques for using promises in web projects as well as Node.js APIs. Let's combine our earlier exercises to build a web application that renders progressively as data is ready and makes use of asynchronous programming on the server to avoid blocking the event loop.

ACTIVITY 12.01: BUILDING A PROMISE APP

In this activity, we're going to build a web application that talks to the API we just built. Although frameworks such as Angular, React, and Vue are very popular, those are covered in later chapters so we will build a very basic TypeScript application with no bells or whistles.

> **NOTE**
>
> This activity provides a UI application that communicates with the backend API we built in *Exercise 12.06, Implementing a RESTful API backed by sqlite*. In order to get the output shown, you will need to have your API running. Return to that exercise for help if you need it.

This UI application will connect to our API and allow us to modify the data we store in our database. We will be able to list out the data we've saved (the promises we make), create new items to save, and delete items. Our UI application will need to make **GET**, **POST**, and **DELETE** calls to our backend API. It will need to use an HTTP client to do that. We could install a library such as **axios** to handle that or we could use the native Fetch API available in all modern web browsers.

Our web application will also need to be able to dynamically update the UI. Modern view libraries such as **react** or **vue** do that for us, but in this case we are framework-free so we'll need to use more DOM (document object model) APIs such as **getElementById**, **createElement**, and **appendChild**. These are natively available in all web browsers with no libraries needed.

Implementing this application using promises will be critical because all of the API calls will be asynchronous. We will perform an action, such as a click, our application will call the API, then it will respond with data and then and only then will the promise resolve and cause a change in the DOM state.

Here are some high-level steps that will enable you to create the app:

NOTE

The code file for this activity can be found here: https://packt.link/RlYli.

1. Create a static **html** page with **css** to be served via **http-server** for local development.

2. Add an **app.ts** file to make a web request to the backend using **fetch** and do the required DOM manipulation based on the response.

3. Transpile the **app.ts** file into **app.js** and test against the local server using a web browser.

4. Make adjustments to **app.ts** and continue testing until all the scenarios are working.

   Once you have completed the activity, you should be able to view the form on **localhost:8080**. An example is shown here:

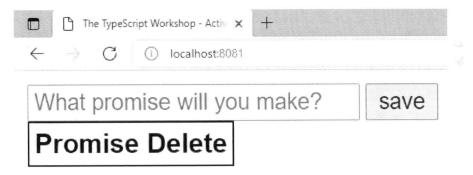

Figure 12.9: Completed form

NOTE

The solution to this activity can be found on page 670.

SUMMARY

We have learned how promises came to be a part of the ECMAScript standard, taken a tour of the native implementation, and worked through sample projects using promises to solve real-world problems. We also explored how TypeScript can enhance the promise spec and how we can polyfill promises when targeting environments that don't include native promise support. We contrasted the Bluebird promise library with native promises. We learned about different ways of interacting with the filesystem using Node.js and we also covered managing asynchronous database connections and queries. In the end, we put all of this together into a working application.

In the next chapter, we will build upon the asynchronous programming paradigm by covering **async** and **await**. We'll discuss when to use these over promises and the place promises still have in the TypeScript ecosystem.

13

ASYNC/AWAIT IN TYPESCRIPT

OVERVIEW

The `async/await` keywords give developers a more concise way to write asynchronous, non-blocking programs. In this chapter, we'll learn all about this syntactic sugar, a term for more concise and expressive syntax, for promises and how it drives modern software development. We will look at common uses of `async/await` and discuss the landscape of asynchronous programming in TypeScript. By the end of this chapter, you will be able to implement async/await keywords in TypeScript and use them to write asynchronous programs.

INTRODUCTION

The previous chapter got you started on promises in TypeScript. While promises improved our ability to write asynchronous code without the ugliness of nested callbacks, developers still wanted a better way to write asynchronous code. The promise syntax is sometimes challenging for programmers with a background in the C family of languages, and so the "syntactic sugar" of **async/await** was proposed to be added to the ECMAScript specification.

In this chapter, we'll learn about the introduction of new asynchronous programming paradigms to the ECMAScript standard, examine the syntax, and look at their use in TypeScript. We'll also cover the new (as of the time of writing) top-level **await** feature, which allows asynchronous programming outside of an **async** function. We will again look at error handling in asynchronous programming and examine the pros and cons of using **async/await** syntax versus promises.

Readers who have been through the prior chapter will see that there is still some nesting involved in promises. While the flow is much easier to manage through multiple promises than it is with nested callbacks, we still have no mechanism by which we can return control to the top level.

For example, consider a **getData** function that returns a promise. The code that invokes this function will look something like this:

```
getData().then(data => {
  // do something with the data
});
```

We don't have any means to propagate the **data** value to the outer scope. We couldn't deal with that value in a subsequent scope. Some programmers may attempt to write code that looks like this:

```
let myData;
getData().then(data => {
  myData = data
});
console.log(myData);
```

This code will always log out **undefined**. It seems like it should work, but it won't because the promise callback won't be invoked until the promise returns. Asynchronous programming like this can be confusing and lead to lots of bugs. **async/await** solve this problem by allowing us to pause the execution of code pending the resolution of a promise. We can rewrite the preceding code using **async/await** syntax:

```
const myData = await getData();
console.log(myData);
```

We've gone from five lines of code to two. The synchronous operation of **console.log** will wait for the promise to resolve. The code is much more understandable, and we can store our variable at the top scope without nesting.

Because TypeScript is transpiled to JavaScript in most cases, we need to make sure that we select the correct target environment in order for our code to run. This topic will be dealt with in greater detail later in the chapter.

EVOLUTION AND MOTIVATION

Although promises moved the needle considerably when it came to asynchronous programming paradigms, there remained a desire for a lighter syntax that relied less on explicitly declaring promise objects. Adding the **async/await** keywords to the ECMAScript specification would allow developers to reduce boilerplate and work with promises. The concept comes from the C# programming language, which in turn borrowed the concept of asynchronous workflows from F#.

An asynchronous function allows a program to continue normal operation even though that function call has yet to return. The program does not wait for that asynchronous function call to complete until the **await** keyword is found. More significantly, using **await** will not block the event loop. Even if we have paused part of a program to await the result of an asynchronous function call, other operations can still complete. The event loop is not blocked. For more on the event loop, return to *Chapter 12, Guide to Promises in TypeScript*.

The great thing about these keywords is that they are immediately compatible with promises. We can await any promise, thereby avoiding having to use the **then()** API. This capability means that along with the concept of promisification (see *Chapter 12, Guide to Promises in TypeScript*), we can use the latest syntax even when integrating with older libraries or modules. To demonstrate this, let's return to an example from the preceding chapter:

```
import { promises } from "fs";

promises.readFile('text.txt').then(file => console.log(file.toString()));
```

This example uses the **promises** API from the **fs** (filesystem) module from Node.js. The code reads a file from the local filesystem and logs the contents to the console. We can use await syntax with this code:

```
import { promises } from "fs";

const text = (await promises.readFile('text.txt')).toString();

console.log(text);
```

Note that in order to run this code, you must be able to use top-level **await**, which, at the time of this writing, requires a bit of extra setup. Refer to the section later in this chapter. The takeaway from this example is that we are still able to use the **promises** API from the **fs** module, even if we prefer **async/await**.

ASYNC/AWAIT IN TYPESCRIPT

The maintainers of TypeScript begin work on supporting ECMAScript features when they are in stages 1 and 2 of the review process, but only formally release them when they reach stage 3.

TypeScript began offering experimental support for **async** functions in version 1.6, released in September 2015, and offered full support in version 1.7, released in November 2015. TypeScript programmers could work with this syntax a full year ahead of official browser and Node.js support.

Use of the **async/await** keywords in TypeScript does not vary much from JavaScript, but we do have an advantage in the ability to be more explicit about which functions should return promises and which should return a resolved value or throw an error.

One thing to be cognizant of when writing modern syntax in TypeScript is that most TypeScript code is transpiled to JavaScript for execution in a runtime, such as a web browser or Node.js. We need to understand the difference between transpilation and a polyfill. **Transpilation** will convert code from one syntax into another. In this case, we can write **async/await** code and transpile to an environment that only supports promise syntax. A **polyfill** adds missing language features. If our target environment doesn't even support promises, then transpiling async/await into promises won't do the trick. We will require a polyfill as well.

EXERCISE 13.01: TRANSPILATION TARGETS

In this exercise, we will use a contrived "Hello World!" example to demonstrate how TypeScript handles the transpilation of the **async /await** keywords:

> **NOTE**
>
> The code files for this exercise can be found here: https://packt.link/NS8gY.

1. Navigate to the **Exercise01** folder and install dependencies with **npm install**:

```
npm install
```

2. That will install TypeScript and the TS Node execution environment. Now, execute the program included by typing **npx ts-node target.ts**. The result will be as follows:

```
World!
Hello
```

World! printed before **Hello**.

3. Open up **target.ts** and inspect the reason for this. This program creates a **sayHello** function, which internally creates a promise that resolves after one millisecond. You may notice that the program does exactly the same thing even if we remove the **await** keyword. That's OK. It's the different transpilation targets here that are interesting. When we run this program using TS Node, this will target the current Node.js version we're running. Assuming that's a recent version, **async/await** will be supported. Instead of doing that, let's try transpiling the code into JavaScript using TypeScript to see what happens.

4. Now, open the **tsconfig.json** file and look at it:

```
{
  "compilerOptions": {
    "target": "es5",
    "module": "commonjs",
    "strict": true,
    "esModuleInterop": true,
    "skipLibCheck": true,
    "forceConsistentCasingInFileNames": true
  }
}
```

5. The **target** option being set to **es5** means that TypeScript will attempt to produce code that conforms to the ECMAScript5 specification. So let's give that a try:

```
npx tsc
```

No output means that it executed successfully.

6. Check out the **target.js** file that was produced by TypeScript. The size of this file may vary depending on your TypeScript version, but the transpiled code module may be more than 50 lines:

```
"use strict";
var __awaiter = (this && this.__awaiter) || function (thisArg, _
arguments, P, generator) {
    function adopt(value) { return value instanceof P ? value : new
P(function (resolve) { resolve(value); }); }
    return new (P || (P = Promise))(function (resolve, reject) {
//….
sayHello();
console.log('World!');
```

> **NOTE**
>
> The complete code can be found here: https://packt.link/HSmyX.

We can execute the transpiled code by typing **node target.js** at the command prompt and we'll see that we get the same output as before.

Promises are not part of the ECMAScript5 specification, so to generate code that will work in an ECMAScript5 environment, the transpiler had to create **__awaiter** and **__generator** functions to support promise-like functionality.

7. Let's switch our target to es6. Open **tsconfig.json** and change the target property to **es6**:

```
{
  "compilerOptions": {
    "target": "es6",
    "module": "commonjs",
    "strict": true,
    "esModuleInterop": true,
    "skipLibCheck": true,
    "forceConsistentCasingInFileNames": true
  }
}
```

8. Invoking the function with **node target.js**, we get exactly the same output as before. Now let's see what TypeScript did when it transpiled our source:

```
"use strict";
var __awaiter = (this && this.__awaiter) || function (thisArg, _
arguments, P, generator) {
    function adopt(value) { return value instanceof P ? value : new
P(function (resolve) { resolve(value); }); }
    return new (P || (P = Promise))(function (resolve, reject) {
        function fulfilled(value) { try { step(generator.next(value));
} catch (e) { reject(e); } }
        function rejected(value) { try { step(generator["throw"]
(value)); } catch (e) { reject(e); } }
        function step(result) { result.done ? resolve(result.value) :
adopt(result.value).then(fulfilled, rejected); }
        step((generator = generator.apply(thisArg, _arguments ||
[])).next());
    });
};
const sayHello = () => __awaiter(void 0, void 0, void 0, function* ()
{
    yield new Promise((resolve) => setTimeout(() => resolve(console.
log('Hello')), 1));
});
sayHello();
console.log('World!');
```

The transpiled code is now 15 lines instead of over 50 because ECMAScript6 is much closer to supporting all the functionality we need than es5 is. The **async/ await** keywords are not supported in ECMAScript6, but promises are, so TypeScript is leveraging promises to make the outputted code more concise.

9. Now, let's change the target to **esnext**, run **npx tsc** one more time, and see what that output looks like:

```
"use strict";
const sayHello = async () => {
    await new Promise((resolve) => setTimeout(() => resolve(console.
log('Hello')), 1));
};
sayHello();
console.log('World!');
```

That's very similar to our source code! Since **async/await** are supported in the latest ECMAScript specification, there's no need to transform.

10. Older versions of TypeScript did not fully polyfill promises and async/await. Downgrade your TypeScript version with **npm i -D typescript@2**, set your compilation target back to es5, and then try transpiling:

```
npx tsc
target.ts:1:18 - error TS2705: An async function or method in ES5/ES3
requires the 'Promise' constructor.  Make sure you have a declaration
for the 'Promise' constructor or include 'ES2015' in your `--lib`
option.


1 const sayHello = async () => {
                   ~~~~~~~~~~~~~~



target.ts:2:13 - error TS2693: 'Promise' only refers to a type, but
is being used as a value here.

2     await new Promise((resolve) =>
                  ~~~~~~~



target.ts:2:22 - error TS7006: Parameter 'resolve' implicitly has an
'any' type.

2     await new Promise((resolve) =>
```

It doesn't work.

11. If you bump up to **es6**, it will still fail:

```
% npx tsc
target.ts:3:30 - error TS2345: Argument of type 'void' is not
assignable to parameter of type '{} | PromiseLike<{}> | undefined'.

3       setTimeout(() => resolve(console.log('Hello')))
```

12. Install the latest version of TypeScript with **npm i -D typescript@latest**
and then everything should work as before.

This aspect of TypeScript can be confusing for newcomers. TypeScript will not provide
a polyfill for missing promises, but it will provide transformations to syntax that is
functionally equivalent.

CHOOSING A TARGET

So how do we choose a compilation target? It's generally safe to use ES2017 or
above unless you need to support outdated browsers, such as Internet Explorer, or
deprecated Node.js versions. Sometimes, we have no choice but to support outdated
browsers due to customer needs, but if we have any control over a Node.js runtime
environment, it's advisable to update to a current, supported version. Doing this
should allow us to use the latest TypeScript features.

SYNTAX

The two new keywords, **async/await**, are often found together, but not always.
Let's look at the syntax for each of them individually.

ASYNC

The **async** keyword modifies a function. If a function declaration or function
expression is used, it is placed before the **function** keyword. If an arrow function
is used, the **async** keyword is placed before the argument list. Adding the **async**
keyword to a function will cause the function to return a promise.

For example:

```
function addAsync(num1: number, num2: number) {
  return num1 + num2;
}
```

Just adding the **async** keyword to this simple function will make this function return a promise, which is now awaitable and thenable. Since there's nothing asynchronous in the function, the promise will resolve immediately.

The arrow function version of this could be written as follows:

```
const addAsync = async (num1: number, num2: number) => num1 + num2;
```

EXERCISE 13.02: THE ASYNC KEYWORD

This exercise illustrates how adding the **async** keyword to a function makes it return a promise:

> **NOTE**
>
> The code files for this exercise can be found here: https://packt.link/BgujE.

1. Examine the **async.ts** file:

```
export const fn = async () => {
  return 'A Promise';
};


const result = fn();


console.log(result);
```

You might expect this program to log out **A Promise**, but let's see what actually happens when we run it:

```
npx ts-node async.ts
Promise { 'A Promise' }
```

2. The **async** keyword wrapped the response in a promise. We can confirm that by removing the keyword and running the program again:

```
npx ts-node async.ts
A Promise
```

3. Modifying our function with **async** is exactly equivalent to wrapping it in a promise. If we wanted to use promise syntax, we could write the program like this:

```
export const fn = () => {
```

```
   return Promise.resolve('A Promise');
};

const result = fn();

console.log(result);
```

4. Again, running the program written this way will log out the unresolved promise:

```
npx ts-node async.ts
Promise { 'A Promise' }
```

Since we're using TypeScript and return types can be inferred, modifying a function with **async** guarantees that TypeScript will always see the function as returning a promise.

The **async** keyword causes the function it modifies to be wrapped in a promise. Whether you choose to do that explicitly by declaring a promise or by using the **async** keyword is often a matter of taste and style.

How can we resolve an **async** function? We'll come to **await** in a moment, but what about using **then** and the promise chaining we learned about in *Chapter 12, Guide to Promises in TypeScript*. Yes, that is also possible.

EXERCISE 13.03: RESOLVING AN ASYNC FUNCTION WITH THEN

This exercise will teach you how to resolve an **async** function using **then**:

> **NOTE**
>
> The code files for this exercise can be found here: https://packt.link/4Bo4c.

1. Create a new file called **resolve.async.ts** and enter the following code:

```
export const fn = async () => {
  return 'A Promise';
};

const result = fn();

result.then((message) => console.log(message));
```

2. Execute this code by entering **`npx ts-node resolve.async.ts`** into your console and you'll see the expected text message logged, not an unresolved promise:

```
A Promise
```

Even though we never explicitly declared a promise object, the use of **async** has ensured that our function will always return a promise.

AWAIT

The second half of this combo perhaps has greater value. The **await** keyword will attempt to resolve any promise before continuing. This will get us out of **then** chaining and allow us to write code that appears to be synchronous. One great benefit of using **await** is if we want to assign the result of an asynchronous call to some value and then do something with the value. Let's look at how that's done in a promise:

```
asyncFunc().then(result => {
  // do something with the result
});
```

That can work fine and, in fact, this kind of syntax is used widely, but it breaks down a little if we need to do something tricky with chaining:

```
asyncFuncOne().then(resultOne => {
  asyncFuncTwo(resultOne).then(resultTwo => {
    asyncFuncThree(resultTwo).then(resultThree => {
      // do something with resultThree
    });
  });
});
```

But wait a minute. I thought promises were supposed to get rid of callback hell?! It's actually not that ideal for this kind of chaining. Let's try using **await** instead:

```
const resultOne = await asyncFuncOne();
const resultTwo = await asyncFuncTwo(resultOne);
const resultThree = await asyncFuncThree(resultTwo);
// do something with resultThree
```

Most programmers would agree that this syntax is much cleaner and, in fact, this is one of the primary reasons why **async/await** were added to the language.

EXERCISE 13.04: THE AWAIT KEYWORD

This exercise will show you how to resolve a promise using **await**:

> **NOTE**
>
> The code files for this exercise can be found here: https://packt.link/mUzGl.

1. Create a file called **await.ts** and enter the following code:

```
export const fn = async () => {
  return 'A Promise';
};

const resolveIt = async () => {
  const result = await fn();
  console.log(result);
};

resolveIt();
```

Here we declare two **async** functions. One of them calls the other using **await** to resolve the promise and it should print out the string, rather than an unresolved promise.

2. Run the file using **npx ts-node await.ts** and you should see the following output:

```
A Promise
```

Why did we need to wrap **await** in a second function? That is because normally, **await** cannot be used outside of an **async** function. We'll discuss the top-level **await** feature later in this chapter, which is an exception to this rule. What about mixing **await** with promises? This can certainly be done.

EXERCISE 13.05: AWAITING A PROMISE

This exercise teaches you how you can use **await** with promises:

1. Create a new file called **await-promise.ts** and enter the following code:

```
export const resolveIt = async () => {
  const result = await Promise.resolve('A Promise');
  console.log(result);
};


resolveIt();
```

2. Execute the code by entering **npx ts-node await-promise.ts** and you'll see the text output:

```
A Promise
```

3. A longer way to write this same code with a more explicit promise declaration would be:

```
export const resolveIt = async () => {
  const p = new Promise((resolve) => resolve('A Promise'));
  const result = await p;
  console.log(result);
};


resolveIt();
```

This code functions exactly the same:

4. Enter **npx ts-node src/await-promise.ts** to verify that you get the following output:

```
A Promise
```

SYNTACTIC SUGAR

The preceding exercises on **async** functions and promises are simply two different ways of expressing the exact same operation in TypeScript. Likewise, using **await** and resolving a promise with **then** are equivalent. The **async/await** keywords are what's known as "syntactic sugar," or code structures that enable more expressive syntax without changing the behavior of the program.

This means it is possible and, at times, even advisable to mix **async/await** syntax with promises. A very common reason for doing this would be because you are working with a library that was written to use promises, but you prefer **async/await** syntax. Another reason for mixing the two would be to handle exceptions more explicitly. We'll deal with exception handling in detail later in this chapter.

EXCEPTION HANDLING

We've been over how to turn **then** chaining into **await**, but what about **catch**? If a promise is rejected, the error will bubble up and must be caught in some way. Failing to catch an exception in the **async/await** world is just as damaging as failing to catch a promise rejection. In fact, it's exactly the same and **async/await** is just syntactic sugar on top of promises.

Failing to handle a rejected promise can lead to system failure where a program running in a web browser crashes, resulting in blank pages or broken functionality, thereby driving users away from your site. A failure to handle a rejected promise on the server side may cause a Node.js process to exit and a server to crash. Even if you have a self-healing system that attempts to bring your server back online, whatever job you were attempting to complete will have failed and frequently repeated restarts will make your infrastructure more expensive to run.

The most straightforward way to handle these errors is with **try** and **catch** blocks. This syntax is not unique to **async/await** and has been part of the ECMAScript specification since ECMAScript3. It is very simple and straightforward to use:

```
try {
  await someAsync();
} catch (e) {
  console.error(e);
}
```

Just as you can catch an error thrown from any of several chained promises, you can implement a similar pattern here:

```
try {
  await someAsync();
  await anotherAsync();
  await oneMoreAsync();
} catch (e) {
  console.error(e);
}
```

There may be cases where finer-grained exception handling is required. It is possible to nest these structures:

```
try {
  await someAsync();
  try {
    await anotherAsync();
  } catch (e) {
    // specific handling of this error
  }
  await oneMoreAsync();
} catch (e) {
  console.error(e);
}
```

However, writing code such as this negates most of the benefits of the **async/await** syntax. A better solution would be to throw specific error messages and test for them:

```
try {
  await someAsync();
  await anotherAsync();
  await oneMoreAsync();
} catch (e) {
  if(e instanceOf MyCustomError) {
    // some custom handling
  } else {
    console.error(e);
  }
}
```

With this technique, we can handle everything in the same block and avoid nesting and messy-looking code structures.

EXERCISE 13.06: EXCEPTION HANDLING

Let's see how we can implement error handling in a simple example. In this exercise, we will intentionally and explicitly throw an error from an **async** function and see how that implements the operation of our program:

> **NOTE**
>
> The code files for this exercise can be found here: https://packt.link/wbA8E.

1. Start by creating a new file called **error.ts** and entering the following code:

```
export const errorFn = async () => {
  throw new Error('An error has occurred!');
};


const asyncFn = async () => {
  await errorFn();
};


asyncFn();
```

2. This program will, of course, always throw an error. When we execute it by entering **npx ts-node error.ts** into the console, we can see quite clearly that the error is not being handled properly:

```
(node:29053) UnhandledPromiseRejectionWarning: Error: An error has
occurred!
    at Object.exports.errorFn (/workshop/async-chapter/src/error.
ts:2:9)
    at asyncFn (/workshop/async-chapter/src/error.ts:6:9)
    at Object.<anonymous> (/workshop/async-chapter/src/error.ts:9:1)
    at Module._compile (internal/modules/cjs/loader.js:1138:30)
    at Module.m._compile (/workshop/async-chapter/node_modules/
ts-node/src/index.ts:858:23)
    at Module._extensions..js (internal/modules/cjs/loader.
js:1158:10)
    at Object.require.extensions.<computed> [as .ts] (/workshop/
async-chapter/node_modules/ts-node/src/index.ts:861:12)
    at Module.load (internal/modules/cjs/loader.js:986:32)
    at Function.Module._load (internal/modules/cjs/loader.js:879:14)
```

```
      at Function.executeUserEntryPoint [as runMain] (internal/modules/
run_main.js:71:12)
(node:29053) UnhandledPromiseRejectionWarning: Unhandled promise
rejection. This error originated either by throwing inside of an
async function without a catch block, or by rejecting a promise
which was not handled with .catch(). To terminate the node process
on unhandled promise rejection, use the CLI flag `--unhandled-
rejections=strict` (see https://nodejs.org/api/cli.html#cli_
unhandled_rejections_mode). (rejection id: 2)
(node:29053) [DEP0018] DeprecationWarning: Unhandled promise
rejections are deprecated. In the future, promise rejections that are
not handled will terminate the Node.js process with a non-zero exit
code.
```

Notice the deprecation warning. Not only is this an ugly stack trace, at some point in the future, exceptions such as this one will cause the Node.js process to exit. We clearly need to handle this exception!

3. Fortunately, we can do so by simply surrounding the call with **try** and **catch**:

```
export const errorFn = async () => {
  throw new Error('An error has occurred!');
};


const asyncFn = async () => {
  try {
    await errorFn();
  } catch (e) {
    console.error(e);
  }
};


asyncFn();
```

4. Now, when we execute the program, we get a more orderly exception and stack trace logged:

```
Error: An error has occurred!
    at Object.exports.errorFn (/workshop/async-chapter/src/error.
ts:2:9)
    at asyncFn (/workshop/async-chapter/src/error.ts:7:11)
    at Object.<anonymous> (/workshop/async-chapter/src/error.ts:13:1)
    at Module._compile (internal/modules/cjs/loader.js:1138:30)
    at Module.m._compile (/workshop/node_modules/ts-node/src/index.
ts:858:23)
```

```
    at Module._extensions..js (internal/modules/cjs/loader.
js:1158:10)
    at Object.require.extensions.<computed> [as .ts] (/workshop/node_
modules/ts-node/src/index.ts:861:12)
    at Module.load (internal/modules/cjs/loader.js:986:32)
    at Function.Module._load (internal/modules/cjs/loader.js:879:14)
    at Function.executeUserEntryPoint [as runMain] (internal/modules/
run_main.js:71:12)
```

Of course, that message only appears because we explicitly logged it out. We could instead choose to throw a default value or perform some other operation instead of logging the error.

5. It's always a good idea to log an error if the system isn't behaving correctly, but depending on your system requirements, you might instead write something like this:

```
const primaryFn = async () => {
  throw new Error('Primary System Offline!');
};

const secondaryFn = async () => {
  console.log('Aye aye!');
};

const asyncFn = async () => {
  try {
    await primaryFn();
  } catch (e) {
    console.warn(e);
    secondaryFn();
  }
};


asyncFn();
```

In this case, we just throw a warning and fall back to the secondary system because this program was designed to be fault-tolerant. It's still a good idea to log the warning so that we can trace how our system is behaving. One more variation of this for now.

6. Let's put our **try** and **catch** blocks at the top level and rewrite our program like this:

```typescript
export const errorFN = async () => {
  throw new Error('An error has occurred!');
};

const asyncFn = async () => {
  await errorFN();
};

try {
  asyncFn();
} catch (e) {
  console.error(e);
}
```

7. This is the output that you get:

```
Error: Primary System Offline!
    at primaryFn (C:\Users\Mahesh\Documents\Chapter13_TypeScript\
Exercise13.06\error-secondary.ts:2:9)
    at asyncFn (C:\Users\Mahesh\Documents\Chapter13_TypeScript\
Exercise13.06\error-secondary.ts:11:11)
    at Object.<anonymous> (C:\Users\Mahesh\Documents\Chapter13_
TypeScript\Exercise13.06\error-secondary.ts:18:1)
    at Module._compile (internal/modules/cjs/loader.js:1063:30)
    at Module.m._compile (C:\Users\Mahesh\AppData\Roaming\npm-cache\_
npx\13000\node_modules\ts-node\src\index.ts:1056:23)
    at Module._extensions..js (internal/modules/cjs/loader.
js:1092:10)
    at Object.require.extensions.<computed> [as .ts] (C:\Users\
Mahesh\AppData\Roaming\npm-cache\_npx\13000\node_modules\ts-node\src\
index.ts:1059:12)
    at Module.load (internal/modules/cjs/loader.js:928:32)
    at Function.Module._load (internal/modules/cjs/loader.js:769:14)
    at Function.executeUserEntryPoint [as runMain] (internal/modules/
run_main.js:72:12)
Aye aye!
```

You may assume that the program might work the same as putting **try** and **catch** inside **asyncFn**, but actually, it will behave the same as no error handling at all. That's because we aren't awaiting the function inside the **try** block.

TOP-LEVEL AWAIT

Top-level **await** is a feature that allows the use of the **await** keyword at the module level, outside of any function. This allows a number of interesting patterns, such as waiting for a dependency to fully load by calling an asynchronous function before attempting to use it. Someday, top-level **await** may support some very exciting functional programming paradigms, but at the time of writing, it is still technically in preview mode, and so is not ready for widespread use. You may be reading this book at a time when top-level **await** is widely available and supported, and if so, you should definitely give it a look!

Writing code with top-level **await** is very straightforward. Here is a very short program that attempts to make use of it:

```
export const fn = async () => {
  return 'awaited!';
};


console.log(await fn());
```

This looks fine. Now let's see what happens when we try to execute it:

```
× Unable to compile TypeScript:
src/top-level-await.ts:5:13 - error TS1378: Top-level 'await' expressions
are only allowed when the 'module' option is set to 'esnext' or 'system',
and the 'target' option is set to 'es2017' or higher.

5 console.log(await fn());
```

It's not supported, but it gives me some pointers. How can we make this work?

Top-level **await** requires NodeJS 14.8 or greater. This version of NodeJS entered LTS (long-term service) in October of 2020 and so is still new at the time of this writing. You can check your NodeJS version on the command line with **node -v**. If you aren't running version 14.8 or greater, there are some good utilities like **nvm** and **n** that will allow you to switch your version easily.

That, however, doesn't fix the problem. It seems that I will need to change my **tsconfig.json target** property to **es2017** or higher and set the **module** property to **esnext**. Adding the **module** property means that I want to use ES modules, which is a relatively new way to handle modules and is beyond the scope of this book. To enable ES modules, I need to set the **type** property in my **package.json** file to **module**.

Now I've updated a couple of JSON files and am ready to try again:

```
TypeError [ERR_UNKNOWN_FILE_EXTENSION]: Unknown file extension ".ts" for /
workshop/async-chapter/src/top-level-await.ts
    at Loader.defaultGetFormat [as _getFormat] (internal/modules/esm/
get_format.js:65:15)
    at Loader.getFormat (internal/modules/esm/loader.js:113:42)
    at Loader.getModuleJob (internal/modules/esm/loader.js:243:31)
    at Loader.import (internal/modules/esm/loader.js:177:17)
```

It still isn't working. I'll need to do one more thing to make this work, and that is to enable the experimental feature in Node.js and instruct TS Node to allow **ES modules (esm)**. This requires a longer command:

```
node --loader ts-node/esm.mjs top.ts
(node:91445) ExperimentalWarning: --experimental-loader is an
experimental feature. This feature could change at any time
(Use `node --trace-warnings ...` to show where the warning was created)
awaited!
```

But it works. Top-level **await** will likely become much easier and more intuitive to work with in the months and years ahead, so make sure to check the latest documentation for your runtime.

PROMISE METHODS

In addition to the standard **next** and **catch** methods exposed by promises, there are a number of other convenience methods, such as **all**, **allSettled**, **any**, and **race**, that make working with promises nicer. How can they be used in the **async/ await** world? They can actually work together quite nicely. For example, here is a use of **Promise.all** that employs **then** and **catch**. Given three promises, **p1**, **p2**, and **p3**:

```
Promise.all([p1, p2, p3])
  .then(values => console.log(values))
  .catch(e => console.error(e));
```

There isn't any kind of **awaitAll** operator, so if we want to execute our promises in parallel, we're still going to need to use **Promise.all**, but we can avoid chaining **then** and **catch** if we choose to:

```
try {
  const values = await Promise.all([p1, p2, p3]);
  console.log(values);
```

```
} catch (e) {
  console.error(e);
}
```

In this case, we might feel like the code isn't improved by the addition of **await**, since we've actually expanded it from three lines to six. Some may find this form more readable. As always, it's a matter of personal or team preference.

EXERCISE 13.07: ASYNC/AWAIT IN EXPRESS.JS

In this exercise, we will build a small web application using the popular Express framework. Although Express was written for the JavaScript language, typings have been published for it and it is fully usable with TypeScript. Express is an unopinionated, minimalist framework for building web applications. It's one of the oldest and most popular frameworks in use today.

For our simple application, we'll start a web server on port **8888** and accept **GET** requests. If that request has a **name** parameter in the query string, we will log the name in a file called **names.txt**. Then we'll greet the user. If there's no name in the query string, we log nothing and print out **Hello World!**:

> **NOTE**
>
> The code files for this exercise can be found here: https://packt.link/cG4r8.

Let's get started by installing the Express framework and typings.

1. Enter **npm i express** to install Express as a dependency and **npm i -D @types/express @types/node** to install the typings that we'll need to support TypeScript.

   Remember the **-D** flag means that it's a **devDependency** that can be managed differently from a production dependency, although its use is optional.

2. With our dependencies installed, let's create a file called **express.ts**. The first thing to do is import **express**, create the app, add a simple handler, and listen on port **8888**:

```
import express, { Request, Response } from 'express';

const app = express();

app.get('/', (req: Request, res: Response) => {
```

```
    res.send('OK');
});


app.listen(8888);
```

This looks very much like your standard starter Express app, other than we're giving types to the **Request** and **Response** objects. This is already enormously useful as we'll be able to use IntelliSense and ascertain what methods we can call on those objects without having to look them up.

Our requirements say that we need to listen for a **name** parameter in the query string. We might see a request that looks like **http://localhost:8888/?name=Matt**, to which we should respond **Hello Matt!**.

The query string is in the **Request** object. If we delve into the typings, it is typed as follows:

```
interface ParsedQs { [key: string]: undefined | string | string[] |
ParsedQs | ParsedQs[] }
```

This basically means that it is a hash of key/value pairs and nested key/value pairs. In our case, we would expect to see a query object that looks like **{ name: 'Matt' }**. Thus, we can get the **name** attribute by using **const { name } = req.query;**. Then we can respond to the request with something like **res.send(`Hello ${name ?? 'World'}!`);**. In this case, we're using the nullish coalesce operator (**??**) to say that we'll fall back to the **World** string if the **name** variable has a nullish (null or undefined) value. We could also use the fallback or logical OR operator, **||**.

3. The updated code now looks like this:

```
import express, { Request, Response } from 'express';


const app = express();


app.get('/', (req: Request, res: Response) => {
  const { name } = req.query;
  res.send(`Hello ${name ?? 'World'}!`);
});


app.listen(8888);
```

4. One requirement is still missing. We need to log the name to a file if it exists. To do that, we'll need to use the **fs** library from Node.js. We'll also use the **path** library to resolve a path to the file we want to write to. First, add the new imports:

```
import { promises } from 'fs';
import { resolve } from 'path';
```

5. Now we'll use the **promises** API from **fs** to asynchronously write to our log file. Since this is a log, we want to append to it, not overwrite it on each request. We'll use **appendFile** and write the name along with a newline character. We want this operation to repeat before returning:

```
if (name) {
    await promises.appendFile(resolve(__dirname, 'names.txt'),
`${name}\n`);
}
```

That's almost it, but we should have a warning by now that our handler function isn't properly async. All we need to do is add the **async** keyword to it.

6. The completed code looks like this:

```
import express, { Request, Response } from 'express';
import { promises } from 'fs';
import { resolve } from 'path';

const app = express();

app.get('/', async (req: Request, res: Response) => {
  const { name } = req.query;
  if (name) {
    await promises.appendFile(resolve(__dirname, 'names.txt'),
`${name}\n`);
  }
  res.send(`Hello ${name ?? 'World'}!`);
});

app.listen(8888);
```

7. Run the program with **npx ts-node express.ts** and try hitting the URL at **http://localhost:8888?name=your_name** a few times. Try hitting that URL with different names and watch your log file increment. Here are a few examples.

8. The following is the browser output for your_name:

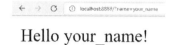

Hello your_name!

Figure 13.1: Browser message for name = your_name

9. The following is the browser output for Matt:

Hello Matt!

Figure 13.2: Browser message for name = Matt

10. The following is the browser output for Albert Einstein:

Hello Albert Einstein!

Figure 13.3: Browser message for name = Albert Einstein

The **names.txt** file will increment as follows:

```
Exercise07 >  ≡ names.txt
     1     your_name
     2     Matt
     3     Albert Einstein
```

Figure 13.4: Log file

EXERCISE 13.08: NESTJS

In contrast to Express, NestJS is a highly opinionated and fully featured framework for building TypeScript applications. NestJS can be used to quickly bootstrap an application. It provides out-of-the-box support for middleware, GraphQL, and Websockets. It ships with ESLint, a dependency injection framework, a test framework, and many other useful things. Some developers really enjoy working with such a full-featured framework and others find all the boilerplate oppressive and prefer to work with something more bare-bones, such as Express:

> **NOTE**
>
> The code files for this exercise can be found here: https://packt.link/blRq3.

Let's bootstrap a new NestJS application and give it a closer look.

1. NestJS applications can be generated by a **command-line interface** (**CLI**) that can be installed via **npm**. Install that package globally:

```
npm i -g @nestjs/cli
```

2. When we use the CLI, it will generate a project by creating a new directory inside the directory we entered the command into, so you may want to change the directory to where you store your projects. Then, generate the project:

```
nest new async-nest
```

Here the project is named **async-nest**. You can name it differently. NestJS will automatically install all dependencies and bootstrap a bare-bones application.

3. Change directory into your new application and start looking at the code. If you pop open **main.ts**, you'll see **async/await** already in use. That module will look something like this:

```
import { NestFactory } from '@nestjs/core';
import { AppModule } from './app.module';

async function bootstrap() {
  const app = await NestFactory.create(AppModule);
  await app.listen(3000);
}
bootstrap();
```

NestJS is built on top of Express. This code will create a new Express application. The internals of Express are not exposed to you as you write NestJS code, but you always have the option to drop down to them if you need something not supported by NestJS.

Let's go over a few useful commands that you can start using immediately. If you type **npm test** (or **npm t**), you'll launch a test run by the Jest framework. This test launches an instance of your application, invokes it, and then shuts it down after verifying the expected response was received. NestJS ships with fixtures that allow a light version of your app to be tested.

It's a great idea to continue adding unit and integration tests to your app as you work on it. TypeScript can help you ensure code correctness, but only tests will guarantee that your app is behaving as it should.

Another useful command is **npm run lint**. This will check your code style and notify you of any issues with it by using the popular ESLint library.

4. Finally, you can type **npm run start:dev** to run the development server in watch mode, which means the server will restart whenever you change a file.

5. Try running that now and navigate to **http://localhost:3000** and you'll see the **Hello World** message. If you open the file called **app.service.ts** and change the message returned there, you can just refresh your browser and you should see the message change.

    Now that we've seen this simple Hello World app done in two very different frameworks, let's add the same greeting and logging functionality that we did in *Exercise 13.07: async/await in Express.js.*

6. To add the custom greeting based on the query param, let's open two files, **app.controller.ts** and **app.service.ts**. Notice that **app.service. ts** implements a **getHello** function that returns the string "Hello World!". We will need to change this function to accept a **name** argument.

7. Add the **name** argument with the **string** type to the function's argument list, and then change the return to a string template and say Hello. You'll have something like this:

```
export class AppService {
  getHello(name: string): string {
    return `Hello ${name}!`;
  }
}
```

This is a simple refactor. If we check **app.controller.ts**, we'll see that our IDE is now telling us that **getHello** needs an argument and we're not done yet.

In the Express application, we found our query parameter on the built-in **Request** object. You could do the same thing in NestJS, but it's more common and preferable to use a decorator. Decorators are special functions that wrap other functions. They are sometimes called higher-order functions and are similar to aspects of languages such as Java.

The decorator we want to use is **@Query**, which takes an argument of the name of the query parameter and then binds that parameter to one of our function arguments.

8. We can import that decorator from **@nestjs/common**. Then we add the function argument to **getHello** and pass it through to the service call. One more thing that's a good idea is to set a default so that we maintain backward compatibility and don't print out **Hello undefined** if we fail to give an argument. Adding the default may prompt a hint that you no longer need the type annotation as it is trivially inferred from the default type. Go ahead and remove it if you like:

```
import { Controller, Get, Query } from '@nestjs/common';

import { AppService } from './app.service';

@Controller()
export class AppController {
  constructor(private readonly appService: AppService) {}

  @Get()
  getHello(@Query('name') name: string = 'World'): string {
    return this.appService.getHello(name);
  }
}
```

9. The dev server should restart and now, if we browse to **http://localhost:3000/?name=Matt**, we'll see **Hello Matt!**:

Hello Matt!

Figure 13.5: Browser message for name = Matt

10. Now let's add the same logging functionality that we implemented in Express.

    In a full-scale application, we'd probably want to build a separate logging service class. For our purposes, we can implement that as a separate **async** method. Add the method to **app.service.ts** and call it with **await** from **getHello**. Test it to be sure that it's working correctly.

    There are a few gotchas here. One is that NestJS is automatically transpiling and serving your code from a folder called **dist**, so you'll find your **names.txt** file in there once you start logging names. But the bigger trick here is that in order to await the logging, we need to make **getHello** in **app.service.ts** into an **async** method. This, in turn, will mean that **getHello** in **app.controller. ts** must also be **async**. What will changing these methods to **async** do to our app? Nothing! NestJS already knows how to resolve the promises before returning the request.

11. One more thing to check out in this exercise is the unit test. Since we've set a default value for the **name** attribute, the test should still work, right? Well actually, it doesn't. Try running **npm test** and you'll see the problem. The issue is that the test isn't expecting **getHello** to be async. That's OK. We can fix it by making the test callback **async** to look like this:

```
describe('root', () => {
  it('should return "Hello World!"', async () => {
    expect(await appController.getHello()).toBe('Hello World!');
  });
});
```

The test should now pass. Try adding another test with an argument.

EXERCISE 13.09: TYPEORM

TypeORM is an object relational mapper written in, and for, TypeScript. TypeORM supports many popular databases, such as MySQL, Postgres, SQL Server, SQLite, and even MongoDB and Oracle. TypeORM is often used in NestJS applications, so in this exercise we will add a local in-memory SQLite database to work with our NestJS application.

In this exercise, you will build another REST service to help us keep track of the promises we make. Since **Promise** is the name of a built-in object in TypeScript, let's use the term "pledge" so we can differentiate domain concepts from language abstractions:

> **NOTE**
>
> The code files for this exercise can be found here: https://packt.link/ZywYh.

1. To get started, let's bootstrap a new NestJS project:

```
nest new typeorm-nest
```

2. NestJS has a powerful module system that lets us build out different functional areas of our application in cohesive chunks. Let's create a new module for pledges:

```
nest g module pledge
```

This command will generate a new module under the **/pledge** subdirectory.

3. We're also going to need a controller and a service for the pledge API, so let's generate those using the NestJS CLI:

```
nest g controller pledge
nest g service pledge
```

4. Finally, we need to install the **typeorm** library, SQLite3, and NestJS integration:

```
npm i @nestjs/typeorm sqlite3 typeorm
```

TypeORM maps database tables to TypeScript entities by means of decorators on plain objects.

5. Let's create **pledge.entity.ts** under **/pledge** and create our first entity:

```
import { Entity, PrimaryGeneratedColumn, Column } from 'typeorm';

@Entity()
export class Pledge {
  @PrimaryGeneratedColumn()
  id: number;

  @Column()
  desc: string;

  @Column()
  kept: boolean;
}
```

For this entity, we're using a few specialized decorators, such as **PrimaryGeneratedColumn**. These decorators can be very powerful but often rely on underlying database functionality. Because SQLite can generate an ID for our table, TypeORM is able to expose that in a declarative way with a decorator, but if it couldn't, this wouldn't work. It's always good to check the documentation before proceeding with a new implementation.

Now that we have an entity, we need to provide configuration to TypeORM about what our database is and where to find it, as well as what entities we want to map. For databases such as MySQL and Postgres, this might include a URI as well as database credentials. Since SQLite is a file-based database, we will just provide the name of the file we want to write.

Note that production database credentials should always be handled safely, and the best practices for doing so are beyond the scope of this book, but suffice to say that they shouldn't be checked into your version control.

6. Let's configure our application to use SQLite. We want to configure TypeORM at the root of our application, so let's import the module into **app.module.ts**:

```
TypeOrmModule.forRoot({
  type: 'sqlite',
  database: 'db',
  entities: [Pledge],
  synchronize: true,
}),
```

7. Doing this will require a couple of more imports at the top of the module:

```
import { TypeOrmModule } from '@nestjs/typeorm';

import { Pledge } from './pledge/pledge.entity';
```

We're letting NestJS know that our application will use a SQLite database and will manage the **Pledge** entity. By setting **synchronize: true**, we are telling TypeORM to automatically create any entities that don't already exist in the database when the application starts. This setting should NOT be used in production as it may cause data loss. TypeORM supports migrations for managing databases in production environments, another topic beyond the scope of this book.

8. If we start our application now with **npm run start:dev**, it will start up and we'll get a new binary file (the SQLite database) called **db**.

9. Before we can use the **Pledge** entity in our new module, we need to do a little more boilerplate. Open up **pledge.module.ts** and add an import so that the module looks like this:

```
import { Module } from '@nestjs/common';
import { TypeOrmModule } from '@nestjs/typeorm';

import { PledgeController } from './pledge.controller';
import { Pledge } from './pledge.entity';
import { PledgeService } from './pledge.service';

@Module({
  controllers: [PledgeController],
  imports: [TypeOrmModule.forFeature([Pledge])],
  providers: [PledgeService],
})
export class PledgeModule {}
```

This will allow the **Pledge** entity to be used by **pledge.service.ts**. Again, NestJS has quite a lot of boilerplate, which may be jarring to developers who are used to unopinionated ExpressJS workflows. This module system can help us to isolate our application into functional areas. It's a good idea to understand the benefits of a structured application before deciding whether a framework such as NestJS is right for your application or team.

We can now start to build out our **Pledge** service. TypeORM supports both Active Record, where an entity itself has methods for reading and updating, and Data Mapper, where such functionality is delegated to a **Repository** object. We will follow the Data Mapper pattern in this exercise.

10. To start, we will add a constructor to the **Pledge** service and inject the repository to expose it as a private member of the class. Once we've done that, we can start to access some of the repository methods:

```
import { Injectable } from '@nestjs/common';
import { Pledge } from './pledge.entity';
import { InjectRepository } from '@nestjs/typeorm';
import { Repository } from 'typeorm';

@Injectable()
export class PledgeService {
```

```
  constructor(
    @InjectRepository(Pledge)
    private pledgeRepository: Repository<Pledge>,
  ) {}


  findAll(): Promise<Pledge[]> {
    return this.pledgeRepository.find();
  }
}
```

We've now exposed a **findAll** method, which will query the database for all the **Pledge** entities and return them in an array.

11. In a production application, it can often be a good idea to implement pagination, but this will do for our purposes. Let's implement some other methods:

```
import { Injectable } from '@nestjs/common';
import { InjectRepository } from '@nestjs/typeorm';
import { DeleteResult, Repository } from 'typeorm';


import { Pledge } from './pledge.entity';


@Injectable()
export class PledgeService {
  constructor(
    @InjectRepository(Pledge)
    private pledgeRepository: Repository<Pledge>,
  ) {}


  delete(id: number): Promise<DeleteResult> {
    return this.pledgeRepository.delete(id);
  }


  findAll(): Promise<Pledge[]> {
    return this.pledgeRepository.find();
  }


  findOne(id: number): Promise<Pledge> {
    return this.pledgeRepository.findOne(id);
```

```
  }

  save(pledge: Pledge): Promise<Pledge> {
    return this.pledgeRepository.save(pledge);
  }
}
```

We can get pretty far using just repository methods, which will generate SQL queries for us, but it's also possible to use SQL or a query builder with TypeORM.

12. Implementing these methods in a service won't expose them to our API, so we need to add matching controller methods in **pledge.controller.ts**. Each controller method will delegate to a service method and NestJS will take care of gluing all the pieces together:

```
import { Body, Controller, Delete, Get, Param, Post } from '@nestjs/
common';
import { DeleteResult } from 'typeorm';

import { Pledge } from './pledge.entity';
import { PledgeService } from './pledge.service';

@Controller('pledge')
export class PledgeController {
  constructor(private readonly pledgeService: PledgeService) {}

  @Delete(':id')
  deletePledge(@Param('id') id: number): Promise<DeleteResult> {
    return this.pledgeService.delete(id);
  }

  @Get()
  getPledges(): Promise<Pledge[]> {
    return this.pledgeService.findAll();
  }

  @Get(':id')
  getPledge(@Param('id') id: number): Promise<Pledge> {
```

```
      return this.pledgeService.findOne(id);
   }


   @Post()
   savePledge(@Body() pledge: Pledge): Promise<Pledge> {
     return this.pledgeService.save(pledge);
   }
}
```

This controller will automatically inject the service and can then easily map service methods to API endpoints using decorators and dependency injection.

13. Since we ran our application with **npm run start:dev**, it should hot reload through all these changes.

14. Check the console and make sure there are no errors. If our code is correct, we can use a REST client such as Postman to start sending requests to our service. If we send a **POST** request with a payload such as **{"desc":"Always lint your code", "kept": true}** to **http://localhost:3000/pledge**, we'll get back a **201 Created** HTTP response. Then we can issue **GET** requests to **http://localhost:3000/pledge** and **http://localhost:3000/pledge/1** to see our record that was stored in SQLite.

In this exercise, we used NestJS and TypeORM to build a real web API that can create and retrieve records from a SQLite database. Doing this isn't very different from using a real production-grade database such as MySQL or PostgreSQL.

ACTIVITY 13.01: REFACTORING CHAINED PROMISES TO USE AWAIT

In this activity, we will refactor a function that chains promises together to use **await**. You are supplied with a starter program that is meant to simulate the creation of DOM elements for a website and render them one after another. In reality, most sites will want to render in parallel, but it's possible that information from one component might inform the rendering of another. It is good enough for example purposes in any case:

> **NOTE**
>
> The code files for this activity can be found here: https://packt.link/L5r76.

1. Start by running the program as-is with **npx ts-node src/refactor.ts**. You'll get each message in sequence.

2. Now, refactor the **renderAll** function to use **async/await**. You shouldn't have to touch any other parts of the code to make this work. When your refactoring is complete, run the program again and verify that the output hasn't changed.

The code for the starter program (**refactor.ts**) is as follows:

```
export class El {
  constructor(private name: string) {}
  render = () => {
    return new Promise((resolve) =>
      setTimeout(
        () => resolve(`${this.name} is resolved`),
        Math.random() * 1000
      )
    );
  };
}


const e1 = new El('header');
const e2 = new El('body');
const e3 = new El('footer');


const renderAll = () => {
  e1.render().then((msg1) => {
    console.log(msg1);
    e2.render().then((msg2) => {
      console.log(msg2);
      e3.render().then((msg3) => {
        console.log(msg3);
      });
    });
  });
};


renderAll();
```

Once you run the program, you should get the following output:

```
header is resolved
body is resolved
footer is resolved
```

> **NOTE**
>
> The solution to this activity can be found on page 678.

SUMMARY

Asynchronous programming has come a long way in the past 10 years and the introduction of **async/await** has continued to move it forward. Although not perfect for every use case, this syntactic sugar has proven very popular with the TypeScript community and has gained widespread acceptance in popular libraries and frameworks.

In this chapter, we went over **async/await** syntax, how it came to be part of the language, and how the use of this syntax is actually complimentary to promises. We then toured several popular frameworks in use by TypeScript developers to see how application developers use promises and asynchronous programming to develop powerful web applications.

This concludes this book's study of language features. The next chapter will look at React for building user interfaces using TypeScript.

14

TYPESCRIPT AND REACT

OVERVIEW

In this chapter, we'll cover the React library and how to build user interfaces enhanced with TypeScript. We'll look at state management solutions for React applications and styling solutions. Then, we will use Firebase, a serverless backend, to build a Hacker News-style application. By the end of this chapter, you will be able to bootstrap React applications using the Create React App command-line interface.

INTRODUCTION

React is a dominant force in web and mobile user interface development. Although it bills itself as "*A JavaScript library for building user interfaces,*" what we often think of as React goes well beyond the core library and includes a wide ecosystem of plugins, components, and other tools. Many developers have chosen to specialize in React and it's a popular topic for code academies. Unlike Angular, React was not developed to use TypeScript and in fact there are a few other typing systems that some developers use with React. However, the popularity of both React and TypeScript made it inevitable that someone would want to marry the two, and writing React with TypeScript has become a standard way to approach user interface development.

React was developed internally by Facebook for their own use and was open sourced in 2013. In contrast to some of the more full-featured frameworks, React has always styled itself as a view library and it relies on other libraries for necessary functionality, such as state management, routing, and web requests.

React uses a declarative, component-based approach. Developers build components that represent different UI elements. These components are typically reusable and can be assembled in different ways to construct web views. Components can be made up of other components and each individual component should be rather simple. Thinking in terms of small, reusable components helps React developers write clean, maintainable code and follow the **Don't Repeat Yourself** (**DRY**) principle.

TYPING REACT

Prior to the dramatic rise in the popularity of TypeScript, React programmers either went without any sort of type system or used libraries such as Flow or PropTypes.

Flow is another library developed by Facebook with the intent of adding types to JavaScript. It has similar goals to TypeScript but takes a different route to achieve them. Instead of being a superset of JavaScript, Flow uses comments and type annotations checked by a language server, which are then removed by a transpiler such as Babel. Since both libraries were developed by Facebook, it was common to use them together, but the popularity of Flow has waned as TypeScript has emerged as the type system of choice for web developers.

PropTypes is another library for enforcing type-checking. In this case, the library is specifically for use with React and has the narrow focus of checking types on React "props," or the parameters that are passed along with components.

TYPESCRIPT IN REACT

While it is technically feasible to use these libraries along with TypeScript, it's not a good idea as they are all essentially trying to solve the same thing. If you're using TypeScript, it's best to avoid Flow and PropTypes.

TypeScript provides many benefits to React programmers. We can achieve all the same aims as the PropTypes library by typing our props using interfaces, and we also get the full IntelliSense experience, which will let us learn more about components and their lifecycles and even let us read developer comments, deprecation notices, and so forth.

TypeScript will help ensure proper use of our components and give us that early feedback loop that makes development much easier.

HELLO, REACT

There are numerous books on React alone. This one chapter in a book on TypeScript cannot cover all the topics relating to React. Readers who aren't already familiar with React but wish to work with React professionally should seek sources beyond this book. That said, to give a very brief overview of how React works, components are written in some flavor of a compile-to-JavaScript language, such as TypeScript, ReasonML, or even JavaScript. The compiled script will be embedded on a web page, hooking into a page element such as a **div**:

```
import React from 'react';
import ReactDOM from 'react-dom';

export interface HelloProps {
  name: string;
}

class HelloComponent extends React.Component<HelloProps, {}> {
  render() {
    return <div>Hello {this.props.name}</div>;
  }
}

ReactDOM.render(
  <HelloTypeScript name="Matt" />,
  document.getElementById('root')
);
```

This script will be loaded into a page with an element that has an ID of **root** and will then print out **Hello Matt**. There are a lot of different ways to structure React applications. Usually, they will be composed of many, many components, each of which is put in a separate file.

React works by keeping a copy of the **Document Object Model (DOM)**, the object tree that translates JavaScript code to a rendered browser page, in memory. This virtual DOM is updated frequently and changes are selectively applied to a render of the actual web page. The virtual DOM allows for performance optimizations and is designed to prevent slow renders or inefficient re-renders.

THE COMPONENT

Inheritance patterns have existed in JavaScript since the beginning, first in the form of prototypal inheritance and then class syntax since ES2015. Some programming paradigms have recommended leveraging inheritance as the primary tool for building complex applications. For example, if we were building a website that included a profile page for a pet kitten, you might think about setting up an inheritance chain such as **KittenProfilePage extends FelineProfilePage extends PetProfilePage extends ProfilePage extends Page**. Indeed, some UI frameworks have attempted to implement models like this. However, in practice, this kind of thinking is quickly revealed as overly rigid, resistant to changing requirements, and forcing you into strange patterns. For example, if we have implemented **whiskerCount** in **FelineProfilePage** and we're now implementing **RodentProfilePage**, do we copy and paste? Does **RodentProfilePage** inherit from **FelineProfilePage**? Should we introduce **WhiskeredPetProfilePage** to the chain in order to share **whiskerCount** according to our model?

That's not to say that modern web frameworks and libraries don't use inheritance. They do! But generally, we are inheriting from a generic base component provided by the library and our inheritance chains are very short. Instead of inheritance, we focus on composition. Composition is the practice of building from many reusable components, most of which have a more general purpose. This doesn't mean that every component must be used more than once, but they are built in such a way that they could be.

This approach is embraced wholeheartedly by React. The basic building block of any React application is the component. There are a few classifications of React component.

STATEFUL COMPONENTS

Stateful components keep track of their own state. Consider a dropdown that tracks whether or not it is open and renders accordingly. Stateful components may use the **this** keyword or enclose other variables for the purpose of keeping the state. In React, the **setState** method may be used in stateful components. A stateful component's state may be set during lifecycle events.

Typically, information about how a component should display can be kept within that component. However, more complex data, such as a user profile, will often require a state management solution that extends beyond the component. See *State Management in React* later in this chapter.

STATELESS COMPONENTS

Stateless components never use the **this** keyword or call **setState**. They may re-render based on props passed in but do not track any data themselves. All normal lifecycle methods are available and stateless components are declared in the same way as stateful components, just without anything that may alter the state.

A dropdown or accordion component could even be stateful if we decided to manage that state in a central location. We typically won't do that for simple components, but we might have some reason, such as an expand/collapse all feature.

PURE COMPONENTS

Pure components are a special optimization for React. They are much like stateless components in terms of how we use them, but they are declared differently (by extending **PureComponent**). Pure components will only re-render when there is a change to their state or props. This is in contrast to most components, which will re-render when a parent component re-renders.

It's a good idea to experiment with pure components. They can dramatically speed up the rendering of a React application but may introduce some unexpected behaviors to those not used to working with them.

HIGHER-ORDER COMPONENTS

Higher-order components (HOCs) are not a library structure but are rather a pattern of wrapping one component with another without mutating the wrapped component. A great example of an HOC is requiring users to authenticate prior to interacting with our components.

Consider the case of a site with a single login page and 99 pages of sensitive information. Following a composition model, how can we implement this? We don't want to inject the details of our authentication into every component we build. Doing that would be sloppy and impractical. We don't want to have to wrap every render with **isUserAuthenticated**. It would be easy to miss one. A better solution to this problem is to use an HOC. Now our components can be written independently of our authentication model.

HOCs are often described as **pure functions** – functions without side effects. Pure functions make many appearances in React programming and are a good model to strive for in general. HOCs are considered to be pure functions because they must not alter the components they wrap. They are not, however, pure components; a pure function is a programming concept while **PureComponent** is an actual part of the React library.

HOCs are a great example of the concept of composition over inheritance. Going back to the authentication example, an inheritance model would likely have us building components that inherit from **RequiresAuthenticationComponent**, a base component that has our auth model built in. However, with composition, we can build our components independently of our authentication system, then apply an HOC around them. Many programmers would see this as a better separation of concerns.

JSX AND TSX

JSX is another innovation from Facebook. It refers to JavaScript enhanced with XML and practically it is JavaScript with HTML templates embedded into it. The following is an example of its use:

```
render() {
   return <div>Hello {this.props.name}</div>;
}
```

This is a function that returns an HTML template. We must use JSX to do this. Normally, this would result in a syntax error as this is not a quoted string nor is it any recognizable object or syntax in TypeScript. JSX allows us to mix our HTML templating in with our code. Some earlier view libraries would use one file for source code and another for templating. This was often confusing to programmers as they needed to flip back and forth between the two.

It is possible to write React without using JSX but that is rarely done and won't be covered in this book. Some other languages, such as Vue, use JSX as well.

When we want to write TypeScript in JSX, we use the **.tsx** file extension instead of **.jsx**. Technically, this is still JSX. To include TypeScript in JSX, all we need to do is set the file extension accordingly and set the **jsx** property in our **tsconfig.json** file to let TypeScript know we're using JSX. Valid values for that property are **react**, **react-native**, and **preserve**. The first two are for targeting a web browser or mobile app, respectively, and the last means that some other transpilation step will handle the JSX.

JSX is not a part of the JavaScript or TypeScript language, but just a language extension that needs to be transpiled. You wouldn't be able to run JSX in most web browsers.

EXERCISE 14.01: BOOTSTRAPPING WITH CREATE REACT APP

Create React App (**create-react-app**) is a library from Facebook that helps developers quickly bootstrap a new React application. It includes a library called **react-scripts** that helps abstract a lot of the tooling that has become standard in web development, like a linter, a test framework, and a bundler (webpack). All of those dependencies are managed by Create React App and **react-scripts**.

In this exercise, we'll bootstrap a new React application using Create React App. We'll run the application, examine the developer experience, and make some minor edits, then see components reload. We'll look at the production build and how that's different from the development build. Then we'll check out the built-in tests:

> **NOTE**
>
> The code for this exercise can be found here: https://packt.link/hMs3v.

1. Create React App ships with a few options and has included a TypeScript option since 2018. It's very easy to create a new application. We don't even need to install anything but can use **npx** to run the latest version of Create React App and start an application. Enter the command line and find a directory where you'd like to create your application and type this:

```
npx create-react-app my-app --template typescript
```

2. Create React App will download from the internet and set up your application, then install dependencies. Create React App will use the **yarn** package manager (also from Facebook) if you have it installed, otherwise it will use **npm**. It doesn't make very much difference which of these you use for the purposes of this book as they provide the same functionality. If you have an old version of **yarn** installed, you may need to update it (**npm i -g yarn**). If you prefer not to use **yarn**, all of these exercises should work fine without it:

```
npx create-react-app my-app --template typescript
npx: installed 67 in 4.26s


Creating a new React app in /Users/mattmorgan/mine/The-TypeScript-
Workshop/Chapter14/Exercise01/my-app.

Installing packages. This might take a couple of minutes.
Installing react, react-dom, and react-scripts with cra-template-
typescript...

yarn add v1.22.10
[1/4] 🔍  Resolving packages...
[2/4] 🚚  Fetching packages...
// […]
warning " > @testing-library/user-event@12.6.2" has unmet peer
dependency "@testing-library/dom@>=7.21.4".
success Uninstalled packages.
✨  Done in 10.28s.


Success! Created my-app at /Users/mattmorgan/mine/The-TypeScript-
Workshop/Chapter15/Exercise15.01/my-app
Inside that directory, you can run several commands:

  yarn start - Starts the development server.

  yarn build - Bundles the app into static files for production.

  yarn test -    Starts the test runner.

  yarn eject    Removes this tool and copies build dependencies,
configuration files and scripts into the app directory. If you do this,
you can't go back!

We suggest that you begin by typing:

  cd my-app

  yarn start


Happy hacking!
```

> **NOTE**
>
> For ease of presentation, only a section of the output is displayed here.

3. The output of **npx create-react-app** will tell you what to do next. **cd** into the directory that was created, and type **yarn start** or **npm start**. Your application will automatically open in a browser window:

```
cd my-app
yarn start
```

You will see the following output:

```
Compiled successfully!
You can now view my-app in the browser.
Local:            http://localhost:3000
On Your Network:  http://192.168.7.92:3000
Note that the development build is not optimized.
To create a production build, use yarn build.
```

4. If you navigate to **http://localhost:3000**, you will see the following:

Figure 14.1: Screenshot of my-app in the browser

5. Examine the source code that was generated in your favorite IDE. You can find an **index.tsx** file that attaches the React application to a **dom** node and an **App.tsx** file, which is the main component in your application so far. Try adding a new message or creating some new components as shown here:

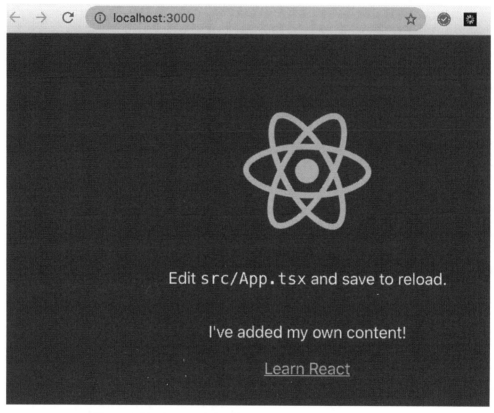

Figure 14.2: Screenshot of my-app after adding App.tsx

6. When you type **npm start**, your application will run in development mode with hot reloads (meaning your page refreshes when you make a change). For running in production, that's obviously not necessary. You can see what a production build looks like by running **yarn build** or **npm run build**. You'll see some output that tells you exactly what is happening and the transpiled JavaScript will be put in a **build** directory. Open the directory and look at the files there. That's what a production React application looks like.

7. Use *Ctrl + C* to stop your local server and try **yarn build** or **npm run build** to run the production build.

8. Production React applications often run on static servers but they can also run on web servers. The concept of server-side rendering in React is beyond the scope of this book but is another topic you may be interested in. Your build should produce a shortened URL that will take you to an article that includes more information about deploying React applications to production:

```
yarn build
yarn run v1.22.10
react-scripts build
Creating an optimized production build...
Compiled successfully.
```

File sizes after **gzip**:

```
41.2 KB   build/static/js/2.311d60e9.chunk.js
1.39 KB   build/static/js/3.73a1c5a5.chunk.js
1.17 KB   build/static/js/runtime-main.f12bc2d0.js
615 B     build/static/js/main.fe0fc6c6.chunk.js
531 B     build/static/css/main.8c8b27cf.chunk.css
```

The project was built assuming it is hosted at **/**. You can control this with the **homepage** field in your **package.json**.

9. The **build** folder is ready to be deployed. You may serve it with a static server:

```
yarn global add serve
serve -s build
Find out more about deployment here:https://cra.link/deployment
✿  Done in 7.88s.
```

10. Type **yarn test** or **npm t** (short for **npm test**). The Jest framework will run a test against your application. The test is very simple but can get you started writing more tests. It's a good idea to write tests for your components as the tests will give you confidence that your application is working. Writing testable code builds strong programming habits:

```
PASS  src/App.test.tsx
  ✓ renders learn react link (23 ms)

Test Suites: 1 passed, 1 total
Tests:       1 passed, 1 total
Snapshots:   0 total
Time:        2.295 s
```

```
Ran all test suites related to changed files.

Watch Usage
 › Press a to run all tests.
 › Press f to run only failed tests.
 › Press q to quit watch mode.
 › Press p to filter by a filename regex pattern.
 › Press t to filter by a test name regex pattern.
 › Press Enter to trigger a test run.
```

And with that, we've covered the basics of Create React App. We've learned how we can quickly bootstrap a new application, looked at the developer experience with hot reloading, and also how to run production builds and tests.

Although Create React App gives you a lot of stuff, it's actually just the tip of the iceberg of what we'll see in the coming sections. For example, our application has no way to handle different kinds of requests or different pages. We don't have any routing. We also have no place to store data and no way to interact with any kind of backend. We'll delve into those concepts in the coming sections.

ROUTING

React doesn't include a solution for routing by default. That's because at its heart it is a view library. Some applications have no need for routing, but most will want the ability to render multiple pages at the very least. Some applications have complicated routing requirements that may involve "deep linking" or linking directly to a particular document. Request or query variables in a URL may contain some identifier that connects to a particular user's record.

While there are some alternatives, most React applications that use routing use React-Router, which is the official Facebook solution.

EXERCISE 14.02: REACT ROUTER

In this exercise, we'll bootstrap another application with Create React App and then enhance it with React Router to be able to support multiple views and navigate between them:

> **NOTE**
>
> The code for this exercise can be found here: https://packt.link/EYBcF.

1. To start, go to the command line where you can create another application:

```
npx create-react-app router-app --template typescript
cd router-app
```

2. To add React Router, let's install the library and typings. If you are not using **yarn**, **yarn add** commands can be replaced with **npm install**:

```
yarn add react-router-dom
yarn add -D @types/react-router-dom
% yarn add react-router-dom
yarn add v1.22.10
[1/4] 🔍  Resolving packages...
[2/4] 🚚  Fetching packages...
[3/4] 🔗  Linking dependencies...
warning " > @testing-library/user-event@12.6.2" has unmet peer
dependency "@testing-library/dom@>=7.21.4".
[4/4] 🔨  Building fresh packages...
success Saved lockfile.
success Saved 8 new dependencies.
info Direct dependencies
└─ react-router-dom@5.2.0
info All dependencies
├─ hoist-non-react-statics@3.3.2
├─ mini-create-react-context@0.4.1
├─ path-to-regexp@1.8.0
├─ react-router-dom@5.2.0
├─ react-router@5.2.0
├─ resolve-pathname@3.0.0
├─ tiny-warning@1.0.3
└─ value-equal@1.0.1
✨  Done in 4.86s.
% yarn add -D @types/react-router-dom
yarn add v1.22.10
[1/4] 🔍  Resolving packages...
[2/4] 🚚  Fetching packages...
[3/4] 🔗  Linking dependencies...
warning " > @testing-library/user-event@12.6.2" has unmet peer
dependency "@testing-library/dom@>=7.21.4".
[4/4] 🔨  Building fresh packages...
```

```
success Saved lockfile.
success Saved 2 new dependencies.
info Direct dependencies
└─ @types/react-router-dom@5.1.7
info All dependencies
├─ @types/react-router-dom@5.1.7
└─ @types/react-router@5.1.11
✨  Done in 4.59s.
```

Now we can start the application with **yarn start** or **npm start**. We'll be editing files as we add these routes and our application will just restart automatically, which makes for a nice developer experience.

We could begin by adding the router, but we currently have nothing to route to, so let's start by adding a few new components. Since components are the building blocks of a React application, a component can be a page. That same component could also be part of another page.

3. Let's create a **/src/pages** subdirectory in our application to hold the new page components. In the **pages** subdirectory, create **Add.tsx**, **Home.tsx**, **SignIn.tsx**, and **Signup.tsx**.

    To start, we'll create some very simple components to route between. In a later section in this chapter, we'll discuss the creation of function components.

4. Create **Add.tsx** using the following code:

```
import React from 'react';

const Add = () => <div>Add a new story</div>;

export default Add;
```

5. Create **Home.tsx** using the following code:

```
import React from 'react';

const Home = () => <div>You are home!</div>;

export default Home;
```

6. Create **SignIn.tsx** using the following code:

```
import React from 'react';

const SignIn = () => <div>Sign in here</div>;

export default SignIn;
```

7. Create **SignUp.tsx** using the following code:

```
import React from 'react';

const SignUp = () => <div>Sign up here</div>;

export default SignUp;
```

These basic components only return some JSX, but they are sufficient to route between. Note that without a router, we could include the components in our main **App.tsx**, but we cannot navigate between pages in a traditional web app sense. That is the responsibility of the router.

8. So, at this point, we have components that we can't yet interact with. Let's add routing to our **App.tsx**.

React Router exposes a few different router types that have mostly narrow use cases. We will focus on **BrowserRouter**. To get started, we will add a few imports to **App.tsx**:

```
import { BrowserRouter as Router, Switch, Route } from 'react-router-dom';
```

By convention, we are renaming **BrowserRouter** to **Router** in our import. We will also use **Switch**, which gives us a declarative way to shift between different components based on the route, and **Route**, which lets us define the component route.

Adding our first (default) route is pretty simple. Before doing that, make sure your local dev environment is running with **npm start**. You should see the spinning React logo in a web browser running at **http://localhost:3000**.

9. Now let's use the other components to build out the first route. We'll remove all the JSX that the **App.tsx** component is currently returning and replace it with the routing:

```
function App() {
  return (
    <Router>
      <Switch>
        <Route exact path="/" component={Home} />
      </Switch>
    </Router>
  );
}
```

You will need to import the **Home** component:

```
import Home from './pages/Home';
```

Your IDE may prompt you to automatically import **Home** as you are typing.

10. If you've got everything working correctly, your view will refresh and you'll see the React logo replaced with **You are home!**.

Let's add some additional routes:

```
<Route path="/add" component={Add} />
<Route path="/signin" component={SignIn} />
<Route path="/signup" component={SignUp} />
```

11. Our **Home** route sets the **exact** property. Routing in React uses a regular expression to match the path starting from the leftmost part of the path. This allows for variable query and route parameters to be matched. The **exact** prop forces an exact match and ensures **"/add"** doesn't match to **"/"**.

12. Now we can test the routing. Type **http://localhost:3000/add** in your browser. You should get the message **Add a new story**. Try visiting the other routes.

13. Of course, it isn't very natural to expect users to manually type all the URLs in a browser to navigate your site. Let's add some links. We can import **Link** from **react-router**. This component will create navigation links that connect to your application routing. Because of this, **Link** must always be used within **Router**.

Link wraps some text and has a **to** prop, which should have the route you want to link to:

```
<Link to="/">home</Link>
```

With that, it's pretty easy to add some navigation elements:

```
<nav>
  <ul>
    <li>
      <Link to="/">home</Link>
    </li>
    <li>
      <Link to="add">add</Link>
    </li>
    <li>
      <Link to="signin">signin</Link>
    </li>
    <li>
      <Link to="signup">signup</Link>
    </li>
  </ul>
</nav>
```

This should give us a nice way to move between our pages. However, pasting a bunch of extra JSX into **App.tsx** isn't a great way to write React, so let's write a **NavBar** component instead.

14. Add a **components** directory under **src**. We'll use this directory to hold components that aren't tied to routes:

```
import React from 'react';
import { Link } from 'react-router-dom';

const NavBar = () => (
  <nav>
    <ul>
      <li>
        <Link to="/">home</Link>
      </li>
      <li>
        <Link to="add">add</Link>
      </li>
```

```
        <li>
          <Link to="signin">signin</Link>
        </li>
        <li>
          <Link to="signup">signup</Link>
        </li>
      </ul>
    </nav>
  );

export default NavBar;
```

15. Now we can simply use this component in **App.tsx**. Here's the finished component:

```
import './App.css';

import React from 'react';
import { BrowserRouter as Router, Route, Switch } from 'react-router-dom';

import NavBar from './components/NavBar';
import Add from './pages/Add';
import Home from './pages/Home';
import SignIn from './pages/SignIn';
import SignUp from './pages/SignUp';

function App() {
  return (
    <Router>
      <NavBar />
      <Switch>
        <Route exact path="/" component={Home} />
        <Route path="/add" component={Add} />
        <Route path="/signin" component={SignIn} />
        <Route path="/signup" component={SignUp} />
      </Switch>
    </Router>
  );
}

export default App;
```

16. Check your browser now and you should see the simple navigation and be able to use it to shift between views:

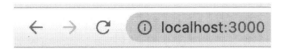

- home
- add
- signin
- signup

You are home!

Figure 14.3: List of folders in the finished component

Adding routing to a React application is easy to do. In this exercise, we showed how to add routes, navigate between them, and also how to share a common component across several routes. One of the real strengths of React is the ability to share components among other components and create reuse patterns that make putting together the building blocks of an application easy.

Routing can also include path and query parameters. Be sure to read the React Router documentation for how to add parameters to your routes.

REACT COMPONENTS

Now let's dig into how these components work. There are several different ways to declare a component in React. You even have the choice to use JSX or not. This book will focus on creating components with function expressions, but we'll go over a few other patterns, so you'll know them when you see them.

CLASS COMPONENTS

This style of component follows a classical (that is, relating to the programming concept of classes) pattern of component declaration. Many older examples will use class components, but they have fallen largely out of fashion due to being more verbose than other patterns. To create a class component, we import the **Component** class from React and extend it while creating our own class:

```
import React, { Component } from 'react';

interface Comp1Props {
```

```
  text: string;
}

export default class Comp1 extends Component<Comp1Props> {
  render() {
    const { text } = this.props;
    return <div>{text}</div>;
  }
}
```

It's a good idea to create your own interface for props and the same can be done for state – for example:

```
import React, { Component } from 'react';

interface Comp1Props {
  text: string;
}

interface Comp1State {
  value: boolean
}

export default class Comp1 extends Component<Comp1Props, Comp1State> {
  render() {
    ...
}
```

Props are accessed via **this.props** and state via **this.state** and **this. setState**. This style of programming may seem comfortable and familiar to those with a background in Java or C++, but the **this** keyword can be troubling to work with in TypeScript and the class-focused declaration style doesn't fit well with some of the functional programming concepts in React, so other patterns have gained popularity in recent years. For more information about the **this** keyword, see *Chapter 3, Functions*.

FUNCTION COMPONENTS (FUNCTION DECLARATION)

It's far more common for React components to be written as function components. The same simple component from the previous section, rewritten as a function component, could look like this:

```
import React from 'react';

interface Comp2Props {
  text: string;
}

export default function Comp2({ text }: Comp2Props) {
  return <div>{text}</div>;
}
```

We've shaved off a couple of lines of code and come to something a bit more like a functional programming style. You won't use **this** very often when using function components, nor do you need to actually import the **Component** class. Props are simply the arguments passed into the function. State can't be handled directly here, but we will see how to manage that in the next section on React Hooks.

FUNCTION COMPONENTS (FUNCTION EXPRESSION WITH ARROW FUNCTIONS)

This book prefers this pattern as a very intuitive and declarative way of creating components. You can even create pure function components as a one-liner. First, let's write the same component again:

```
import React from 'react';

interface Comp3Props {
  text: string;
}

const Comp3 = ({ text }: Comp3Props) => <div>{text}</div>;

export default Comp3;
```

Scoping rules do not allow the **const** and **default** keywords to be on the same line (avoiding absurd code such as **export default const a=1, b=2, c=3;**, which would otherwise be allowed), so we need to export the component on a separate line.

If we really want to slim the code down, we could write it like this:

```
import React from 'react';

export const Comp3 = ({ text }:{ text: string }) => <div>{text}</div>;
```

This is a pure function component that is stateless and has no other side effects. Most programmers prefer to use an interface for the props as it helps with readability, but that declaration can be done inline as in the preceding snippet (**{ text: string }**) if we really want to make the component small.

NO JSX

Any of the preceding methods can use **createElement**. Here's a quick example of why you probably don't want to use that:

```
import { createElement } from 'react';

interface Comp4Props {
  text: string;
}

const Comp4 = ({ text }: Comp4Props) => createElement('div', null, text);

export default Comp4;
```

The arguments to **createElement** are the element tag to create, its props, and its children. It doesn't take long to realize that creating nested elements with **createElement** would be *substantially* more difficult than using JSX, so JSX is almost always used. If we decide not to use JSX, we can use the **.ts** file extension instead of **.tsx**. This is a very small benefit!

STATE IN FUNCTION COMPONENTS

This book recommends function components over class components. We cannot access state directly in a function component, nor is there a **setState** method to call. However, we do have access to the excellent **useState** and so we hardly miss **this** or **setState** at all.

useState is part of React Hooks, available since React version 16.8. React Hooks introduced several functions that greatly enhance working with function components. Let's start by coming up with a simple component that uses the class constructor, **this**, and **setState**:

```
import React, { Component } from 'react';

interface Comp1Props {
  text: string;
}

interface Comp1State {
  clicks: number;
}

export default class Comp1 extends Component<Comp1Props, Comp1State> {
  constructor(props: Comp1Props) {
    super(props);
    this.state = { clicks: 0 };
  }
  handleClick = () => {
    this.setState({ clicks: this.state.clicks + 1 });
  };
  render() {
    const { text } = this.props;
    return (
      <div>
        {text}
        <div>
```

```
           <button onClick={this.handleClick}>{this.state.clicks} clicks</
button>
         </div>
       </div>
     );
   }
}
```

We've defined interfaces for props and state as well as an event handler to count up the clicks. We are using **setState** to increment our counter in the state. It looks a bit weird that **handleClick** uses an arrow function while **render** does not, yet they both refer to **this**. This is due to the strangeness of interpreting **this** references in TypeScript. Without an arrow function, **handleClick** will not find our component when accessing **this** but will instead get an **undefined** reference. This sort of issue has cost a lot of developers a lot of time and so framework authors have sought after solutions that simply avoid language constructs that so many find confusing. Let's rewrite this component as a function component:

```
import React, { useState } from 'react';

interface Comp2Props {
  text: string;
}

export default function Comp2({ text }: Comp2Props) {
  const [clicks, setClicks] = useState(0);
  const handleClick = () => setClicks(clicks + 1);
  return (
    <div>
      {text}
      <div>
        <button onClick={handleClick}>{clicks} clicks</button>
      </div>
    </div>
  );
}
```

This function component does exactly the same thing as the class component. Let's look at the differences. For one, we're starting to see substantial savings in terms of lines of code. The function component is 18 lines while the class component is 30.

Next, we are avoiding the troublesome **this** keyword. We are also avoiding having to define an interface for the state. It may seem counterintuitive, but this is actually a good thing. In class components, state, as a single object, may often combine several unrelated things into one state. State is really just a place for any and all local variables. By declaring each of these variables independently from the others, we can establish much better programming paradigms.

The **useState** function takes an argument, which is the default state, and returns an array of **const** pointing to the value and a method used to update the state. The stateful value is **const** because it cannot be updated without re-rendering our component. If we call **setClicks**, the component will re-render with a newly initialized **const clicks**. You can have several **useState** calls in a single function component. Each one manages its own part of the state independently.

Your state can still be strongly typed when using **useState**. In our case, TypeScript infers the type of number for clicks, based on how we've initialized it with a number. However, if we wanted to, we could add a type hint such as **useState<number>(0)** or **useState<MyType>(0)** to handle more complex types.

STATE MANAGEMENT IN REACT

State is a bit of an overloaded term in the UI development world. Thus far, the state we've been referring to is a local state inside of a component. Going back to the clicks example, while that value could be passed to a child component via the usual means (as a prop), there's no easy way to pass the value to a parent component or some distant "cousin" component elsewhere in the DOM tree.

The management of global state is a problem much older than React. It's always been fairly simple to create some kind of widget that can internally manage its own data, but that widget gets extremely complicated when new requirements are introduced that connect the widget's data to other parts of an application. Often applications were written in an imperative fashion with hand-coded "events" to try to propagate data through some global scope. This approach can work, but bugs are common and managing change can be extremely difficult. A likely outcome of an ad hoc approach to state management is unmaintainable spaghetti code.

React does have a "brute force" approach to state management, which is that all data is stored in some parent component and passed (along with any necessary methods to update the data) to all children and all of their descendants. Doing this in a complex application can be really challenging, with long lists of props that must always be passed through. For this reason, most developers choose another solution.

Redux is a popular library introduced in 2015 that aimed to solve the problem of state management by introducing functional programming concepts such as the reducer. The concept behind Redux is that an immutable state is stored somewhere in the application. Different parts of the application can dispatch actions that will produce a new state to replace the old one. Because each version of the immutable state can be stored and is immutable (meaning nothing outside this framework can change it), it is possible to time-travel through different application states, something that can be very useful for development but may also have use in production applications, such as an "undo" feature. Redux can be used with almost any web application and is not tied to React, but it's very common to find the two of them together in an application.

Redux is powerful but receives criticism for being overly complex and using a lot of boilerplate. It also typically requires additional libraries (such as **redux-saga** or **redux-thunk**) to make asynchronous calls to a backend server. All of these libraries can be very intimidating to newcomers and even challenging to use for experienced programmers.

React Hooks provides a simpler way using React context. React context allows us to set root-level data stores and actions and make them available to components deep in the DOM tree without having to pass props all the way through (sometimes known as "prop drilling"). The difference between Redux and context is tantamount to going from class components and **setState** to function components and **useState**. Like the prior example, we are moving from a single state object and complexity managing it to multiple contexts that can be managed more simply.

EXERCISE 14.03: REACT CONTEXT

Let's get some experience with context. For this exercise, you can either bootstrap a new **create-react-app** instance or use the one from the previous sections. In this exercise, we'll create two new components and one provider. Technically, providers are components too, but they are actually specialized HOCs:

> **NOTE**
>
> The code for this exercise can be found here: https://packt.link/rUfr4.

1. Let's start with the provider. Create **/components** and **/providers** subdirectories under your **/src** directory. In the **/providers** directory, create a file called **ClickProvider.tsx**. This component will manage our clicks and provide its context to descendants.

2. Unlike most components, a provider will export a context and a provider. Some guides will create **Context** and then export **Consumer** and **Provider**. Rather than using **Consumer**, we will use **useContext**, another React Hook. When using **useContext**, the **Consumer** object is not referenced directly:

```
export const ClickContext = createContext();
```

3. That's the basic signature for creating **Context**. We will need to add a type hint and a default value. Let's come to that in a moment after adding **Provider**:

```
export const ClickProvider = ({ children }) => {
  const [clicks, setClicks] = useState(0);
  return (
    <ClickContext.Provider value={{ clicks, setClicks }}>
      {children}
    </ClickContext.Provider>
  );
};
```

This component takes some props, which are child nodes. It uses **useState** to create a **clicks** value and an **update** function, then it returns **Provider** with the value and the function.

4. This is the basic provider we need, but it's not yet good TypeScript. We need to add some more types:

```
interface Clicks {
  clicks: number;
  setClicks: Dispatch<SetStateAction<number>>;
}


interface ContextProps {
  children: ReactNode;
}
```

5. **ClickContext** will be the type for the value our **Provider** returns and **ContextProps** works as a basic prop type for any HOC with children. With these types, we can fill out the rest of **Provider**:

```
import React, {
  createContext,
  Dispatch,
  ReactNode,
  SetStateAction,
  useState,
} from 'react';

interface Clicks {
  clicks: number;
  setClicks: Dispatch<SetStateAction<number>>;
}

interface ContextProps {
  children: ReactNode;
}

export const ClickContext = createContext<Clicks>({
  clicks: 0,
  setClicks: () => {},
});

export const ClickProvider = ({ children }: ContextProps) => {
  const [clicks, setClicks] = useState(0);
  return (
```

```
        <ClickContext.Provider value={{ clicks, setClicks }}>
          {children}
        </ClickContext.Provider>
    );
};
```

6. Now let's add **Clicker.tsx** and **Display.tsx** in the
   components directory:

```
import React, { useContext } from 'react';
import { ClickContext } from '../providers/ClickProvider';

const Clicker = () => {
  const { clicks, setClicks } = useContext(ClickContext);
  const handleClick = () => setClicks(clicks + 1);
  return <button onClick={handleClick}>Add a click</button>;
};

export default Clicker;
```

7. This component renders a button and uses the **setClicks** method
   from **Provider**:

```
import React, { useContext } from 'react';
import { ClickContext } from '../providers/ClickProvider';

const Display = () => {
  const { clicks } = useContext(ClickContext);
  return <div>{clicks}</div>;
};

export default Display;
```

Display.tsx just grabs the **clicks** value from the context and displays it.

8. Now that we have a couple of simple components that work with our provider,
   let's add them to **App.tsx** and see how our app looks.

9. Delete the default code from **App.tsx** and replace it with **Provider** and the new components:

```
import './App.css';

import React from 'react';

import Clicker from './components/Clicker';
import Display from './components/Display';
import { ClickProvider } from './providers/ClickProvider';

function App() {
  return (
    <ClickProvider>
      <Clicker />
      <Display />
    </ClickProvider>
  );
}

export default App;
```

Run the app and click the button several times. The counter will increment. It's not that amazing to make a counter increment on a website, but our components are nicely decoupled and this approach will scale well to much larger apps:

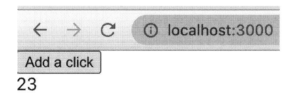

Figure 14.4: App displaying the click counter

In this exercise, we used React context to manage state in an application. We showed how different components can interact with the state and how it can be passed to components without the need for nested props.

React applications can contain multiple contexts or a single tree of data. React context will even keep the current state while a modified component reloads in development mode so you can keep coding without interrupting the application flow.

FIREBASE

Firebase is a mobile and web development platform owned by Google. Firebase includes a web API so you can add authentication, analytics, a database, and more to a web application. Firebase can be used as the backend of a modern web application, allowing developers to focus on user experience. It includes a free tier that we will use for the following exercise.

EXERCISE 14.04: GETTING STARTED WITH FIREBASE

In this exercise, we'll set up a database and authentication using Firebase. We'll need to register a free account. We'll also get the required payload that we'll need to complete an activity using Firebase later in this chapter:

> **NOTE**
>
> The code files for this exercise can be found here: https://packt.link/bNMr5.

1. Firebase requires a Google account, but using it doesn't require a credit card or any payment. To get started, navigate to https://firebase.google.com/ and click **Get started**.

    You should find yourself at the Firebase console. Click **Add project** and work through the wizard. You can name your project whatever you like – Firebase will make the name unique if you don't.

2. Don't enable Google Analytics, unless you already have an account you want to use.

    You'll need to wait a minute and then you'll find yourself at your project dashboard. There you will find several services you can deploy to help build out your application. We will focus only on Authentication and Firestore.

3. First, go to **Authentication** and click **Get Started**. Choose **Email/ Password** and enable it. All the other authentication methods require additional setup steps. Go ahead and work through those steps if you like. The documentation on the Firebase website should be sufficient. Save your changes.

4. Now click on **Firestore Database** and **Create database**. Choose the **Start in test mode** option and then choose a region to deploy to. The region doesn't really matter, but you probably want to choose something that is close to you for faster responses. Finish creating the database.

5. One last thing we need to do in the Firebase console is find our app config. The way Firebase works is that a config object with a bunch of IDs will live in your app and manage connections to your Firebase backend; however, the security rules that govern which users can affect which data are all set up in the console (or the CLI, which this book doesn't cover). This config is not actually secret because if your app is set up correctly, there's nothing a malicious user can do that you haven't allowed.

6. To get your app config, you first must register your app. You can add an app either from **Project Overview** (the **</>** symbol) or via the gear next to **Project Overview**. Add a web app, name it anything you like, and skip the web hosting option. Go into your app config (gear icon) and find the config. Go with config over CDN (content delivery network) and you'll find something that looks like this:

```
const firebaseConfig = {
  apiKey: "abc123",
  authDomain: "blog-xxx.firebaseapp.com",
  projectId: "blog-xxx",
  storageBucket: "blog-xxx.appspot.com",
  messagingSenderId: "999",
  appId: "1:123:web:123abc"
};
```

Hang on to that config. We will need it later, but for now we are done in the Firebase console. You may wish to return to it later to view your database, manage your users, or even upgrade or delete your apps and projects, but you won't need to do so again in this chapter.

Getting started with Firebase is easy. We'll be able to use Firebase to sign up, authenticate and track users, and store data, without having to write our own backend service.

STYLING REACT APPLICATIONS

A modern UI developer has a lot of different options when it comes to styling applications. The traditional approach of creating a few **Cascading Style Sheets (CSS)** files and including them is not great for scaling or for building a unified presentation layer. Modern web applications and React in particular offer so many different options for styling that we can't hope to cover all of them. Here are a few popular techniques.

MASTER STYLESHEET

We have a **styles.css** file with all the styles. Styles are global and will affect all components. This can work very well for a small application but has some serious scaling problems as you add more styles and components. When new styles are added, we may start to see existing components break as they are influenced by the new styles.

COMPONENT-SCOPED STYLES

With this approach, we create a style for each component that needs styling and use the **import** keyword to add the style to your component. A build system such as webpack will prefix all of the style names so they don't "pollute" the global scope and wind up styling other components. This is the approach you get out of the box with Create React App, which uses webpack internally.

This approach works well if you can effectively use plain CSS or a stylesheet compiler like Sass. Some developers don't like it because display elements are spread across CSS and JSX files.

CSS-IN-JS

CSS-in-JS is an approach that has produced popular libraries such as Styled Components and Emotion. The approach is simply that we write our CSS in our JavaScript (or TypeScript, in our case, as most of these libraries publish typings), thereby combining our styling with our display layer.

This approach works well for teams that create lots of custom components. The downside is another build dependency to maintain.

COMPONENT LIBRARIES

Component libraries deliver fully usable components ready to be plugged into an application. Component libraries are great for building a nice-looking application very quickly. Many of them have been around for a lot of years. Some examples of component libraries are Twitter Bootstrap, Semantic UI, and Material-UI. All of these libraries publish versions designed to work with popular web systems such as Angular, Vue, and of course React.

Working with a component library is a lot like working with your own components. You import the components and use them as you would any other component. Doing this can really speed up your development cycles as you have common components ready to go. Some teams find the components from the component library too inflexible and don't like to deal with the additional dependencies.

The upcoming activity will use Material-UI for a quick and attractive build.

ACTIVITY 14.01: THE BLOG

Now that we have some experience with **create-react-app** and Firebase, let's create a blog! In this activity, we will use all the tools and techniques covered earlier in this chapter. We will use **create-react-app** to quickly create a React project. We will use Material-UI to design an attractive app and write some of our own function components. We will use **react-router** to enable routing between the different pages of our application. We'll manage state with the React context API. Finally, we'll use Firebase to have a backend service we can use to authenticate users and save and share data between visits to the blog.

Let's go through the high-level steps for creating this blog. It sounds like a lot, but it won't be all that challenging when we break it down into individual tasks:

> **NOTE**
>
> The code files for this activity can be found here: https://packt.link/qqlXz.

1. Create a new React application using **create-react-app**, as described earlier in this chapter. You could even reuse an application you began earlier in this chapter. Start your application so you can watch the implementation appear before your eyes.

2. Refer back to your Firebase application from *Exercise 14.04, Getting Started with Firebase*, or complete that exercise if you haven't yet. Find your config data in Firebase and follow the instructions to add the **firebase** dependency to your React application, then add the app-specific config from the Firebase console.

3. Implement the Firebase **auth** and **firestore** services, then add React context and providers for each to maintain state.

Install **react-router** and **material-ui** to build some UI components and create some routes. Start by creating a sign-up route and page:

Figure 14.5: Landing page

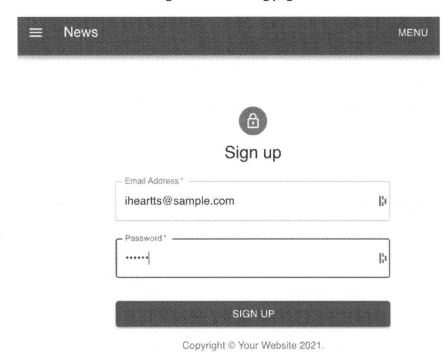

Figure 14.6: Sign-up page

4. Create a route to add pages and add UI components to be able to set the title and link for a new story:

Figure 14.7: Page for adding stories

5. Using your React context and provider and Firebase Firestore, persist your data to the cloud and implement other features such as comments:

Figure 14.8: Commenting features

Figure 14.9: Posting a comment

If this activity took some time, don't worry. If you needed to check the solution on GitHub, don't worry about that either. This one was particularly challenging because it included so many different pieces, but if you managed to pull them all together into a working app, that's a great step forward. You've built a full-stack application with an attractive UI, authentication, and a database.

> **NOTE**
>
> The solution to this activity can be found on page 680.

SUMMARY

TypeScript is becoming a popular tool for writing web applications and while it wasn't always prevalent in React, it is now well supported. Developers no longer need to only add types to props but can gain the benefit of type safety and IntelliSense while working across all parts of an application.

React has a very rich and varied ecosystem, but many TypeScript-friendly solutions such as React Hooks and React context are becoming go-to choices to keep an application simple but powerful. With TypeScript supported in `create-react-app`, it's simple to get started and you can be building your app in minutes.

Developers who want to know more about React will need more than just this book, but this chapter serves to show why you want to stay with TypeScript when you write applications using React.

APPENDIX

CHAPTER 01: TYPESCRIPT FUNDAMENTALS

ACTIVITY 1.01: CREATING A LIBRARY FOR WORKING WITH STRINGS

Solution:

Here are the steps that will help you create all the functions listed in the activity problem statement.

TOTITLECASE

The **toTitleCase** function will process a string and capitalize the first letter of each word, but will make all the other letters lowercase.

Test cases for this function are as follows:

```
"war AND peace" => "War And Peace"
"Catcher in the Rye" => "Catcher In The Rye"
 "tO kILL A mOCKINGBIRD" => "To Kill A MockingBird"
```

Here are the steps to help you write this function:

1. This function will take a single parameter that is a string and return a string as well:

```
function toTitleCase (input:string) : string {
```

2. First off, we will split the input into an array of strings using the split string method. We'll split on every space character:

```
// split the string into an array on every occurrence of
//  the space character
const words = input.split(" ");
```

3. Next, we will define a new array that will hold each word as we transform it into title case, and use a for..of loop to loop through the array of words:

```
const titleWords = [];
// loop through each word
for (const word of words) {
```

4. For each word we will extract the first character and the rest of the characters using the slice string method. We will transform the initial to uppercase, and the rest of the characters to lowercase. Next, we'll join them back together to form a complete word and push the result to the holding array:

```
    // take the first character using `slice` and convert it to
uppercase
    const initial = word.slice(0, 1).toLocaleUpperCase();
    // take the rest of the character using `slice` and convert them
to lowercase
    const rest = word.slice(1).toLocaleLowerCase();
    // join the initial and the rest and add them to the resulting
array
    titleWords.push(`${initial}${rest}`);
```

5. At last, we will join all the processed words together, with a separating space, and we have our result:

```
    // join all the processed words
    const result = titleWords.join(" ");
    return result;
}
```

6. Next, we can test whether the function gives the expected results for the given test inputs:

```
console.log(`toTitleCase("war AND peace"):`);
console.log(toTitleCase("war AND peace"));

console.log(`toTitleCase("Catcher in the Rye"):`);
console.log(toTitleCase("Catcher in the Rye"));

console.log(`toTitleCase("tO kILL A mOCKINGBIRD"):`);
console.log(toTitleCase("tO kILL A mOCKINGBIRD"));
```

7. We should receive the results:

```
toTitleCase("war AND peace"):
War And Peace
toTitleCase("Catcher in the Rye"):
Catcher In The Rye
toTitleCase("tO kILL A mOCKINGBIRD"):
To Kill A Mockingbird
```

COUNTWORDS

Here are the steps to help you write this function:

1. The countWords function will count the number of separate words within a string. Words are delimited by spaces, dashes (-), or underscores (_). Test cases for this function are as follows:

```
"War and Peace" => 3
"catcher-in-the-rye" => 4
"for_whom the-bell-tolls" => 5
```

2. Create the **countWords** function using the following code:

```
function countWords (input: string): number {
```

3. Split the words using a regex that will match any occurrence of a space, underscore, or dash character:

```
const words = input.split(/[ _-]/);
```

4. Return the length of the array that is the result of the split:

```
    return words.length;
}
```

5. Test the function and console out the results:

```
console.log(`countWords("War and Peace"):`);
console.log(countWords("War and Peace"));

console.log(`countWords("catcher-in-the-rye"):`);
console.log(countWords("catcher-in-the-rye"));

console.log(`countWords("for_whom the-bell-tolls"):`);
console.log(countWords("for_whom the-bell-tolls"));
```

TOWORDS

The **toWords** function will return all the words that are within a string. Words are delimited by spaces, dashes (−), or underscores (_).

Test cases for this function are as follows:

```
"War and Peace" => [War, and, peace]
"catcher-in-the-rye" => [catcher, in, the, rye]
"for_whom the-bell-tolls" => [for, whom, the, bell, tolls]
```

This function is very similar to the previous one we developed. The significant difference is that we need to return not only the number of words but also the actual words themselves. So, instead of a number, this function will return an array of strings:

1. Here is the code to create this function:

```
function toWords (input: string): string[] {
```

2. Once more, we will need to split the input into an array of strings using the split string method, using the [_-] regular expression. Split the words using a regular expression that will match any occurrence of a space, underscore, or dash character:

```
const words = input.split(/[ _-]/);
```

3. Once we have the words, we can just return them:

```
// return the words that were split
return words;
}
```

4. Next, we can test whether the function gives the expected results for the given test inputs:

```
console.log(`toWords("War and Peace"):`);
console.log(toWords("War and Peace"));

console.log(`toWords("catcher-in-the-rye"):`);
console.log(toWords("catcher-in-the-rye"));

console.log(`toWords("for_whom the-bell-tolls"):`);
console.log(toWords("for_whom the-bell-tolls"));
```

5. We should receive the results:

```
toWords("War and Peace"):
[ 'War', 'and', 'Peace' ]
toWords("catcher-in-the-rye"):
[ 'catcher', 'in', 'the', 'rye' ]
toWords("for_whom the-bell-tolls"):
[ 'for', 'whom', 'the', 'bell', 'tolls' ]
```

REPEAT

repeat will take a string and a number and return that same string repeated that number of times.

Test cases for this function are as follows:

```
„War", 3 => „WarWarWar"
„rye", 1 => „rye"
„bell", 0 => „"
```

Here are the steps to help you write this function:

1. This function will take two parameters, one that is a string and a second one that is a number, and return a string as well:

```
function repeat (input: string, times: number): string {
```

There are many ways to implement this function, and we'll illustrate one approach. We can create an array with the required number of elements, and then use the array's **fill** method to fill it with the value of the string. In that way, we will have an array of **times** elements, and each element will have the **input** value:

```
// create a new array that with length of `times`
// and set each element to the value of the `input` string
const instances = new Array(times).fill(input);
```

2. Next, we just need to join all the instances, using an empty string as the delimiter. That way, we're making sure that no spaces or commas are inserted between the strings:

```
// join the elements of the array together
const result = instances.join("");
return result;
}
```

3. Next, we can test whether the function gives the expected results for the given test inputs:

```
console.log(`repeat("War", 3 ):`);
console.log(repeat("War", 3 ));

console.log(`repeat("rye", 1):`);
console.log(repeat("rye", 1));

console.log(`repeat("bell", 0):`);
console.log(repeat("bell", 0));
```

4. We should receive the following results:

```
repeat("War", 3 ):
WarWarWar
repeat("rye", 1):
rye
repeat("bell", 0):
```

ISALPHA

isAlpha returns **true** if the string only has alpha characters (that is, letters). Test cases for this function are as follows:

```
"War and Peace" => false
"Atonement" => true
"1Q84" => false
```

Here are the steps to help you write this function:

1. This function will take a single parameter that is a string and return a Boolean:

```
function isAlpha (input: string): boolean {
```

2. For this function to work, we need to check whether each character is a lower- or uppercase letter. One of the best ways to determine that is to use a regular expression that checks it. In particular, the character group [a-z] will check for a single character and if we use the star quantifier (*), we can tell the regular expression to check for all the characters. We can add the i modifier to the regular expression to make the match case-insensitive, so we don't need to worry about letter casing:

```
// regex that will match any string that only has upper and  //
lowercase letters
    const alphaRegex = /^[a-z]*$/i
```

3. Next, we need to actually test our input. Since we only need to know whether the string matches, we can use the test method of the regular expression and return its result:

```
    // test our input using the regex
    const result = alphaRegex.test(input);
    return result;
}
```

4. Next, we can test whether the function gives the expected results for the given test inputs:

```
console.log(`isAlpha("War and Peace"):`);
console.log(isAlpha("War and Peace"));

console.log(`isAlpha("Atonement"):`);
console.log(isAlpha("Atonement"));

console.log(`isAlpha("1Q84"):`);
console.log(isAlpha("1Q84"));
```

5. We should receive the results:

```
isAlpha("War and Peace"):
false
isAlpha("Atonement"):
true
isAlpha("1Q84"):
false
```

ISBLANK

isBlank returns **true** if the string is blank, that is, it consists only of whitespace characters.

Test cases for this function are as follows:

```
"War and Peace" => false
"          " => true
"" => true
```

Here are the steps to help you write this function:

1. This function will take a single parameter that is a string and return a Boolean:

```
function isBlank (input: string): boolean {
```

2. For this function to work, we need to check whether each character in the string is a whitespace character. We can use a regular expression to determine that, or we can use some kind of looping construct that will iterate through the string. One approach would be to test whether the first character is a space, and if it is, slice it off:

```
// test if the first character of our input is an empty space
    while (input[0] === " ") {
// successively slice off the first character of the input
        input = input.slice(1);
    }
```

3. This loop will execute until it reaches a non-whitespace character. If it does not encounter one, it will only stop when there is no first element of the string, that is, when the string is the empty string. If that's the case, our original input only contained whitespace, and we can return true. Otherwise, we should return false:

```
// the loop will stop on the first character that is not a //space.
// if we're left with an empty string, we only have spaces in // the
input
    const result = input === "";
    return result;
```

4. Next, we can test whether the function gives the expected results for the given test inputs:

```
console.log(`isBlank("War and Peace"):`);
console.log(isBlank("War and Peace"));

console.log(`isBlank("          "):`);
console.log(isBlank("         "));

console.log(`isBlank(""):`);
console.log(isBlank(""));
```

5. We should receive the following results:

```
isBlank("War and Peace"):
false
isBlank("         "):
true
isBlank(""):
true
```

Note that there are multiple ways to implement all the preceding functions. The code shown is just one way to implement them, and these implementations are mostly for illustrative purposes. For example, a proper string utility library will need to have much more robust and extensive test suites.

CHAPTER 02: DECLARATION FILES

ACTIVITY 2.01: BUILDING A HEAT MAP DECLARATION FILE

Solution:

In this activity, we'll be building a TypeScript application named **heat map log system** that will track the baseball pitch data and ensure the integrity of the data. Perform the following steps to implement this activity:

1. Visit the following GitHub repository at https://packt.link/dqDPk and download the activity project containing the specs and configuration elements.

2. Open the Visual Studio Code editor and then open the terminal.

3. Change to the **activity-starter** directory in the terminal or command prompt by writing the following command:

```
cd activity-starter
```

4. Run the following command to install the dependencies:

```
npm install
```

You will now see the following files in the **activity-starter** directory:

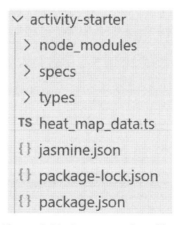

Figure 2.19: Starter project files

5. Open the **HeatMapTypes.d.ts** declaration file in the **types/** directory, define a module called **HeatMapTypes**, and export the interface named **Pitcher**. Define three attributes for the **Pitcher** module: **batterHotZones**, **pitcherHotZones**, and **coordinateMap**. The data structures should be the same for all three attributes, **Array<Array<number>>**, but **coordinateMap** should be optional. Write the following code to accomplish this:

```
declare module "HeatMapTypes" {
  export interface Pitcher {
    batterHotZones: Array<Array<number>>;
    pitcherHotZones: Array<Array<number>>;
    coordinateMap?: Array<any>;
  }
}
```

The preceding code in the editor looks like this:

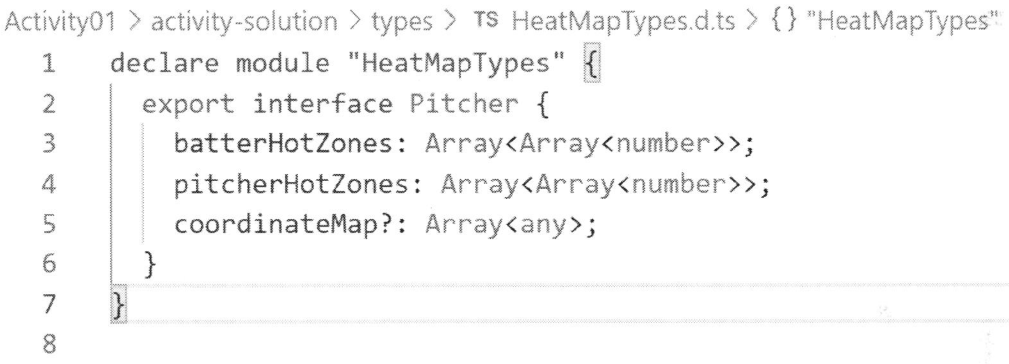

Activity01 > activity-solution > types > TS HeatMapTypes.d.ts > {} "HeatMapTypes"

```
1    declare module "HeatMapTypes" {
2      export interface Pitcher {
3        batterHotZones: Array<Array<number>>;
4        pitcherHotZones: Array<Array<number>>;
5        coordinateMap?: Array<any>;
6      }
7    }
8
```

Figure 2.20: Creating a pitcher interface

6. Open **heat_map_data.ts** and import the declaration files. Create and export a **let** variable called **data** and assign it to the **Pitcher** type. You will need to import the **lodash** library, which was installed when you initially ran **npm install**. Write the following code to do this:

```
/// <reference path="./types/HeatMapTypes.d.ts"/>
import hmt = require('HeatMapTypes');
import _ = require('lodash');
export let data: hmt.Pitcher;
```

7. Add values to the **data** variable that adhere to the declaration rules. Assign nested arrays as values to both the **batterHotZones** and **pitcherHotZones** attributes. Add the following code to do this:

```
data = {
   batterHotZones: [[12.2, -3], [10.2, -5], [3, 2]],
   pitcherHotZones: [[3, 2], [-12.2, 3], [-10.2, 5]],
};
```

8. Create a new function named **findMatch()** that takes in both the **batterHotZones** and **pitcherHotZones** arrays and utilize the **lodash** function, **intersectionWith()**, to return the identical nested array. Finally, store the value of the **findMatch()** function in the **coordinateMap** attribute that was defined in the declaration file. Write the following code to do this:

```
export const findMatch = (batterHotZones, pitcherHotZones) => {
   return _.intersectionWith(batterHotZones, pitcherHotZones,
_.isEqual);
};

data.coordinateMap = findMatch(data.batterHotZones, data.
pitcherHotZones);
console.log(data.coordinateMap);
```

9. Now, in the terminal, type the following commands to generate the JavaScript code and run it:

```
tsc heat_map_data.ts
node heat_map_data.js
```

Once we run the preceding commands, the following output is displayed in the terminal:

```
[[3,2]]
```

In the preceding output, the common values from both the attributes are fetched and then printed. In this case, the common values are [3, 2].

10. Now, change the values of both the attributes. Write the following code:

```
data = {
    batterHotZones: [[12.2, -3], [10.2, -5], [3, 2]],
    pitcherHotZones: [[3, 2], [-12.2, 3], [10.2, -5]],
};
```

11. Now, in the terminal, type the following commands to generate the JavaScript code and run it:

```
tsc heat_map_data.ts
node heat_map_data.js
```

Once we run the preceding commands, the following output is displayed in the terminal:

```
[[10.2, -5], [3, 2]]
```

In the preceding output, the common values are [10.2, -5] and [3, 2]. Finally, we built a heat map log system that will track the baseball pitch data and ensure the integrity of the data.

CHAPTER 03: FUNCTIONS

ACTIVITY 3.01: BUILDING A FLIGHT BOOKING SYSTEM WITH FUNCTIONS

Solution:

1. Start with the stubs provided in code samples. We have three files: **index.ts**, **bookings.ts**, and **flights.ts**. The **index.ts** file is a bit abstract and will just represent some of the transactions we push into our system. **bookings.ts** handles the user-facing activities of managing a booking, and **flights.ts** is the back office of filling up flights and making sure that everybody has a seat.

2. The **index.ts** file won't change unless you feel like changing it and adding some new scenarios. Let's run it without adding any code:

```
npx ts-node index.ts
Not implemented!
```

So we have work to do. Several functions are not yet implemented. Let's start by looking at **flights.ts**. There is a partial implementation there as we have an interface called **Flights** that describes the attributes of a flight, a list of available flights implementing that interface, and even a method to fetch the flights, called **getDestinations**. We need to implement logic to check to see whether the number of seats we want to book are still available, logic that can hold seats while we confirm a reservation, and logic that converts those seats held into reserved seats once our payment has been processed.

3. To check availability, we should see whether the number of seats we're requesting exceeds the number of remaining seats while holding any held seats in reserve. We can express this as **seatsRequested <= seatsRemaining - seatsHeld**, which is a Boolean expression that can be returned by the function. This can be written as an arrow function in the **flights.ts** file:

```
export const checkAvailability = (
  flight: Flight,
  seatsRequested: number
): boolean => seatsRequested <= flight.seatsRemaining - flight.
seatsHeld;
```

4. The **holdSeats** function should confirm that the requested seats are available and hold them if they are. If there aren't enough seats remaining, we need to throw an error and interrupt the flow:

```
export const holdSeats = (flight: Flight, seatsRequested: number):
Flight => {
  if (flight.seatsRemaining - flight.seatsHeld < seatsRequested) {
    throw new Error('Not enough seats remaining!');
  }
  flight.seatsHeld += seatsRequested;
  return flight;
};
```

5. To round out **flights.ts**, we have **reserveSeats**. This function operates similarly to **holdSeats**, but it confirms that the seats we wish to reserve have been held, and then converts them into reserved seats by increasing the **seatsHeld** property and reducing the **seatsRemaining** property by the same amount:

```
export const reserveSeats = (
  flight: Flight,
  seatsRequested: number
): Flight => {
  if (flight.seatsHeld < seatsRequested) {
    throw new Error('Seats were not held!');
  }
  flight.seatsHeld -= seatsRequested;
  flight.seatsRemaining -= seatsRequested;
  return flight;
};
```

That should do it for **flights.ts**. However, our program still won't run until we implement **bookings.ts**.

6. First of all, we're going to use a factory pattern for creating bookings. That means we'll have a function that returns a function to create bookings. We'll employ currying to create a closure so that we can initialize the **createBooking** function with **bookingNumber** in order to give each booking a unique identifier. The factory could look like this:

```
const bookingsFactory = (bookingNumber: number) => (
  flight: Flight,
  seatsHeld: number
): Booking => ({
  bookingNumber: bookingNumber++,
  flight,
  paid: false,
  seatsHeld,
  seatsReserved: 0,
});
```

Our factory takes **bookingNumber** as an argument to initialize this value and then increments the number each time it creates a new booking. We assign some default values to the booking to confirm to the **Booking** interface already provided in the module.

7. To call the factory and get a **createBooking** function with **bookingNumber** already curried into it, we can simply write the following:

```
const createBooking = bookingsFactory(1);
```

8. We have yet to write functions to start the booking process, handle the payment, and complete the booking, thereby reserving the seats on a flight. To begin the booking, we need to check availability on the flight we've chosen based on the number of seats we're requesting. If that is successful, we can create the booking and hold the seats. Otherwise, we can raise an error to alert the user to the fact that the booking cannot be completed:

```
export const startBooking = (
flight: Flight,
seatsRequested: number
): Booking => {
  if (checkAvailability(flight, seatsRequested)) {
    holdSeats(flight, seatsRequested);
    return createBooking(flight, seatsRequested);
  }
```

```
    throw new Error('Booking not available!');
};
```

9. In order to check flight availability and hold seats, we need to import these functions from **flights.ts**. This has already been done at the top of the **bookings.ts** module. The **export** keyword is used throughout these modules to make functions available to other modules. Some functions lack the **export** keyword, and so can only be invoked from within the module, effectively making them private.

10. We'll cheat a little with our **processPayment** function since we aren't implementing a payment system. We will just mark the booking as paid and return it:

```
export const processPayment = (booking: Booking): Booking => {
  booking.paid = true;
  return booking;
};
```

11. To complete the booking, we call **reserveSeats** in the **flights** module and then update our counts:

```
export const completeBooking = (booking: Booking): Booking => {
reserveSeats(booking.flight, booking.seatsHeld);
booking.seatsReserved = booking.seatsHeld;
booking.seatsHeld = 0;
return booking;
};
```

12. With all the functions implemented, we can invoke our program again and see the output:

```
npx ts-node index.ts
Booked to Lagos {
  bookingNumber: 1,
  flight: {
    destination: 'Lagos',
    flightNumber: 1,
    seatsHeld: 0,
    seatsRemaining: 29,
    time: '5:30'
  },
  paid: true,
  seatsHeld: 0,
```

```
    seatsReserved: 1
  }
  //...
  Istanbul flight {
    destination: 'Istanbul',
    flightNumber: 7,
    seatsHeld: 0,
    seatsRemaining: 0,
    time: '14:30'
  }
  Booking not available!
```

ACTIVITY 3.02: WRITING UNIT TESTS

Solution:

1. In the **describe** block, fetch the destinations for this scenario and then cache the first one as **flight**. Now, we can write a simple test to test that the correct number of destinations were returned:

```
test('get destinations', () => {
  expect(destinations).toHaveLength(7);
});
```

We could test each of the individual destinations and their properties as well.

2. Check the availability of several of the destinations. We can introduce all sorts of scenarios. Here are a few:

```
test('checking availability', () => {
  const destinations = getDestinations();
  expect(checkAvailability(destinations[0], 3)).toBeTruthy();
  expect(checkAvailability(destinations[1], 5)).toBeFalsy();
  expect(checkAvailability(destinations[2], 300)).toBeFalsy();
  expect(checkAvailability(destinations[3], 3)).toBeTruthy();
});
```

The first destination has at least three seats available. The second does not have five available, and so on.

3. Try holding some seats in the next test. We should test both success and failure scenarios:

```
test('hold seats', () => {
  expect.assertions(3);
  flight = holdSeats(flight, 3);
  expect(flight.seatsHeld).toBe(3);
  flight = holdSeats(flight, 13);
  expect(flight.seatsHeld).toBe(16);
  try {
    holdSeats(flight, 15);
  } catch (e) {
    expect(e.message).toBe('Not enough seats remaining!');
  }
});
```

Note that in order to ensure that the **catch** block was reached, we're expecting three assertions in this test. Without that, the test would still turn green even if, for some reason, the last call to **holdSeats** didn't throw an error.

4. Finish up the flights test with a unit test to reserve seats:

```
test('reserve seats', () => {
  expect.assertions(3);
  flight = reserveSeats(flight, 3);
  expect(flight.seatsRemaining).toBe(27);
  flight = reserveSeats(flight, 13);
  expect(flight.seatsRemaining).toBe(14);
  try {
    reserveSeats(flight, 1);
  } catch (e) {
    expect(e.message).toBe('Seats were not held!');
  }
});
```

This test runs through a few scenarios, including another error condition. In some cases, it might be appropriate to put error conditions in separate tests. A good rule of thumb for this is that each of your tests should be easy to comprehend and maintain. If any module or function gets to be too big, just break it up.

5. Now, write some tests for bookings using the same principles:

```
describe('bookings tests', () => {
  test('create a booking', () => {
    const booking = startBooking(destinations[0], 3);
    expect(booking).toEqual({
      bookingNumber: 1,
      flight: destinations[0],
      paid: false,
      seatsHeld: 3,
      seatsReserved: 0,
    });
  });
  test('pay for a booking', () => {
    let booking = startBooking(destinations[0], 3);
    booking = processPayment(booking);
    expect(booking.paid).toBe(true);
  });
  test('complete a booking', () => {
    let booking = startBooking(destinations[0], 3);
    booking = processPayment(booking);
    booking = completeBooking(booking);
    expect(booking.paid).toBe(true);
    expect(booking.seatsReserved).toBe(3);
  });
});
```

6. Let's now try running the tests and see how things look:

```
npm test
> jest --coverage --testRegex="^((?!-solution).)*\\.test\\.tsx?$"


 PASS   ./bookings.test.ts
 PASS   ./flights.test.ts
-------------|---------|----------|---------|---------|--------------
-----
File         | % Stmts | % Branch | % Funcs | % Lines | Uncovered
Line #s
-------------|---------|----------|---------|---------|--------------
-----
All files    |   97.14 |    83.33 |     100 |   96.97 |
 bookings.ts |   94.74 |       50 |     100 |   94.44 | 34
 flights.ts  |     100 |      100 |     100 |     100 |
```

```
--------------|---------|----------|---------|---------|--------------
-----
Test Suites: 2 passed, 2 total
Tests:       7 passed, 7 total
Snapshots:   0 total
Time:        1.782 s
Ran all test suites.
```

The tests passed! But we haven't hit 100% line coverage yet. We can actually open up the coverage report, which will be inside the **coverage/lcov-report** directory in the root of our project. The coverage tool (Istanbul) that comes bundled with Jest will produce an HTML report that we can open in any browser. This will show us the exact piece of code that hasn't been covered:

```
26 1x  export const startBooking = (
27         flight: Flight,
28         seatsRequested: number
29     ): Booking => {
30 3x     E if (checkAvailability(flight, seatsRequested)) {
31 3x       holdSeats(flight, seatsRequested);
32 3x       return createBooking(flight, seatsRequested);
33       }
34       throw new Error('Booking not available!');
35     };
```

Figure 3.2: HTML report produced by the tool

7. We've missed one error scenario. Let's add that as a new **describe** block to avoid further complicating the tests we've already written:

```
describe('error scenarios', () => {
  test('booking must have availability', () => {
    expect.assertions(1);
    try {
      startBooking(destinations[6], 8);
    } catch (e) {
      expect(e.message).toBe('Booking not available!');
    }
  });
});
```

There's no particular need to have a new **describe** block, but in this case, it might make the code a bit cleaner. Use **describe** and test blocks for readability and maintenance.

8. Let's now run the tests again:

```
npm test


> jest --coverage --testRegex="^((?!-solution).)*\\.test\\.tsx?$"
 PASS  ./bookings-solution.test.ts
 PASS  ./flights-solution.test.ts
-------------|---------|----------|---------|---------|--------------
-----
File         | % Stmts | % Branch | % Funcs | % Lines | Uncovered
Line #s
-------------|---------|----------|---------|---------|--------------
-----
All files    |     100 |      100 |     100 |     100 |
 bookings.ts |     100 |      100 |     100 |     100 |
 flights.ts  |     100 |      100 |     100 |     100 |
-------------|---------|----------|---------|---------|--------------
-----


Test Suites: 2 passed, 2 total
Tests:       8 passed, 8 total
Snapshots:   0 total
Time:        0.694 s, estimated 1 s
Ran all test suites.
```

We've hit our goal of 100% line coverage!

CHAPTER 04: CLASSES AND OBJECTS

ACTIVITY 4.01: CREATING A USER MODEL USING CLASSES, OBJECTS, AND INTERFACES

Solution:

In this activity, we'll be building a user authentication system that will pass login data to a backend API to register and sign users into our baseball scorecard application. Perform the following steps to implement this activity:

1. Visit the following GitHub repository and download the activity project containing the specs and configuration elements: https://packt.link/oaWbW.

    The **activity-solution** directory contains the completed solution code, and the **activity-starter** directory provides the basic start code to work with.

2. Open the Visual Studio Code editor and then open the terminal. Change into the **activity-starter** directory in the terminal or command prompt and run the following command to install the dependencies:

```
npm install
```

    You will now see the following files in the **activity-starter** directory:

Figure 4.10: Activity project files

3. Open the **auth.ts** file inside the **activity-starter** folder and create an interface named **ILogin** containing two string attributes, namely, **email** and **password**. Write the following code to accomplish this:

```
interface ILogin{
    email: string;
    password:string;
}
```

4. Create a **Login** class that takes in an object that contains the string attributes of **email** and **password**. Also, pass the **ILogin** interface as a parameter to the **constructor** function inside the **Login** class:

```
export class Login{
    email: string;
    password: string;

    constructor(args: ILogin){
        this.email = args.email;
        this.password = args.password;
    }
}
```

5. Create an interface named **IAuth** containing two attributes, **user** and **source**. Here, the **user** attribute will be of the **Login** type, and the **source** attribute will be of the **string** type. Write the following code to implement this:

```
interface IAuth{
    user: Login;
    source: string;
}
```

6. Create an **Auth** class that takes in an object containing the attributes of **user** and **source**. Also, create a **constructor** function that will take the **IAuth** interface as a parameter. Write the following code to accomplish this:

```
export default class Auth{
    user: Login;
    source: string;
```

```
    constructor(args: IAuth){
        this.user = args.user;
        this.source = args.source;
    }
}
```

7. Next, we'll add a **validUser()** method to the **Auth** class, which returns a string stating that the user is authenticated if **email** is equal to **admin@ example.com**, and if **password** is equal to **secret123**. If either of those values doesn't match, the function will return a string stating that the user is not authenticated. Write the following code to define this function:

```
validUser(): string{
    const { email, password } = this.user;
    if(email === "admin@example.com"
      && password === "secret123"){
        return `Validating user…User is authenticated: true`;
    } else {
        return `Validating user…User is authenticated: false`;
    }
}
```

8. Create two objects of the **Login** class, namely, **goodUser** and **badUser**. For the **goodUser** object, set the **email** value to **admin@example.com** and **password** to **secret123**. For the **badUser** object, set the **email** value to **admin@example.com** and **password** to **whoops**. Write the following code to accomplish this:

```
const goodUser = new Login({
    email: "admin@example.com",
    password: "secret123"
});

const badUser = new Login({
    email: "admin@example.com",
    password: "whoops"
});
```

9. Create two objects of the **Auth** class, namely, **authAttemptFromGoodUser** and **authAttemptFromBadUser**. For the first object, assign the **goodUser** object of the **Login** class to the **user** attribute and **Google** to the **source** attribute. For the second object, assign the **badUser** object of the **Login** class to the **user** attribute and **Google** to the **source** attribute. Once both objects are created, call the **validUser()** function of the **Auth** class and print the results in the terminal. Write the following code to accomplish this:

```
const authAttemptFromGoodUser = new Auth({
    user: goodUser,
    source: "Google"
});

console.log(authAttemptFromGoodUser.validUser());

const authAttemptFromBadUser = new Auth({
    user: badUser,
    source: "Google"
});

console.log(authAttemptFromBadUser.validUser());
```

10. Now, in the terminal, type the following commands to generate the JavaScript code and run it:

```
tsc auth.ts
node auth.js
```

Once we run the preceding commands, the following output is displayed in the terminal:

```
Validating user...User is authenticated: true
Validating user...User is authenticated: false
```

In the preceding output, the **validUser()** function returns a **true** value when the correct details of **user** and **password** are passed. When incorrect details are passed, the function returns a **false** value.

CHAPTER 05: INTERFACES AND INHERITANCE

ACTIVITY 5.01: BUILDING A USER MANAGEMENT COMPONENT USING INTERFACES

Solution:

1. Create a user object interface with the following properties: **email :
   string**, **loginAt : number**, and **token : string**. Make **loginAt** and
   token optional:

```
interface UserObj {
    email: string
    loginAt?: number
    token?: string
}
```

2. Build a class interface with a global property user and use the interface created
   in *Step 1* to apply user object rules. You need to define a **getUser** method
   that returns the user object. Use the interface to ensure that the return object
   is a user object. Finally, define a **login** method that takes a **user** object and
   password(type string) as arguments. Use the user object interface as the
   user argument type:

```
interface UserClass {
    user: UserObj
    getUser(): UserObj
    login(user: UserObj, password: string):UserObj
}
```

3. Declare a class called **UserClass** that implements the class interface from
   Step 2. Your login method should assign the local function's **user** argument
   to the global user property and return the global user. The **getUser** method
   should return the global user:

```
class User implements UserClass {

    user:UserObj

    getUser(): UserObj {
        return this.user
    }
```

```
        login(user:  UserObj, password: string): UserObj {
            // set props user object
            return this.user = user
        }
    }
```

4. Create an instance of your class, as declared in *Step 2*:

```
const newUserClass:UserClass = new User()
```

5. Create a user object instance:

```
const newUser: UserObj = {
    email: "home@home.com",
    loginAt: new Date().getTime(),
    token: "123456"
}
```

6. Console out our methods to ensure that they are working as expected:

```
console.log(
    newUserClass.login(newUser, "password123")
)

console.log(
    newUserClass.getUser()
)
```

The expected output is as follows:

```
{ email: 'home@home.com', loginAt: 1614068072515, token: '123456' }
{ email: 'home@home.com', loginAt: 1614068072515, token: '123456' }
```

This user management class is a central location where you can isolate all your application's user-related functions and rules. The rules you have crafted by using interfaces to implement your code will ensure that your code is better supported, easier to work with, and bug-free.

ACTIVITY 5.02: CREATING A PROTOTYPE WEB APPLICATION FOR A VEHICLE SHOWROOM USING INHERITANCE

Solution:

1. Create a parent class that will hold all common methods and properties for a base vehicle, define a constructor method that allows you to initialize the base properties of this class, and add a method that returns your properties as an object. If necessary, add an access modifier to properties and class methods you want to control access to:

```
class Motor {
    private name: string
    wheels: number
    bodyType: string

    constructor(name: string, wheels: number, bodyType: string) {
        this.name = name
        this.wheels = wheels
        this.bodyType = bodyType
    }

    protected getName(): string {
        return this.name
    }

    buildMotor() {
        return {
            wheels: this.wheels,
            bodyType: this.bodyType,
            name: this.name
        }
    }
}
```

2. Derive two child classes from your parent class that are types of vehicles, for example, **Car** and **Truck**. Override your constructor to add some unique properties to your child classes based on the type of vehicles:

```
class Car extends Motor {
    rideHeight: number
    constructor(name: string, wheels: number, bodyType: string,
```

```
        rideHeight: number) {
                super(name, wheels, bodyType)
                this.rideHeight = rideHeight
        }
        _buildMotor() {
                return {
                        ...super.buildMotor,
                        rideHeight: this.rideHeight
                }
        }
}
class Truck extends Motor {
        offRoad: boolean
        constructor(name: string, wheels: number, bodyType: string,
offRoad: boolean) {
                super(name, wheels, bodyType)
                this.offRoad = offRoad
        }
        _buildMotor() {
                return {
                        wheels: this.wheels,
                        bodyType: this.bodyType,
                        offRoad: this.offRoad
                }
        }
}
```

3. Derive a class from one of the child classes created in *Step 3*, for example, **Suv**, which will have some of the things a truck might have, so it would be logical to extend **Truck**:

```
class Suv extends Truck {
        roofRack: boolean
        thirdRow: boolean

        constructor(name: string, wheels: number, bodyType: string,
                offRoad: boolean, roofRack: boolean, thirdRow: boolean) {
                super(name, wheels, bodyType, offRoad)
```

```
        this.roofRack = roofRack;
        this.thirdRow = thirdRow


    }
}
```

4. Instantiate your child class:

```
const car: Car = new Car('blueBird', 4, 'sedan', 14)
const truck: Truck = new Truck('blueBird', 4, 'sedan', true)
const suv: Suv = new Suv('xtrail', 4, 'box', true, true, true)
```

5. Console out our child class instance:

```
console.log(car)
console.log(truck)
console.log(suv)
```

You will obtain the following output:

```
Car { name: 'blueBird', wheels: 4, bodyType: 'sedan', rideHeight: 14
}
Truck { name: 'blueBird', wheels: 4, bodyType: 'sedan', offRoad: true
}
Suv {
  name: 'xtrail',
  wheels: 4,
  bodyType: 'box',
  offRoad: true,
  roofRack: true,
  thirdRow: true
}
```

In this activity, you created the bare minimum classes that we require for the web application. We have shown how we can build complexity, reuse, and extend application code with inheritance in TypeScript.

CHAPTER 06: ADVANCED TYPES

ACTIVITY 6.01: INTERSECTION TYPE

Solution:

1. Create a **Motor** type, which will house some common properties you may reuse on their own or in combination with other types to describe a vehicle object. You can use the following properties as a starting point: **color**, **doors**, **wheels**, and **fourWheelDrive**:

```
type Motor = {
    color: string;
    doors: number;
    wheels: number;
    fourWheelDrive: boolean;
}
```

2. Create a **Truck** type with properties common to a truck, for example, **doubleCab** and **winch**:

```
type Truck = {
    doubleCab: boolean;
    winch: boolean;
}
```

3. Intersect the two types to create a **PickUpTruck** type:

```
type PickUpTruck = Motor & Truck;
```

4. Build a **TruckBuilder** function that returns our **PickUpTruck** type and also takes **PickUpTruck** as an argument:

```
function TruckBuilder (truck: PickUpTruck): PickUpTruck {
    return truck
}

const pickUpTruck: PickUpTruck = {
    color: 'red',
    doors: 4,
    doubleCab: true,
    wheels: 4,
```

```
        fourWheelDrive: true,
        winch: true
    }
```

5. Console out the function return:

```
console.log (
        TruckBuilder(pickUpTruck)
)
```

You should see the following output once you run the file:

```
{
  color: 'red',
  doors: 4,
  doubleCab: true,
  wheels: 4,
  fourWheelDrive: true,
  winch: true
}
```

ACTIVITY 6.02: UNION TYPE

Solution:

1. Build a **LandPack** and an **AirPack** type. Make sure to have a literal to identify the package type:

```
type LandPack = {
    height: number,
    weight: number,
    type: "land",
    label?: string };

type AirPack = {
    height: number,
    weight: number,
    type : "air",
    label?: string };
```

2. Construct a union type, **ComboPack**, which can be **LandPack** or **AirPack**:

```
type ComboPack = LandPack | AirPack
```

3. Make a **Shipping** class to process your packages. Make sure to use your literal to identify your package types and modify your package with the correct label for its type:

```
class Shipping {
    Process(pack: ComboPack) {
        // check package type
        if(pack.type === "land") {
            return this.ToLand(pack);
        } else {
            return this.ToAir(pack);
        }
    }
    ToAir(pack: AirPack): AirPack {
        pack.label = "air cargo"
        return pack;
    }
    ToLand(pack: LandPack): LandPack {
        pack.label = "land cargo"
        return pack;
    }
}
```

4. Create two package objects of the **AirPack** and **LandPack** types. Then, instantiate your **Shipping** class, process your new objects, and console out the modified objects:

```
const airPack: AirPack = {
    height: 5,
    weight: 10,
    type: "air",
};

const landPack: LandPack = {
    height: 5,
    weight: 10,
    type: "land",
};

const shipping = new Shipping;
```

```
console.log(
    shipping.Process(airPack)
);


console.log(
    shipping.Process(landPack)
);
```

Once you run the file, you will obtain the following output:

```
{ height: 5, weight: 10, type: 'air', label: 'air cargo' }
{ height: 5, weight: 10, type: 'land', label: 'land cargo' }
```

ACTIVITY 6.03: INDEX TYPE

Solution:

1. Build your **PackageStatus** index type using an interface with a **status** property of the **string** type and a value of the **Boolean** type:

```
interface PackageStatus {
    [status: string]: boolean;}
```

2. Create a **Package** type that includes a property of the **PackageStatus** type and some common properties of a typical package:

```
type Package = {
    packageStatus: PackageStatus,
    barcode:   number,
    weight: number
}
```

3. Make a class to process your **Package** type, which takes the **Package** type on initialization, has a method to return your **packageStatus** property, and a method that updates and returns the **packageStatus** property:

```
class PackageProcess {

    pack: Package

    constructor(pack: Package) {
        this.pack = pack;
    }

    Status () {
```

```
            return this.pack.packageStatus;
    }
    UpdateStatus(status: string, state: boolean) {
        this.pack.packageStatus[status] = state;
        return this.Status();}
}
```

4. Create a **Package** object called **pack**:

```
const pack: Package = {
    packageStatus: {"shipped": false, "packed": true, "delivered":
true},
    barcode: 123456,
    weight: 28
};
```

5. Instantiate your **PackageProcess** class with your new **pack** object:

```
const processPack = new PackageProcess(pack)
```

6. Console out your **pack** status:

```
console.log(processPack.Status());
```

7. Update your **pack** status and console out your new **pack** status:

```
console.log(
    processPack.UpdateStatus("shipped", true)
);
```

Once you run the file, you should obtain the following output:

```
{ shipped: false, packed: true, delivered: true }
{ shipped: true, packed: true, delivered: true }
```

The first line in the preceding output displays the original **pack** status, whereas the second line displays the updated **pack** status.

CHAPTER 07: DECORATOR

ACTIVITY 7.01: CREATING DECORATORS FOR CALL COUNTING

Solution:

1. Create a class called **Person** with the public properties **firstName**, **lastName**, and **birthday**.

2. Add a constructor that initializes the properties via the constructor parameters:

```
class Person {
        constructor (public firstName: string,
                     public lastName: string,
                     public birthDate: Date) {

        }
}
```

3. Add a private field called **_title** and expose it via a **getter** and **setter** as a property called **title**:

```
    private _title: string;

    public get title() {
        return this._title;
    }

    public set title(value: string) {
        this._title = value;
    }
```

4. Add a method called **getFullName** that will return the full name of person:

```
    public getFullName() {
        return `${this.firstName} ${this.lastName}`;
    }
```

5. Add a method called **getAge** that will return the current age of the person (by subtracting the birthday from the current year):

```
    public getAge() {
        // only sometimes accurate
        const now = new Date();
        return now.getFullYear() - this.birthDate.getFullYear();
    }
```

6. Create a global object called **count** and initialize it to the empty object:

```
const count = {};
```

7. Create a constructor wrapping decorator factory called **CountClass** that will take a string parameter called **counterName**:

```
type Constructable = { new (...args: any[]): {} };

function CountClass(counterName: string) {
    return function <T extends Constructable>(constructor: T) {
        // wrapping code here
    }
}
```

8. Inside the wrapping code, increase the **count** object's property defined in the **counterName** parameter by 1 and then set the prototype chain of the wrapped constructor:

```
    const wrappedConstructor: any = function (...args: any[]) {
        const result = new constructor(...args);
        if (count[counterName]) {
            count[counterName]+=1;
        } else {
            count[counterName]=1;
        }
        return result;
    };
    wrappedConstructor.prototype = constructor.prototype;
    return wrappedConstructor;
```

9. Create a method wrapping decorator factory called **CountMethod** that will take a string parameter called **counterName**:

```
function CountMethod(counterName: string) {
    return function (target: any, propertyName: string,
                    descriptor: PropertyDescriptor) {
        // method wrapping code here
    }
}
```

10. Add checks for whether the descriptor parameter has **value**, **get**, and **set** properties:

```
if (descriptor.value) {
    // method decoration code
}
if (descriptor.get) {
    // get property accessor decoration code
}
if (descriptor.set) {
    // set property accessor decoration code
}
```

11. In each respective branch, add code that wraps the method:

```
// method decoration code
const original = descriptor.value;
descriptor.value = function (...args: any[]) {
    // counter management code here
    return original.apply(this, args);
}
// get property accessor decoration code
const original = descriptor.get;
descriptor.get = function () {
    // counter management code here
    return original.apply(this, []);
}
// set property accessor decoration code
const original = descriptor.set;
descriptor.set = function (value: any) {
    // counter management code here
    return original.apply(this, [value]);
}
```

12. Inside the wrapping code, increase the **count** object's property defined in the **counterName** parameter by 1:

```
// counter management code
if (count[counterName]) {
    count[counterName]+=1;
} else {
    count[counterName]=1;
}
```

13. Decorate the class using the **CountClass** decorator, with a **person** parameter:

```
@CountClass('person')
class Person{
```

14. Decorate **getFullName**, **getAge**, and the **title** property getter with the **CountMethod** decorator, with the **person-full-name**, **person-age**, and **person-title** parameters, respectively:

```
@CountMethod('person-full-name')
public getFullName() {
@CountMethod('person-age')
public getAge() {
@CountMethod('person-title')
public get title() {
```

15. Write code outside the class that will instantiate three **person** objects:

```
const first = new Person("Brendan", "Eich", new Date(1961,6,4));
const second = new Person("Anders", "Hejlsberg ", new Date(1960,11,2));
const third = new Person("Alan", "Turing", new Date(1912,5,23));
```

16. Write code that will call the **getFullName** and **getAge** methods on the objects:

```
const fname = first.getFullName();
const sname = second.getFullName();
const tname = third.getFullName();

const fage = first.getAge();
const sage = second.getAge();
const tage = third.getAge();
```

17. Write code that will check whether the **title** property is empty and set it to something if it is:

```
if (!first.title) {
    first.title = "Mr."
}


if (!second.title) {
    second.title = "Mr."
}


if (!third.title) {
    third.title = "Mr."
}
```

18. Write code that will log the **count** object to the console:

```
console.log(count);
```

Once you run the file, you will obtain the following output on the console:

```
{
  person: 3,
  'person-full-name': 3,
  'person-age': 3,
  'person-title': 6
}
```

ACTIVITY 7.02: USING DECORATORS TO APPLY CROSS-CUTTING CONCERNS

Solution:

1. Create the code for the **BasketBallGame** class:

```
interface Team {
    score: number;
    name: string;
}


class BasketBallGame {
    private team1: Team;
    private team2: Team;

    constructor(teamName1: string, teamName2: string) {
```

```
            this.team1 = { score: 0, name: teamName1 };
            this.team2 = { score: 0, name: teamName2 };
        }


        getScore() {
            return `${this.team1.score}:${this.team2.score}`;
        }


        updateScore(byPoints: number, updateTeam1: boolean) {
            if (updateTeam1) {
                this.team1.score += byPoints;
            } else {
                this.team2.score += byPoints;
            }
        }
    }
```

2. Create a class decorator factory called **Authenticate** that will take a
   permission parameter and return a class decorator with constructor
   wrapping. The class decorator should load the **permissions** metadata
   property (array of **strings**), then check if the passed parameter is an element
   of the array. If the passed parameter is not an element of the array, the class
   decorator should throw an error, and if present, it should continue with the
   class creation:

```
    type Constructable = { new (...args: any[]): {} };


    function Authenticate(permission: string) {
        return function <T extends Constructable>(constructor: T) {
            const wrappedConstructor: any = function (...args: any[])
{
                if (Reflect.hasMetadata("permissions",
wrappedConstructor)) {
                    const permissions = Reflect.
getMetadata("permissions",

wrappedConstructor) as string[];
                    if (!permissions.includes(permission)) {
                        throw Error(`Permission ${permission} not
present`);
                    }
                }
```

```
                const result = new constructor(...args);
                return result;
            };
            wrappedConstructor.prototype = constructor.prototype;
            return wrappedConstructor;
        };
    }
```

3. Define a metadata property of the **BasketballGame** class called **permissions** with the value ["**canUpdateScore**"]:

```
    Reflect.defineMetadata("permissions", ["canUpdateScore"],
BasketBallGame);
```

4. Apply the class decorator factory on the **BasketballGame** class with a parameter value of "**canUpdateScore**":

```
    @Authenticate("canUpdateScore")
    class BasketBallGame {
```

5. Create a method decorator called **MeasureDuration** that will use method wrapping to start a timer before the method body is executed and stop it after it's done. You need to calculate the duration and push it to a metadata property called **durations** for the method:

```
    function MeasureDuration() {
        return function (target: any, propertyName: string,
                                    descriptor: PropertyDescriptor)
{
            if (descriptor.value) {
                const original = descriptor.value;
                descriptor.value = function (...args: any[]) {
                    const start = Date.now();
                    const result = original.apply(this, args);
                    const end = Date.now();
                    const duration = end-start;
                    if (Reflect.hasMetadata("durations", target,
propertyName)) {
                        const existing = Reflect.getMetadata("durations",
                                            target,
propertyName) as number[];
                        Reflect.defineMetadata("durations", existing.
concat(duration),
                                            target,
propertyName);
                    } else {
```

```
                        Reflect.defineMetadata("durations", [duration],
                                                target,
    propertyName)
                    }
                 return result;
              }
           }
         }
       }
```

6. Apply the **MeasureDuration** method decorator on the **updateScore** method:

```
    @MeasureDuration()
    updateScore(byPoints: number, updateTeam1: boolean) {
```

7. Create a method decorator factory called **Audit** that will take a message parameter and return a method decorator. The method decorator should use method wrapping to get the arguments and the return value of the method. After the successful execution of the original method, it should display the audit log to the console:

```
    function Audit(message: string) {
        return function (target: any, propertyName: string,
                            descriptor: PropertyDescriptor)
    {
            if (descriptor.value) {
                const original = descriptor.value;
                descriptor.value = function (...args: any[]) {
                    const result = original.apply(this, args);
                    console.log(`[AUDIT] ${message} (${propertyName})
    called with:`)
                    console.log("[AUDIT]", args);
                    console.log("[AUDIT] and returned result:")
                    console.log("[AUDIT]", result);
                    return result;
                }
            }
        }
    }
```

8. Apply the **Audit** method decorator factory on the **updateScore** method, with a parameter value of **Updated score**:

```
@MeasureDuration()
@Audit("Updated score")
updateScore(byPoints: number, updateTeam1: boolean) {
```

9. Create a parameter decorator called **OneTwoThree** that will add the decorated parameter in the **one-two-three** metadata property:

```
function OneTwoThree(target: any, propertyKey: string,
                                    parameterIndex: number) {
    if (Reflect.hasMetadata("one-two-three", target, propertyKey))
{
        const existing = Reflect.getMetadata("one-two-three",
                                    target, propertyKey) as
number[];
        Reflect.defineMetadata("one-two-three",
                    existing.concat(parameterIndex), target,
propertyKey);
        } else {
        Reflect.defineMetadata("one-two-three",
                                [parameterIndex], target,
propertyKey);
        }
    }
```

10. Create a method decorator called **Validate** that will use method wrapping to load all values for the **one-two-three** metadata property, and for all marked parameters, check their value. If the value is 1, 2, or 3, you should continue the execution of the original method. If not, you should stop the execution with an error:

```
function Validate() {
    return function (target: any, propertyKey:string,
                                    descriptor: PropertyDescriptor)
{
        const original = descriptor.value;
        descriptor.value = function (...args: any[]) {
            // validate parameters
            if (Reflect.hasMetadata("one-two-three",
                                    target, propertyKey)) {
                const markedParams = Reflect.getMetadata("one-two-
three",
                                    target, propertyKey) as
number[];
```

```
                    for (const marked of markedParams) {
                        if (![1,2,3].includes(args[marked])) {
                            throw Error(`The parameter at position
${marked} can only be 1, 2 or 3`);
                        }
                    }
                }
                return original.apply(this, args);
            }
        }
    }
```

11. Apply the **OneTwoThree** decorator to the **byPoints** parameter of **updateScore** and apply the **Validate** decorator to the **updateScore** method.

```
    @MeasureDuration()
    @Audit("Updated score")
    @Validate()
    updateScore(@OneTwoThree byPoints: number, updateTeam1: boolean)
{
```

12. Create a **game** object and update its score a few times:

```
const game = new BasketBallGame("LA Lakers", "Boston Celtics");
game.updateScore(3, true);
game.updateScore(2, false);
game.updateScore(2, true);
game.updateScore(2, false);
game.updateScore(2, false);
game.updateScore(2, true);
game.updateScore(2, false);
```

When you run the file, the console should reflect the application of all decorators:

```
[AUDIT] Updated score (updateScore) called with arguments:
[AUDIT] [ 3, true ]
[AUDIT] and returned result:
[AUDIT] undefined
[AUDIT] Updated score (updateScore) called with arguments:
[AUDIT] [ 2, false ]
[AUDIT] and returned result:
[AUDIT] undefined
```

```
[AUDIT] Updated score (updateScore) called with arguments:
[AUDIT] [ 2, true ]
[AUDIT] and returned result:
[AUDIT] undefined
[AUDIT] Updated score (updateScore) called with arguments:
[AUDIT] [ 2, false ]
[AUDIT] and returned result:
[AUDIT] undefined
[AUDIT] Updated score (updateScore) called with arguments:
[AUDIT] [ 2, false ]
[AUDIT] and returned result:
[AUDIT] undefined
[AUDIT] Updated score (updateScore) called with arguments:
[AUDIT] [ 2, true ]
[AUDIT] and returned result:
[AUDIT] undefined
[AUDIT] Updated score (updateScore) called with arguments:
[AUDIT] [ 2, false ]
[AUDIT] and returned result:
[AUDIT] undefined
  7:8
```

CHAPTER 08: DEPENDENCY INJECTION IN TYPESCRIPT

ACTIVITY 8.01: DI-BASED CALCULATOR

Solution:

In this activity, we will build a basic calculator that utilizes DI to evaluate mathematical expressions, as well as logging its output to either the console or a file:

1. To start things off, define the basic building block of our calculator – an operator. This is defined via an interface, which actual implementations can rely on:

```
export interface Operator {
    readonly symbol: string;

    evaluate(a: number, b: number): number;
}
```

You need to create this file in the **src/interfaces** folder and save it as **operator.interface.ts**.

2. Next, implement the first operator – the addition operator. This will be a class that implements the **Operator** interface:

```
import { Operator } from '../interfaces/operator.interface';

export class AddOperator implements Operator {
    readonly symbol = '+';

    public evaluate(a: number, b: number) {
    return a + b;
    }
}
```

The preceding code needs to be written in a file called **add.operator.ts** in **src\operators**.

3. Make this operator available for injection by InversifyJS by adding the @ **injectable** decorator to the class:

```
import { injectable } from 'inversify';
import { Operator } from '../interfaces/operator.interface';

@injectable()
export class AddOperator implements Operator {
```

```
    readonly symbol = '+';

    public evaluate(a: number, b: number) {
        return a + b;
    }
}
```

4. Next, since interfaces don't exist at runtime, we need to create some runtime representation of our abstraction for **AddOperator**. This is usually done using symbols, and will be used by InversifyJS at runtime to understand what needs to be injected. We'll define it under a **TYPES** constant, which we'll be able to add other symbols for later:

```
export const TYPES = {
    AddOperator: Symbol.for('AddOperator'),
};
```

This code needs to be written in a new file saved in the **src\types** folder. We have named this file **index.ts**.

5. Now, build a first draft for our calculator, which will use **AddOperator**, via DI:

```
import { injectable, inject } from 'inversify';
import { TYPES } from '../types';
import { AddOperator } from '../operators/add.operator';

@injectable()
export class Calculator {
    constructor(@inject(TYPES.AddOperator) private addOperator:
AddOperator) {}

    evaluate(expression: string) {
        const expressionParts = expression.match(/[\d\.]+|\D+/g);
        if (expressionParts === null) return null;

        // for now, we're only going to support basic expressions:
X+Y
        const [operandA, operator, operandB] = expressionParts;
        if (operator !== this.addOperator.symbol) {
            throw new Error(`Unsupported operator. Expected ${this.
addOperator.symbol}, received: ${operator}.`);
        }
```

```
        const result = this.addOperator.evaluate(Number(operandA),
Number(operandB));


        return result;
    }
}
```

Here, we implement a **Calculator** class that has a single method –
evaluate, which takes in an expression as a string, and returns the result for
that expression. This code needs to be written in a new file called **index.ts**,
saved in the **src/calculator** folder.

> **NOTE**
>
> The current implementation only supports expressions in the form of X+Y
> (where X and Y can be any numbers). We'll fix that later in the activity.

Calculator gets **AddOperator** in DI, and in order to evaluate the expression,
it first runs through a regular expression to split it by numbers, and then
it *destructures* the result array. Lastly, it uses the **evaluate** method of
AddOperator to perform the final expression evaluation.

This means that the calculator's responsibility is only to destructure the
expression into its individual parts, and then pass it off to **AddOperator** to
handle the math evaluation logic. This demonstrates how using DI helps to retain
the single responsibility principle of SOLID.

6. Configure the IoC container (in the **src/ioc.config.ts** file) so that
   Calculator can receive **AddOperator** when it asks for **TYPES.
   AddOperator**:

```
import { Container } from 'inversify';
import { Calculator } from './calculator/index';
import { Operator } from './interfaces/operator.interface';
import { AddOperator } from './operators/add.operator';
import { TYPES } from './types';


export const container = new Container();


container.bind<Operator>(TYPES.AddOperator).to(AddOperator);
container.bind(Calculator).toSelf();
```

7. Finally, our main file (**src/main.ts**), which will kick things off when we run the application, is as follows:

```
import 'reflect-metadata';

import { Calculator } from './calculator/index';
import { container } from './ioc.config';

const calculator = container.get(Calculator);

try {
    const result = calculator.evaluate('13+5');
    console.log('result is', result);
} catch (err) {
    console.error(err);
}
```

This is just using our previously defined IoC container and asking it for a **Calculator** instance. This is how we ask for instances of symbols explicitly in InversifyJS in an imperative API, which we need here, since we want to kick things off. Since InversifyJS is the one creating **Calculator**, it also looks at its constructor and sees that we've asked for a **TYPES.AddOperator**, which it then looks up in the IoC container again to resolve and gives that to the calculator's constructor.

Once you run this file, you should obtain the following output:

```
result is 18
```

Note that you can either run the code by executing **npm start** in the **activity-starter** folder or by executing **npx ts-node main.ts** in the **src** folder.

> **NOTE**
>
> If the **AddOperator** class were also to require dependencies using @ **inject**, the same process described above would be repeated again to get them, and so on recursively until all dependencies have been resolved.

8. Next, we can implement the other operators, similar to how we did with **AddOperator** – just replace the symbol with the relevant one (**-**, *****, **/**) and the evaluate method's implementation with the relevant math operation:

9. Here is the code for **SubtractOperator** (**subtract.operator.ts**):

```
// operators/subtract.operator.ts
import { injectable } from 'inversify';
import { Operator } from '../interfaces/operator.interface';

@injectable()
export class SubtractOperator implements Operator {
    readonly symbol = '-';

    public evaluate(a: number, b: number) {
        return a - b;
    }
}
```

10. Here is the code for **MultiplyOperator** (**multiply.operator.ts**):

```
// operators/multiply.operator.ts
import { injectable } from 'inversify';
import { Operator } from '../interfaces/operator.interface';

@injectable()
export class MultiplyOperator implements Operator {
    readonly symbol = '*';

    public evaluate(a: number, b: number) {
        return a * b;
    }
}
```

11. Here is the code for **DivideOperator** (**divide.operator.ts**):

```
// operators/divide.operator.ts
import { injectable } from 'inversify';
import { Operator } from '../interfaces/operator.interface';

@injectable()
```

```
export class DivideOperator implements Operator {
    readonly symbol = '/';

    public evaluate(a: number, b: number) {
        return a / b;
    }
}
```

Now, instead of creating an injection token for each **Operator**, injecting each one into **Calculator**, and then acting on each, we can create a more generic implementation of **Calculator** with the help of the **@multiInject** decorator. This decorator allows an injection token to be specified and an array of all implementations registered for that token to be obtained. This way, **Calculator** is not even coupled to an abstraction for any specific operator and only gets a dynamic list of operators, which can have any implementation as long as it conforms to the **Operator** interface.

12. Update the **types/index.ts** file with the following code:

```
export const TYPES = {
    Operator: Symbol.for('Operator'),
};
```

This replaces our **AddOperator** symbol from earlier with a more generic one.

13. Update the calculator app code (**src/calculator/index.ts**):

```
import { injectable, multiInject } from 'inversify';
import { Operator } from '../interfaces/operator.interface';
import { tryParseNumberString, tryParseOperatorSymbol } from "../
utils/math";
import { TYPES } from '../types';

@injectable()
export class Calculator {
    constructor(@multiInject(TYPES.Operator) private operators:
Operator[]) {}

    evaluate(expression: string) {
        // same as before...
    }
}
```

Note that in further steps, you will need to modify the preceding code to include two functions, **tryParseNumberString** and **tryParseOperatorSymbol**. Both these functions are created in the **math.ts** file placed in the **src/utils** folder.

14. Update the **ioc.config.ts** file:

```
import { Container } from 'inversify';
import { Calculator } from './calculator';
import { Operator } from './interfaces/operator.interface';
import { AddOperator } from './operators/add.operator';
import { DivideOperator } from './operators/divide.operator';
import { MultiplyOperator } from './operators/multiply.operator';
import { SubtractOperator } from './operators/subtract.operator';
import { TYPES } from './types';


export const container = new Container();


container.bind<Operator>(TYPES.Operator).to(AddOperator);
container.bind<Operator>(TYPES.Operator).to(SubtractOperator);
container.bind<Operator>(TYPES.Operator).to(MultiplyOperator);
container.bind<Operator>(TYPES.Operator).to(DivideOperator);


container.bind(Calculator).toSelf();
```

15. Next, fix the naïve **evaluate** method of **Calculator** to be more generic, too. First, instead of relying on a specific token, **map** all expression parts and parse them:

```
evaluate(expression: string) {
    // ...
    const parsedExpressionParts = expressionParts.map(part => {
        const numberParseResult = tryParseNumberString(part);
        if (numberParseResult.isNumberString) return
numberParseResult.number;
        const operatorParseResult = tryParseOperatorSymbol(part,
this.operators);
        if (operatorParseResult.isOperatorSymbol) return
operatorParseResult.operator;

        throw new Error(`Unexpected part: ${part}`);
    });
}
```

This will give us back an array of numbers and operators.

> **NOTE**
>
> Try to implement **tryParseNumberString** and **tryParseOperatorSymbol** yourself. However, you can refer to **utils/math.ts** to help you complete this step.

16. Then, reduce this array to get our final result:

```
evaluate(expression: string) {
    // ...
    const { result } = parsedExpressionParts.reduce<{ result: number;
queuedOperator: Operator | null }>((acc, part) => {
        if (typeof part === 'number') {
            // this is the first number we've encountered, just set
the result to that.
            if (acc.queuedOperator === null) {
                return { ...acc, result: part };
            }


            // there's a queued operator - evaluate the previous
result with this and
            // clear the queued one.
            return {
                queuedOperator: null,
                result: acc.queuedOperator.evaluate(acc.result,
part),
            };
        }

        // this is an operator - queue it for later execution
        return {
            ...acc,
            queuedOperator: part,
        };
    }, { result: 0, queuedOperator: null });

    return result;
}
```

17. Simplify the code in the **ioc.config.ts** file even further by leveraging barrels. Create **operator/index.ts** with the following code:

```
// operators/index.ts
export * from './add.operator';
export * from './divide.operator';
export * from './multiply.operator';
export * from './subtract.operator';
```

18. Update the **ioc.config.ts** file:

```
// ioc.config.ts
import { Container } from 'inversify';
import { Calculator } from './calculator';
import { Operator } from './interfaces/operator.interface';
import * as Operators from './operators';
import { TYPES } from './types';

export const container = new Container();

Object.values(Operators).forEach(Operator => {
    container.bind<Operator>(TYPES.Operator).to(Operator);
});

container.bind(Calculator).toSelf();
```

This means we now import an **Operators** object from the barrel file, which includes everything that's exposed there. We take the values of that barrel object and bind each one to **TYPES.Operator**, generically.

This means that adding another **Operator** object only requires us to create a new class that implements the **Operator** interface and add it to our **operators/index.ts** file. The rest of the code should work without any changes.

19. Our **main.ts** file is changed to a slightly more complicated expression:

```
import 'reflect-metadata';

import { Calculator } from './calculator';
import { container } from './ioc.config';
```

```
    const calculator = container.get(Calculator);

    try {
        const result = calculator.evaluate('13*10+20');
        console.log('result is', result);
    } catch (err) {
        console.error(err);
    }
}
```

When you run the **main.ts** file (using **npx ts-node main.ts**), you should obtain the following output:

```
result is 150
```

Bonus:

1. As a bonus, let's say that we want some reporting on the operations performed in the calculator. We can add logging pretty easily without too many changes. We'll create two reporting implementations, one to the console and another to a filesystem:

    > **NOTE**
    >
    > The filesystem implementation will only work in a Node.js environment, since it will use some modules only available to it.

2. Define the **Logger** interface:

```
export interface Logger {
    log(message: string, ...args: any[]): void;
    warn(message: string, ...args: any[]): void;
    error(message: string, ...args: any[]): void;
}
```

This will serve as the public API that the consumers wanting a logger can use, and that our implementations will need to adhere to.

3. Create the console-based implementation of **Logger** first:

```
import { injectable } from 'inversify';
import { Logger } from '../interfaces/logger.interface';

@injectable()
```

```
export class ConsoleLogger implements Logger {
    log(message: string, ...args: any[]) {
        console.log('[LOG]', message, ...args);
    }

    warn(message: string, ...args: any[]) {
        console.warn('[WARN]', message, ...args);
    }

    error(message: string, ...args: any[]) {
        console.error('[ERROR]', message, ...args);
    }
}
```

This is a simple wrapper class around the **console** object that's built into browser engines and Node.js. It adheres to our **Logger** interface, and so allows consumers to depend on it. For the example, we've also added the type of the message to the beginning of the actual output.

4. Next, create an injection token for it, and register it in our container. The updated code for the **types/index.ts** file is as follows:

```
// types/index.ts
export const TYPES = {
    Operator: Symbol.for('Operator'),
    Logger: Symbol.for('Logger'),
};
```

The updated code for the **src/ioc.config.ts** file is as follows:

```
// ioc.config.ts
import { Container } from 'inversify';
import { Calculator } from './calculator';
import { Logger } from './interfaces/logger.interface';
import { Operator } from './interfaces/operator.interface';
import { ConsoleLogger } from './logger/console.logger';
import * as Operators from './operators';
import { TYPES } from './types';

export const container = new Container();

Object.values(Operators).forEach(Operator => {
    container.bind<Operator>(TYPES.Operator).to(Operator);
```

```
    });


    container.bind(Calculator).toSelf();


    container.bind<Logger>(TYPES.Logger).to(ConsoleLogger);
```

5. Finally, use the logger in our **Calculator** class:

```
import { injectable, multiInject, inject, optional } from
'inversify';
import { Operator } from '../interfaces/operator.interface';

import { TYPES } from '../types';

import { tryParseNumberString, tryParseOperatorSymbol } from '../
utils/math';

import { Logger } from '../interfaces/logger.interface';


@injectable()
export class Calculator {
    constructor(
        @multiInject(TYPES.Operator) private operators: Operator[],
        @inject(TYPES.Logger) @optional() private logger?: Logger
    ) {}


    evaluate(expression: string) {
        // ...


        const { result } = parsedExpressionParts.reduce<{ result:
number; queuedOperator: Operator | null }>( ... );


        this.logger && this.logger.log(`Calculated result of
expression: ${expression} to be: ${result}`);


        return result;
    }
}
```

Notice that we use the **@optional** decorator to indicate to InversifyJS that **Calculator** doesn't *require* a **Logger** to operate, but if it has one it can inject, **Calculator** can use it. This is also why it's marked as an optional argument in the constructor, and why we need to check whether it exists before calling the **log** method.

The output to the console when running it should be as follows:

```
[LOG] Calculated result of expression:13*10+20 is 150
```

Now, let's say we want to replace our console-based logger with a file-based one, which will persist across runs so that we can track the calculator's evaluation history.

6. Create a **FileLogger** class that implements **Logger**:

```
import fs from 'fs';
import { injectable } from 'inversify';
import { Logger } from '../interfaces/logger.interface';

@injectable()
export class FileLogger implements Logger {
    private readonly loggerPath: string = '/tmp/calculator.log';

    log(message: string, ...args: any[]) {
        this.logInternal('LOG', message, args);
    }

    warn(message: string, ...args: any[]) {
        this.logInternal('WARN', message, args);
    }

    error(message: string, ...args: any[]) {
        this.logInternal('ERROR', message, args);
    }

    private logInternal(level: string, message: string, ...args:
any[]) {
        fs.appendFileSync(this.loggerPath, this.
logLineFormatter(level, message, args));
    }

    private logLineFormatter(level: string, message: string, ...args:
any[]) {
        return `[${level}]: ${message}${args}\n`;
    }
}
```

7. And finally, all we need to do in order to replace our console-based logger with a file-based one is a single-line change in our IoC container configuration.

    For console-based logging, use this command:

    ```
    container.bind<Logger>(TYPES.Logger).to(ConsoleLogger);
    ```

    For file-based logging, use this command:

    ```
    container.bind<Logger>(TYPES.Logger).to(FileLogger);
    ```

    Make sure to import this logger correctly in the **ioc.config.ts** file.

    The final output to the file is as follows:

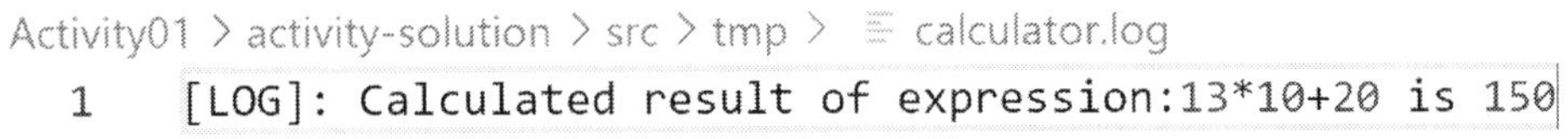

    Activity01 > activity-solution > src > tmp > ≡ calculator.log

    ```
    1    [LOG]: Calculated result of expression:13*10+20 is 150
    ```

Figure 8.8: Final output of the file-based logger in activity-starter/src//tmp/calculator.log, after changing the app to use it

CHAPTER 09: GENERICS AND CONDITIONAL TYPES

ACTIVITY 9.01: CREATING A DEEPPARTIAL<T> TYPE

Solution:

Let's build this type up, step by step:

1. First, let's create a **PartialPrimitive** type:

```
type PartialPrimitive = string | number | boolean | symbol | bigint |
Function | Date;
```

2. Then, let's start by defining a basic **DeepPartial<T>** type:

```
type DeepPartial<T> = T extends PartialPrimitive ? T : Partial<T>;
```

Next, we need to handle more complex structures – such as arrays, sets, and maps. These require using the **infer** keyword, and in addition to that, require some more "manual wiring" for each of these types.

3. Let's start with adding handling for the **Array** type:

```
type DeepPartial<T> =
     T extends PartialPrimitive
     ? T
     : T extends Array<infer U>
     ? Array<DeepPartial<U>>
     : Partial<T>;
```

This would've worked, but due to current limitations in TypeScript at the time of writing, this doesn't compile, since **DeepPartial<T>** circularly references itself:

```
21    type DeepPart  type DeepPartial<T> = any
22          T extend
23          ? T          Type 'DeepPartial' is not generic. ts(2315)
24          : T exte  Peek Problem    No quick fixes available
25          ? Array<DeepPartial<U>>
26          : Partial<T>;
```

Figure 9.17: Current TypeScript version limitation not allowing generic types to reference themselves

To work around this, we'll create a helper type, **DeepPartialArray\<T\>**, and use it:

```
interface DeepPartialArray<T> extends Array<DeepPartial<T>> {}

type DeepPartial<T> =
    T extends PartialPrimitive
    ? T
    : T extends Array<infer U>
    ? DeepPartialArray<U>
    : Partial<T>;
```

This works around the problem and compiles fine.

4. Next, to support a **Set**, a similar approach to what we did in the previous step is needed, so we'll create an **interface** to serve as a "middle-man" for building the entire generic type:

```
interface DeepPartialArray<T> extends Array<DeepPartial<T>> {}
interface DeepPartialSet<T> extends Set<DeepPartial<T>> {}

type DeepPartial<T> = T extends PartialPrimitive
    ? T
    : T extends Array<infer U>
    ? DeepPartialArray<U>
    : T extends Set<infer U>
    ? DeepPartialSet<U>
    : Partial<T>;
```

5. Similarly to arrays and sets, maps also need the approach wherein we need create an **interface** to serve as a "middle-man" for building the entire generic type:

```
interface DeepPartialArray<T> extends Array<DeepPartial<T>> {}
interface DeepPartialSet<T> extends Set<DeepPartial<T>> {}
interface DeepPartialMap<K, V> extends Map<DeepPartial<K>,
DeepPartial<V>> {}

type DeepPartial<T> = T extends PartialPrimitive
    ? T
    : T extends Array<infer U>
    ? DeepPartialArray<U>
    : T extends Map<infer K, infer V>
```

```
      ? DeepPartialMap<K, V>
      : T extends Set<infer U>
      ? DeepPartialSet<U>
      : Partial<T>;
```

> **NOTE**
>
> This workaround is no longer needed as of TypeScript 3.7.

6. Lastly, let's make our **DeepPartial\<T\>** type support objects too:

```
type DeepPartial<T> = T extends PartialPrimitive
    ? T
    : T extends Array<infer U>
    ? DeepPartialArray<U>
    : T extends Map<infer K, infer V>
    ? DeepPartialMap<K, V>
    : T extends Set<infer U>
    ? DeepPartialSet<U>
    : T extends {}
    ? { [K in keyof T]?: DeepPartial<T[K]> }
    : Partial<T>;
```

This completes the **DeepPartial\<T\>** implementation.

A great use case for the **DeepPartial\<T\>** type is in a server-side **PATCH** method handler, which updates a given resource with new data. In **PATCH** requests, all fields are usually optional:

```
import express from 'express';

const app = express();

app.patch('/users/:userId', async (req, res) => {
    const userId = req.params.userId;
    const userUpdateData: DeepPartial<User> = req.body;
```

```
        const user = await User.getById(userId);
    await user.update(userUpdateData);


    await user.save();


    res.status(200).end(user);
});
```

Notice that we use **DeepPartial<User>** to correctly type the body of the
request, before passing it in the **update** method:

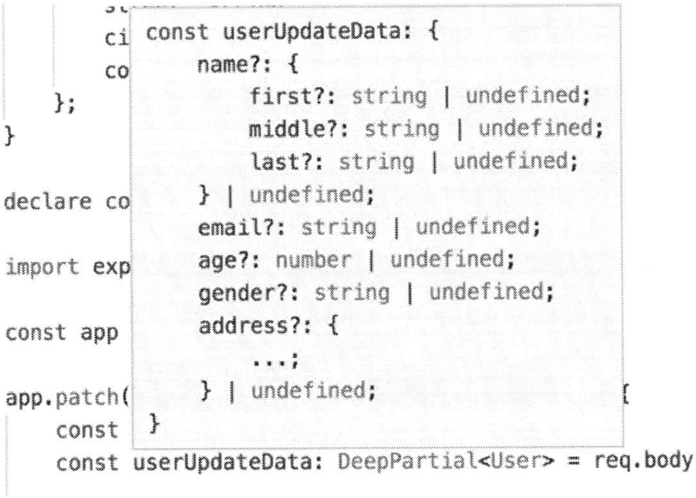

```
const userUpdateData: {
    name?: {
        first?: string | undefined;
        middle?: string | undefined;
        last?: string | undefined;
    } | undefined;
    email?: string | undefined;
    age?: number | undefined;
    gender?: string | undefined;
    address?: {
        ...;
    } | undefined;
}
const userUpdateData: DeepPartial<User> = req.body
```

Figure 9.18: The correctly typed request body

As can be seen in the preceding figure, due to the usage of **DeepPartial<T>**,
the request's body is typed correctly, such that all fields are optional, including
nested ones.

CHAPTER 10: EVENT LOOP AND ASYNCHRONOUS BEHAVIOR

ACTIVITY 10.01: MOVIE BROWSER USING XHR AND CALLBACKS

Solution:

1. In the **script.ts** file, locate the **search** function and verify that it takes a single string parameter and that its body is empty.

2. Construct a new **XMLHttpRequest** object:

```
const xhr = new XMLHttpRequest();
```

3. Construct a new string for the search result URL using the **getSearchUrl** method:

```
const url = getSearchUrl(value);
```

4. Call the **open** and **send** methods of the **xhr** object:

```
xhr.open('GET', url);
xhr.send();
```

5. Add an event handler for the **xhr** object's **onload** event. Take the response and parse it as a JSON object. Store the result in a variable of the **SearchResultApi** interface. This data will have the results of our search in a **results** field. If we get no results, this means that our search failed:

```
xhr.onload = function() {
    const data = JSON.parse(this.response) as SearchResultApi;
}
```

6. If the search returned no results, call the **clearResults** method:

```
if (data.results.length === 0) {
    clearResults(value);
}
```

7. If the search returned some results, just take the first one and store it in a variable, ignoring the other ones:

```
else {
    const resultMovie = data.results[0];
}
```

8. Inside the **onload** handler, in the successful search branch, create a new **XMLHttpRequest** object:

```
const movieXhr = new XMLHttpRequest();
```

9. Construct a new string for the search result URL using the
    getMovieUrl method:

    ```
    const movieUrl = getMovieUrl(resultMovie.id);
    ```

10. Call the **open** and **send** method of the constructed **xhr** object:

    ```
    movieXhr.open('GET', movieUrl);
    movieXhr.send();
    ```

11. Add an event handler for the **xhr** object's **onload** event. Take the
    response and parse it as a JSON object. Store the result in a variable of the
    MovieResultApi interface. This response will have the general data for our
    movie, specifically, everything except the people who were involved in the movie.
    We will need to have another call to the API to get the data about the people:

    ```
    movieXhr.onload = function () {
        const movieData: MovieResultApi = JSON.parse(this.response);
    ```

12. Inside the **onload** handler, create a new **XMLHttpRequest** object:

    ```
    const peopleXhr = new XMLHttpRequest();
    ```

13. Construct a new string for the search result URL using the
    getPeopleUrl method:

    ```
    const peopleUrl = getPeopleUrl(resultMovie.id);
    ```

14. Call the **open** and **send** method of the constructed **xhr** object:

    ```
    peopleXhr.open('GET', peopleUrl);
    peopleXhr.send();
    ```

15. Add an event handler for the **xhr** object's **onload** event. Take the
    response, and parse it as a JSON object. Store the result in a variable of the
    PeopleResultApi interface. This response will have data about the people
    who were involved in the movie:

    ```
    const data = JSON.parse(this.response) as PeopleResultApi;
    ```

16. Now we actually have all the data we need, so we can actually create our own
    object, inside the people **onload** handler, which is inside the movie **onload**
    handler, which is inside the search **onload** handler.

    The people data has **cast** and **crew** properties. We'll only take the first six cast
    members, so first sort the **cast** property according to the **order** property of
    the cast members. Then slice off the first six cast members into a new array:

    ```
    data.cast.sort((f, s) => f.order - s.order);
    const mainActors = data.cast.slice(0, 6);
    ```

17. Transform the cast data (which is **CastResultApi** objects) into your own **Character** objects. We need to map the **character** field of **CastResultApi** to the **name** field of **Character**, the **name** field to the **actor** name, and the **profile_path** field to the **image** property:

```
const characters: Character[] = mainActors.map(actor => ({
    name: actor.character,
    actor: actor.name,
    image: actor.profile_path
}))
```

18. From the **crew** property of the people data, we'll only need the director and the writer. Since there can be multiple directors and writers, we'll get the names of all directors and writers and concatenate them, respectively. For the directors, from the **crew** property, filter the people who have a **department** of **Directing** and a **job** of **Director**. For those objects, take the **name** property, and **join** it together with an **&** in between:

```
const directors = data.crew
    .filter(person => person.department === "Directing" && person.
job === "Director")
    .map(person => person.name)
    const directedBy = directors.join(" & ");
```

19. For the writers, from the **crew** property, filter the people who have a **department** of **Writing** and a **job** of **Writer**. For those objects, take the **name** property, and **join** it together with an **&** in between:

```
const writers = data.crew
    .filter(person => person.department === "Writing" && person.
job === "Writer")
    .map(person => person.name);
    const writtenBy = writers.join(" & ");
```

20. Create a new **Movie** object (using object literal syntax). Fill in all the properties of the **Movie** object using the data from the movie and people responses we've prepared so far:

```
const movie: Movie = {
    id: movieData.id,
    title: movieData.title,
    tagline: movieData.tagline,
    releaseDate: new Date(movieData.release_date),
    posterUrl: movieData.poster_path,
    backdropUrl: movieData.backdrop_path,
    overview: movieData.overview,
    runtime: movieData.runtime,
```

```
        characters: characters,
        directedBy: directedBy,
        writenBy: writtenBy
    }
```

21. Call the **showResults** function with the movie we constructed:

```
    showResults(movie);
```

22. In your parent directory (**Activity01** in this case), install dependencies with **npm i**.

23. Compile the program using **tsc ./script.ts ./interfaces.ts ./ display.ts**.

24. Verify that the compilation ended successfully.

25. Open **index.html** using the browser of your choice.

    You should see the following in your browser:

Figure 10.5: The final web page

ACTIVITY 10.02: MOVIE BROWSER USING FETCH AND PROMISES

Solution:

1. In the **script.ts** file, locate the **search** function and verify that it takes a single string parameter and that its body is empty.

2. Above the **search** function, create a helper function called **getJsonData**. This function will use the **fetch** API to get data from an endpoint and format it as JSON. It should take a single string called **url** as a parameter, and it should return a promise:

```
const getJsonData = (url: string):Promise<any> => {
}
```

3. In the body of the **getJsonData** function, add code that calls the **fetch** function with the **url** parameter, and **then** call the **json** method on the returned response:

```
const getJsonData = (url: string):Promise<any> => {
    return fetch(url)
        .then(response => response.json());
}
```

4. In the **search** method, construct a new string for the search result URL using the **getSearchUrl** method:

```
const searchUrl = getSearchUrl(value);
```

5. Call the **getJsonData** function with **searchUrl** as a parameter:

```
return getJsonData(searchUrl)
```

6. Add a **then** handler to the promise returned from **getJsonData**. The handler takes a single parameter of the type **SearchResultApi**:

```
return getJsonData(url)
    .then((data:SearchResultApi) => {
    }
```

7. In the body of the handler, check whether we have any results and if we don't, throw an error. If we do have results, return the first item. Note that the handler returns an object with **id** and **title** properties, but the **then** method actually returns a promise of that data. This means that after the handler, we can chain other **then** calls:

```
.then((data:SearchResultApi) => {
    if (data.results.length === 0) {
        throw Error("Not found");
    }
```

```
            return data.results[0];
    })
```

8. Add another **then** call to the previous handler. This handler will take a
   movieResult parameter that contains the **id** and **title** of the movie. Use
   the **id** property to call the **getMovieUrl** and **getPeopleUrl** methods to,
   respectively, get the correct URLs for the movie details and for the cast and crew:

```
    })
    .then(movieResult => {
        const movieUrl = getMovieUrl(movieResult.id);
        const peopleUrl = getPeopleUrl(movieResult.id);
    })
```

9. After getting the URLs, call the **getJsonData** function with both
   of them, and assign the resulting values to variables. Note that
   the **getJsonData(movieUrl)** call will return a promise of
   MovieResultApi, and **getJsonData(peopleUrl)** will return a promise
   of **PeopleResultApi**. Assign those result values to variables called
   dataPromise and **peoplePromise**:

```
    const movieUrl = getMovieUrl(movieResult.id);
    const peopleUrl = getPeopleUrl(movieResult.id);
    const dataPromise: Promise<MovieResultApi> =
getJsonData(movieUrl);
    const peoplePromise: Promise<PeopleResultApi> =
getJsonData(peopleUrl);
```

10. Call the static **Promise.all** method with **dataPromise** and
    peoplePromise as parameters. This will create another promise based on
    those two values, and this promise will be resolved successfully if and only if
    both (that is, all) promises that are contained within resolve successfully. Its
    return value will be a promise of an array of results:

```
    const resultPromise = Promise.all([dataPromise, peoplePromise]);
```

11. Return the promise generated by the **Promise.all** call from the handler:

```
        return resultPromise;
    })
```

12. Add another **then** handler to the chain. This handler will take the array
    returned from **Promise.all** as a single parameter:

```
    })
    .then(dataResult => {
    });
```

13. Deconstruct the parameter into two variables. The first element of the array should be the **movieData** variable of type **MovieResultApi**, and the second element of the array should be the **peopleData** variable of type **PeopleResultApi**:

```
const [movieData, peopleData] = dataResult // we can actually let
TypeScripts type inference pick out the types
```

14. The people data has **cast** and **crew** properties. We'll only take the first six cast members, so first sort the **cast** property according to the **order** property of the cast members. Then slice off the first six cast members into a new array:

```
peopleData.cast.sort((f, s) => f.order - s.order);
const mainActors = peopleData.cast.slice(0, 6);
```

15. Transform the cast data (which is **CastResultApi** objects) into our own **Character** objects. We need to map the **character** field of **CastResultApi** to the **name** field of **Character**, the **name** field to the **actor** name, and the **profile_path** field to the **image** property:

```
const characters :Character[] = mainActors.map(actor => ({
    name: actor.character,
    actor: actor.name,
    image: actor.profile_path
}))
```

16. From the **crew** property of the people data, we'll only need the director and the writer. Since there can be multiple directors and writers, we'll get the names of all directors and writers and concatenate them, respectively. For the directors, from the **crew** property, filter the people who have a **department** of **Directing** and a **job** of **Director**. For those objects, take the **name** property, and **join** it together with an **&** in between:

```
const directors = peopleData.crew
    .filter(person => person.department === "Directing" && person.
job === "Director")
    .map(person => person.name)
const directedBy = directors.join(" & ");
```

17. For the writers, from the **crew** property, filter the people who have a **department** of **Writing** and a **job** of **Writer**. For those objects, take the **name** property, and **join** it together with an **&** in between:

```
const writers = peopleData.crew
    .filter(person => person.department === "Writing" && person.
job === "Writer")
    .map(person => person.name);
const writtenBy = writers.join(" & ");
```

18. Create a new **Movie** object (using object literal syntax). Fill in all the properties of the **Movie** object using the data from the movie and people responses we've prepared so far:

```
const movie: Movie = {
    id: movieData.id,
    title: movieData.title,
    tagline: movieData.tagline,
    releaseDate: new Date(movieData.release_date),
    posterUrl: movieData.poster_path,
    backdropUrl: movieData.backdrop_path,
    overview: movieData.overview,
    runtime: movieData.runtime,
    characters: characters,
    directedBy: directedBy,
    writenBy: writtenBy
}
```

19. Return the **Movie** object from the handler:

```
    return movie;
});
```

Note that we did not do any UI interactions in our code. We just received a string, did some promise calls, and returned a value. The UI work can now be done in UI-oriented code. In this case, that's in the **click** event handler of the **search** button. We should simply add a **then** handler to the **search** call that will call the **showResults** method, and a **catch** handler that will call the **clearResults** method:

```
search(movieTitle)
    .then(movie => showResults(movie))
    .catch(_ => clearResults(value));
```

The output should be the same as the previous activity.

ACTIVITY 10.03: MOVIE BROWSER USING FETCH AND ASYNC/AWAIT

Solution:

1. In the **script.ts** file, locate the **search** function and verify that it takes a single string parameter and that its body is empty. Note that this function is now marked with the **async** keyword, which allows us to use the **await** operator:

```
const getJsonData = (url: string):Promise<any> => {
}
```

2. In the body of the **getJsonData** function, add code that calls and **await**s the **fetch** function with the **url** parameter, and then call calls the **json** method on the returned response:

```
const getJsonData = (url: string):Promise<any> => {
    const response = await fetch(url);
    return response.json();
}
```

3. In the **search** method, construct a new string for the search result URL using the **getSearchUrl** method:

```
const url = getSearchUrl(value);
```

4. Call the **getJsonData** function with the **searchUrl** as a parameter, and **await** the result. Place the result in the **SearchResultApi** variable:

```
const data: SearchResultApi = await getJsonData(url);
```

5. Check whether we have any results and if we don't, throw an error. If we do have results, set the first item of the **result** property in a variable called **movieResult**. This object will contain the **id** and **title** properties of the movie:

```
if (data.results.length === 0) {
    throw Error("Not found");
}
const movieResult = data.results[0];
```

6. Use the **id** property to call the **getMovieUrl** and **getPeopleUrl** methods to, respectively, get the correct URLs for the movie details and for the cast and crew:

```
const movieUrl = getMovieUrl(movieResult.id);
const peopleUrl = getPeopleUrl(movieResult.id);
```

7. After getting the URLs, call the **getJsonData** function with both and assign the resulting values to variables. Note that the **getJsonData(movieUrl)** call will return a promise of **MovieResultApi**, and **getJsonData(peopleUrl)** will return a promise of **PeopleResultApi**. Assign those result values to variables called **dataPromise** and **peoplePromise**:

```
    const dataPromise: Promise<MovieResultApi> =
getJsonData(movieUrl);
    const peoplePromise: Promise<PeopleResultApi> =
getJsonData(peopleUrl);
```

8. Call the static **Promise.all** method with **dataPromise** and **peoplePromise** as parameters. This will create another promise based on those two values, and this promise will be resolved successfully if and only if both (that is, all) promises that are contained within resolve successfully. Its return value will be a promise of an array of results. **await** this promise, and place its result in a variable of type array:

```
    const dataArray = await Promise.all([dataPromise,
peoplePromise]);
```

9. Deconstruct that array into two variables. The first element of the array should be the **movieData** variable of type **MovieResultApi**, and the second element of the array should be the **peopleData** variable of type **PeopleResultApi**:

```
    const [movieData, peopleData] = dataArray;
```

10. The people data has **cast** and **crew** properties. We'll only take the first six cast members, so first sort the **cast** property according to the **order** property of the cast members. Then slice off the first six cast members into a new array:

```
    peopleData.cast.sort((f, s) => f.order - s.order);
    const mainActors = peopleData.cast.slice(0, 6);
```

11. Transform the cast data (which is **CastResultApi** objects) into our own **Character** objects. We need to map the **character** field of **CastResultApi** to the **name** field of **Character**, the **name** field to the **actor** name, and the **profile_path** field to the **image** property:

```
    const characters :Character[] = mainActors.map(actor => ({
        name: actor.character,
        actor: actor.name,
        image: actor.profile_path
    }))
```

12. From the **crew** property of the people data, we'll only need the director and the writer. Since there can be multiple directors and writers, we'll get the names of all directors and writers, and concatenate them, respectively. For the directors, from the **crew** property, filter the people who have a **department** of **Directing** and a **job** of **Director**. For those objects, take the **name** property, and **join** it together with an **&** in between:

```
const directors = peopleData.crew
    .filter(person => person.department === "Directing" && person.
job === "Director")
    .map(person => person.name)
const directedBy = directors.join(" & ");
```

13. For the writers, from the **crew** property, filter the people who have a **department** of **Writing** and a **job** of **Writer**. For those objects, take the **name** property, and **join** it together with an **&** in between:

```
const writers = peopleData.crew
    .filter(person => person.department === "Writing" && person.
job === "Writer")
    .map(person => person.name);
const writtenBy = writers.join(" & ");
```

14. Create a new **Movie** object (using object literal syntax). Fill in all the properties of the **Movie** object using the data from the movie and people responses we've prepared so far:

```
const movie: Movie = {
    id: movieData.id,
    title: movieData.title,
    tagline: movieData.tagline,
    releaseDate: new Date(movieData.release_date),
    posterUrl: movieData.poster_path,
    backdropUrl: movieData.backdrop_path,
    overview: movieData.overview,
    runtime: movieData.runtime,
    characters: characters,
    directedBy: directedBy,
    writenBy: writtenBy
}
```

15. Return the **Movie** object from the function:

```
return movie;
```

16. Note that we did not do any UI interactions in our code. We just received a string, did some promise calls, and returned a value. The UI work can now be done in UI-oriented code. In this case, that's in the **click** event handler of the **search** button. We should simply **await** the result of the **search** call and then call the **showResults** method with it. We can use a standard **catch** expression to handle any errors:

```
try {
    const movie = await search(movieTitle);
    showResults(movie);
} catch {
    clearResults(movieTitle);
}
```

The output should be the same as the previous activity.

CHAPTER 11: HIGHER-ORDER FUNCTIONS AND CALLBACKS

ACTIVITY 11.01: HIGHER-ORDER PIPE FUNCTION

Solution:

In this activity, we'll build a higher-order **pipe** function that accepts functions as arguments, and composes them from left to right, returning a function that accepts the arguments of the first function, and returns the type of the last function. When the returned function is run, it iterates over the given functions, feeding the return value of each function to the next one:

1. Let's start by defining a type definition for the supported functions to compose, a function that accepts one argument of type **T** and returns one of type **R**:

```
type UnaryFunction<T, R> = T extends void ? () => R : (arg: T) => R;
```

   As mentioned, we'll only support functions accepting up to one argument, for simplicity.

   Note that in order to deal with the special case of 0 arguments, we need to check whether **T extends void** and returns a parameterless function.

2. Next, let's start by writing a simple implementation of the **pipe** function, one that supports only a single function, making it essentially an identity function:

```
function pipe<R>(fn: UnaryFunction<void, R>): UnaryFunction<void, R>;
function pipe<T, R = T>(fn: UnaryFunction<T, R>): UnaryFunction<T, R>
{
    return fn;
}
```

   Note that we require two overloads for the function, one for the special case of no parameters, and another for a single-parameter function.

3. Let's expand this to support two functions by adding another overload:

```
function pipe<R>(fn: UnaryFunction<void, R>): UnaryFunction<void, R>;
function pipe<T, R = T>(fn: UnaryFunction<T, R>): UnaryFunction<T,
R>;
function pipe<T, A, R>(fn1: UnaryFunction<T, A>, fn2:
UnaryFunction<A, R>): UnaryFunction<T, R>;
function pipe<T, A, R>(fn1: UnaryFunction<T, A>, fn2?:
UnaryFunction<A, R>) {
    // TODO: Support two functions

}
```

The previous implementation no longer works, since we need to support both a single function, as well as multiple functions, so we can no longer just return **fn**. We'll add a naïve implementation for now and expand it to a more generic solution in the next steps.

4. The naïve implementation for supporting two functions is to simply check whether **fn2** is **undefined** – if it is, we only have a single function at hand, and can simply return **fn1**. Otherwise, we need to return a function that composes **fn1** and **fn2** on the given argument:

```
function pipe<R>(fn: UnaryFunction<void, R>): UnaryFunction<void, R>;
function pipe<T, R = T>(fn: UnaryFunction<T, R>): UnaryFunction<T,
R>;
function pipe<T, A, R>(fn1: UnaryFunction<T, A>, fn2:
UnaryFunction<A, R>): UnaryFunction<T, R>;
function pipe<T, A, R>(fn1: UnaryFunction<T, A>, fn2?:
UnaryFunction<A, R>) {
  if (fn2 === undefined) {
    return fn1;
  }

  return (arg: T) => {
    return fn2(fn1(arg));
  };
}
```

5. We can persist with the preceding approach, but it is tedious, and supporting more functions means changing the implementation. Instead, we can make the actual implementation accept an array of functions and reduce them, starting with **arg** as the initial value, and running the current function, **fn**, on the accumulator (the previous result). Let's do that, while still only supporting up to two functions:

```
function pipe<R>(fn: UnaryFunction<void, R>): UnaryFunction<void, R>;
function pipe<T, R = T>(fn: UnaryFunction<T, R>): UnaryFunction<T,
R>;
function pipe<T, A, R>(fn1: UnaryFunction<T, A>, fn2:
UnaryFunction<A, R>): UnaryFunction<T, R>;
function pipe<T>(...fns: UnaryFunction<any, any>[]):
UnaryFunction<any, any> {
  return (arg: T) => {
    return fns.reduce((prev, fn) => fn(prev), arg);
  };
}
```

6. Lastly, we can expand our support for more functions by only needing to change the function declaration by adding another overload with the correct type:

In the case of three functions:

```
function pipe<T, A, B, R>(
    fn1: UnaryFunction<T, A>,
    fn2: UnaryFunction<A, B>,
    fn3: UnaryFunction<B, R>,
): UnaryFunction<T, R>;
```

In the case of four functions:

```
function pipe<T, A, B, C, R>(
    fn1: UnaryFunction<T, A>,
    fn2: UnaryFunction<A, B>,
    fn3: UnaryFunction<B, C>,
    fn4: UnaryFunction<C, R>,
): UnaryFunction<T, R>;
```

In the case of five functions:

```
function pipe<T, A, B, C, D, R>(
    fn1: UnaryFunction<T, A>,
    fn2: UnaryFunction<A, B>,
    fn3: UnaryFunction<B, C>,
    fn4: UnaryFunction<C, D>,
    fn5: UnaryFunction<D, R>,
): UnaryFunction<T, R>;
```

In each overload, we have the first generic as **T** – this is the type of argument that the returned function will have, and **R** – the return type of the returned function. Between them we have **A, B, C,** and so on, as the interim return type/ argument type of the second...second to last functions. For all the preceding steps, make sure to export the functions by adding **export** before the **function** keyword.

Finally, we can use our **pipe** function to compose any functions we want, while staying completely type-safe:

```
const composedFn = pipe(
  (x: string) => x.toUpperCase(),
  x => [x, x].join(','),
  x => x.length,
  x => x.toString(),
  x => Number(x),
);


console.log('result is:', composedFn('hello'))
```

Running the this code should result in the following output:

```
result is: 11
```

CHAPTER 12: GUIDE TO PROMISES IN TYPESCRIPT

ACTIVITY 12.01: BUILDING A PROMISE APP

Solution:

1. We can get started the same way we started building our API from the sample from GitHub:

```
npm i
```

The only dependencies we're using here are **http-server** to power our web application and **typescript** to transpile our code. Now that our project is set up, let's quickly create an **index.html** file:

```
<html>
  <head>
    <title>The TypeScript Workshop - Activity 12.1</title>
    <link href="styles.css" rel="stylesheet"></link>
  </head>
  <body>
    <input type="text" placeholder="What promise will you make?"
id="promise-input"> <button id="promise-save">save</button>
    <div>
        <table id="promise-table"></ul>
    </div>
  </body>
  <script type="module" src="app.js"></script>
</html>
```

2. And then a **styles.css** file:

```
body {
  font-family: Arial, Helvetica, sans-serif;
  font-size: 12px;
}


input {
  width: 200;
}


table {
  border: 1px solid;
}
```

```
td {
  overflow: hidden;
  white-space: nowrap;
  text-overflow: ellipsis;
}
```

Now we will create an **app.ts** file and create a very rough client library that implements a **fetch** abstraction similar to what we created in *Chapter 3, Functions*. Because TypeScript doesn't run natively in a web browser, we will need to use **tsc** to transpile our TypeScript code into JavaScript. There are some advanced tools such as webpack and Parcel that can help with this, but those are out of scope for this chapter so we will keep this simple and just use a single **app.ts** file.

3. We'll use our **PromiseModel** interface again in our web app and create a **fetchClient** function using currying:

```
interface PromiseModel {
  id?: number;
  desc: string;
}

const fetchClient = (url: string) => (resource: string) => (method:
string) => (
  body?: PromiseModel
) => {
  return fetch(`${url}/${resource}`, {
    body: body && JSON.stringify(body),
    headers: { "Content-Type": "application/json" },
    method,
  });
};
```

4. Building on the model of curried **fetch** functions, let's create some resources:

```
const api = fetchClient("http://localhost:3000");

const resource = api("promise");

const getAction = resource("get");

const postAction = resource("post");
```

5. These functions handle invoking the resources and updating page elements:

```
const deleteItem = (id: number) => {
  const resource = api(`promise/${id}`);
  resource("delete")().then(loadItems);
};


const loadItems = () => {
  getAction().then((res) => res.json().then(renderList));
};


const saveItem = () => {
  const input = document.getElementById("promise-input") as
HTMLInputElement;
  if (input.value) {
    postAction({ desc: input.value }).then(loadItems);
    input.value = "";
  }
};
```

6. Finally, we'll do some ugly HTML manipulation to update the UI:

```
const renderList = (data: PromiseModel[]) => {
  const table = document.getElementById("promise-table");
  if (table) {
    table.innerHTML = "";
    let tr = document.createElement("tr");
    ["Promise", "Delete"].forEach((label) => {
      const th = document.createElement("th");
      th.innerText = label;
      tr.appendChild(th);
    });
    table.appendChild(tr);
    data.forEach((el) => {
      table.appendChild(renderRow(el));
    });
  }
};


const renderRow = (el: PromiseModel) => {
  const tr = document.createElement("tr");
  const td1 = document.createElement("td");
```

```
    td1.innerHTML = el.desc;
    tr.appendChild(td1);
    const td2 = document.createElement("td");
    const deleteButton = document.createElement("button");
    deleteButton.innerText = "delete";
    deleteButton.onclick = () => deleteItem(el.id!);
    td2.appendChild(deleteButton);
    tr.appendChild(td2);
    return tr;
};


document.getElementById("promise-save")?.addEventListener("click",
saveItem);
loadItems();
```

7. Altogether, the **app.ts** file looks like this:

```
interface PromiseModel {
    id?: number;
    desc: string;
}


const fetchClient = (url: string) => (resource: string) => (method:
string) => (
    body?: PromiseModel
) => {
    return fetch(`${url}/${resource}`, {
        body: body && JSON.stringify(body),
        headers: { "Content-Type": "application/json" },
        method,
    });
};


const api = fetchClient("http://localhost:3000");


const resource = api("promise");


const getAction = resource("get");


const postAction = resource("post");


const deleteItem = (id: number) => {
```

```
    const resource = api(`promise/${id}`);
    resource("delete")().then(loadItems);
};


const loadItems = () => {
  getAction().then((res) => res.json().then(renderList));
};


const saveItem = () => {
  const input = document.getElementById("promise-input") as
HTMLInputElement;
  if (input.value) {
    postAction({ desc: input.value }).then(loadItems);
    input.value = "";
  }
};


const renderList = (data: PromiseModel[]) => {
  const table = document.getElementById("promise-table");
  if (table) {
    table.innerHTML = "";
    let tr = document.createElement("tr");
    ["Promise", "Delete"].forEach((label) => {
      const th = document.createElement("th");
      th.innerText = label;
      tr.appendChild(th);
    });
    table.appendChild(tr);
    data.forEach((el) => {
      table.appendChild(renderRow(el));
    });
  }
};


const renderRow = (el: PromiseModel) => {
  const tr = document.createElement("tr");
  const td1 = document.createElement("td");
  td1.innerHTML = el.desc;
  tr.appendChild(td1);
  const td2 = document.createElement("td");
  const deleteButton = document.createElement("button");
```

```
    deleteButton.innerText = "delete";
    deleteButton.onclick = () => deleteItem(el.id!);
    td2.appendChild(deleteButton);
    tr.appendChild(td2);
    return tr;
};


document.getElementById("promise-save")?.addEventListener("click",
saveItem);
loadItems();
```

It's not hard to see why view frameworks are popular; however, this should do the trick for putting together a full-stack application.

8. Now let's compile and run our web application. In one Command Prompt window, enter the following:

```
npx tsc -w.
```

This will transpile the TypeScript code in watch mode so that it restarts when changes are made.

9. Start the HTTP server in another window with **npx http-server . -c-1** as we did in *Exercise 12.03, Promise.allSettled*.

Now navigate a web browser to **http://localhost:8080/**. You should see a form like the one that follows:

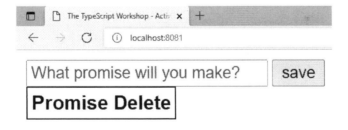

Figure 12.10: Initial load

> **NOTE**
>
> If you don't see "Promise Delete" then it could be that your API from Exercise 6, Implementing a RESTful API backed by sqlite isn't running. Return to that exercise and follow the steps there.

You can add and delete promises. Here are some examples:

10. Add the promise **`Always lint my code`** and save it. You should see the following:

Figure 12.11: One promise made

11. Add the promise **`Never block the event loop`** and save it:

Figure 12.12: Text entered

You should see the following promise saved:

Figure 12.13: Text saved

Figure 12.14 and *Figure 12.15* show some more examples:

Figure 12.14: Another promise saved

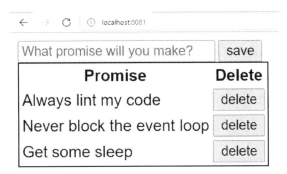

Figure 12.15: Another promise saved

Try to add to the application and make use of the API to get a single promise or update promises.

CHAPTER 13: ASYNC/AWAIT IN TYPESCRIPT

ACTIVITY 13.01: REFACTORING CHAINED PROMISES TO USE AWAIT

Solution:

Let's go over what needed to change in order to make this work:

1. First of all, the **await** keyword can only be used inside an **async** function, so we must add that keyword to the function declaration:

```
const renderAll = async () => {
```

2. Now we have to replace **then** with **await**. Let's look again at what the **render** function does. In our simple case, it just returns a promise that resolves to a string, but in the real world, it would render something in a web browser and then resolve to a string. Since we want to log out that string, we can actually resolve the promise inside a **console.log** statement. Even though **console.log** is a synchronous operation, putting **await** inside it will cause the function to print out the resolved promise value, exactly as we would hope.

The refactored program is six lines shorter and eliminates nesting:

```
export class El {
  constructor(private name: string) {}
  render = () => {
    return new Promise((resolve) =>
      setTimeout(
        () => resolve(`${this.name} is resolved`),
        Math.random() * 1000
      )
    );
  };
}

const e1 = new El('header');
const e2 = new El('body');
const e3 = new El('footer');
```

```
const renderAll = async () => {
  console.log(await e1.render());
  console.log(await e2.render());
  console.log(await e3.render());
};

renderAll();
```

3. Run the file using **npx ts-node refactor.ts**. You should get the following output:

```
header is resolved
body is resolved
footer is resolved
```

CHAPTER 14: TYPESCRIPT AND REACT

ACTIVITY 14.01: THE BLOG

Solution:

1. Create a new React application as outlined earlier in this chapter.

2. Prepare a Firestore database with authentication on Firebase as outlined in *Exercise 14.04, Getting Started with Firebase.*

3. Install the Firebase client with **npm i firebase**. Firebase includes typings so we won't need to install those separately.

4. Create a directory called **services** under **src** and a file called **firebase.ts** there. The Firebase integration can be pretty basic:

```
import firebase from 'firebase';

const config = {
  apiKey: 'abc123',
  authDomain: 'blog-xxx.firebaseapp.com',
  projectId: 'https://blog-xxx.firebaseio.com',
  storageBucket: 'blog-xxx.appspot.com',
  messagingSenderId: '999',
  appId: '1:123:web:123abc',
};

firebase.initializeApp(config);
export const auth = firebase.auth();
export const db = firebase.firestore();
```

5. Make sure to use the values from the Firebase dashboard. This will expose Firebase's authentication and database capabilities to the rest of your application.

6. Set up two providers under **src/providers** called **StoriesProvider.ts** and **UserProvider.ts**. Now, **UserProvider.ts** will be simpler, so let's do that one first. Like *Exercise 14.03, React Context*, we'll employ **createContext** and **useState**, but we'll also need **useEffect**:

```
import firebase from 'firebase';
import React, { createContext, ReactNode, useEffect, useState } from
'react';

import { auth } from '../services/firebase';

interface ContextProps {
```

```
    children: ReactNode;
}

export const UserContext = createContext<Partial<firebase.User |
undefined>>(
  {}
);

export const UserProvider = (props: ContextProps) => {
  const [user, setUser] = useState<firebase.User>();

  useEffect(() => {
    auth.onAuthStateChanged((userAuth) => {
      setUser(userAuth ?? undefined);
    });
  });

  return (
    <UserContext.Provider value={user}>{props.children}</UserContext.
Provider>
  );
};
```

7. **StoriesProvider.ts** is responsible for persisting stories (the blog links) and comments on the stories. To make this work, start by creating interfaces for comments and stories. Comments should belong to stories. Here's a sample of how that could be done:

```
export interface CommentModel {
  comment: string;
  timestamp: number;
  user: string;
}

export interface StoryModel {
  comments: CommentModel[];
  id: string;
  link: string;
  title: string;
  user: string;
}
```

With those interfaces created, we need to implement some methods in our provider, namely methods for adding comments and stories as well as a method that will fetch all the stories. To do that, we'll need to access a collection in our database. This can be done with a single line of code:

```
const storiesDB = db.collection('stories');
```

This code will create the collection if it doesn't exist. The **storiesDB** object we created has methods for fetching, adding, and updating documents from the collection. With those methods implemented, we add our stories data and the methods that handle the data to our provider value. This means that components that use **StoriesContext** will be able to call those methods or access that data.

Again, the solution to this somewhat complicated provider is available on GitHub.

8. Raw document data is a bit difficult to work with, but Firebase has the concept of a converter that we can create, which will tell it how to map document fields to our TypeScript objects. Create and export a converter implementing the **fromFirestore** and **toFirestore** methods. Using those should eliminate some type errors and avoid us needing to use **any**.

9. Install React Router (**react-dom** and **react-router-dom**). Set the default route to a home page. Then, create **Add**, **Signin**, and **Signup** pages. Put the pages under **src/pages**. Just put some text on them in a basic function component to verify routing is working as expected.

10. Build out the **Signup** page first as it's hard to sign in without having signed up. Now we'll use Material-UI. Install **@material-ui/core** and **@material-ui/icons** and we can start building components.

11. Our **Signup** page can be created using **Container**, **TextField**, and **Button**, which are all available components in Material-UI. How your page ultimately looks is up to you, but you will need two **TextField** components. One of those should have both a **type** and **name** of **"email"** and the other should have **"password"** for both of those props.

    We'll track the state of both the email and password fields using **useState** and an **onChange** event.

    When the button is clicked, we should call a method on the **auth** object we exported from our Firebase service earlier to create a new user using the given email address and password.

12. Upon successfully signing in, let's send the user back to the home page with the **useHistory** React Hook.

13. The **Signin** page will be a lot like the **Signup** page. It also needs to capture the user's email address and password and have a button to submit the form. This time we should call a method on **auth** to sign the user in via an email and password.

14. Our **Add** page creates new posts to the blog. We'll capture the title of the post and a link. Add additional fields if you like. This will work similarly to the prior two pages, but now we will use **StoriesContext** instead of **UserContext** to expose the method to add stories.

15. For the home page, we can just load up all the stories and display them as a Material-UI **List**. It's possible to just output the **story** object and wrap it in HTML tags to make it look presentable, but a better solution is to create a **Story** component that can better encapsulate the object. Add a **Story** component to **src/components** and use that for your story display.

16. To manage comments, each story should have its own comments. It's a good idea to create this as a separate component that each story will contain. The **Comments** component can contain a list of each individual comments (another component!) as well as controls for grabbing that method to add comments from **StoriesContext**.

17. At this point, everything is working quite well, but we should add some navigation elements so users don't have to key in the different routes. We can use the **AppBar**, **Toolbar**, **Menu**, **MenuItem**, and **Button** components from Material-UI to create some attractive navigation options. Navigation itself can be performed via the **useHistory** React Hook.

Ben Grynhaus

Jordan Hudgens

Rayon Hunte

Matt Morgan

Wekoslav Stefanovski

HEY!

We're Ben Grynhaus, Jordan Hudgens, Rayon Hunte, Matt Morgan, and Wekoslav Stefanovski, the authors of this book. We really hope you enjoyed reading our book and found it useful for learning TypeScript.

It would really help us (and other potential readers!) if you could leave a review on Amazon sharing your thoughts on *The TypeScript Workshop*.

Go to the link https://packt.link/r/1838828494.

OR

Scan the QR code to leave your review.

Your review will help us to understand what's worked well in this book and what could be improved upon for future editions, so it really is appreciated.

Best wishes,

Ben Grynhaus, Jordan Hudgens, Rayon Hunte, Matt Morgan, and Wekoslav Stefanovski

INDEX

Made in the USA
Las Vegas, NV
12 February 2022

43778699R00391